International Association of Legislation (IAL)
Deutsche Gesellschaft für Gesetzgebung (DGG)

Edited by
Prof. Dr. Ulrich Karpen

Volume 18

Patricia Popelier | Helen Xanthaki | William Robinson
João Tiago Silveira | Felix Uhlmann (eds.)

Lawmaking in Multi-level Settings

Legislative Challenges in Federal Systems and the European Union

Nomos

HART
PUBLISHING

The Deutsche Nationalbibliothek lists this publication in the Deutsche Nationalbibliografie; detailed bibliographic data are available on the Internet at http://dnb.d-nb.de

ISBN 978-3-8487-5957-6 (Print)
978-3-7489-0086-3 (ePDF)

British Library Cataloguing-in-Publication Data
A catalogue record for this book is available from the British Library.

ISBN: HB (Hart) 978-1-5099-3605-2

Library of Congress Cataloging-in-Publication Data
Popelier, Patricia / Xanthaki, Helen / Silveira, João Tiago / Uhlmann, Felix / Robinson, William (eds.)
Lawmaking in Multi-level Settings
Legislative Challenges in Federal Systems and the European Union
Patricia Popelier / Helen Xanthaki / João Tiago Silveira / Felix Uhlmann / William Robinson (eds.)
317 pp.

ISBN 978-1-5099-3605-2 (hardcover Hart)

1st Edition 2019

Table of Contents

Introduction to Lawmaking in Multi-Level Settings

Patricia Popelier, Helen Xanthaki, William Robinson, João Tiago Silveira and Felix Uhlmann

Law making is a difficult task in itself, even in a simple national setting. Multi-level settings complicate matters still further and present major challenges. At the central or upper level, laws must respect the autonomy and diversity of the component units, yet be effective, coherent, simple and accessible. At the decentralized or lower level, law makers must implement laws from outside their own system, drafted at the central level, within a given time-frame and integrate them in their own legislative framework. There are problems of principles and theory as well as practical and technical problems. How to secure the autonomy of subnational entities or Member States? How to ensure that law making is effective, both at the central level and the decentralized level? In the specific context of the European Union (EU), how to ensure timely transposition of EU directives, reduce red tape and avoid bureaucracy? How to include the practical knowledge of the "lower" level in the legislative process of the "upper" level? How to balance the legal drafting traditions and practices of the "lower" and "upper" levels?

These challenges – and the solutions to them – are discussed in the present edited volume, which contains selected papers from the International Association of Legislation's 2018 Conference held at the University of Antwerp. The book covers all multi-tiered systems, but the many of the contributions focus on the European Union, where all those tensions are on display, in particular that between autonomy and efficacy.

In this volume, we take a broad approach to 'multi-level settings', i.e. systems where law-making is a shared responsibility assigned to various levels of authority. It encompasses all multi-tiered systems, including federal states, regionalized systems, as well as multi-level governance systems such as the European Union. While the key focus is on the latter, challenges and instruments in multi-tiered states are discussed as well.

In Part I, all different types of multi-level settings are discussed, with the purpose of establishing a theoretical framework to categorize multi-level lawmaking systems and instruments for effective multi-level law-making.

In Chapter 1, Uhlmann and Popelier give an overview of the forms of multi-tiered systems and the challenges that ensue for law-making at the upper and lower levels. In this chapter, the connecting threads that surface in the following chapters are brought together to make categorizations, emphasize common problems, and map instruments for better law-making in multi-tiered systems. Multi-tiered systems are categorized according to the degree to which the upper level of authority depends upon the lower levels to make its laws effective, and on the degree of autonomy that is left for the lower-level law-maker. Effectiveness and autonomy are derived from this categorization as the main concerns of lawmakers in multi-level systems, which are both linked to quality concerns. Given the advantages and disadvantages that are linked with all types of instruments presented to overcome efficiency and/or autonomy concerns, a mixture of enforcement and sanctioning instruments, participatory instruments, and coordination instruments is recommended.

Schmid examines the upper level perspective in multi-tiered systems. In Chapter 2, she seeks commonalities in techniques to ensure effective legislative implementation at the lower levels, resulting in four categories of mechanisms: (1) substitute performance by the upper level, (2) court enforcement, (3) financial liability, and (4) oversight and cooperation measures. From this upper level perspective, autonomy concerns are acknowledged and taken seriously. In multi-level systems where the powers of the upper level result from a conferral of powers by the lower levels, important autonomy concerns are portrayed as a legitimacy problem. As Schmid stresses, when delegating powers to the upper level, lower-level authorities should be aware that multi-level law-making inevitably encroaches upon autonomy, and should secure legitimacy for these consequences. For all types of multi-level systems, autonomy concerns may also result from of the fact that the benefits of cooperation are – or are perceived to be – unevenly distributed.

Chapter 3 focuses on the lower level perspective. Griglio and Lupo distinguish political and judicial mechanisms to resolve the coordination problems derived from misaligned behaviours and asymmetrical positions between the different entities. They consider four legislative procedures in this respect, situated, respectively, in the context of a multi-level governance system, and in the context of a multi-tiered state. The first two, in the European Union context, concern first the legislative initiative and inter-institutional programming and second the Early Warning system, including the role of the Court of Justice of the European Union regarding the principle of subsidiarity. For the last two, the regionalized Italian state is selected to study the role of the Constitutional Court on Regional/

Central State legislation as well as the drafting rules at both levels. The authors conclude that difficulties increase when local needs and specificities are not duly taken into account in a timely manner in the legislation approved by the upper level, and that judicial checks cannot effectively replace political dialogue between upper-level and lower-level legislators.

Part II and III are dedicated to the functioning of the European Union system in particular. Part II examines the perspective of the European Union, whereas Part III takes the perspective of the Member States.

Part II is subdivided into three sections. The first gives a broad of the European Commission's Better Regulation policy (Chapter 4). The next section concentrates on drafting policy and techniques (Chapters 5, 6 and 7). In a third section, various tools are discussed, such as consultations and soft law (Chapters 8, 9 and 10).

Part II opens with an overview, in Chapter 4, of the Better Regulation toolkit. In view of the tensions between the European Union's quest for legitimacy and coherence while respecting the Member States' autonomy concerns, Mousmouti addresses the connection between Better Regulation and subsidiarity. She asserts that while the subsidiarity principle holds a clear position in the institutional context of the European Union and its Better Regulation agenda, a closer look at the legislative practice suggests that so far the application of that principle has not lived up to expectations: it has not functioned as a 'doorstopper', acting as a brake on lawmaking activity, for the European Union lawmaker nor as a catalyst for improving the tense relationship between European Union and national legal order, nor has it contributed to a common law-making culture. The author recommends strengthening the principle's strategic orientation and ensuring that upper-level legislation clearly defines common results and standards and leaves sufficient room to lower-level rules to regulate to achieve those results and standards in the most effective way.

Chapter 5 gives an internal view on the European Union legislative process, with insights from within the European Commission's Legal Service. Banks discusses the 2016 Interinstitutional Agreement on Better Law-Making, the Task Force on Subsidiarity, Proportionality and "Doing Less More Efficiently", and access to documents, to illustrate the difficulties the Commission encounters in its efforts to engage in Better Regulation. The author admits that the process of EU law-making is 'a work in progress', but stresses that it depends on all actors sharing a common purpose.

Continuing on the theme that European Union law-making is 'a work in progress', Whelanova, in Chapter 6, identifies three types of problems related to the drafting of EU laws that complicate the Member State's implementation tasks: ambiguity, incompleteness, and defects of form. The author contends that while the 1998 Interinstitutional Agreement on common guidelines for the quality of drafting of EU legislation provides a sound basis for good drafting, in practice the formal quality of EU legislation is jeopardized by political issues during the negotiation phase, thus confirming that the responsibility for effective law-making is shared by the different actors in the multi-level system.

In Chapter 7, these problems are viewed from the angle of linguistics. Faced with the difficulty of adopting EU legislation in 24 different languages, which then has to be implemented in the legal languages of the 28 Member States, Doczekalska examines how legal languages interact at national and EU level and defines the characteristics of the EU legal language. She describes processes of hybridization and deculturalization at the EU level, and processes of further hybridization, dehybridization and culturalization of legal language at the national levels.

Moving to the discussion of specific tools and instruments, Chapters 8 and 9 discuss soft law and its relation with 'hard' law-making. In Chapter 8, Andone and Coman-Kund propose a normative framework for assessing the prescriptive content of hard law and soft law and discuss the implications of the blurred distinction between both instruments for the quality of EU law, with concerns related to the principles of legal certainty, legality, conferral and institutional balance, and judicial review. The authors advocate a clearer delineation between the European Union's soft law and hard law through an increased role for argumentation as a means to foster compliance. One specific type of soft law is the focus of Chapter 9 in which Lancos discusses the case of hybrid recommendations. The author is highly critical of the tendency to use instruments such as deadlines, reporting and monitoring tasks usually linked with hard law obligations in EU Directives and stresses the importance of the persuasion factor as an incentive for national implementation.

Another tool for multi-level law-making is discussed in Chapter 10, where Koutras examines consultations as a tool for multi-level governance. The argument is that a multi-level approach through public consultation can be beneficial for policy makers both at the level of the European Union and in the Member States because different societal layers are involved and because it creates a dynamic of an integrated approach. The argument is tested in a case study on copyright. The author concludes that while several requirements for proper multi-level consultations are met – such as a broad variety of stakeholders and the distribution over old and new Member States – its potential is undermined by the tendency of the European Union Institutions to focus on their own discussions rather than engaging with the outcomes of wide consultations.

Part III considers the perspective of the Member States of the European Union.

Chapter 11 discusses how the national Parliaments in the Member States can contribute to the overall legitimacy of multi-level EU legislation. Voermans suggests that, although their positions and traditions vary substantially, national Parliaments have been able to give a voice to the Member State's electorate separate from the one of governments. He asserts that the role of national Parliaments in the legislative process leading up to EU Directives has shifted from that of bystanders to team players, as may be read from the number of opinions national Parliaments have delivered to the European Commission since 2006, the way national Parliaments have organized their scrutiny procedures on proposals for EU legislation, the rise of scrutiny reserves throughout the Member States since the entry into force of the Lisbon Treaty and the practice of giving governments of the Member States (formal) mandates and instructions on positions to be taken in negotiations on EU legislation.

Chapter 12 takes up the discussion of drafting quality, by examining the differences between the legislative drafting rules and practices of the European Union and those of the Member States. Lanceiro holds that certain mechanisms, reinforced by the Court of Justice of the EU, lead to the implementation of EU drafting rules and the loss of diversity of national traditions, creating problems in certain Member States. The author pleads for a cross-fertilisation and harmonization of EU and national practices by letting the national entities responsible for the formal legal drafting of implementing acts participate in the EU law-making procedure.

In Chapter 13, de Graaff and Verheij show how EU legislation, and in particular Regulations, interferes with renewed codification trends in Member States. The authors express concern for the impact this has on the clarity, accessibility and coherence of private law. To address that concern, they make recommendations for authorities at both the national and the EU level, including, amongst other proposals, reconnecting with the idea of a European Civil Code.

Part III concludes with a case study. In Chapter 14, Van Nieuwenhove illustrates the concerns of EU legislative quality and implementation problems by discussing the implementation of the General Data Protection Regulation (GDPR). The author concludes that the replacement of a Directive by a Regulation, the actual content of the GDPR, and the wide margin of appreciation left for the Member States have complicated the implementation processes in the Member States. Like other contributors though, the author also stresses that the quality of multi-level law-making is a responsibility shared by both the European Union and the Member States.

Having mapped the theoretical challenges as well as the practical problems that come with multi-level law-making and having discussed the instruments to address these problems, the final chapter, reconnecting with the idea of shared responsibility, concludes on a more positive note. In his afterword, Naundorf reflects on the virtues of law-making in multilevel systems as an innovative, collaborative task involving all stakeholders and academics too. Setting the agenda for future research in the field of legislative studies, he calls upon scholars to complement the scientific study of legislation with 'a more practical, impact-oriented and forward-looking point of view'. This combination of theoretical insights and more practical perspectives is exactly what this edited volume aims at offering its readership.

Part I.
Lawmaking in Multi-level Settings: A Theoretical Framework

Chapter 1: Multi-level Lawmaking. Form, Arrangement and Design in Theory and Practice

Felix Uhlmann (University of Zürich) and Patricia Popelier (University of Antwerp)

I. Introduction

Legislative studies are often concerned with one type of legislation in one particular country. While such an approach does have its uses, it does not adequately reflect the complexity of modern legal systems. Many legal questions cannot be answered by consulting just one particular piece of legislation. This holds true within one state entity, where laws are often supplemented by secondary legislation and must take account of higher ranking norms such as constitutional provisions, but it becomes especially complex when states are embedded in global governance. This raises particular issues for lawmakers. At the lower level, the lawmaker has to take into account the upper-level legal framework or is required to take measures to implement upper-level laws, which impinges on its autonomy to make laws. At the upper level, the lawmaker has to take account of the interests of lower-level authorities and their capacity to observe and implement its laws and respect areas of autonomy. Thus, lawmaking at different levels is characterized by a tension between the autonomy to act and the constraints established by the other levels.[1] Moreover, instruments to deal with this tension must also take into account the interest of individual persons in the accessibility of the entire legislative complex.

The purpose of this chapter is to give an overview of the main types of multi-level systems, the prevalent types of problems that lawmakers encounter at the different levels of authority in such systems, and the main instruments to address these problems. It is structured as follows. First, in

1 C Tietje, 'Autonomie und Bindung der Rechtsetzung in gestuften Rechtsordnungen' in *Bundesstaat und europäische Union zwischen Konflikt und Kooperation* (VVDStRL 66, De Gruyter 2007) 52. See, for autonomy as the constitutive element of a level M Zürn, S Wälti and H Enderlein 'Introduction' in M Zürn, S Wälti and H Enderlein (eds), *Handbook on Multi-level Governance* (Edward Elgar 2010) 3.

the introduction, we define the dimensions of relationships between authorities with lawmaking powers within multi-level systems and explain the terminology of 'upper' and 'lower' levels used in this paper (I). We go on to offer a typology of multi-level systems based on power, tasks and legal sources (II), followed by the identification of the typical concerns of lawmakers in multi-level systems (III). Next, we give an overview of instruments to deal with the concerns of the different levels in lawmaking activities, taking into account the specificities of the different types of multi-level systems (IV). Finally we draw some brief conclusions (V).

1. *Multi-level Systems*

The term 'multi-level systems' in this article means systems that disperse lawmaking power over different levels of authority. This resembles Hooghe's and Marks' classification of Type I systems of Multi-level Governance, characterized by the dispersion of power over a limited number of territorial, non-intersecting and general-purpose jurisdictions.[2] While this type of multi-level governance system is closely connected to federal systems, there are some fundamental differences based on what is defined by Piattoni as the 'centre-periphery', the 'state-society' and the 'domestic-international' axes.[3] In this paper, both federal systems and more complex multi-level governance systems are covered by the term 'multi-level systems', but we are only concerned with the relations between levels of public authority with lawmaking powers. Multi-level governance systems are more complex because of the multiplication of relevant actors and, as a result, the multiplication of dynamics between these actors. Yet, if we focus on levels of public authority, the difference between federal systems and multi-level governance systems is less straightforward, because federal systems can be part of the multi-level governance system, and because the dynamics within federal systems are not confined to the federal and the subnational level; in some federal systems different types of subnational entities co-exist, and decentralized levels of authority are established within federations.

2 L Hooghe and G Marks, 'Unraveling the Central State, but How? Types of Multi-Level Governance' (2003) 97(2) Am. Pol. Sc. Rev. 236–238.

3 S Piattoni, *The theory of multi-level governance: conceptual, empirical and normative challenges* (OUP 2010) 26–31.

Multi-level systems, then, can be found in different contexts,[4] with four dimensions of growing complexity. These dimensions concern:

1. the relationships between national government and local authorities;
2. the relationships between the federal government and subnational governments – and added to that the relationships between the federal government, subnational governments, and local authorities;
3. the relationships between international law and national states (including levels of authority within these states) – and added to that the relationships between international law, states, subnational entities if any, and local authorities;
4. the relationship between supranational organizations and their Member States – and added to that the relationships between international law, supranational organizations, Member States, subnational entities, and local authorities.

This structure shows that complexity arises when the lower-level authorities have ultimate legislative powers in their own autonomous legal system while they form, at the same time, part of broader legal systems, but not necessarily in a strictly hierarchical way. This multiplication of relationships comes in particular to the fore within federal systems (dimension 2) and with respect to the European Union (dimension 4), with traces of federations and international intergovernmental institutions[5]. Complexity arises in particular when both dimensions intertwine, i.e. when federal states are Members of the European Union and EU law is enacted within the sphere of competence of the exclusive or shared powers of the subnational government within a federal state. The interaction between the norms enacted by these governments defines the powers between the different federal levels.

---

4 See GF Schuppert, *Governance und Rechtsetzung – Grundfragen einer modernen Regelungswissenschaft* (Nomos 2011) 329f; E Pache, 'Verantwortung und Effizienz in der Mehrebenenverwaltung' in *Bundesstaat und europäische Union zwischen Konflikt und Kooperation* (VVDStRL 66, De Gruyter 2007) 107; H Aden, 'Nationale, europäische und internationale Verrechtlichung in wechselseitiger Abhängigkeit. Mehrebenenrecht und Machtverschiebung zur Exekutive' in M Becker and R Zimmerling (eds), *Politik und Recht* (Springer VS 2006) 357ff. For the meaning of 'level' see GB Doern and R Johnson, Conclusion, in GB Doern and R Johnson (eds), *Rules, Rules, Rules, Rules: Multi-Level Regulatory Governance* (University of Toronto Press 2006) 360.

5 See the Lisbon Judgment of the German Constitutional Court of June 30, 2009, BVerfGE 123, 267.

2. Upper and Lower Level

For the sake of academic classification it is necessary to define the different levels of the system. We differentiate between the 'upper' and the 'lower' level. 'Upper' and 'lower' describe *the size and scope of the level*. Upper-level law applies to more than one lower-level entity, such as federal law applies to all subnational entities on the federal territory, international law to more than one state (i.e. a country) and EU law to all Member States (and beyond). Upper-level law is the law of the larger entity. The term, however, does not necessarily encompass a hierarchal relationship between the upper and the lower level. It may be often the case that upper-level law overrides lower-level law but there are notable exceptions. Hence, 'upper' and 'lower' do not describe a system of power but rather a system of size and scope as every upper level typically has more than one lower level.

It should also be noted that upper and lower level are *relative terms*. They change depending on the perspective. Subnational law is lower-level law when compared with federal law but upper-level law when communal law is the point of reference. Federal law is lower-level law with regard to EU law and EU law is – arguably – lower-level law in relation to some sources of international law.[6]

Such a chain of upper and lower levels illustrates the complexity of the modern legal world. Many legal issues involve more than two legal orders. This holds true e.g. for government procurement. A local authority in a federal country must consider communal law (if applicable), subnational law, inter-regional law, federal law, EU law (by membership or by bilateral treaties) as well as the GPA (Government Procurement Agreement?), the latter sources typically directly applicable on the national level.[7] One might add complexity by considering that on the subnational and on the federal level the sources often consist of primary and secondary legislation as well as of constitutional principles (economic freedom, equal treatment etc.). Often, cases of public procurement pose questions of procedure that necessitate the consultation of federal and subnational administrative procedure laws (and again, of secondary legislation and of constitutional prin-

6 See II.1.1 below.

7 See, e.g., AR Ziegler 'Subtle but Enduring – The Role of Domestic Courts in the Shaping of International Economic Law through Proper Interpretation of Domestic Law: The WTO Agreement before Swiss Courts' in OK Fauchald and A Nollkaemper (eds), *The Practice of International and National Courts and the (De-)Fragmentation of the International Law* (Hart Publishing 2012) 338.

ciples). In a common case of public procurement, one might easily count five to ten different legal sources from different governmental entities.[8]

Multi-level lawmaking and application are daily routine. They often involve more than two levels. This paper focuses on two levels, simply denominated as 'upper' and 'lower' levels but one should keep in mind that this covers a much more complex reality of interwoven levels of authority.

II. Forms of Multi-Level Systems

In this part, we identify different types of multi-level systems according to different bases for classification: (1) power, (2) tasks and (3) the predominant legislator. These classifications are relevant for the lawmaking activity as they determine the degree of autonomy and dependency of the levels of lawmaking authority. This, in turn, determines the concerns that rise from each level of authority, which are discussed in the next section.

1. Classification of Multi-level Systems Based on Power

A first classification characterizes multi-level systems by considering the *powers* that each level possesses in relation to the other. 'Power' refers to competences and the instruments to exercise them, such as legislative or administrative powers. The relationship between the upper and the lower level may be hierarchical (1.1.) or non-hierarchical (1.2.). Within these types, relations can be balanced or point to a dominant actor at either the lower or the upper level. Sometimes, different types can be found within the same legal system. This is because relations between levels may differ according to the policy domain in which the lawmaking activity occurs. As a result, the upper level can be dominant in some areas but have a weaker position in others.

8 See for the 'rise of the regulatory state' in the context of multi-level regulation R Baldwin, M Cave and M Lodge, *Understanding Regulation* (2nd edn, OUP 2012) 373ff.

1.1. Hierarchical Systems

In a hierarchical relationship,[9] two features are characteristic for upper-level legislation: direct effect and priority over lower-level legislation.

Direct effect means that upper-level legislation is in force in the lower-level jurisdiction with no need for a political process on the lower level to transform upper-level law into lower-level law. Within one multi-tiered state entity, the direct effect of the central level is undisputed. Within intergovernmental systems, it is the national system that decides whether the upper level-legislation has direct effect, while in the European Union, it is the upper level that claims direct effect of its norms.[10] Direct effect reduces the upper level's dependency, but does not entirely do away with it. For one thing, in transnational systems, the national jurisdiction must enable the intrusion of upper-level legislation.[11] Further, upper-level law may still depend on lower-level law for its realization. For example, as both Van Nieuwenhove and Whelanova point out further in this volume, EU Regulations often require national measures for their completion.

Priority means that in case of conflict, upper-level law overrides lower-level law. This is undisputed in more centralized multi-tiered systems, but in federal systems as well, federal law usually trumps subnational law. The Swiss Supreme Court has even attributed the status of a fundamental right to the principle of preeminence of federal law over cantonal law.[12] Federal systems, however, are not by definition hierarchical systems. Mostly, the relationship is more complex and balanced, and hierarchy slips in where – and to the extent that – the federal and subnational entities have concur-

---

9 See for the notion of hierarchy T Kovziridze, *Hierarchy and Interdependence in Multi-level Structures* (Brussels UP 2008) 45.

10 See art 288(ii) Consolidated version of the Treaty on the Functioning of the European Union [2012] OJ C326/47 (TFEU): 'A regulation shall have general application. It shall be binding in its entirety and directly applicable in all Member States.' See also Case 6/64 *Costa v ENEL* [1964] ECR 585.' For a reconceptualization, see A Von Bogdandy, 'Pluralism, direct effect, and the ultimate say: On the relationship between international and domestic constitutional law' (2008) 6 Int. J. Const. L. 397–413.

11 See for example on 'Europe clauses' that enable the direct effect of EU law in national jurisdictions: M Claes, 'Constitutionalizing Europe at its Source: the 'European Clauses' in National Constitutions: Evolution and Typology' (2005) 24 Yearbook of European Law 81–125; P Popelier, 'Europe Clauses' and Constitutional Strategies in the Face of Multi-Level Governance' (2014) 21 Maastricht J. of European and Comparative Law 300.

12 BGE 138 I 468, consid. 3.2.1; BGE 138 I 356, consid. 5.4.2.

rent powers. In these cases, a priority rule must resolve conflicts that rise when a matter is regulated in different ways by different levels of authority; this is further developed in the contribution of Griglio and Lupo, further in this volume. In most – but not all[13] – cases, priority is given to the upper level. In such cases the autonomy of the lower level depends on whether the upper level takes legislative action, and on the intensity of that action. The dominance of the upper level, however, can be constrained by subsidiarity rules that require the upper level to justify its action on the basis of necessity.[14]

The question of whether a system can be described as hierarchical is sometimes a matter of perspective. For example, the Court of Justice of the EU, arguing from a European Union perspective, has asserted the priority of EU law over national laws and constitutions.[15] From a national perspective, however, the EU system is not always defined in terms of hierarchy. Instead, as a system of constitutional pluralism[16] or composite constitutionalism,[17] the predominance of EU legislation within the national legal system derives from the national constitution which may limit the primacy

13 Cf art 72(3) of the Basic Law for the Federal Republic of Germany ('Grundgesetz'), as last amended by art 1 of the Act of 23 December 2014 (Federal Law Gazette I 2438), which enumerates matters where the *Länder* may enact laws at variance with federal legislation.

14 This can be found in the EU and in several federal states such as Germany and Switzerland. For a discussion of the enforcement of the necessity clause which forms part of the subsidiarity principle, see W Vandenbruwaene, 'The Judicial Enforcement of Subsidiarity: the Comparative Quest for an Appropriate Standard' in P Popelier, A Mazmanyan and W Vandenbruwaene (eds), *The Role of Constitutional Courts in Multilevel Governance* (Intersentia 2013) 131–164.

15 Cf, inter alia, Case 6/64 *Costa v ENEL* [1964] ECR 585.

16 See, for example, M Avbelj and J Komárek (eds), *Constitutional Pluralism in the EU and Beyond* (Hart Publishing 2012); N Krisch, *Beyond Constitutionalism. The Pluralist Structure of Postnational Law* (OUP 2010); K Jaklic, *Constitutional Pluralism in the EU* (Oxford: OUP 2014); A von Bogdandy, 'Pluralism, Direct Effect, and the Ultimate Say: On the Relationship Between International and Domestic Constitutional Law' (2008) 6 Int'l J. Const. Law, 397–413.

17 LFM Besselink, 'National Parliaments in the EU's composite constitution: a plea for a shift in paradigm', in Ph Kiiver (ed), *National and Regional Parliaments in the European Constitutional Order* (Europa Law Publishing 2006) 117–131; M Kumm, 'How does European Union Law Fit into the World of Public Law? Costa, Kadi and Three Conceptions of Public Law' in J Neyer and A Wiener (eds), *Political Theory of the European Union* (OUP 2011).

of EU legislation based on *ultra vires* or constitutional identity doctrines.[18] These, however, are limitations that are invoked only in exceptional cases, and primacy of EU law remains the general rule on a day to day basis.[19]

1.2. Non-hierarchical Systems

In non-hierarchical systems, the power relationship between upper and lower levels varies. In some systems, the lower level takes the upper hand. In other cases, the relationship is more balanced.

On one side of the spectrum, one finds situations in which the upper level is particularly weak. The upper level will merely try to influence the lower level by enacting soft law[20] or producing uniform codes that the lower level may use for its own legislation – or may simply ignore.[21] The power of the upper level merely consists of persuasion, possibly supported by the fact that many lower-level entities have followed its example and that practical considerations suggest to the lower level that it should bring its legislation into line with the majority of the other lower-level entities (and of course, with what the upper level is proposing).[22]

---

18 For a critical appraisal see, amongst many others, M Kumm and V Ferreras Comella, 'The Primacy Clause of the Constitutional Treaty and the Future of Constitutional Conflict in the European Union' (2005) 3 Int'l J. Const. L. 473–492.

19 See, in the context of financial aids during the sovereign debt crisis, for the tendency of the EU Member States to avoid the EU level and act intergovernmentally, F Schorkopf 'Finanzkrisen als Herausforderung der internationalen, europäischen und nationalen Rechtsetzung' in *Grundsatzfragen der Rechtsetzung und Rechtsfindung* (VVDStRL 71, De Gruyter 2012) 208ff.

20 See, for the notion of soft law, L Senden, *Soft Law in European Community Law* (Hart Publishing 2004) passim; M Knauff, *Der Regelungsverbund: Recht und Soft Law im Mehrebenensystem* (Mohr Siebeck 2010) 214ff; see, for the tendency to use informal instruments to compensate lacking legislative competence, Schuppert (n 4) 340. In the EU, for example, namely the non-binding recommendations (art 288(iv) TFEU) serve as (formal) steering instrument, cf Schuppert (n 4) 346; see, for a typology of the then EC-soft law, A Peters, 'Typology, Utility and Legitimacy of European Soft Law' in A Epiney, M Haag and A Heinemann (eds), *Die Herausforderung von Grenzen – Le défi des frontiers – Challenging boundaries* (Nomos 2007) 413.

21 Further, it is conceivable that the lower level adopts upper level law without being obliged to do so, cf A Rochvarg, 'State Adoption of Federal Law – Legislative Abdication or Reasoned Policymaking?' (1984) 35 Adm. Law Rev. 277ff.

22 See, for examples, Schuppert (n 4) 344ff.

In such systems, the upper level does not possess the means to enforce its regulation but must convince the lower level of the benefits of its proposals. Possibly, as it is often the case in federal systems, the 'deal' with the upper level is 'sweetened' by financial incentives such as public subsidies. The form of multi-level relationship, however, remains cooperative.

Dual federations form a specific type of non-hierarchical systems. In these systems, the division between the upper and lower levels is based on equality and autonomy. The prototype of such system is the Belgian federation, where the federal government and the subnational entities are defined on the basis of equality, and, apart from some rare exceptions, competences are distributed on the basis of exclusivity.[23] In such a system, ideally a matter is regulated by one or the other level of authority, and conflicts can be solved merely on the basis of tracing to which authority the matter was assigned. In practice, however, exclusivity easily leads to fragmentation, as matters are split in parts, with some parts being attributed to one level, and other parts attributed to other levels of authority. Fragmentation prevents each level from developing comprehensive and coherent policies, and obliges the different entities to collaborate after all, but on a basis of equality, for example in the form of intra-federal cooperation agreements. This may even lead to innovative forms of legislation, such as the 'double decrees' in Belgium, which are discussed in inter-parliamentary committees but then approved by each subnational assembly alone.[24]

2. *Classification of Multi-level Systems Based on Tasks*

Another classification of multi-level systems, relevant from the angle of lawmaking, is based on the types of tasks that are fulfilled on each level. Here, the locus of attention is the lower level which, in relation to the upper level, acts as (2.1) a co-legislator, (2.2.) an executive authority or (2.3.) an implementing actor.

---

23 See P Popelier, 'Zuständigkeitsteilung in Belgien: Kompetenzverteilung als Kennzeichlichen multinationalen Konfliktsmanagement', in A Gamper et al. (eds), *Föderale Kompetenzverteilung in Europa* (Baden-Baden, Nomos 2016) 154–159.

24 P Caboor and H El Bachiri, 'De gezamenlijke decreten en ordonnanties schieten uit de startblokken' (2018) 21 Tijdschrift voor Wetgeving 150–154.

2.1. Co-legislator

As co-legislators, the upper and lower level both have lawmaking powers with regard to the same policy domain. The precise interaction depends on the power relations as described in the previous section. One possibility is that the upper level defines the framework within which the lower level can legislate. Another option is that each level can act, but with a priority rule in favor of (mostly) the upper level. In other cases both levels work together to produce collective rules inserted in, for example, cooperation agreements.

2.2. Execution

Lower levels are often charged with the execution of upper-level legislation.[25] This may be explained by the simple fact that the lower level is 'closer' to the persons affected by legislation.[26] It is obvious that, again taking the case of public procurement at the communal level, such decisions are taken by the authority directly involved with the project and not by a remote administrative unit. Still, closeness is often prone to more or less subtle forms of corruption. It is no coincidence that Swiss federal zoning law requires a subnational authority – and not a communal one – to grant exceptions to build a house outside the predefined building zones.[27]

This is the dominant allocation of powers technique in so-called 'executive federalism'. It generates a form of cooperative federalism, because the upper level is dependent upon the lower level for the execution of its laws and will therefore be more inclined to involve the lower level in the lawmaking procedure.[28]

---

25 G Biaggini, *Theorie und Praxis des Verwaltungsrechts im Bundesstaat* (Helbing & Lichtenhahn 1996) 39. See art 291 TFEU in the EU.

26 See, for the evolution in the EC and EU, respectively, Pache (n 4) 108ff.

27 Art 25(ii) of the Swiss Federal Act on Spatial Planning of June 22, 1979.

28 Cf for the German model of the 'unitarian federal state' FW Scharpf, 'Legitimität im europäischen Mehrebenensystem' (2009) 37 Leviathan – Berliner Zeitschrift für Sozialwissenschaft 251. See also for the subsidiarity principle realized in art 291 TFEU M Gellermann, in R Streinz (ed), *Kommentar EUV/AEUV* (3rd edn, C.H. Beck 2018) art 291 TFEU para 3.

2.3. Implementation

The term 'implementation' suggests that the lower level must embed upper-level law in the context of lower-level regulation.[29] In implementing upper-level law, the lower-level authority is in a position between co-legislator and executive authority. On the one hand, the lower level enjoys more discretion to decide on means and principles to obtain the results pursued by the upper level than is the case with mere execution. On the other hand, its autonomy is more restricted than where it acts as co-legislator, both as to the decision to act or not and as to the content of the rules, thus taking a much more limited role than acting as co-legislator.

3. Classification of Multi-level Systems Based on the Predominant Legislator

Another way to classify multi-level systems from the vantage point of lawmaking is by examining which level of authority is the predominant regulator of a policy area. Here, one may take a more systemic approach, or single out a specific policy area. The classification, then, may vary according to the policy area. The allocation of competences is of key importance, both as to content and technique. As for content, the questions arise of which policy areas are allocated to which level, and the degree of detail in which these areas are delineated.[30] The upper-level powers may be defined more broadly if not comprehensively, restricted only by some exceptions for lower-level powers or by a vague but difficult to enforce notion of subsidiarity.[31] The main techniques for the allocation of powers are exclusivi-

---

29 Cf the directives in EU law, see art 288(iii) TFEU; such implementation can be interpreted as some form of 'delegated lawmaking', see S Kadelbach, 'Autonomie und Bindung der Rechtsetzung in gestuften Rechtsordnungen' in *Bundesstaat und europäische Union zwischen Konflikt und Kooperation* (VVDStRL 66, De Gruyter 2007) 31f.

30 The principle of conferral applies, for example, in the EU (art 5(ii) Consolidated version of the Treaty on European Union [2012] OJ C326/13: 'Under the principle of conferral, the Union shall act only within the limits of the competences conferred upon it by the Member States in the Treaties to attain the objectives set out therein. Competences not conferred upon the Union in the Treaties remain with the Member States.') and in Switzerland (art 42(i) of the Swiss Federal Constitution of April 18, 1999 ('Bundesverfassung'): 'The Confederation shall fulfil the duties that are assigned to it by Federal Constitution.').

31 Cf Vandenbruwaene (n 14) 162 for the necessity of substantiating the vague notion of subsidiarity to enable judicial enforcement.

ty, framework powers, and concurrent powers. The choice of technique is determinant for the position of dependency and autonomy. In the case of exclusivity, each level of authority can act autonomously, and in the case of fragmentation, co-legislation is adopted on the basis of equality. In the case of framework powers, the upper level depends upon the lower level for the completion and implementation of its legislation. In the case of concurrent powers[32], the autonomy of (mostly) the lower level depends upon the activity grade of the upper level.

3.1. Predominantly Upper Level

Predominant upper-level law means that a specific policy area is mostly covered by upper-level regulation. Lower-level law will supplement upper-level law and facilitate its application on the lower level. Private individuals, administrative authorities, courts etc. turn mainly to upper-level legal sources. Lower-level law may provide answers to questions of procedure and to technical details.[33]

3.2. Predominantly Lower Level

Particular policy areas can be covered mostly by lower-level law. Upper-level law may not be directly applicably, may be of limited normative effect (soft law), or may be restricted in scope and relevant only for very specific questions.[34] It is also possible that upper-level law is explicitly designed to apply only if lower-level law has been enacted. In the case of soft law, upper-level law may influence the way in which lower-level law is understood and applied, e.g. by giving a fuller description of the goals of the regulation in place.[35]

---

32 'Concurrent powers' are attributed to both the upper and the lower level; if the upper level, however, legislates, the lower level set of rules ceases to be in force.

33 See, for instance, bylaws in the United Kingdom.

34 In Switzerland, e.g., in the area of spatial planning, federal law concerns only specific areas (such as building activities outside construction zones, cf art 24ff of the Swiss Federal Act on Spatial Planning of June 22, 1979).

35 See n 20.

3.3. Both Upper and Lower Level

Often, as is the case in many federal states and in the European Union, the legal sources form a complex web between upper-level and lower-level law. A concrete legal question may be capable of being answered only by reference to both upper-level and lower-level law. This does not rule out the possibility that upper-level law overrides lower-level law in the event of a conflict[36] but it means that in a typical case administrative authorities and courts will turn to both upper-level and lower-level law.[37]

A typical division of tasks between the upper level and the lower level consists of upper-level law that defines the broad outline – the *skeleton* – of the regulation in place, through framework powers. Lower-level law fills in the gaps and leads towards a tailored solution on the lower level.[38]

It may also be that upper-level law sets *minimal standards* that lower-level law must respect. Lower-level law may go beyond the minimum and prescribe higher standards.[39] Such multi-level regulation is often found in areas such as safety, public health, environmental policy, etc.

3.4. Hybrid Systems

It is possible that the upper level and lower level together create new legal norms that can be attributed neither to the upper level nor to the lower level. Upper-level and lower-level organs of the state may engage in some sort of contractual relationship; such contracts may encompass norms that are directly applicable to private parties, administrative authorities and courts alike. It is also possible that upper-level and lower-level organs of the state establish institutions straddling both levels that are capable of enacting legal norms. These norms, as well as contracts between the two levels with direct effect on third parties, should be classified as hybrid norms. They are joint legislation and no level can claim sole authorship.

Such highly complex structures may be found in fields such as higher education where the upper level and the lower level typically have parallel competencies, meaning that both the upper level and the lower level may

---

36 See II.1.1 above.

37 See n 7.

38 Such finding is true in particular in the case of EU directives (art 288(iii) TFEU).

39 See for the so-called 'gold-plating' W Robinson, 'EU Legislation' in U Karpen and H Xanthaki (eds), *Legislation in Europe* (Hart Publishing 2017) 234; Tietje (n 1) 61.

lay down rules on universities but coordination between the two levels may suggest common rules (e.g. on admission standards).[40] Another example relates to cooperation agreements between a federal government and regional authorities, for example in the fight against climate change, which affects a broad range of policy fields.

III. *Effectiveness, Autonomy and Quality as the Key Concerns of Lawmakers in Multi-level Systems*

It follows from the previous section that the power relations, the interaction and the activity in the regulation of a given policy area vary, and that this variety puts the levels of lawmaking authority in different positions of dependency towards each other. These positions indicate to what extent the upper level depends upon the lower level to regulate a policy area, which, in turn, dictates the key concerns that the upper level and the lower level have in multi-level lawmaking: effectiveness, autonomy and quality.

1. *Effectiveness and Quality*

Effectiveness is the most important concern at the upper level. The more the upper level is dependent upon the lower level, the more impediments it meets, which puts the effectiveness of legislation at risk.[41] The upper-level law will not achieve its goals if the lower level fails to implement or execute it, if the quality of lower level legislation is deficient, or if the lower level pursues different policy goals. And the consistency of the law and the equality of legal subjects will be undermined if the implementation of the upper-level law in the different lower-level jurisdictions is uneven. Of course, upper-level law may define the extent to which lower-level law may deviate from upper-level law, thus leaving room for and accepting differing measures of lower-level law. This is often the case when the upper level

---

40 In Switzerland, e.g., the Federation and certain Cantons entered into an agreement with respect to the cooperation in the area of university level education, thus creating the Swiss University Conference.

41 Cf for the requirement of state implementation plans EA Young, 'Federalism as a Constitutional Principle' (2015) 83 University of Cincinnati Law Review 1057 1074.

implements rules that seek to harmonize the various lower-level laws.[42] If dependency is so strong that lower-level authorities act as co-legislators, the effectiveness of the law is less at risk, once it is adopted. However, it becomes harder to adopt laws in the first place, because of the number of players with a veto.

The lower level may, however, also be concerned about the effectiveness of its legislation. In such a case, provided the upper level grants freedom to do so, the lower level may adopt more restrictive rules when implementing the upper-level law (so-called 'gold-plating'[43]). In the case of co-legislation, both levels share the same concern of how to succeed in adopting effective and high-quality legislation, but the interpretation of what this means in practice may vary. Also, the lower level may find the effectiveness of its own legislation is jeopardized by the constraints set by the upper level.

Finally, the presence of diverse legal cultures complicates effective lawmaking. European Union law faces the challenge of how to be effective in all Member States notwithstanding the differences in legal culture. The differences may be minor, such as whether or not there is a tradition of using legal definitions, but also major if different Member States have different traditions of statutory interpretation or different drafting styles.[44] This is further developed in the contributions to this volume by Doczekalska and Lanceiro.

In a multi-level setting, cases of doubts that arise as to the extent and the reach of upper-level legislation affect the implementation at the lower level and the consistency across jurisdictions. A simple example illustrates this point: Assume that the upper level defines a speed limit on highways of 120 kilometers per hour. From the lower-level perspective, such regulation

42 Art 1 of the Swiss Federal Act on the Harmonization of Direct Cantonal and Communal Taxes of December 14, 1990, for example, states that the Act determines the direct taxes to be levied by the cantons and lays down the principles according to which cantonal legislation is to be shaped (para 1). Simultaneously, it provides that cantonal law shall apply to the structuring of cantonal and municipal taxes to the extent that the Act does not contain any rules. In particular, it remains the responsibility of the cantons to determine, inter alia, the tax rates and tax allowances (para 3).

43 See G Müller and F Uhlmann, *Elemente einer Rechtssetzungslehre* (3rd edn Schulthess 2013) para 381 n 979.

44 Some scholars complain, for example, that the drafting style of EU legislation has shifted from 'the 'fuzzy' or general-principles style familiar to many countries of continental Europe towards the 'fussy' or more detailed draft style familiar to common law countries', Robinson (n 39) 247.

poses the question whether this is a minimal standard or not. If it is a minimal standard, the lower-level regulation may be stricter and prescribe a general speed limit of 100 kilometers per hour. But that is not all. Even if the lower-level authority indeed concludes that the upper-level regulation has fixed a general speed limit of 120 kilometers as a compromise between safety and market demand, i.e. not a minimum standard, this does not necessarily answer the question whether lower speed limits are permissible, e.g. for the sake of noise reduction, environmental policy etc. Hence, simple rules may easily become challenging if considered in a multi-level setting.

2. *Autonomy and Quality*

For the lower level, the key concern is autonomy. Autonomy, in fact, is the counterpart of dependency. The less dependent the upper level is upon the lower level, the more the lower level experiences a loss of autonomy.

In the first place, the lower-level authority may feel concerned about the reduction of its sphere of competences. The perception of the lower level, be it in the national, EU or international context, is often that powers shift gradually from the lower to the upper level.[45] The discussion of the principle of subsidiarity is just an obvious example for a larger trend that shifts legislative competencies from the lower to the upper level.[46] The lament of regional authorities has a striking resemblance to the one national authorities formulate when confronted with the abundance of new EU and international regulations. However, in the case of the EU, the participation of the Member States in EU lawmaking may also be understood as an increase of power, as the Member States can participate in areas that extend their own geographical scope.[47] We will return to this in the next section.

As a consequence, the possible encroachment of upper-level law into lower-level competences is the steady source of concern from the lower-level perspective. A key question within the balance of powers is what the consequences are if the lower level contends that such an encroachment has taken place. May the lower level just suspend upper-level law and cause the upper-level authorities to sue the lower level authorities, possibly in

45 Schuppert (n 4) 340. See, however, for a differentiated consideration Tietje (n 1) 53.

46 Kadelbach (n 29) 14.

47 Kadelbach (n 29) 26.

their own courts? Or conversely does the upper-level law remain in force as long as the lower-level authority has not successfully challenged it in the upper-level courts? Or is there no legal remedy at all, with the result that it is only the upper level that decides unilaterally on the validity of its own law?

Secondly, the lower level's concern for autonomy is, in fact, also a concern for the quality of the law. The more the lower level is constrained by upper-level law, the more the quality of the upper level-law affects the quality of the lower-level law. As Whelanova's contribution points out, further in this volume, if upper-level legislation is of bad quality, lower-level lawmakers face a dilemma. They may just copy out or directly apply upper-level law but legal certainty is adversely affected if upper-level law leaves questions unanswered. Lower-level law may try to 'improve' upper-level law but this will typically raise the question whether parallel legislation on the lower level just clarifies upper-level law or is intended to amend it.[48] Moreover, the quality of lower-level law may be affected due to unrealistic timelines for implementation. Lower-level authorities may also feel that upper-level law is not practicable because it is designed and drafted by upper level-lawmakers who are remote from the needs of daily administrative work.

Thirdly, specific difficulties arise when policy choices underpinning upper-level legislation do not coincide with those for lower-level legislation. Even if these laws co-exist in parallel, the one may affect the other. For example, a system of environmental taxes at the upper level may interfere with a recycling policy at the lower level, if this means that the lower level encourages manufacturers to invest in recycling mechanisms for certain products, whereas the upper level stimulates them to invest in alternative products. More difficulties arise if the lower level has to implement the legislation adopted at the upper level. For example, the new scope and focus of EU legislation may thwart the delicate political compromises upon which national legislation rests. This creates problems, especially when the national level is required to scale its policy down.[49] The problems are less if the national level can simply scale its policy up, but even then finding coherence and a political balance is challenging. Conversely, if the scope of the policy at the upper level aligns with policy aspirations at the lower lev-

48 See for the quality of EU legislation in general C Grüner, *Quantität und Qualität der europäischen Rechtsetzung* (Lang 2011); cf also Robinson (n 39) 250ff.

49 DG Dimitrakopoulos, 'The Transposition of EU Law: "Post-Decisional Politics" and Institutional Autonomy' (2001) 7 European Law Journal 445.

el, the implementation of legislation goes more smoothly and can even be used as a lever to push through a broader reform.[50]

IV. Instruments

The key question, then, is how effectiveness, autonomy and legislative quality are secured in multi-level lawmaking. A range of instruments are in place to monitor this, but the choice is related to the type of multi-level system – with instruments of control more common in hierarchical systems – and the degree of trust between the levels of lawmaking authority. In this part, we give an overview of instruments within a spectrum with instruments of control or distrust at one end, and instruments of coordination or trust at the other. This is further developed in the contributions of Schmid, and Griglio and Lupo, further in this volume.

1. Instruments of Control

1.1. Notification, Reporting, Oversight and Permission Requirements

One way to exert direct control over the execution or implementation of upper-level law by lower-level law is to impose a duty upon the lower levels to notify draft norms, to ask for approval prior to the adoption of lower-level legislation, or to report on compliance with upper-level law.[51] For example, in the EU, a system of notification of (draft) norms that grant State aid is in place.[52] The Swiss Constitution makes provision for the Federal Council to approve cantonal legislation when required by federal law.[53] And when the deadline for the transposition of an EU Directive expires, Member States are obliged to report to the European Commission on their national implementing measures. Finally, oversight is often exercised in administratively decentralized systems, but it can also be found in federal systems. For example, in Belgium, the Federal Government may suspend and the House of Representatives may annul ordinances of the

50 For an example, see K Geeraerts and P Bursens, 'Van Kaderrichtlijn water tot decreet integraal waterbeheer. Impact van binnenlandse factoren op de Vlaamse aanpassing aan Europese regelgeving' (2007) 4 Burger bestuur & beleid 135–137.

51 Müller and Uhlmann (n 43) para 390.

52 Art 108 TFEU.

53 Art 186(2) Swiss Federal Constitution.

Brussels Region concerning urban development, town planning, public works or transport, to secure the international and metropolitan status of Brussels.[54]

These requirements sometimes blend. For example, in the European Union the notification of draft rules on State aid implies that these norms are not to come into force unless the European Commission finds that the measure does not constitute State aid or grants an exemption.

The system of notification and prior approval is helpful in so far as it is clear that the lower-level law conflicts with the upper-level legislation. In practice, the conflict is not always obvious and may only arise in administrative and court practice. Also, the technique of approval is only effective if the conflict with lower level-law relates to legislation in the same area. This is not necessarily the case. Federal regulation on aviation, for example, may be severely restricted not only by subnational regulation explicitly targeting air transport and airports but also by regional regulation on zoning, environmental policy, noise, etc. In such cases, subnational regulation addresses the same issues but from a different perspective.[55]

1.2. Enforcement and Sanctioning Instruments

An additional benefit of notification and reporting requirements is that it allows upper-level authorities to detect failures to comply with upper-level legislation. Other instruments are needed, however, to ensure enforcement of upper-level legislation through sanctions and invalidation. This requires

54 Art 45 Special majority law concerning the Brussels Institutions.

55 In Switzerland, the canton of Appenzell-Innerrhoden (lower level) implemented legislation which restricted – among other sports activities – the starting and landing of delta flyers or hang-gliders in certain alpine areas. The legislation on aviation is within the competence of the Swiss Federation (upper level, Art 87 Swiss Federal Constitution). The canton of Appenzell Innerrhoden justified its act with the interest in maintaining the ecological balance and aspects of nature conservation for which the cantons are competent. The Swiss Supreme Court had to decide whether the cantonal act violated federal law and the order of competence, respectively. It reasoned that federal law does not conclusively regulate the protection of nature or alpine areas from impairments caused by take-off and landing of hang-gliders although the Federation had the competence to do so. Because of the Federation not using this competence fully, the cantons remained competent to legislate in this area. The Court thus rejected the appeal against the act (BGE 122 I 70, consid 2ff); cf also Müller and Uhlmann (n 43) para 387.

a hierarchical system, where upper-level legislation has priority over lower-level legislation.

Sanctions can be imposed by administrative or judicial upper-level bodies. Judicial bodies may invalidate lower-level legislation that does not comply with upper-level legislation. Additional rules may support the controlling function of upper-level authorities, e.g. by giving upper-level administrative authorities standing in lower-level court cases,[56] or by allowing upper-level authorities to take action against lower-level legislation.

In this scenario, lower-level courts are often deployed to ensure the effectiveness and preeminence of upper-level law. This is an important component of the EU enforcement system.[57] In prevailing on national courts to play their full part in that system, however, issues of legal culture may arise. Especially in countries with a dualist tradition, and in countries where courts are restrained from reviewing statutes, the shift to a system of direct applicability of supranational law under the judicial review of courts is not without difficulties. Tensions arise especially where upper-level legislation has little legitimacy – e.g. secondary legislation in a technical area – and collides with norms of the lower level with high legitimacy – e.g. a national constitution. The potential for conflict is regularly mitigated by a mechanism for an interpretation of the lower-level law that is in line with the upper-level law.[58] Even then, lower-level courts may not easily accept the supremacy of the upper-level norm in such cases. This is especially true

56 In Switzerland, for example, federal agencies have standing in state court cases contingent the challenged decision could affect the federal legislation in their respective scope of duties (cf art 89(2)(a) in connection with art 111(1) of the Federal Act on the Swiss Federal Tribunal of June 17, 2005).

57 Cf, inter alia, Case 6/64 *Costa v ENEL* [1964] ECR 585 and Case 106/77 *Amministrazione delle Finanze dello Stato v Simmenthal SpA* (*Simmenthal II*) [1978] *ECR* 629; Case C-282/10 *Dominguez v. Centre Informatique du Centre Ouest Atlantique* [2012] ECR I-000, para 27; Young (n 41) 1071; I Härtel, *Handbuch Europäische Rechtsetzung* (Springer 2006) § 15 para 5; A McDonnell, 'The Hierarchy of Norms in EU Law – Empowering and controlling the Commission' in A Epiney, M Haag and A Heinemann (eds), *Die Herausforderung von Grenzen – Le défi des frontiers – Challenging boundaries* (Nomos 2007) 372ff. In Switzerland, art 49 of the Swiss Federal Constitution states that '(f)ederal law takes precedence over any conflicting provision of cantonal law.'.

58 See for the interpretation of national law in conformity with EU law Case C-282/10 *Dominguez v. Centre Informatique du Centre Ouest Atlantique* [2012] ECR I-000, para 24ff. The same principle applies in Switzerland between the Federation and the Cantons, cf G Biaggini, *Kommentar Bundesverfassung der Schweizerischen Eidgenossenschaft* (2nd edn, Orell Füssli 2017) art 49 para 4. Cf also the 'presumption against preemption' in US law, Young (n 41) 1073.

if fundamental rights are concerned. The 'Solange' cases of the German Constitutional Court[59] were just the start of a much broader counter-reaction against the supremacy of EU law, presently under the label of constitutional identity.[60]

This shows that the system goes both ways. Invalidation of upper-level law by courts is an instrument to secure the lower level's autonomy. Here, the key question is which court has the power to assess and invalidate upper-level norms. Usually, this is attributed to the upper-level courts, but procedural rules may enable lower-level authorities to be given standing or take action. The more hierarchical the system, the less room there is for judicial review by lower-level courts. The most that can be done is to introduce a system of preliminary references, allowing lower-level courts to refer questions to the upper-level court when doubts on the validity of upper-level legislation arise. By contrast, as mentioned above, in systems of constitutional pluralism, constitutional courts, in exceptional circumstances, do review upper-level legislation against constitutional norms and principles.

To conclude, enforcement and sanctioning rights are focused on the effectiveness of, mostly, upper-level laws and less concerned with autonomy issues. This may, however, lead to counter-reactions, especially when fundamental values at the lower level are at stake. Also, if the upper level cannot be confident of compliance by the lower-level entities, it has to invest in a sophisticated enforcement program, which is often difficult to apply.[61]

2. *Participation in the Lawmaking Process*

An instrument to secure both the effectiveness of higher-level law and the autonomy of lower-level authorities is the participation of lower-level representatives in the upper-level lawmaking process.[62] Lower-level authorities will thereby be in a better position to execute, implement or transpose

---

59 BVerfGE 37, 271ff (Solange I); BVerfGE 73, 339ff (Solange II).

60 Cf LFM Besselink, 'National and constitutional identity before and after Lisbon' (2010) 6(3) Utrecht Law Review 36–49.

61 For a discussion of the EU monitoring system of compliance, see TA Börzel, 'Non-compliance in the European Union: pathology or statistical artefact?' (2001) 8 Journal of European Public Policy 803–824.

62 See, for the participation rights of the Swiss cantons in the federal lawmaking process Müller and Uhlmann (n 43) para 382ff.

upper-level legislation because their involvement increases the legitimacy of the upper-level law and allows them to better prepare for their task.

There are several ways to secure participation by lower-level authorities. This function is generally attributed to upper chambers in federal states, although the requirements in terms of composition and powers are often not met in practice and executive-based institutions have proven more effective.[63] Also, representation in upper houses provides for collective representation and collective veto rights,[64] whereas particular subnational interests are better secured through instruments that give them individual participation or veto rights.[65] Individual veto rights are in place in the case of co-legislation: when unanimity is required to pass binding rules, which is usually the case in intergovernmental international systems,[66] or when cooperative agreements are required to regulate a matter. In other systems as well, some or all lower-level entities may have the individual right to intervene in the lawmaking process, for example if they are of the opinion that their interests are threatened by a draft law. Systems often incorporate a mixture of participation and representation mechanisms. For example, in the EU system, the Council of Ministers consists of representatives of Member State's governments, whereas national Parliaments participate through the Early Warning System under Article 12 TEU and Protocol (No 2) on the Application of the Principles of Subsidiarity and Proportionality.[67]

Hence, even if the upper level is in a strong position by virtue of passing legislation that must be enforced by the lower level, focusing just on the upper level may cloud the fact that the lower level has considerable influ-

63 F Palermo, 'Beyond Second Chambers: Alternative Representation of Territorial Interests and Their Reasons' (2018) 10 Perspectives on Federalism 51–61.

64 Cf art 142(ii) of the Swiss Federal Constitution: 'Proposals that are submitted to the vote of the People and Cantons are accepted if a majority of those who vote and a majority of the Cantons approve them.'.

65 Palermo (n 63) 61–64.

66 See, however, for the evolution from decision-making by unanimity to majority voting in international organizations and the constitutionalization of international law, respectively, HG Schermers and NM Blokker, 'International Organizations or Institutions, Voting Rules and Procedures', *Max Planck Encyclopedia of Public International Law* (April 2009), para 8 <http://opil.ouplaw.com/view/10.1093/law:epil/9780199231690/law-9780199231690-e467?prd=EPIL> accessed 4 March 2019; C Humrich and B Zangl, 'Global governance through legislation' in M Zürn, S Wälti and H Enderlein (eds), *Handbook on Multi-level Governance* (Edward Elgar 2010) 348ff; U Karpen, Introduction, in U Karpen and H Xanthaki (eds), *Legislation in Europe* (Hart Publishing 2017) 7.

67 [2010] OJ C 83/206.

ence on the decision-making process of the upper level.[68] Participation, then, comes with the risk of decision traps, pointing to the risk that veto players may make it difficult for the upper level to adopt measures.[69] Also, the influence of lower-level entities is often asymmetrical in nature. In the international context, small states often complain about decisions that are taken by a small number of powerful states, leaving little room for smaller states to do other than comply with such rules.[70] Asymmetry, then, can be the result of informal power relations, but it may also result from legal arrangements. This is often the case in multinational systems, where some groups are privileged as a means to secure room for the development of their regional identity.[71]

Conversely, the upper level is sometimes involved in rule making at the lower level. This is obviously the case when co-legislation applies, but other examples can be cited. Hence, in non-hierarchical dual federations, the right to interfere in another Parliament's lawmaking process may apply both ways. For example, in Belgium, Parliaments of the subnational entities (Communities and Regions) may suspend the federal lawmaking process for negotiations when they are of the opinion that a bill is likely to harm their interests, but the federal Parliament may also interfere in the lawmaking process of the subnational Parliaments.[72]

Complexity is added when the legislative activity involves more than two layers. This is the case when for example the European Union intervenes in domains that fall under the exclusive or shared powers of federal states. In principle, the EU identifies the national authorities as its direct discussion partners, considering that they incorporate the further strands of governance.[73] It is left to the Member States to involve the subnational

68 See for the risk of blocking upper level legislation Schuppert (n 4) 353.

69 F Scharpf, 'The joint decision trap. Lessons from German federalism and European integration' (1988) 66 Public Adm. 239–278.

70 See, e.g., with respect to the working methods of the UN Security Council the initiative of a group of small states called 'ACT' (Accountability, Coherence and Transparency) and the 'Small Five Group', respectively.

71 On the link between constitutional asymmetry and multinationalism; P Popelier and M Sahadzic, 'Conclusion. A Country Studies-Based Deliberation on Constitutional Asymmetry in Multi-tiered Multinational Systems', in P Popelier and M Sahadzic (eds), *Constitutional Asymmetry in Multinational Federalism* (Cham, Palgrave MacMillan 2019) 492–498.

72 Art 143 Constitution, art 32 Law on the reform of institutions, art 67 law 31 December 1983 on the reform of institutions of the German-speaking Community.

73 GB Peters, 'The Future of the State: Comparative Perspectives', (2007) Revista General de Derecho Público Comparado 3.

authorities. The EU framework may facilitate the involvement of lower levels of authority, but may also establish constraints. For example, the eight-week time limit for the adoption of reasoned opinions under the Early Warning System[74] is short in itself, but particularly so where regional parliaments have to be involved in the process and coordinated.

3. *Coordination Instruments*

While enforcement and sanctioning instruments are mostly concerned with the upper level's efficiency needs, coordination instruments aim at effectiveness with respect for the lower level's autonomy. Here, compliance is pursued through softer mechanisms. Soft mechanisms can prove very effective in practice, for example if nudging or consulting leads to outcomes in which the lower-level lawmaker feels acknowledged. However, they require goodwill on all sides, and therefore a fair amount of trust.

This category may consist of instruments that help the lower level to implement higher-level law, for example through financial aid, education, manuals etc. This category also includes harmonization of lower-level laws, as well as the consultation of affected entities or the establishment of working groups – which comes close to the category of participatory instruments, but is a weaker and less visible form of involvement.

The loyalty principle can be seen as a legal translation of this type of instruments that is more interested in ways to adopt effective laws that balance all interests and secures the autonomy of each entity. This principle involves a duty for the lawmaker to take account of the impact of its laws on other entities, even if it remains within its sphere of competences. In practice, this principle often comes down to a duty to consult the affected parties or to involve them in other ways.[75]

---

74 See art 6(i) of the Protocol (No 2) on the Application of the Principles of Subsidiarity and Proportionality [2010] OJ C 83/206.

75 See for the principle of loyalty within federalist states P Egli, *Die Bundestreue – Eine rechtsvergleichende Untersuchung* (DIKE 2010) 21ff (for Germany), 169ff (for Switzerland) and 338ff (for the United States of America). For the very outspoken implementation of loyalty as a proportionality principle, see P Popelier, 'Zuständigkeitsteilung in Belgien: Kompetenzverteilung als Kennzeichen multinationalen Konfliktmanagements' in A Gampe, P Bußjäger, F Karlhofer, G Pallaver and W Obwexer (eds), *Föderale Kompetenzverteilung in Europa* (Nomos 2016) 176. Art. 4(3) TEU on the principle of sincere cooperation can also be seen as an expression of the loyalty principle, see M. Klamert, *The principle of loyalty in the EU* (Oxford, Oxford University Press 2014).

V. Conclusion

The purpose of this paper was to give an overview of types of multi-level systems, the types of problems that lawmakers encounter at the different levels of authority, and the means to address these problems.

Multi-level systems were distinguished on the basis of power, tasks and legal sources. These categories do not always apply to the system in its entirety; sometimes they characterize a multi-level system only with regard to certain policy domains.

The main denominator here was the degree to which the upper level of authority depends upon the lower levels to make its laws effective, and on the degree of autonomy that is left for the lower levels. As a result, effectiveness and autonomy were identified as the main concerns of lawmakers in multi-level systems, which are both linked to quality concerns.

To address these concerns, different types of instruments were presented, one category more focused on effectiveness, another on autonomy, and an intermediate category focused on participation as a means to secure both autonomy and effectiveness. At the same time, some drawbacks were noticed. Enforcement and sanctioning instruments may lead to counter-reactions at the lower level, and cannot be relied on for the entire lawmaking activity. Participation instruments may lead to decision traps. And coordination instruments rely upon the goodwill of all actors involved, which is a condition that is not always met in practice. Ultimately, a mixture of instruments is recommended, the exact combination of which is determined by the type of multi-level system.

Chapter 2: How Upper Levels Strive to Influence Law-Making at the Lower Levels and Why Lower Levels Can't Have Cake and Eat It

Evelyne Schmid (University of Lausanne)[*]

I. Introduction

In this chapter, I ask whether there are commonalities of how various upper levels attempt and often succeed in ensuring legislative implementation at the lower levels and what this means for the complex situation in which domestic legislators find themselves in today's multi-level settings. I claim that it is possible to discern four groups of approaches that upper levels employ to assert legislative implementation. My starting point is the inevitable challenge of every legal system to allocate competences and responsibilities and to employ at least some mechanisms by which the upper level can secure the actual observance of its legal sources – ideally while accommodating the competing interests of autonomy of legislative actors situated at a lower level. I am exclusively concerned with obligations that require lower level legislators to engage, i.e. legislative obligations rather than obligations to execute. Why this choice? Legislative obligations are particularly salient for the purpose of this book as they raise thorny questions in relation to the autonomy of those making laws at the lower level. As soon as we have multiple normative levels, the need to secure the effectiveness of upper level legal sources at the lower level raises the question of how and under what circumstances upper levels can take steps to achieve such effectiveness. As a corollary, questions of the separation of power at each level and between levels emerge. Moreover, legislative obligations are also particularly interesting because they are a consequence of political communities entrusting upper levels with additional tasks. In a domestic jurisdiction, for instance, legislative obligations arise notably when we demand that the state is taking some sort of positive action to protect natural or legal persons and other interests (such as the environment) against risks or abuses. Similarly, states have created additional international or region-

* I thank Nitya Duella, BSc, BLaw, for proofreading the manuscript.

al legal sources because they concluded that certain goals can best be pursued by regulating at the upper level. This increased normative density at upper levels naturally increases the relevance and political and legal salience of the question of how, and at what price, upper level legal sources can be rendered effective at the lower levels.

In terms of methodology, I look at the tools available to each upper level vis-à-vis lower level. When referring to upper levels, this chapter takes the perspectives of public international law, EU law and federal law in federal domestic legal systems as three relevant variants of upper levels. I thus look at the tools available for the federation vis-à-vis the lower level of the sub-units; the EU vis-à-vis Member States and public international law vis-à-vis states.

Legislative studies have so far usually analysed upper level perspectives within a single set of relations between two levels, e.g. the implementation of public international law at the national level, EU law in Member States or federal law in a federal system. Moreover, when international lawyers have been concerned with implementation in national legal systems, they have disproportionately focused on domestic courts to the neglect of domestic legislators.[1] The traditional approach to look at upper level perspectives in isolation is not entirely unjustified. Indeed, to a large extent it makes sense to look at the various sets of interactions in isolation, let alone because of the complexity of each of them and the inherent difficulties of comparative attempts. Yet, by considering various upper levels in the same chapter, we gain a better understanding of the idea that many of the dilemmas in ambitious multi-level settings are shared and sometimes unavoidable. Such a macroscopic view shows that we cannot have the cake and eat it. When normative ambitions increase at the upper levels, the strive for effectiveness and the associated use of upper level mechanisms almost axiomatically increase as well and potentially limit legislative autonomy at the lower levels. Against this background, the present chapter does not intend to outline a deterministic meta-theory that would necessarily fit all multi-level interactions between any upper level and any legislator situated at a lower level. Nonetheless, I claim that it is still possible to identify some commonalities and that these commonalities reveal something about the inherent challenges of law-making in a multilevel setting.

The chapter is structured as follows. In a first step, I explain the selection of three variants of normative levels that can play the role of upper

1 E Schmid and T Altwicker, 'International Law and (Swiss) Domestic Law-Making Processes' (2015) SRIEL 501.

levels: 1) federal law in a federal country, 2) EU law and 3) public international law and I sketch the argument that all three of these upper levels – through a variety of conceptual manifestations – strive to ensure the effectivity of their legal sources at the lower level (section II). If they would not do so, we would consider them dysfunctional. Based on this premise, I then present, in section III, four groups of mechanisms and instruments that these upper levels employ in order to increase the chances that lower level legislators comply. For each group of approaches, I identify the most common concerns from the perspective of the lower level. The chapter concludes with some reflections on this state of affairs and its relationship with the current backlash against international and regional law.

Complexity, terminology and limitations

A few remarks on terminology are required. Readers of this chapter will have to bear with terminological simplifications in this paper. A few points must be made. First, as Felix Uhlmann and Patricia Popelier point out in their contribution, the term 'upper level' does not necessarily denote a hierarchically superior level but refers to the entity with the community of the larger size.[2]

Second, one and the same normative level can simultaneously be upper and lower depending on the legal question or the perspective one takes. For instance, federal law in a federation can be situated at the upper level vis-à-vis sub-national legislators but at the lower level vis-à-vis European or international law.

Third, the term 'level' comes with the inaccurate connotation that there are neatly separated 'zones' of norm creation and subsequent legislative engagement. In reality, the norms of one level can originate conjunctively at upper and lower levels with the participation of actors from both.[3] Moreover, as far as international law is concerned, domestic legal systems can decide to treat international legal sources as 'the land of the law', and therefore as a part of lower level law, as soon as they acquire domestic legal validity (monism), or they can conceive them as two separate legal spheres

2 F Uhlmann and P Popelier, 'Multi-Level Law-Making: Form, Arrangement and Design in Theory and Practice' in P Popelier and others (eds), *Law-Making in Multilevel Settings* (Hart 2019) 25, 28.

3 Uhlmann and Popelier (n 2),37.

(dualism), each time with many possible nuances between these two basic options.

Fourth, the chapter maintains distinct vocabulary for multilevel governance and federalism. I use the term federalism to apply exclusively to a polity that encompasses several territorial jurisdictions within a single nation state whereas I use the term multilevel governance independently of whether or not the territorial lower levels operate within a single state.

Fifth, it is beyond the scope of this chapter to debate to what extent EU law as a sui generis legal order constitutes international law. Those who argue that EU law is essentially part of public international law (rather than some sort of entirely self-contained regime) shall be reassured that I do not wish to take issue with their point of view. Nevertheless, it is justified to consider EU law as a separate level in the analysis of this chapter, be it because it is regional law and thus 'in-between' international law and national law, or because EU law is particularly relevant if we want to assess whether there are commonalities in upper level approaches.

II. The three upper levels and their strive for effectiveness

This section sketches the following three selected variants of upper level perspectives, namely A) federal level in a federal country, B) EU law and C) public international law. For each of them, the major manifestations of how they seek effective legislative implementation at the lower level(s) is briefly outlined.

1. The federal level in federations

The first upper level considered in this contribution is federal law in a federal (or devolved) country. In any federal legal system, some issues are governed by upper level law that the sub-units (Länder, states, cantons etc.) are expected to comply with. Of course, the extent to which matters are governed at the level of federal law is very variable across systems. The default competence can be situated either at the lower level (as, for instance, in the US, Germany or Switzerland) or at the upper level (as with devolution in the UK or in India for residual subjects).

That said, generalisations across federal systems are almost taboo. There is a wide variety of the upper levels within federal states, each with different histories, forms, mechanism, procedures, legal cultures and constituencies. Moreover, there is variation across domains and political salience of one and the same pattern of interaction even within a single jurisdiction.[4] Yet, it seems permissible to conclude that some sort of pre-eminence of federal constitutional and other federal law is shared across federal systems. Even if the concrete arrangements and practices vary considerably, and existing research has largely focused on a U.S.- and Western-centric perspective in examining supremacy as exercised by domestic constitutional courts in federal systems,[5] it is safe to observe that federal upper levels rely on pre-eminence to ensure the effectiveness of upper level legal sources. Such pre-eminence is sometimes combined with commitments to subsidiarity.

2. *European Union law*

The second upper level to be considered is EU law. As is well known, EU law depends to a significant extent on lower level (national) law-making, especially when it comes to the implementation of EU Directives. Directives are the primary instrument when an ambition is placed upon the 'EU upper level' in scenarios in which there is widespread agreement that a one-size fits all solution is not desirable or not acceptable to Member States. At least as conceptually conceived, directives thus leave discretion to Member States as to *how* a certain objective is best reached but leave no discretion as to *whether* to legislate and very little when it comes to the question of *when* to legislate given that directives contain a timeframe within which states must have implemented it.

As in federal states, a combination of supremacy and subsidiarity are the bedrock concepts of how EU law interacts with the lower levels, i.e. the Member States. As is well-known since *Van Gen den Loos*, EU law – or at least how it has been interpreted by the Court of Justice of the European Union (ECJ) – must be treated as superior to any national legal sources.[6] At the same time, in the spheres of non-exclusive powers, the Treaty on

4 For an overview, T Hueglin and A Fenna, *Comparative Federalism* (2nd edn, Toronto University Press 2015).

5 M Mate, 'Judicial Supremacy in Comparative Constitutional Law' (2017) 92 Tul L Rev, 395.

6 Including national constitutions. Case C-11/70 *International Handelsgesellschaft v Einfuhr- und Vorratsstelle Getreide* [1970], ECR 1125. Case 26/62 *NV Algemene Transport- en Expeditie Onderneming van Gend & Loos v Netherlands Inland Revenue Administration* (1963) ECR 1.

European Union (TEU) explicitly requires subsidiarity as a general constitutional principle of the EU. The 'Union shall act only if and in so far as the objectives of the proposed action cannot be sufficiently achieved by the Member States'.[7]

3. *Public international law*

Contemporary international law regularly requires domestic legislators to change existing or adopt new domestic legislation. International human rights law, in particular, contains ambitious obligations that require the engagement of domestic legislators, such as legislative measures to eradicate discrimination or measures to allocate competences and resources to fully realise rights. This situation implies that domestic legislators have a decisive influence – and clear obligations – shaping the extent to which international legal ambitions translate into tangible outcomes.

Yet, one of the thorny problems that international law continues to face is precisely its limited ability to influence the behaviour of domestic legislators and the 'relative impermeability of national systems to international legal imperatives'.[8] If 'the future of international law is domestic', as Slaughter and Burke-White claim, legislative implementation at the domestic level becomes even more decisive.[9]

International law places obligations upon domestic legislations in essentially two ways. I distinguish international legislative obligations that arise directly at the international level from other legislative obligations that arise in the interaction with the domestic constitutional framework. The former are obligations for which international law itself says that the domestic legislator must take action (sometimes it does so explicitly, sometimes implicitly). The latter are obligations that might or might not require domestic legislative engagement depending on the domestic division of competences.[10]

---

7 Consolidated Version of the Treaty on European Union [2008] OJ C115/13, art 5.

8 A Cassese, 'Towards a Moderate Monism: Could International Rules Eventually Acquire the Force to Invalidate Inconsistent National Laws?' in A Cassese (ed), *Realizing Uotpia: The Future of International Law* (OUP 2012) 187, 188.

9 A-M Slaughter and W Burke-White, 'The Future of International Law Is Domestic (or, The European Way of Law)' (2006) 47 HarvInt'l LJ 327.

10 For a more detailed explanation of this classification and examples, see E Schmid, 'The Identification and Role of International Legislative Duties in a Contested

The central manifestation of how public international law operates in relation to lower level law-makers is state responsibility. International law leaves it to each domestic legal system to decide how precisely international legal sources are treated within the national system. What counts is the state's compliance with international obligation. Failure to conform with what is required by an international obligation by a state results – in the absence of circumstances precluding wrongfulness – in the responsibility of the state for internationally wrongful acts.[11] It does not matter whether the breach is caused by an act or an omission.[12] The conduct of a domestic legislator – whether national or sub-national – is squarely attributable to the state.[13]

4. *What all three upper levels share: A common appetite for effectiveness*

As an intermediary finding of this short outline of the three selected upper levels, it is warranted to note that the three upper levels share a common strive for effectiveness. All three upper levels depend to some extent on lower level legislators and all three of them therefore need to ensure that the lower levels comply with upper level legal sources.[14]

There is, however, a qualification to be made. The assumption that upper levels seek to achieve the effectiveness of their legal sources does not always need to hold true. Consider a new upper legal source that resulted from a hard-fought compromise. At least some of the actors at the upper level may not fully back the new legal norms and might be rather indifferent or even spoil the implementation of the new legal source at the lower level. Similarly, a federation may decide to ratify an international treaty that requires legislative implementation at the sub-national level. If a treaty was ratified with 'mixed feelings', it is well possible that federal actors will not push for implementation at the lower level in their state but rather adopt a 'wait-and-see-approach', notably if there is no international institution that can make a binding legal finding of non-compliance. Hence, the

---

Area: Must Switzerland Legislate in Relation to «Business and Human Rights»?' (2015) SRIEL 563.

11 ILC Articles on State Responsibility, Annex to GA Res. 56/83, 12 December 2001, art 12 in conjunction with arts 1 and 2 [subsequently cited as ARSIWA].

12 ARSIWA, art 2.

13 ARSIWA, art 4; J Crawford, *State Responsibility: the General Part* (Cambridge University Press 2013) 120.

14 Uhlmann and Popelier (n 2), 38.

assumption that upper levels unequivocally strive for legislative implementation at the lower level is a friendly oversimplification. Despite this qualification, if all goes well, an upper level normally does and should strive for the effectiveness of its legal sources at the lower level(s). In the next section, we thus consider the types of instruments and mechanisms upper levels can employ and how these tools lead to at least some concerns from the lower levels.

III. *What upper levels can do to secure effectiveness and the common concerns at the lower levels*

Upper levels dispose of various mechanisms to incentivise, push or otherwise influence law-making at 'their' respective lower levels. I propose to classify these mechanisms into four groups: (1) substitute performance by the upper level, (2) court enforcement, (3) financial liability and (4) a fourth group containing a range of oversight and cooperation measures. The following sections sketch each of these groups of mechanisms. I then examine to what extent a group of mechanisms exists in all three upper levels and I then present each time the main concerns that are raised when an upper level resorts to one of the mentioned mechanisms.

Before I begin, I must explain why I do not consider supremacy/pre-eminence as a mechanism. Supremacy (or the absence thereof) is an intervening factor that plays out in relation to almost any of the mechanisms discussed below. In addition, even where pre-eminence exists, pre-eminence alone will not be sufficient to secure the effectiveness of lower level legal sources without concrete mechanisms. Hence, supremacy is not a mechanism but a transversal factor that influences interactions in multi-level settings.

1. *Vertical[15] substitute performance*

In some cases, upper levels can resort to substitute performance and legislate *in lieu* of the lower level legislator. Some federations foresee or at least do not exclude the possibility of vertical substitute performance by the fed-

15 As mentioned in the introduction, horizontal mechanisms are not discussed here. Suffice it to say that substitute performance at the same level is perceived as less problematic and is an option in many systems (e.g. legislative competence tem-

eral level for failures of the sub-units to implement federal law.[16] In a number of federations, the federal level as the 'mid-level' between sub-units and international law installs a substitute mechanism for the implementation of international or EU law by the sub-national legislators. In Austria, for instance, art 16(4) of the federal constitution allows the federation to legislate on behalf of the Länder. Failure to comply 'promptly' with the obligation to implement international treaties results in the passage of the competence for such measures, 'especially the enactment of the necessary laws', to the Federation.[17] In Belgium, the Constitution foresees that the federal state can (or could) exceptionally take over and carry out obligations of a sub-national unity that fails to carry out Belgium's international obligations within the federated entity's sphere of competence.[18] But a high threshold must be met and the process has apparently not yet been used.[19] It does not require much imagination to note that this is an exceptional mechanism that is unfriendly towards lower level federal interests. In the Indian Constitution, the federal parliament even has the power to legislate for any part of India in order to 'implement any treaty, agreement or convention with any other country or countries or any decision made at any international conference, association or other body'.[20] Note that the provision is not limited to treaties in the sense of the Vienna Conventions on the Law of Treaties (between states or with international organisations) but includes international decisions as well. The Indian constitutional provision has the advantage to provide a powerful safeguard for the federal level for the legislative implementation of upper (international) level norms at all levels of the Indian domestic legal system. The provision, however, comes with obvious disadvantages from the point of view of the autonomy of the subnational level. Given the contemporary density of in-

---

porarily passing to the executive level if the sub-national legislator fails to comply with an upper level obligation).

16 But at least in Switzerland, the eventuality of such a substitute performance by the federal level substituting cantonal legislators has little to no practical significance. E Schmid, 'Völkerrechtliche Gesetzgebungsaufträge in den Kantonen' (2016) 135 ZSR 3, 15-16.

17 Austrian Federal Constitution (Bundes-Verfassungsgesetz) of 19 December 1945, art 16(4).

18 Belgian Constitution, Belgian Official Gazette of 29 November2017, Art. 169.

19 C Panara, *The Sub-national Dimension of the EU: A Legal Study of Multilevel Governance* (Springer 2015), 29 n 50. G Hernández, 'Federal States' in André Nollkaemper and Ilias Plakokefalos (eds), *The Practice of Shared Responsibility in International Law* (CUP 2017), 40, n 92.

20 The Constitution of India of 26 November 1949, art 253.

ternational law, the lower level must – at least in theory – nearly always expect that the federal level asserts some legislative competence. These few examples aside, federations in many systems constitutionally lack competence to implement international law on sub-unit matters without the co-operation of the lower units.[21] Yet, the absence of explicit provisions on such substitute performance does not necessarily mean that the federal level does not – in some extreme cases – dispose of (implicit or emergency) powers to legislate *in lieu* of the lower level legislator.

In the other two types of upper levels, vertical substitute performance in the area of law-making is equally perceived as a tool of last resort, if it is available at all. The only conceivable and contested constellation that comes close to a substitute performance at the level of public international law vis-à-vis states would be situations in which the UN Security Council (UNSC) adopts a resolution under Chapter VII of the UN Charter if it has previously determined the 'existence of any threat to the peace, breach of the peace, or act of aggression' in accordance with art 39 of the Charter. With the exception of the 15 members of the UNSC, the lower level does not participate in the law-making at the upper level. But it is only an approximation to vertical substitute performance because the UNSC does not legislate in the Member States. But the last word has probably not yet been spoken on the controversy as to what extent the UNSC has the power to take legislative action interfering with domestic legal systems. In the aftermath of the 9/11 terrorist attacks, and beginning with Resolution 1373 of 28 September 2001, the UNSC has exercised quasi-legislative functions that led to arguably compulsory legislative changes by domestic legislators by virtue of the interpretation that articles 25 and 103 of the UN Charter leave states no choice.[22]

In the EU, upper level institutions cannot adopt legislation on behalf of the Member States. If the legislative competence is with the Member States (and thus the lower level), the EU institutions cannot resort to a vertical substitute performance *in lieu* of the Member States' legislators. For shared competences, the Member States can legislate as long as the EU level has

21 For an overview, W Rudolf, 'Federal States' in R Wolfrum (ed), *Max Planck Encyclopedia of Public International Law* (MPIL 2011) para 30.

22 Suffice to refer to some scholarly analyses: S Talmon, 'The Security Council as World Legislature' (2005) 99 AJIL 175. A Tzanakopoulos, *Disobeying the Security Council: Countermeasures against Wrongful Sanctions* (OUP 2011).

not done so, but not vice versa.[23] For supporting competences, there is also no vertical substitute performance.[24]

Despite the largely unavailable vertical substitute performance in international law and EU law, both of these upper levels – with the participation of the lower levels – can, however, adopt statute-like norms that are so precise that the lower level legislator is essentially bypassed or arguably degraded to a simple executioner.[25] EU Regulations are the commonly used tool in the EU. International law provisions usually leave considerable discretion to national law-makers and other domestic actors but there are significant exceptions. Some obligations leave almost no discretion to the national legislator.[26] Jacob Katz Cogan argues that the number of such obligations is increasing.[27] In any event, the phenomenon of adopting precise statute-like norms at the upper level must be clearly distinguished from substitute performances as these situations concern the nature of the upper level norm and not the mechanisms to implement the norm at the lower level, albeit both phenomena lead to similar concerns.

The major worries with substitute performance are rather obvious. Vertical substitute performance of the lower level legislator dramatically reduces or even eradicates the autonomy of the lower level legislator and constitutes a harsh form of interference into the areas of competence of the lower level. The use of quasi-legislative wording in UNSC resolutions is perceived as problematic as only few countries are members of the UNSC and some provisions in some resolutions stand in tension with states' other international obligations.[28] In any case, lower level law-making in these circumstances is by-passed or does at least not correspond to the ideal of parliamentarism in which democratically accountable representatives deliberate and then make choices.

Compared to substitute performance, the enforcement of legislative obligations in courts, considered next, is more common but also raises concerns.

---

23 Consolidated version of the Treaty on the Functioning of the European Union (TFEU) [2016] OJ C202/1, art 4.

24 TFEU (n 23), art 6.

25 S Kadelbach, *Allgemeines Verwaltungsrecht unter europäischem Einfluss* (Mohr Siebeck 1999) 300.

26 Maritime Labour Convention (adopted 23 February 2006, entered into force 20 August 2013), 2952 UNTS I -51299, Standard A1.1 (hat tip to Anna Petrig for bringing this example to my attention).

27 JK Cogan, 'The Regulatory Turn in International Law' (2011) 52 HarvInt'l LJ 321.

28 See (n 22).

2. *Vertical court enforcement*

Under what circumstances can upper level courts enforce legislative implementation at the lower level? This section discusses the basic issues with enforcing upper level legislative obligations through upper level courts. Court enforcement through financial sanctions is discussed separately in sub-section III.3. As with the other mechanisms, a basic methodological problem concerns comparability. As Ran Hirschl has persuasively argued, it is impossible to compare the roles of courts in different polities without fully understanding the social, economic and political context in which those courts operate.[29] Yet, even if we cannot 'compare' mechanisms, we can arguably identify – in broad brushstrokes – the types of approaches most commonly invoked.

2.1. The importance of admissibility rules

Admissibility rules, and particularly rules on standing, are crucially important to help secure effectiveness of upper level norms through court enforcement: if private individuals or upper level institutions have standing in courts[30] to challenge lower level law-makers because of normative conflicts with upper level law, this is a powerful tool to support upper level law. This is even more powerful if the admissibility rules also foresee standing to invoke negative conflicts, i.e. the absence of lower level legislation on a certain point of law.[31]

Domestically, private individuals may be given standing to support upper level law in (upper and lower level) courts. Given that this chapter focuses on upper level mechanisms, it is particularly important to note that the principle of supremacy of federal law over subnational law in federal states is sometimes treated as a fundamental right, which implies that individuals can challenge subnational legislation in any procedure, including at the upper level courts. An individual can therefore claim that a subnational piece of legislation is in conflict with upper level (federal) law, as is

29 R Hirschl, *Towards Juristocracy: the Origins and Consequences of the New Constitutionalism* (Harvard University Press 2007) 151.

30 For reasons of simplicity, this chapter primarily looks at upper level courts but such standing can also be granted at lower level courts (e.g. federal authorities having standing in state court cases).

31 And such standing may ultimately form the basis for a ruling on liability, see section III.3.

the case in Switzerland.[32] The limitation of this arrangement on standing rules, while powerful, is that it is difficult to use if the conflict is negative in nature, i.e. if the lower level fails to engage in law-making in a given area (as opposed to 'positive' conflicts in which the lower level adopts legislation that infringes upper level principles). Rules of procedure in court proceedings tend to be better equipped to deal with 'bad' legislation at one and the same level rather than with the lack of legislation required by an upper level.

EU law and the ECJ sometimes require Member States to set aside national rules on standing in order to grant individuals access to court and remedies foreseen at the upper level.[33] As with other mechanisms, this approach is in a way at the crossroads between delegating tasks to secure effectiveness to lower level courts against lower level legislators while it is backed up with infringement procedures at the upper level.

Public international law does not dictate admissibility rules at the lower level, i.e. at the domestic level of states. However, states have themselves recognised in some cases that they should grant individuals standing in national courts in order to increase the effectiveness of international law in their own legal order and in order to avoid state responsibility.[34] States have also sometimes accepted supervisory mechanisms at the international level that provide standing for individuals. The European Court of Human Rights currently goes farthest in this regard (although the actual admissibility of applications is low, and the overwhelming majority of applications do not reach the merits stage). With the exception of art. 34 (6) of the Protocol to the African Charter on Human and Peoples' Rights on the Establishment of the African Court on Human and Peoples' Rights, the Inter-American and the African human rights system 'filter' applications at the level of a commission who decides whether a case can reach the regional court. Supervisory mechanisms at the United Nations (treaty-bodies) to various extents also provide for standing of individuals at the international level.[35] Although the outcomes of proceedings before treaty bodies (so

32 Uhlmann and Popelier (n 2), 45.

33 M Eliantonio and others, *Standing up for Your Right(s) in Europe: A Comparative Study on Legal Standing (Locus Standi) Before the EU and Member States' Courts* (Intersentia 2013).

34 As was, for instance, the case in Switzerland. Decision of the Swiss Federal Tribunal of 26 July 1999, 125 II 417.

35 For an overview of regional human rights systems and UN supervisory mechanisms, see, e.g., D Moeckli, S Shah and S Sivakumaran (eds), *International Human Rights Law* (OUP 2018) 369-481.

called 'views') are not legally binding, the provision of standing to bring claims at the upper level can influence the decision-making at lower levels and increase the effectiveness of upper level norms.[36]

2.2. Direct applicability and vertical direct effect

In all our three upper levels, courts[37] at any level can sometimes stipulate that upper level norms are directly applicable or have direct effect. I hope EU lawyers will not be shocked by my discussion of these two concepts in one and the same section. Direct applicability and direct effect are not the same and the criteria to identify them can vary across systems. Direct applicability refers to the idea that upper law legislation becomes part of the law of the lower level without the need for implementing legislation. As is well-known, this is the case for EU regulations because the treaties so provide (art 288(2) TFEU). Vertical direct effect on the other hand refers to the function of allowing a court to protect an upper level right without being dependent on prior or subsequent lower level legislation pertaining to that particular right.[38] In EU law, direct applicability is thus a consequence of the legal *classification* of an EU act while direct effect can only be ascertained by looking at the nature of the provision on a case-by-case basis. This is why EU lawyers insist on the need to keep these two concepts separate.[39] In domestic legal systems, however, direct applicability and direct effect (of international law or of federal law vis-à-vis lower level law) are sometimes one and the same or at least very close relatives.

In one way or another, the tool of direct applicability/direct effect exists at all of the three upper levels: in a federal domestic legal system, domestic courts at all levels can and sometimes must directly apply federal law (e.g. state courts applying directly applicable provisions of the federal constitu-

36 For the most recent addition to the empirical research on this claim, see C Conrad and E Hencken Ritter, *Contentious Compliance: Dissent and Repression Under International Human Rights Law* (2019).

37 Direct applicability can also function as a tool outside courts. If an upper level norm is directly applicable at the lower level, the authorities at the lower level can (or should) base administrative decisions directly on that upper level norm, notably when supremacy is affirmed.

38 A Nollkaemper, 'The Duality of Direct Effect of International Law' (2014) 25 EJIL 105, 108.

39 For the argument that the ECJ 'wrongly alluded to the idea that direct effect without direct application was possible', see R Schütze, *European Constitutional Law* (1st edn, Cambridge University Press 2012) 324.

tion). If domestic courts conclude that an upper level norm is directly applicable/has direct effect, they examine whether the upper level law can be used as a direct basis for a decision. Although the precise criteria to identify direct effect (or direct applicability in the sense used outside EU law) vary in nuance, the common criteria is the level of concreteness and unconditionality of the concerned norm and its relationship with individual rights, i.e. whether the norm is sufficiently precise to solve a concrete legal question about the conferral of rights.

Courts in EU Member States must directly apply EU regulations. If an EU provision is not directly applicable, vertical direct effect is a powerful tool to secure the effectiveness of upper level sources. If the implementation period for Member States has ended and if a provision is sufficiently clear and precisely stated; unconditional and not dependent on any other legal provision; and it confers a specific right upon which a citizen can base a claim, an individual can obtain a remedy based on the upper level legal source.[40] In other words, when the lower level (Member State) lawmaker fails to do its job, vertical direct effect attenuates the law-making failure in support of the upper level legal source.

As far as international law is concerned, domestic courts in monist jurisdictions can directly apply at least some international legal provisions. If courts find international norms directly applicable or directly effective, this is one way in which they can pave the way to arrive at an outcome that is compatible with the upper level norm.[41] In the interaction between public international law and national law, this association is particularly relevant in monist countries in which courts recognise the supremacy of international law over national law.[42]

2.3. Invalidation by upper level courts

When a court finds an upper level norm to be directly applicable, it has sometimes the power to set aside conflicting lower level laws. If an upper level court can invalidate lower level legislation, the upper level legal

40 Case 41-74 *van Duyn v Home Office* [1974] ECR 1337, para 13. Case 148/78 *Publico Ministero v Ratti* [1979] ECR 1629, para 24.

41 And can use direct applicability as a 'sword' in the sense of Nollkaemper (n 38).

42 But see Nollkaemper for the ways in which in this constellation national courts can and regularly do also use direct applicability as a 'shield' to control, i.e. limit, the relevance of international law in the domestic legal system. Nollkaemper (n 38).

source is rendered effective through a harsh and powerful mechanism.[43] Federal supreme courts can often invalidate lower level legislation if incompatible with federal law to enforce pre-eminence. The mechanism of invalidation is, however, not directly available at the level of EU law and PIL, although the practical effects of some alternative approaches at the EU level resemble invalidation: In *Simmenthal* in 1978, the ECJ famously stipulated the duty of Member States not to apply a national provision conflicting with EU law. Although the EU courts cannot invalidate national legislation, the combination of the *Simmenthal* finding on supremacy, the enforcement actions against Member States and the remedies available for non-implementation attenuate (or maybe even eradicate) the need for EU institutions to dispose of the delicate power to invalidate lower level (Member States) legislation. What about public international law? The short answer is that international tribunals such as the ICJ cannot invalidate national laws. We should not necessarily view this state of affairs as negative but, in Nollkaemper's words, 'as a strategy that provides checks and balances that are lacking at the international level, and which supports the system of international law and its overall legitimacy'.[44] In any event, invalidations of legislation at lower level are certainly difficult to reconcile with federal interests of autonomy.

2.4. If norms are not directly applicable

Even if a norm is not deemed directly applicable, several types of court enforcement are conceivable.

a) Between appeals to the legislator and judge-made law

If direct applicability and direct effect are not an option (or not one that courts prefer to seize),[45] upper level courts can 'tell' lower level legislators to legislate and they can do so with various degrees of deference. Courts may appeal to legislators by 'merely' identifying the obligation, or courts

43 The exception being complete legislative omissions. Invalidation is not useful if there is no lower level law to invalidate.

44 Nollkaemper writes about national practices that limit the direct effect of international law, but the same remark is useful to discuss the absence of the ability of international courts to invalidate national legislation. Nollkaemper (n 38) 121.

45 In other words, if direct effect is used as a 'shield': ibid 115.

can outline the precise scope of such obligations, they can sometimes render a declaration of incompatibility as in the British legal system in cases of contravention with the Human Rights Act. Sometimes courts recommend or prescribe precise guidelines, sometimes courts set a time-frame, courts may sometimes be involved in monitoring the enforcement of a judgment in a follow-up process or they may at times conclude that there is a gap that the courts can legitimately fill with judge-made law.[46] On this spectrum, we find domestic courts in federations, the ECJ as well as international tribunals who have all, with highly variable degrees of specificity, at least requested lower level legislators to make laws in accordance with obligations from an upper level.

b) Requiring consistent interpretation

Another tool at the disposal of upper levels is the prescription or encouragement of consistent interpretation. Consistent interpretation occurs when lower level authorities or courts interpret lower level law consistent with upper level law. While the exercise of consistent interpretation happens at the lower level, consistent interpretation can be an upper level mechanism if the upper level prescribes or otherwise incentivises such consistent interpretation, again with supremacy as an intervening factor. Despite the lack of teeth, consistent interpretation can go a long way to avoid normative conflict in favour of upper level norms.[47] Let us look at the three selected upper levels in turn:

Federal law can prescribe the principle of consistent interpretation either explicitly or it can follow as a corollary from the supremacy of federal law vis-à-vis the law adopted at the level of the sub-units.[48] Upper levels can notably incentivise consistent interpretation through the deterrent of invalidation or federal oversight. In EU law, consistent interpretation is

---

46 For a comparative overview, see European Commission for Democracy through Law (Venice Commission), *Special Bulletin: Legislative Omission - General Report of the XIVth Congress of the Conference of European Constitutional Courts on Problems of Legislative Omission in Constitutional Jurisprudence* (Council of Europe Publishing 2008).

47 And should therefore not be (mis)understood as a technical doctrine. A von Bogdandy, 'Pluralism, Direct Effect, and the Ultimate Say: On the Relationship Between International and Domestic Constitutional Law' (2008) 6 ICON, 398.

48 For examples, see A Gamper, 'Constitutional Courts, Constitutional Interpretation, and Subnational Constitutionalism' (2014) 6 Special Issue: Re-Exploring Subnational Constitutionalism, A Special Issue of Perspectives on Federalism 24.

mandatory under the doctrine of indirect effect developed by the ECJ. The doctrine of indirect effect requires national courts to interpret the domestic law of the Member States consistently with EU Directives.[49]

In public international law, consistent interpretation has no special vocabulary but is equally known. It can be viewed as a corollary of primary obligations and the idea that any non-compliance with an obligation – in the absence of circumstances precluding wrongfulness, amounts to a breach of international law. If states achieve compliance by interpreting their national laws consistently with international law, states avoid state responsibility. Public international law also incentivises consistent interpretation though the customary norm that a state may not invoke its national law as a justification for non-implementation of an international obligation.[50]

2.5. Common concerns with court enforcement

Of course, court enforcement regularly causes concerns for the lower levels. The critiques focus on separation of powers arguments (courts being ill-suited to 'replace' democratically legitimised legislators) as well as arguments of subsidiarity and legitimacy. Even with presumably 'softer' mechanisms such as consistent interpretation, upper level courts are essentially asking the lower level courts to perform tasks which arguably belong to law-makers at the lower level. Particularly in cases in which positive obligations must be fulfilled by the legislator, the intervention of courts is viewed with suspicion given the potential resource implications of court decisions in polycentric cases and such concerns arise even if we are not in a multi-level setting.[51]

---

49 Case 14/83 *von Colson v Land Nordrhein-Westfalen* [1984] ECR 1891, para 26.

50 Vienna Convention on the Law of Treaties, 1155 UNTS 331, 23 May 1969 (entered into force 27 January 1980), art 27. ARSIWA, art 3.

51 For arguments on both sides of this debate, the literature on social rights is particularly recommended. Against judicial review e.g. J Waldron, *Law and disagreement* (OUP 2004). For opposing views, e.g. A Nolan, *Children's socio-economic rights, democracy and the courts* (Hart 2011). D Kyritsis, 'Representation and Waldron's Objection to Judicial Review' (2006) 26 Oxford Journal of Legal Studies 733. J King, *Judging Social Rights* (Cambridge University Press 2012).

3. *Financial liability (as a sub-type of court enforcement)*

If courts cannot always make legislators act, they can sometimes impose financial liability as a replacement option that often aims to operate as a deterrent against non-implementation of the upper level legal sources with the idea that lower level law-making will happen more swiftly if the stick of a financial sanction is present.

Financial liability is most famously known at the level of EU law. As is well-known, directives have no horizontal direct effect.[52] In the absence of national law implementing the directive, the individual cannot rely on EU law against a private actor as this would undermine the idea that directives require the engagement of the lower level legislator. As is known to any student of EU law, the ECJ famously decided in the *Francovich* case that national courts must provide the individual with compensation for the non-implementation of a directive in order to mitigate against the rejection of horizontal direct effect from the point of view of the affected individual.[53]

In public international law, financial compensation is a possible consequence of state responsibility. Art 36(1) of the Articles on State Responsibility foresees that a state responsible for an internationally wrongful act 'is under an obligation to compensate for the damage caused thereby, insofar as such damage is not made good by restitution'.[54] However, financial compensation as a form of reparation under the law of state responsibility is only available between states – and to a less well-established extent – in the relationship between states or international organisations.[55] International law moreover contains obligations of states to provide individuals with reparation. Such obligations at times explicitly require financial compensation for non-compliance. The right to a remedy in international human rights law sometimes contains an explicit financial compensation aspect.[56] Yet, it is generally fair to say that access to financial remedies is very difficult for victims of human rights violations (or violations of interna-

---

52 Case 152/84 *Marshall v Southampton and South-West Hampshire Area Health Authority* [1986] ECR 723.

53 Cases C-6/90 and C-9/90, *Andrea Francovich and Danila Bonifaci and others v. Italy* [1991] ECR I-5357, para 33.

54 ARSIWA (n 11).

55 Articles on the Responsibility of International Organisations, Annex to A/RES/66/100 of 27 February 2012 art 38.

56 E.g. International Covenant on Civil and Political Rights (adopted 16 December 1966, entered into force 23 March 1976) 999 UNTS 171 (ICCPR) art 14(6). A bit dated but still an excellent overview: D Shelton, *Remedies in International Human Rights Law* (2nd edn, OUP 2005).

tional humanitarian law) and even more so when the problem is the lack of implementation by law-makers.

At the domestic level, financial liability for non-implementation of federal law in a federation seems to be hardly existing but it is not entirely unheard of. Where there is domestic state liability, it tends to concern infringements of the state and less so omissions and even less so omissions by legislative actors.[57] That said, it would at least seem legally conceivable to see courts provide remedies for law-making failures based on the logic of '*effet utile*' in domestic legal systems. Yet, we don't see such cases often. There are procedural hurdles to litigate omissions and many judges and lawyers are more familiar with cases of state interference with human rights (negative obligations) rather than with positive obligations requiring the state to adopt a certain conduct. Moreover, it is almost needless to say that financial liability is controversial notably for its consequences of public spending and because of the fact that courts and law-makers may sometimes choose a different political emphasis when interpreting legal sources. In sum, financial consequences are available at least to some extent in all three upper levels while they clearly play the most prominent role in EU law.

In addition to substitute performance, court proceedings and financial sanctions, a range of mechanisms are available that rely on some forms of oversight and cooperation exercised by the upper level vis-à-vis the lower level.

4. *Oversight and cooperation*

The fourth group of mechanisms regroups approaches that use oversight and cooperation with an aim to induce, motivate or otherwise enhance the lower level law-makers' zeal to implement upper level sources. Many of these mechanisms are cooperative in nature, but there are others that rely on sticks rather than carrots. We will see that a vast range of them is available at all three upper levels.

---

57 E.g. A-C Favre, 'Le droit de la responsabilité de l'État: les enjeux' in A-C Favre, V Martenet and E Poltier (eds), *La responsabilité de l'État* (Schulthess 2012) 9, n 21. T Jaag, 'La responsabilité de l'État en tant que législateur en Suisse' in Institut Suisse de droit comparé (ed), *Rapports suisses présentés au XVème Congrès international de droit comparé* (Schulthess 1998) 255, 228, concluding that financial liability against legislative omissions in the Swiss legal system cannot be ruled out even in the absence of cases.

4.1. Approval requirements

A very direct approach to oversight is one that requires the lower level to seek permission from the upper level before enacting law. Approval requirements can be designed as vetoes or as a requirement of a positive level of support from the upper level. Of course, approval requirements are only helpful if the upper level – at the time of approval – recognises the inadequacy of the lower level legislation. If the (positive or negative) conflict only arises later on, this mechanism is no longer helpful – unless a system would foresee periodic approvals and re-evaluations over time. In practice, approval requirements exist in federal domestic systems but not in EU law or public international law. In federations, there are approval requirements for sub-national law (e.g. state constitutions) as well as approval requirements for international and interstate/intercantonal agreements (and potentially other forms of cooperation) concluded by sub-units.

4.2. Loyalty principles, duties to consult, inform and involve

Loyalty principles are a common feature of domestic federal systems. They usually contain a duty for both upper and lower levels to take into account how the exercise of their own competences affects the other entities. Outside of domestic federal states, we also find loyalty principles in the EU in the form of the 'principle of sincere cooperation'[58] and – with some creativity and to a less-well established extent – we also find the idea in public international law, notably if we combine good faith,[59] the principle of non-interference[60] and the idea of *erga omnes* obligations that states owe towards the international community as a whole. In all of these, there is at the core a bi-directional idea of mutual respect of one level towards the other which implies that upper levels can legitimately exercise some oversight and seek cooperation for the implementation of their legal sources at the lower level.

As corollaries of the loyalty principle, probably all federal or multi-level systems foresee some duties to consult and inform the respective other lev-

58 4 (3) TEU. For an analysis M Klamert, *The Principle of Loyalty in EU Law* (OUP 2014).

59 Charter of the United Nations, 1 UNTS XVI, 26 June 1945 (entered into force 24 October 1945), art 2(2).

60 UN Charter (n 59) art 2(7).

el of law-making developments. Some approaches go further than informing and consulting and formalise the involvement of the lower level in the decision-making. The deepening of the involvement of the EU Member States' parliaments in EU law-making is the prime example of this approach.[61] In domestic federations, the lower level parliaments often have a say in the upper level law-making by representation in an upper chamber or by the provision of specific rights for the sub-units (such as parliamentary participation or state initiatives).

4.3. Financial and other incentives

This chapter would be incomplete without a mention of the financial incentives the upper level can employ to spur law-making at the lower level. If the upper level offers money to incentivise law-making at the lower level, this is a presumably lenient mechanism. But one should not underestimate the fact that de facto autonomy hinges to a large extent on financial arrangements (and upper level financial aid is always tempting and can be difficult to turn down), as has been noted in Germany during the reform on federalism.[62] Financial and other incentives are also important at the level of EU law and public international law where they are, however, more relevant horizontally given the absence of a central enforcement system (i.e. between states, reciprocity, diplomatic consequences, reputational incentives) rather than between international institutions and nation states.

4.4. Oversight mechanisms

In any multi-level setting, some oversight mechanisms aim to ensure that lower-level law-making takes place as the upper level would like it to happen. Oversight mechanisms can range from friendly educational information to friendly reminders, bulletins, ombudspersons, manuals or guidelines to supervision in a more formal sense of the term. As the 'guardian of

61 C Hefftler and others (eds), *The Palgrave Handbook of National Parliaments and the European Union* (Palgrave Macmillan 2015).

62 See the new wording of art 104a of the German Grundgesetz, 'Änderung Artikel 104a GG' (1 September 2006) <http://www.buzer.de/gesetz/5041/al1813-0.htm> ac cessed 15 July 2019.

the Treaties', the EU Commission is vested with supervisory powers vis-à-vis the lower level, i.e. the Member States.[63] Oversight mechanisms also exist in public international law, e.g. in international and regional human rights law, environmental law, anti-corruption or other fields. Non-binding mechanisms such as treaty bodies, committees or other types of groups or individual experts monitor law-making at lower levels and sometimes have the right to undertake country visits or make investigations or inspections.

4.5. Common concerns with oversight and cooperation

Even though mechanisms based on cooperation and oversight tend to raise less concerns than substitute performance, financial liability or some court enforcement mechanisms, it is fair to say that even oversight and cooperation can lead to common concerns. These concerns usually relate to interrogations on how far the mechanism should go and how paternalistic they may legitimately be without eroding lower level autonomy.

IV. Conclusions

We have examined the various types of approaches that upper levels can use to influence legislative implementation at the lower level(s). I sketched four types of approaches, most of them with sub-groups of mechanisms. Almost all of them are available to all three upper levels, albeit with a lot of variation of the relative weight, acceptance or prominence both at the various upper levels and within federations at the domestic level.

We also considered how the use of each group of mechanisms raises a group of common, or at least similar, concerns from the perspective of the lower levels. No matter what relationship we look at, the common worry pertains to the reduction of autonomy left to the lower level. Such reduction is unequal for each legal source and in relation to each of the mechanisms, of course, but from the perspective of lower levels, attempts to influence legislators' choices at the lower level are viewed with suspicion. This finding implies that concerns of reduced federalism should not be seen in isolation from international and European normative developments and vice-versa. From the point of view of the lower levels, any assertion of the

63 TFEU (n 23), art 258.

upper levels is met with at least some concerns. It would be wrong, however, to only mention concerns without also noting that upper level assertiveness is not just a concern but, depending on the perspective, also a cause of celebration. Andrea Franchovich, his colleagues and the many who benefit from upper levels' struggles for effectiveness would certainly agree.

Where does this leave us and how do these findings relate to the current backlash against EU law, other regional and international law? This chapter argued that upper levels inevitably strive for implementation at the lower levels and that this situation leads – equally inevitably – to some concerns at the lower level. Lower levels cannot 'have cake or eat it'. It is not possible to effectively pursue higher normative ambitions at the upper level without expecting some reduction of autonomy at the lower level. Yet, does this conclusion explain the current pushback against international law and notably against international and regional human rights law? I do not believe that it does. It is one thing to say that more upper level law raises autonomy concerns at the lower level but it is quite something else to suggest that this state of affairs explains Brexit or the opposition to human rights law and its institutions as is sometimes suggested. I do not want to deny that a relationship exists and that this relationship deserves to be analysed more seriously but I do not believe that such deterministic and monocausal shortcuts are permissible.[64] As additional or alternative explanations for the current backlash, we need to consider several other possibilities. Actors at the lower level might not have secured sufficient legitimacy for delegating certain issues towards the upper level, the gains from the benefits of cooperation may not be evenly distributed at the lower levels,[65] these benefits may not be sufficiently visible and palpable or there may be actors who do not support the goals pursued by upper level sources and therefore choose to undermine them.

If anything, the observation that there are common mechanisms and common associated challenges and concerns should provide caution

---

64 C Kaempfer, S Thirion and E Schmid, 'Switzerland Rejects a Popular Initiative 'Against Foreign Judges'' (*OpinioJuris*, 17 December 2018) <http://opiniojuris.org/2018/12/17/switzerland-rejects-a-popular-initiative-against-foreign-judges/> accessed 13 March 2019.

65 As economic theory on free trade arrangements suggests (B Ohlin, *Interregional and International Trade* (Harvard University Press 1933)), gains from trading and arguably other exchanges that require some upper level regulation can be unevenly distributed within communities even if the overall size of the pie increases. How we deal with these effects is a political question.

against the idea that a fruitful debate can be held whether one is 'in favour' or 'against' legal sources of any upper level. Upper level legislative obligations exist because a political community had reasons to believe that solutions should be found at an upper level. This is usually the case when 'we' (or some of us) see cooperation at the upper level as necessary or desirable to solve problems that cross the boundaries of the community at the lower level, be it in relation to trade, environmental problems, criminality, values, the coordination of viewpoints in foreign affairs or anything else that sub-units in a federation, Member States in the EU or states at the international level entrust the upper level to take care of. The benefits of such higher-level cooperation come at the price of a certain loss of autonomy for law-making at the lower level. It would be an oversimplification to state that this relationship is entirely axiomatic – it is not.[66] But in the big picture of things, it should not come as a surprise that higher expectations at the upper level will also require at least some mechanisms to secure effectiveness.

66 See section II.4.

Chapter 3: Legislative Challenges in Multi-level Settings from a Lower Level Perspective

Elena Griglio and Nicola Lupo (LUISS)

I. Introduction. Law-making in multi-level settings: a problem of coordination

In multi-level settings, law-making is normally allocated to different territorial entities.[1] This arrangement is a constitutional choice pursued in order to harmonise the requirements and needs of the upper level with the specific interests and demands of the lower levels.[2]

In contemporary democracies, the multi-level arrangement transcends the boundaries of the national and subnational dimensions, including the supranational and international ones. In federal and quasi-federal States, the supranational, national and subnational dimensions are closely intertwined, as the upper layers of authority exert a strong influence upon the subnational dimension.[3]

In this 'multi-level' regulatory framework, rules emerge from different legal orders whose dividing lines are not always easy to define;[4] consequently, the organisation and exercise of the law-making function raise several coordination challenges.

Difficulties in coordinating law-makers arise due to legal, political, sociological and economic factors. Law-making authorities are often called upon to respond simultaneously – although asymmetrically – to the same inputs and social needs. In many cases, competing and contrasting behaviours and policies are implemented by the upper and lower levels, each

---

1 On the notion of 'multi-level governance' referring to a variety of forms of decision-making or regulation characterised by a complex interweaving of actors operating at different levels of authority, see L Hooghe and G Marks, *Multilevel Governance and European Integration* (Rowman & Littlefield 2001).

2 D Fontana, 'Federal Decentralization' (2018) 104 *Virginia Law Review* 727 ff.

3 P Popelier, 'Subnational multilevel constitutionalism' (2014) 6 *Perspectives on Federalism* 1 ff. See also C Panara, *The Sub-national Dimension of the EU: A Legal Study of Multilevel Governance* (Springer 2015).

4 RA Wessels and J Wouters, 'The Phenomenon of Multilevel regulation: Interactions between Global, EU and National Regulatory Spheres' (2007) *International Organizations Law Review* 257 ff.

one attempting to provide timely and more appropriate responses to these needs. In a society that moves faster than ever, this feature is obviously accentuated. Sometimes, lower-level legislators react first, but not necessarily all at the same time. In other cases, when upper-level reacts first, lower-level law-making may become the setting for the revival of interests which were disregarded at the central level (especially in the implementation phase).

Coping with these misalignments is the main challenge for multi-level settings. The task is made even harder by existing asymmetries in the access to information, timeframe and duration of the legislative process, technical expertise, financial and economic capacity, and political motivation among the different law-making 'levels' and 'bodies'.

In multi-level legal orders, two types of mechanisms are usually provided to resolve the coordination problems deriving from misaligned behaviours and asymmetrical positions between the different territorial entities.

On the one hand, political mechanisms are based on the dialogue and cooperation between representatives of the upper and lower levels.[5] Political coordination unfolds not through legally binding acts, but rather through soft and informal procedures and instruments aimed at preventing controversies and accommodating the interests of the different parts.

On the other hand, judicial mechanisms provide for the intervention of courts as the ultimate authority to resolve the coordination issues arising from the above-mentioned misalignments and asymmetries.

These two types of mechanisms rely upon two rather opposing theories, respectively labelled 'Political Safeguards of Federalism' and 'Judicial Safeguards of Federalism'. The former entrusts to politics the reconciliation of the upper and lower levels' requirements.[6] One main pillar of the political safeguards of federalism is the participation of lower levels in the national political process through the Upper House.[7] The latter theory argues that judicial review serves not only to guarantee the lower levels' constitutional

---

5 LD Kramer, 'Putting the Politics Back Into the Political Safeguards of Federalism' (2000) 100 *Columbia Law Review* 215 ff. PJ Weiser, 'Towards a Constitutional Architecture for Cooperative Federalism' (2001) 79 *North Carolina Law Review* 663 ff.

6 The theory of the 'Political Safeguards of Federalism' was developed by some US scholars: H Wechsler, 'The Political Safeguards of Federalism: The Role of the States in the Composition and Selection of the National Government' (1954) 54 *Columbia Law Review* 543; JH Choper, 'The Scope of National Power Vis-à-Vis the States: The Dispensability of Judicial Review' (1977) 80 *Yale Law Review* 1552.

7 Wechsler, n. 6, 549.

status, but also to protect their ability to promote and preserve the rights and liberty of the people.[8]

The combined effect of these mechanisms in the daily practice of multi-level systems[9] demonstrates that the weaknesses and gaps in the 'dialogue' between law-makers are usually filled by the courts, which ordinarily intervene at a later stage, when legislation has already been approved.

With this general framework in mind, this contribution addresses two main research questions. First, it attempts to identify and assess the cases in which there is a heightened risk of deficiencies in the dialogue amongst multi-level law-makers; and second, it investigates whether and how courts are able to resolve these deficiencies. In particular, how far can the courts penetrate into legislative decisions affecting the distribution of power in multi-level settings that should be arranged on a political basis?

Answering these questions is made even harder by the fact that multi-level law-making is now mirrored by a multi-level system of judicial courts.[10] Sometimes, it is not self-evident which court is competent to judge a certain case affecting multi-level law-making.

The article addresses these issues not from an abstract perspective, but through a 'bottom-up' approach, based on the analysis of four benchmark cases selected to represent different instances of multi-level law-making, both at the European Union and at the national level.

The article specifically covers four challenging cases related to multi-level law-making: legislative initiative and inter-institutional programming in the EU; the Early Warning System and the role of the Court of Justice of the European Union on the respect of the subsidiarity principle; the dynamics of multi-level law-making in Italian regionalism, specifically considering the role of the Italian Constitutional Court; and the rules regarding quality of legislation in the Italian multi-level law-making framework.

Case studies have been selected in order to satisfy different qualitative criteria. First, they cover the dimension of multi-level law-making both at the EU and at the domestic level. Second, they highlight that, within the framework of the EU, law-making extends from the integration between

---

8 JC Choo, 'The Judicial Safeguards of Federalism' (1996) 70 *California Law Review* 1311 ff. and LA Baker and EA Young, 'Federalism and the Double Standard of Judicial Review' (2001) 51 *Duke Law Journal* 75 ff.

9 For an application of this debate to the EU, see R Schütze, 'Subsidiarity after Lisbon: Reinforcing the Safeguards of Federalism?' (2009) 68 *The Cambridge Law Journal* 525 ff.

10 P Popelier, A Mazmanyan and W Vandenbruwaene (eds), *The Role of Constitutional Courts in Multilevel Governance* (Intersentia 2013).

European and national actors, rules and procedures.[11] Third, they are all based on the principle of 'loyal cooperation', applied both to inter-institutional and to inter-territorial relations.[12] Fourth, they demonstrate the close interaction between political authorities and courts in multi-level law-making processes.

Italy is selected as a reference national case due to the combination of two factors: the Italian territorial system is not an example of fully-fledged federalism and yet the level of decentralisation of the legislative and executive powers, as foreseen by the Constitution as amended in 2001, is comparable to the arrangement of some advanced European federalisms. As a consequence, it shows in a clear fashion existing difficulties in coordinating upper and lower levels that arise from recently developed multi-level settings that are devoid of the typical safeguards of federalism.

II. Legislative initiative and inter-institutional programming in the EU

The European Communities were conceived, since their origins, as multi-level settings. That is why the first case study of this contribution relates to these Communities, then European Union, in order to verify how the processes of law-making and agenda-setting in such a legal order could be arranged in a manner which is consistent with this feature. The original decision was, indeed, to entrust the main supranational institution, the European Commission, with a monopoly of the legislative initiative, and to make it the engine of the European integration process.

According to what is now Article 17, para 2, TEU, "Union legislative acts may only be adopted on the basis of a Commission proposal, except where the Treaties provide otherwise".[13] The exceptions to this general rule have gradually been extended, but overall they are still rather limited.[14] However, because of them, some authors refer to a "near-

11 L Besselink, *A Composite European Constitution* (Europa Law Publishing 2007); A Manzella and N Lupo (eds), *Il sistema parlamentare euro-nazionale. Lezioni* (Giappichelli 2014).

12 On the principle of federal loyalty, *Bundestreue*, *fideltè féderale* or *leale collaborazione*, see M Finck, 'Loyalty Towards Federation' (2016) 296 *Max Planck Encyclopedia of Comparative Constitutional Law*. On the application of this principle to EU law, see M Klamert, *The Principle of Loyalty in EU Law* (OUP 2014).

13 For non-legislative acts the criterion is inverted, as the Commission's initiative needs to be specifically provided for by the Treaties.

14 For an accurate reconstruction of the exceptions, introduced by the Treaty of Rome and then revised by the Treaty of Maastricht and by the Treaty of Lisbon,

monopoly", a "quasi-monopoly", a "quasi-exclusive right", or use similar expressions.[15]

This monopoly or near-monopoly represents one of the blueprints of the so-called 'community method'. The right to submit formal proposals of legislative acts was not assigned to the intergovernmental body, the Council (of Ministers), which originally exercised the legislative functions. Nor was it attributed to the European Parliament, which since 1979 has acquired a direct popular legitimacy and has gradually increased, during the subsequent years, its legislative powers. It was, instead, reserved to a supranational institution, not controlled by any Government, "completely independent", and called upon to "promote the general interest of the Union" (Article 17, paras 3 and 1, respectively, TEU).

This arrangement pursued three different aims. The first is the intention of the founders not to bestow an advantage, in the drafting process of EU legislation, on any Member State, or on a political party, as the Commission "was supposed to be able to adopt legislative proposals that would be based on the most advanced national legislation or on innovative regulation that pursued the interest of the entire Community/Union".[16] Secondly, the legislative initiative allows the Commission to make the crucial choice about which legal basis must be used in order to adopt each legislative proposal: a choice that clearly involves many implications, first and foremost regarding the procedure to be followed and the majority required in the Council. Thirdly, this setting was also fully consistent with the high level of technical complexity, on average, of the legislative texts to be adopted – which often went together with the low level of their political relevance – and with the need to take proper care with respect to their multilingualism. In substantive terms, this made the Commission the institution that all interest groups needed, and still need, to address in order to have their voices heard in the process that leads to the enactment of a legislative act.[17]

This setting has worked rather well when there has been a high level of homogeneity which has permitted the Commission to more easily identify

---

see P Ponzano, C Hermanin and D Corona, 'The Power of Initiative of the European Commission: A Progressive Erosion?' (2012) 89 *Notre Europe* 8.

15 See, respectively, T Konstadinides, *Division of Powers in European Union Law: The Delimitation of Internal Competence Between the EU and the Member States* (Kluwer 2009) 63 f.; O Costa and N Brack, *How the EU really works* (Farnham, 2014) 73.

16 Ponzano, Hermanin and Corona, n 10, 7.

17 See, among many, D Coen and J Richardson (eds.), *Lobbying the European Union: Institutions, Actors, and Issues* (OUP, 2009).

the general interests of the Union, when the choice of the legal basis did not call into question the competence of the Communities to pursue a certain policy and when the political relevance of the acts so initiated was deemed low. When these factors changed, however, so too was the Commission's monopoly called into question. It is not surprising that a crisis of the 'community method' has been detected and that Member States since the Treaty of Maastricht have often preferred to follow other procedures, mainly intergovernmental, which, especially thanks to the role of the European Council, they could keep under closer control. According to some scholars, the new intergovernmental procedures have deeply altered the Constitution of the Union and endangered the features on which it built its own success, thus determining a too strong imbalance among Member States.[18]

Developing inter-institutional procedures for agenda-setting has represented a means of resolving this dissociation, for coordinating the initiatives taken by the Commission and the priorities set by the European Council, and also for taking into greater consideration the Member States' requests and priorities. The idea is that all EU institutions, each Member State, and even national parliaments and sub-national institutions can take part in these inter-institutional programming procedures.

The main principles that govern these procedures are now included in the inter-institutional agreement on better law-making between the European Parliament, the Council of the European Union and the European Commission of 13 April 2016.[19]

Preliminarily, the three EU institutions agreed to "reinforce the Union's annual and multi-annual programming in line with Article 17(1) of the Treaty on the European Union, which entrusts the Commission with the task of initiating annual and multi-annual programming". First, they decided to take advantage of the fact that every new Commission, following its appointment and its vote by the European Parliament, would have a longer timeframe: so they foresee an exchange of views "on the principal policy objectives and priorities of the three Institutions for the new term", possibly leading to joint conclusions and in any event to a mid-term review, always "on the Commission's initiative". Then, there is a detailed procedure established for the annual programming, which is still based on the "Commission Work Programme". However, this document is preced-

18 See, among many, S Fabbrini, *Which European Union? Europe after the Euro Crisis* (CUP, 2015) ch 5.

19 Official Journal of the European Union, L 123/1, 12 May 2016.

ed and followed by a series of inter-institutional interactions, in which, according to the said inter-institutional agreement, the European Parliament and the Council are also fully involved.

Furthermore, the Juncker Commission also decided to engage national parliaments in the procedure for the adoption of its first work programme. This means that the 2015 work programme (called "A new start") was sent by First Vice-President Timmermans to the chairs of the European affairs committees in all national parliaments and, in response, attracted 26 opinions: more precisely, individual opinions by 12 chambers, as well as a joint opinion from 14 chambers in which each chamber identified its own priorities among the initiatives proposed by the Commission. In its replies to the opinions received, the Commission welcomed national parliaments' expressions of interest in the work programme, as well as the opportunity presented by the work programme to have an early exchange of views with national parliaments with respect to priorities.[20]

This inter-institutional approach to agenda-setting has found formal support in the Court of Justice of the European Union. In general terms, the principle of inter-institutional balance – which also extends to the dynamics between upper and lower levels – has been elaborated upon for the first time in the Court's case law.[21] Moreover, more specifically, the Court has been called upon to resolve a dispute regarding the Commission's power to withdraw legislative initiatives. In the judgment of 14 April 2015, case C-409/13 Council v Commission, notwithstanding the silence of the Treaties, the Court recognised this power as belonging to the Commission. At the same time, in order to avoid surprises, it required a kind of "parliamentarisation" of the procedure adopted to withdraw the proposals and highlighted the importance of inter-institutional cooperation even in the exercise of the power to withdraw legislative proposals.[22]

Therefore, the inter-institutional programming procedures can be deemed a useful way of ensuring a dialogue among legislators at different

---

20 See the Annual report 2015 on 'Relations between the European Commission and National Parliaments' (COM (2016) 471 final, 15 July 2016) 4 f.

21 K Lenaerts, 'L'évolution du Cadre Juridique-Institutionnel de l'Union Européenne', in A Tizzano (ed), *Verso i 60 anni dai trattati di Roma* (Giappichelli 2016) 5, 9 f highlights the importance that the principle of institutional balance – as opposed to the principle of separation of powers – plays in the EU institutional system, both at the stage of legislative initiative and, following the judgment of the Court of Justice, at the eventual stage of the withdrawal.

22 See N Lupo, 'The Commission's power to withdraw legislative proposals and its 'parliamentarisation', between technical and political grounds' (2018) 2 *European Constitutional Law Review* 311 f.

level, without dismantling the main and successful features of the community method.[23] It still needs, indeed, to be better tuned with financial multi-annual programming, which is still based on a 7-year timeframe and thus not effectively coordinated with the 5-year electoral cycle at the EU level.[24]

III. The Early Warning System and the principle of subsidiarity in the jurisprudence of the European Court of Justice

The principle of subsidiarity is one of the instruments through which a certain legal order forces law-makers to take into consideration the multi-level setting. It appeared rather late in the EU, with the Maastricht Treaty, entered into force in 1993 (Article 5 TEC). After more than 15 years of application of this principle, which were indeed rather deceiving, the Treaty of Lisbon, entered into force in 2009, reformulated it following two main directions: a) taking into explicit consideration sub-national levels of government; and b) establishing a specific procedural mechanism aimed at better enforcing it at the political level through the involvement of national parliaments that are called upon to check whether it is being respected, by scrutinising the Commission's legislative proposals (the so-called Early Warning System).

In slightly more detail, the original formulation of the principle was varied, providing that "the Union shall act only if and in so far as the objectives of the proposed action cannot be sufficiently achieved by the Member States, *either at central level or at regional and local level*, but can rather, by reason of the scale or effects of the proposed action, be better achieved at Union level" (art. 5, par. 3, TEU).

Furthermore, before the Lisbon Treaty, the principle had not yet been protected by the Court of Justice, which was rather reluctant to exercise

23 On the contribution of the inter-institutional and multi-level programming procedures to the requirements of better law-making, see E. Griglio, 'Better Law-Making and the Integration of Impact Assessment in the Decision-Making Process: The Role of National Parliaments', in A. De Feo e B. Laffan (eds), *Scrutiny of EU Policies* (Fiesole, European University Institute, 2017) 63 ff.

24 On this, also on the light of Art. 312 TFEU, see C Fasone, N Lupo, *The Union Budget and the Budgetary Procedure*, in R Schüteze, T Tridimas (eds), *Oxford Principles of EU Law* (OUP 2018) 809 ff. A proposal to move financial planning on a 5+5 year scheme has been recently put forward.

such a control.[25] This reluctance should be of no surprise, as the Court of Justice, since its inception, has naturally encouraged the process of "competence creep" traditionally taking place at the EU level. In any case, this explains why the Treaty of Lisbon established an *ad hoc* procedural instrument, the EWS, aimed precisely at "ensuring compliance with the principle of subsidiarity", as indicated by Art. 5, par. 3, TEU itself, and regulated by Protocol no. 2, on the application of the principles of subsidiarity and proportionality.

In order to balance the non-activation of a judicial safeguard, a political safeguard was put in place: this is the EWS, which asks national parliaments to assess the respect given to the principle of subsidiarity, by issuing "reasoned opinions", addressed to the EU institution on all draft legislative acts, which produce procedural effects only in the event that a certain number of parliaments raise concerns regarding subsidiarity ("yellow card" and "orange card"). It is up to each national parliament, then, "to consult, where appropriate, regional parliaments with legislative powers" (Art. 6 of Protocol no. 2). The insufficiency and the drawbacks of the CJEU's judicial control over the exercise of the legislative competences, and especially their compliance with the principle of subsidiarity, have therefore opened the door for national parliaments to become directly involved in European decision-making processes.[26]

Art. 5 of Protocol no. 2 also provided that all draft legislative acts must include a detailed statement regarding their compliance with the principles of subsidiarity and proportionality. This statement should provide an assessment of the proposal's financial impact and, in the case of a directive, of its implications on the transposition and implementation of rules to be put in place at the Member States' level, including, where necessary, a reference to the implications on regional legislation.

---

25 See G de Búrca, 'The principle of subsidiarity and the Court of Justice as an institutional actor' (1998) 36 *Journal of Common Market Studies* 217; W Vanderbruwaene, 'The Ambivalent methods of subsidiarity review' in M Cartabia, N Lupo and A Simoncini (eds), *Democracy and Subsidiarity in the EU. National parliaments, Regions and civil society in the decision-making process* (Il Mulino 2013) 371 ff; F Fabbrini, 'The Principle of Subsidiarity', in R Schütze and T Tridimas (eds), *Oxford Principles of European Union Law. I. The European Union Legal Order* (OUP 2018) 221 f.

26 See C Fasone and N Lupo, 'Constitutional Review and The Powers of National Parliaments in EU Affairs. Erosion or Protection?', in D Jancic (ed), *National Parliaments after the Lisbon Treaty and the Euro Crisis. Resilience or Resignation?* (OUP 2017) 59 ff.

In order to connect the political and legal safeguards of the principle of subsidiarity, specific procedural mechanisms to involve the Court of Justice have been provided by Art. 8 of Protocol no. 2: an action complaining of an infringement of the principle of subsidiarity may be brought by the Member States "on behalf of their national parliament or a chamber thereof" and a similar action can also be commenced by the Committee of Regions.

Almost 10 years later, the overall picture looks clearly negative, since these instruments to activate the Court of Justice have never been used.[27] By contrast, many national parliaments have shown a certain interest in the Early Warning System. The overall number of reasoned opinions is quite high (470 reasoned opinions from 1 December 2009 to 4 November 2018), and most of them have been issued on draft proposals of a certain relevance. However, only in three cases has the minimum threshold (that is, the threshold required for raising a yellow card) been reached and only in one of those three did the Commission actually decide to withdraw its proposal.

Scholars have offered contrasting interpretations of this procedure and of the scope of parliamentary scrutiny.[28]

Some argue that national parliaments are called upon to play the role of mere legal advisors regarding compliance with the principle of subsidiarity, which is to be given a strict interpretation.[29] In this way, these scholars have sought to diminish the impact of national parliaments' direct involvement in EU decision-making by claiming that they are heterogeneous and

---

27 Cf K Granat, 'Institutional Design of the Member States for the ex post Subsidiarity Scrutiny', in Cartabia, Lupo and Simoncini (eds), n 18, 427 ff.

28 See M Goldoni and A Jonsson Cornell, 'The Trajectory of the Early Warning System', in A Jonsson Cornell and M Goldoni (eds), *National and Regional Parliaments in the EU-Legislative Procedure Post-Lisbon* (Hart 2017) 335–355; I Cooper, 'Is the Early Warning Mechanism a Legal or a Political Procedure? Three Questions and a Typology', ivi, 18–49 (remarking that the EWS has been studied by both law and political science scholars).

29 See, although with different approaches, P Kiiver, *The Early Warning System for the Principle of Subsidiarity: Constitutional Theory and Empirical Reality* (Routledge 2012) (referring to national parliaments as a sort of 'Council of State'); and F Fabbrini and K Granat, '"Yellow card, but no foul": The role of the national parliaments under the Subsidiarity Protocol and the Commission proposal for an EU regulation on the right to strike' (2013) 50 *Common Market Law* Review 115 (criticising the broad interpretation of the principle of subsidiarity adopted by national parliaments in the first yellow card).

potentially dangerous when inserted into the logic of European integration.

On the contrary, other scholars maintain that, in order to better fulfil the function of "reconnecting" the EU democracy by bringing more national politics into largely Europeanized policies, it is preferable that the Early Warning System should be read and used as a political, rather than merely as a legal, instrument.[30] This implies that each national parliament – and even each House, in bicameral systems – is relatively free to interpret the parameters of its own assessment and to determine the scope of its interventions.

By its very nature, the principle of subsidiarity appears notoriously ambiguous and multifaceted, residing somewhere between law and politics, legal analysis and political assessment.[31] Consequently, it comes as no surprise that in some cases parliaments have acted almost like legal advisors, interpreting in a strict sense their role as guardians of the principle of subsidiarity; while in other cases they have used the reasoned opinions based on the principle of subsidiarity as a means of raising political objections to a given proposal.[32]

As is often the case, the overall assessment depends largely on expectations. The EWS has demonstrated itself as being incapable of fully addressing the concerns underlying the EU's democratic deficit, even if it "provides an effective but limited avenue for national parliaments to influence EU legislation".[33] This "avenue" is in addition to pre-existing channels available to national parliaments, consisting in the setting of political di-

30 See M Goldoni, 'The Early Warning System and the Monti II Regulation: The Case for a Political Interpretation' (2014) 10 *European Constitutional Law Review* 90 ff and N Lupo, 'National parliaments in the European integration process: re-aligning politics and policies', in Cartabia, Lupo and Simoncini (eds), n 18, 107–132.

31 The principle of subsidiarity is defined as 'politically complex and legally uncertain' by de Búrca, n 18, 217. See also M Evans and A Zimmermans, 'Editors' Conclusions: Future Directions for Subsidiarity', in M Evans and A Zimmermans (eds), *Global Perspectives on Subsidiarity* (Springer 2014) 221, 223, who argue that the principle is 'somewhat of a chameleon'.

32 The case of the third yellow card looks particularly telling, as it was used almost exclusively by the Parliaments of Eastern and Central European Member States to oppose a directive on the posted workers which their Governments opposed: see Jancic, n 25, 299–312, and D Fromage and V Kreilinger, 'National parliaments' third yellow card and the struggle over the revision of the posted workers directive' (2017) 10 *European Journal of Legal Studies* 125 ff.

33 See K Granat, *The Principle of Subsidiarity and its Enforcement in the EU Legal Order. The Role of National Parliaments in the Early Warning System* (Hart, 2018) 227 ff.

rections and scrutiny of their own governments, which still proves the easiest way, and which has benefited from the direct channel established by the EWS and by the "political dialogue". The latter procedure, established through a sort of constitutional convention by the Barroso Commission (with the active involvement of COSAC), has indeed showed the most evident success, also in terms of quantity (resulting in more than five times the number of reasoned opinions: 2,747 contributions, from 1 December 2009 to 4th November 2018).

Once more, this experience has demonstrated that the direct channels of communication between the lower and upper level legislators are in all cases beneficial and work better than the judicial ones.

IV. *Challenges of multi-level law-making in Italian regionalism: the role of the Constitutional Court*

Italian regionalism offers a relevant case for testing the challenges met by law-making in multi-level contexts.

The constitutional criteria for the distribution of legislative and administrative competences between the State and the Regions were substantially revised in 2001. The new arrangement resulting from the constitutional law no. 3/2001 led Italian regionalism to reach, at least on the basis of constitutional provisions, levels of decentralisation not too different from those of the most advanced federalisms.[34] Nevertheless, this shift was not supported by the counter-powers which exist in federal systems to protect national interests and requirements and to ensure some level of participation of Member States in Federal decisions.[35]

---

34 On federalism as a doctrine that features different territorial systems, regardless of the formal definition of the State as a Federation in the Constitution, see G De Vergottini, 'Stato federale', in *Enciclopedia del diritto* (XLIII, Giuffrè 1990) 832 ff.

35 The origins of Italian regionalism are quite recent, dating back to the 1970s. The process of political decentralisation has been extremely fast and it has resulted in a system defined as 'polycentric' – M Olivetti, 'Lo Stato policentrico delle autonomie', in T Groppi and M Olivetti (eds), *La Repubblica delle autonomie. Regioni ed enti locali nel nuovo titolo V* (Giappichelli 2001) 39 ff. – or 'multi-level', also having regard to the interconnections with the international and supranational levels – F Pizzetti, *L'ordinamento costituzionale italiano fra riforme da attuare e riforme da completare* (Giappichelli 2003) 88 ff. On these trends, see also E Griglio, *Principio unitario e neo-policentrismo. Le esperienze italiana e spagnola a confronto* (Cedam, 2008).

Broadly speaking, the reform of Italian regionalism was not supported by the introduction of an effective multi-level governance.[36]

On the one hand, the constitutional distribution of legislative power was only apparently self-implementing:[37] the existence of overlapping spheres of competence, gaps and ambiguous labels in the subjects listed by art. 117 Const. paved the way for widespread interpretative issues.[38]

On the other hand, the lack of any structural representation of Regions at the national level prevented the consolidation of political mechanisms capable of anticipating and resolving in a conciliatory manner the interpretative issues affecting the distribution of the legislative power.

A number of factors inhibited the establishment of an authentic system of multi-level representation of lower levels' interests at the upper level.

First, the symmetrical nature of Italian bicameralism comprises two Houses directly elected by the citizens that do not offer any form of territorial representation of Regional interests.[39] Since the 1980s, many attempts have been made to revise the arrangement of Italian bicameralism. However, all the proposals launched over the decades have dramatically failed. Even the provision introduced by the 2001 constitutional amendment, which provided for the inclusion of regional representatives on the Bicameral committee for regional affairs, remained unfulfilled.[40] In subsequent years (2006 and 2016), two broader constitutional reforms were approved by the parliament containing provisions aimed at – *inter alia* – revising and correcting some elements of the multi-level arrangement intro-

---

36 The notion of multi-level *governance* can be referred back to G Marks, 'Structural policy and multilevel governance in the EC', in A Cafruny and SG Rosenthal (eds), *The State of the European Community. Vol. 2, The Maastricht Debate and Beyond* (Lynne Rienner 1993) 390. See also I Bache and M Flinders (eds), *Multi-level governance* (OUP 2004) and S Fabbrini, *Compound democracies. Why the United States and Europe are becoming similar* (OUP 2007).

37 According to L Paladin, 'Problemi legislativi e interpretativi nella definizione delle materie di competenza regionale' (1971) III *Foro amministrativo* 3–4, this feature was also typical of the original distribution of legislative competences provided by the Constitution of 1948.

38 A D'Atena, 'Materie legislative e tipologia delle competenze' (2003) 1 *Quaderni costituzionali* 20.

39 C Mortati, 'Il potere legislativo: unicameralismo o bicameralismo', in Id., *Raccolta di scritti,* I (Milano, Giuffrè, 1972) 429; G Ferrara, 'Le Camere', in G Branca (ed), *Commentario alla Costituzione,* I, art. 55–63 (Zanichelli, 1984) 5; F Rescigno, *Disfunzioni e prospettive di riforma del bicameralismo italiano: la Camera delle Regioni* (Giuffrè, 1995) 12.

40 R Bifulco, 'In attesa della seconda Camera federale', in T Groppi and M Olivetti (eds), *La Repubblica delle autonomie* (Giappichelli, 2001) 211 ff.

duced by the 2001 reform. However, both these reforms – approved with a parliamentary majority that exceeded 50%+1 of the members of the two Houses, but not 2/3s of them – were the subject of popular referendums that did not confirm the proposals approved by the parliament.[41]

Secondly, existing gaps in territorial representation at the national level have partially been filled via ad hoc and rather informal mechanisms of political cooperation involving State and regional executives. The Italian network of relationships between the State and territorial entities is characterised by the existence of a "Conference system": a plurality of intergovernmental conferences operating, in a vertical sense, as cooperative bodies for the coordination of State, regional and local interests.[42] The Conference system consists of the permanent State-Regions-Autonomous Provinces Conference ("*Conferenza permanente per i rapporti tra lo Stato, le Regioni e le Province autonome di Trento e Bolzano*", hereinafter State-Regions Conference), the State-Municipalities-Local Autonomies Conference ("*Conferenza Stato, Città, Autonomie locali*"), and the State-Regions-Autonomous Provinces-Municipalities-Local Autonomies Conference (also known as the Unified Conference, "*Conferenza unificata*"). All these bodies are composed of representatives of the executive branch of each different territorial level, and require each level to be able to coordinate its internal position before approaching the negotiating table with the State.

This Conference system is the outcome of a longstanding process,[43] finally codified by the legislative reforms of 1997,[44] which significantly ex-

41 The 2016 constitutional amendment rejected by the referendum provided for a structural reform of the Upper House, which would have transformed it into an assembly entirely composed of regional representatives, excluded from the confidence circuit and with a limited power of intervention in the law-making process. See N Lupo, 'On the failed reform of the Italian Senate', in P Paczolay, GF Ferrari and F Tanács-Mandák (eds), *Constitutional Issues and Challenges in Hungary and Italy*, forthcoming.

42 On the role and origins of the intergovernmental conferences, see E Ceccherini, 'Intergovernmental relations in Italy: the Permanent State-Regions-Autonomous Provinces Conference' (2009) 4 *Revista de la Facultad de Ciencias Sociales y Jurídicas de Elche* 216- 238.

43 Following the establishment of a provisional and non-permanent form of State-Regions Conference with the Prime Minister's Decree of 12 October 1983, the Conference was given legislative status by art. 12 of law n. 400 of 1988, which completed the structure of the organism, chaired by the Prime Minister and composed of the Presidents of all Regions and Autonomous Provinces.

44 Pursuant to the delegation provided by art. 9 of law n. 69 of 1997, the Government adopted the legislative decree n. 281 of 1997, which can be considered to be the founding norm of the Conference system.

panded the role and functions of these intergovernmental bodies. Apart from their advisory role, the Conferences are permitted to adopt agreements, which turn out in many cases, however, only to be 'weak' tools of cooperation,[45] since they do not necessarily require the compliance of all parts (for example, the government can operate even without the agreement of the Regions).[46]

On the whole, the political mechanisms of multi-level governance in Italy turn out to be extremely weak and unbalanced: in the case of any conflicts between the interests of the upper and lower levels, no effective political guarantee is offered to regional entities, because the national Parliament is free to ignore the voices of sub-national representatives while exercising the law-making function. The only constraining safeguard for territorial interests is therefore to be found at the judicial level.

The Italian Constitutional Court has played a fundamental role vis-à-vis the political gaps in the multi-level governance. It has actually assumed a substitutive role in interpreting the constitutional distribution of competences and filling in the voids of the State-Regional cooperation.[47] However, the results achieved throughout the last two decades may be considered deceiving, at least from a multi-level governance perspective.

On the one hand, the Court has reinterpreted the constitutional distribution of competences through largely discretionary criteria (such as the criteria of the 'unitary interests'),[48] which expand the areas into which

---

45 S Agosta, 'Dall'intesa in senso debole alla leale collaborazione in senso forte? Spunti per una riflessione alla luce della più recente giurisprudenza costituzionale tra (molte) conferme e (qualche) novità' (2004) 2 *Quaderni regionali* 703–728.

46 The evolution of this vertical form of cooperation amongst different territorial entities was accompanied by the gradual emergence of forms of horizontal cooperation amongst bodies belonging to the same levels of government: the Conference of Regions *(Conferenza delle Regioni)*, and the Conference of Presidents of Regional Councils *(Conferenza dei Presidenti dei Consigli regionali)*. See S Cassese and D Serrani, 'Regionalismo moderno: cooperazione tra Stato e Regioni e tra Regioni in Italia' (1980) 3 *Le Regioni* 398–418.

47 G Rolla and T Groppi, 'Between Politics and the Law: the Development of Constitutional Review in Italy', in W Sadurski (ed), *Constitutional Justice, East and West* (Kluwer Law International, 2002); LF Del Duca and P Del Duca, 'An Italian Federalism? The State, its Institutions and National Culture as Rule of Law guarantor' (2006) 54 *American Journal of Comparative Law* 799 ff.; V Barsotti, PG Carozza, M Cartabia, A Simoncini, *Italian Constitutional Justice in Global Context* (OUP, 2016) 194 ff.

48 The reference is to renowned sentence no. 303/2003, through which the Italian Constitutional Court has started a new jurisprudential interpretation of art. 117

State legislation is permitted to intervene.[49] When State legislation is authorised to intervene, regardless of the formal distribution of competences, in order to protect unitary interests, an agreement between the State and the Regions is required via the State-Regions Conference, which, however, represents only the executives.[50]

On the other hand, the interpretative techniques employed by the Constitutional Court have produced an intense fragmentation of legislation between the State and the regional levels. In each subject-matter, it is not always easy to predict which is the 'competent' legislator (this also depends on the nature of the interests involved).[51] The volume of constitutional litigation has remained high for a long time, fostering a case-by-case approach that has hindered the development of a fully-fledged system of multi-level governance.

During the last few years, jurisprudential interpretation has contributed to defining the effective distribution of the legislative power between the State and the Regions: the resulting position demonstrates a clear re-centralisation of legislation at the State level, not only with respect to what is affirmed by the constitutional provisions currently in force, but sometimes even when compared to the original constitutional text.[52]

Const, aimed at introducing elements of flexibility and protection of unitary interests in the distribution of the legislative competences. See A D'Atena, 'L'allocazione delle funzioni amministrative in una sentenza ortopedica della Corte costituzionale' (2003) *Giurisprudenza costituzionale* 2776 ff.

49 Italian scholars have argued that the restatement of the State's role in the protection of unitary interests has actually deprived regional competences of their substance, thereby transforming the 2001 amendment into a 'paper Constitution'; see T Groppi, 'Il Titolo V cinque anni dopo, ovvero la Costituzione di carta' (2007) 3–4 *Le Regioni* 421 ff and, similarly, E Carloni, 'Teoria e pratica della differenziazione: federalismo asimmetrico ed attuazione del Titolo V' (2008) 1 *Le istituzioni del federalismo* 78.

50 G Carpani, 'Tra Stato e regioni. La via per disciplinare le funzioni amministrative' (2003) 8 *Parlamenti regionali* 77 ff.

51 P Cavaleri, 'La definizione e la delimitazione delle materie di cui all'art. 117 della Costituzione', in R Tarchi (ed), *Le competenze normative statali e regionali tra riforme della Costituzione e giurisprudenza costituzionale. Un primo bilancio* (Giappichelli 2006) 31.

52 On the state-of-the-art of the constitutional jurisprudence affecting the distribution of the legislative power between the State and the Regions, see R Bifulco and A Celotto (eds), *Le materie dell'art. 117 nella giurisprudenza costituzionale dopo il 2001* (Napoli, Editoriale Scientifica, 2015) and F Benelli, 'Recenti tendenze della giurisprudenza costituzionale sul riparto per materie tra Stato e Regioni e sul declino del principio di leale collaborazione' (2012) *Le Regioni* 623 ff.

V. *Quality of legislation between the State and Regions in Italy: the multi-level legislator unbound*

As already remarked, multi-level law-making is not a unitary practice in Italy, because there is no institutions and mechanisms (as in the case of the German *Bundesrat*) able to support, on the one hand, the participation of the lower levels in the national law-making and, on the other hand, the control of the upper level on the territorial implementation and follow-up of national legislation.

In Italy, the process of legislative production is fragmented between the national and the regional levels. Furthermore, art. 5 Const. – one of its fundamental principles –, after recognizing local autonomy and decentralization, explicitly provides that "the Republic adapts the principles and methods of the legislation to the requirements of autonomy and decentralisation".[53] The meaning, scope and implications of this fundamental principle are open to several interpretations, affecting not just the respect of constitutional competences, but also the involvement of the lower levels in the legislative process. In actual fact, this constitutional statement has not yet experienced exhaustive implementation.[54]

A correct interpretation and a complete implementation of the fundamental principle embedded in art. 5 Const. would imply that every single piece of State and regional legislation would be subject to a preliminary assessment, based on the constitutional distribution of competences between the State and the regional legislation. In reality, the law-making process at both national and regional levels does not seem to respect this requirement. This situation produces several problems.

On the one hand, it does not contribute to filling the gaps exposed by the lack of permanent structures of vertical cooperation involving the legislative authorities of the different 'levels'. The lack of a participatory structure at the national level for regional law-making authorities does not prevent, but rather should foster, the promotion of procedures capable of

53 On the provision by art. 5 Const. as a substantial criterion of self-limitation and economy in the exercise of legislative powers, see the intervention by L. Violante in Seminario istituzionale *"Nuovi metodi della legislazione tra Stato e Regioni"* – Resoconto stenografico (Camera dei Deputati 2000) 3.

54 On the continuous conflict between the reasons of unity and autonomy in the implementation of art. 5 Const., see R Bifulco, 'Art. 5', in R Bifulco, A Celotto, M Olivetti (eds), *Commentario alla Costituzione*, I (UTET 2006) 136 ff. and G Rivosecchi, 'Articolo 5', in F Clementi et al (eds), *La Costituzione italiana, Commento articolo per articolo*, I (Il Mulino 2018) 41 ff.

structurally integrating regional entities in the legislative process. The existence of integrated and multi-level procedures of this kind would represent an appropriate means of implementation of art. 5 Const.[55] Through such procedures, Regions would be permitted to act not solely as political actors but also as co-managers of the 'policies'.[56]

On the other hand, this scenario hinders the endorsement of high-quality legislation and the planning of a consistent multi-level 'regulatory cycle'.[57] A number of factors, affecting both the formal production of legal norms and the evaluation of their substantial impact on the affected policy area,[58] contribute to this outcome.

From the point of view of the formal production of legal norms, legislative drafting rules are independently established at State and regional levels.

At the State level, since 1986, legislative drafting has been addressed on the basis of an inter-institutional approach involving all the national bodies participating in the law-making activity,[59] that is, the houses of parliament and the executive branch. This process resulted in the adoption, in 2001, some months before the referendum that approved the constitutional reform, of rather exhaustive legislative guidelines comprising conven-

---

55 F Cocozza, *Collaborazioni preliminari al procedimento legislativo* (Milano, Giuffré, 1998) 165. See also E De Marco, *La "negoziazione legislativa"* (CEDAM, 1984) 39.

56 P Caretti and M Morisi (eds), 'Parlamento e politiche pubbliche. Il caso della Commissione bicamerale per l'attuazione della legge n. 59 – rapporto sulla rilevazione svolta nell'ambito del Seminario 2000', in *Quaderno n. 11 – Seminario 2000* (Giappichelli, 2001) 198. On this perspective, see P Pietrangelo, 'Parlamento e assemblee regionali: scheda sulla conferenza di Montecitorio del 12 febbraio 2001' (2001) 1 *Parlamenti regionali* 84 ff.

57 On 'legisprudence' (or 'legistics') as a theoretical and practical science dealing with law production and aiming at improving the quality of norms through a focus on the whole regulation cycle, see P. Noll, *Gesetzgebungslehre* (Reinbeck, 1973). On the 'comprehensive approach to legislation', whereby the entry into force of the statutory act continues in the law enforcement stage where the premises for the inception of future legislative initiatives are also set, *see* L Mader, 'Evaluating the Effects: A Contribution to the Quality of Legislation' (2001) 22 *Statute Law Review* 119 ff.

58 U. Karpen, 'Good Governance through Transparent Application of the Rule of Law' (2009) 11 *European Journal of Law Reform* 219.

59 This activity has benefited from the comparative research carried out by Rodolfo Pagano, see R Pagano, *Le Direttive di tecnica legislative in Europa* (Camera dei Deputati, 1997) and Id, 'Legislative drafting techniques', in U Karpen and EM Wenz (eds), *National legislation in the European framework: proceedings of the second congress of the European association of legislation (EAL) in Rome, March 24–29, 1995* (Nomos 1998) 203–226.

tions, principles, and good and bad practices on how to draft a legal rule.[60] However, regional law-making authorities have been excluded from this process.

'Regional' drafting rules were first adopted separately by some Regions[61] and then at the inter-regional level through the Conference of the Presidents of Regional Councils.[62] Initially, only regional Councils were involved, thereby side-lining the executives (*Giunte*).

Attempts to coordinate the two legislative levels have been made (especially by the Committee on Legislation of the Chamber of Deputies), but they have failed, therefore generating inconsistencies and asymmetries.[63]

Apparently, this outcome appears to be consistent with the formal independence and autonomy of each level of law-making. In reality, however, it raises several contradictions from the perspective of multi-level legislation. Drafting rules which are adapted to the multi-level dimension are rather exceptional.[64] Consequently, regional interests and perspectives are often disregarded by State legislation; conversely, regional lawmakers are usually lacking a comprehensive vision, inclusive of national unitary needs.

---

60 Currently, see Presidenza del Consiglio dei Ministri, Circolare 20 aprile 2001, n. 10888 'Regole e raccomandazioni per la formulazione tecnica dei testi legislative'. More exhaustive criteria, including examples of best practices, are available in the Guide on the drafting of legislative acts (Presidenza del Consiglio dei Ministri, Circolare 2 maggio 2001, n. 1/1.1.26/10888/9.92, 'Guida alla redazione dei testi normativi').

61 See the textbook on legislative drafting released by the Regione Toscana, 'Suggerimenti per la redazione dei testi normativi' (1985) *Le Regioni* 319 ff. Further guidelines were adopted by other Regions, following the precedent of the Regione Toscana.

62 See the Volume "Regole e suggerimenti per la redazione dei testi normativi", adopted by the Conference of the Presidents of Regional Councils in the reunion of 24 January 1992. Currently, the rules followed by the regional legislative assemblies are included in the 3rd Edition of the Volume (available: http://oli.consiglio.regione.toscana.it/documento/regole-e-suggerimenti-per-la-redazione-dei-testi-normativi-terza-edizione-dicembre-2007/). For further details, see R Libertini, 'Il drafting e le tecniche legislative nell'esperienza regionale', in P Costanzo (ed), *Codificazione del diritto e ordinamento costituzionale* (Jovene 1999) 255–269.

63 N Lupo, 'Tecnica e politica della legislazione nelle circolari sulla redazione degli atti normativi' (2004) 1 *Quaderni regionali* 97 ff.

64 By way of example, the Guide on the drafting of legislative acts (4.10) provides that any State laws that confer, delegate or transfer tasks or functions to territorial entities or place a burden on them should not identify in detail the body responsible and the type of act required for the enactment. However, this rule is often disregarded in the actual legislative practice.

Further critical elements arise from the perspective of the so-called "substantial" legislative drafting.

Firstly, legislation at both State and regional levels is not subject to any form of legislative planning. There is no structural ex ante / ex post evaluation of the legislative requirements and deficiencies[65] capable of providing for the coordination of legislative interventions in a multi-level perspective.[66] Secondly, from a formal point of view, the "ex ante" consideration of the formal constitutional constraints on the distribution of legislative competences turns out to be rather weak. This is true both for the two national Houses and for regional Councils.

Thirdly, occasional practices of post-legislative scrutiny (review and sunset clauses)[67] are kept strictly separate by State and Regional law-making authorities.

In this vein, it can be argued that, in Italy, the multi-level legislator is unbound from more effective regulation constraints.

VI. Conclusions

Multi-level law-making is a complex process that calls for structures and mechanisms capable of coordinating and integrating the requirements of different 'levels' of legislation. The lower levels' perspective is the one which principally suffers from the violations and impositions of the upper level: the latter maintains the ultimate control over the rules and procedures that preside over the multi-level governance.

The first case study offers an example of good practice in coping with the challenges of multi-level law-making. This deals with the crisis of the EU Commission's monopoly on the legislative initiative, further propelled by the influences emerging from the lower level. The answer to this crisis has been the development of inter-institutional and multi-level procedures for agenda-setting at the EU level as a means not only of coordinating the

---

65 The regulatory cycle includes four phases: drafting and initiating, deliberation and adoption, implementation and enforcement, control and amendment. See U Karpen, 'Introduction', in U Karpen and H Xanthaki (eds), *Legislation in Europe. A Comprehensive Guide for Scholars and Practitioners* (Hart 2017) 20.

66 On the law as the outcome of the interaction between the multiple sub-systems that comprise the social community, see A La Spina, *La decisione legislativa – lineamenti di una teoria* (Giuffrè, 1989) 35 ff.

67 A Kouroutakis, *The Constitutional Value of Sunset Clauses: An Historical and Normative Analysis* (Routledge 2017).

initiatives taken by the Commission and the priorities set by the European Council, but also for giving greater attention to the requests and priorities of the Member States.

The second case study also provides a positive precedent of multi-level law-making by highlighting the effective but limited channel offered by the EWS for national parliaments to influence EU legislation. The same goes for the political dialogue. These mechanisms confirm that the direct channels of communication between the lower and upper level legislators are, in all cases, beneficial and more effective than the judicial ones.

The Italian case demonstrates the difficulties inherent in coping with a multi-level framework of law-making which incorporates no real system of multi-level governance. The weaknesses of the Italian experience can be tested both at the structural and at the procedural level. On the one hand, the intense decentralisation of the legislative power carried out in 2001 has not been supported and balanced by central structures capable of integrating regional law-making authorities in the national decision-making processes. On the other hand, these structural gaps have not been filled by systematic procedures capable of involving regional entities in the drafting, scrutiny, approval, enactment and ex post evaluation of national legislation. The outcome is that the national and the regional lawmakers are mutually unbound from a procedural point of view.

On the basis of this comparative analysis, the evaluation of political and judicial mechanisms for solving problems related to multi-level law-making offers two main pieces of evidence.

On the one hand, vertical cooperation/integrated regulatory procedures are of utmost importance in order to prevent legislative stalemates and controversies in multi-level settings.

From a lower-level viewpoint, difficulties increase when local requirements and specificities are not duly and efficiently taken into account in the legislation approved by the upper-level.

In this vein, the access to political mechanisms of vertical cooperation may contribute to the evaluation of the territorial impact of a certain provision prior to the rule being approved by State bodies. This purpose should be supported by the sharing between the upper and lower levels of integrated regulatory procedures capable of incorporating national and regional law-making into a process of better regulation, which is cognisant of the multi-level impact of each legislative provision.[68]

---

68 P Popelier, 'Governance and Better Regulation: Dealing with the Legitimacy Paradox' (2011) 17 *European Public Law* 55 ff.

On the other hand, when political mechanisms of multi-level governance are inadequate or do not operate properly, judicial safeguards tend to gain major momentum.[69] The role of Constitutional Courts in checking (from a judicial perspective) the respect given to the distribution of legislative competences is fostered by the lack of an effective political dialogue and cooperation between local and central law-making institutions.

The judicial safeguard may operate as a temporary substitute, but it cannot perfectly replace the political safeguards of federalism or regionalism. Courts' systematic involvement in the dynamics of multi-level law-making raises several problems, affecting both the timeline of the intervention and the dominant case-by-case approach. Judicial decisions are binding on the various arms and levels of government and they always tend to create 'precedents', but they are not always capable of promoting systematic dialogue and virtuous behaviours amongst law-making authorities, thereby preventing stalemates and future controversies.

The challenge exists in relation to defining which types of political safeguards are required to prevent, limit and, in some cases, assist the intervention of Courts. This question, which has given rise to major debates in fully-fledged federal systems,[70] does not actually seem to attract satisfactory answers in other types of multi-level contexts, such as in Italy and the EU.

---

69 For a comparative perspective on the role of Courts in decentralised systems, see E Orban (ed), *Fédéralisme et cours suprêmes/Federalism and Supreme Courts* (Les Presses de l'Université de Montréal 1991); O Mireku, *Constitutional Review in Federalised System of Government: A Comparison of Germany and South Africa* (Nomos 2000).

70 With respect to the US, see L Kramer, 'Understanding Federalism' (1996) 47 *Vanderbilt Law Review* 1485 ff. For a comparison between Germany and the US, see SR Ackerman, 'Environmental Policy and Federal Structure: A Comparison of the United States and Germany', ivi, 1599 ff.

Part II.
Lawmaking in European Multi-level governance: The EU Perspective

Chapter 4: Multi-level lawmaking and Better Regulation in the European Union: a critical approach

Maria Mousmouti (University of London)

I. Law-making in multi-level contexts: setting the scene

Lawmaking takes place nowadays at international, intergovernmental, national and sub-national levels. The nature, decision making processes and outputs of forums that can generate legislation or regulation range from intergovernmental organisations like the United Nations, intergovernmental bodies with specific (technical) mandates, treaty-based conferences, informal cooperative structures, private organisations (e.g. the International Organisation for Standardisation), European institutions and agencies and entities that produce soft law (e.g. the International Institute for the Unification of Private Law). The list becomes even longer if one adds the national and sub-national entities and agencies that have the mandate to produce rules. To give an indicative example of the magnitude of players involved, only in the EU, around 74 regional assemblies, 280 regions and 80,000 municipal authorities are directly involved in applying Union legislation[1].

The scholarship on 'multilevel governance' has studied for some time now the multiple interactions and processes taking place between the actors involved. Legal studies have been slower in analysing multilevel normative processes and the extent to which they affect the creation, interpretation and application of norms beyond the boundaries of national legal systems[2]. Governance, with its focus on efficient and effective achievement of goals, generates important changes in the legal landscape and the nature, the formulation and the content of rules. These 'new' rules are dependent on consensus on aims, enable the production of policies, but cannot

1 European Union, Active Subsidiarity. A new way of working. Report on the Task Force on Subsidiarity, Proportionality and 'Doing Less More Efficiently' 2018 at 7.

2 Jan Wouters, Ramses Wessel and Andreas Follesdal, Multilevel Regulation and the EU: A Brief Introduction in A Follesdal, R Wessel and J Wouters (eds), *Multilevel Regulation and the EU: The Interplay between Global, European and National Normative Processes* (Martinus Nijhoff 2008) at 1–6.

serve as compromises between conflicting interests, are hard to reconcile with the traditional principles of legal certainty and equality, and go hand in hand with proportionality, subsidiarity, transparency and accountability[3]. 'Multilevel regulation'[4], intersystemic or dialectical rule making[5] involves regulatory activity in a specific sector or topic, with actors operating at different administrative levels who interact to produce substantive and procedural norm-setting rules, standards or principles that govern conduct. Multi-level law-making adds to the 'traditional' challenges of law-making questions of institutional balance, boundaries between distinct levels with the mandate to set binding norms, respect for autonomy and diversity, legitimacy, coherence, substantive and normative harmony[6].

In our complex world, legislative activity rarely takes place in a vacuum. Rules of different origin and texture are always in a dynamic interaction. Multi-level law-making has three unique features. Firstly, it is by default an *extrovertive*, outward looking, open-ended, process of interaction between different actors in norm formation, enforcement and adjudication[7]. Secondly, it requires a *strategic cooperation* in the design and the application of rules, whereby lawmaking at higher level acquires stronger *strategic* features and at lower levels more focus on effectiveness, hence the *achievement of results*. Thirdly, in multi-level contexts, rules at different levels use distinct techniques, styles, languages, forms and structure, but nevertheless need to converse and interact harmoniously. In other words, multilevel lawmaking needs to sustain a dynamic *dialogue* and interaction between legal systems, legislative styles, drafting traditions and practices.

This relation of interdependence and dialogue raises an additional concern: the quality of rules produced at each level is a critical factor for the overall effectiveness of multi-level systems. Legislative quality is a 'tricky' concept, not only because it is a broad term, difficult to link to specific standards but, most importantly, because unanimous definitions are rare. Quality can encompass anything from sophisticated legal principles like legitimacy, subsidiarity, proportionality, legal security and transparency to standards of design and drafting like clarity, simplicity, consistency, conci-

3 Pauline Westerman, 'Governing by Goals: Governance as a Legal Style' (2007) 1:1 Legisprudence at 51–72.
4 Wouters et al (n 2) at 338.
5 R. Ahdieh, 'Dialectical Regulation' (2006) 38 Connecticut Law Review 863.
6 Ibid.
7 Nupur Chowdhury, Ramses A. Wessel, 'Conceptualising Multilevel Regulation in the EU: A Legal Translation of Multilevel Governance?' (2012) 18:3 European Law Journal 335–357 at 336.

sion, precision etc and factual criteria like efficacy, effectiveness and efficiency[8]. Apart from the fact that these are often elusive, relative and lack concrete content they might contradict each other and be challenging to operationalise[9]. To complicate matters more, perceptions of quality are contextual and intrinsically linked to the features of legal systems and legal orders. From the perspective of *multi-level law-making, legislative quality becomes a vertical rather than horizontal concept that can be jeopardized, undermined or reversed if not consistently upheld at all levels*[10]. This means that all levels and actors involved in multi-level law-making need to share common -or at least compatible- understandings of legislative quality and actively promote it through compatible processes and drafting traditions.

To conclude, multi-level law-making raises unique challenges in terms of effective formulation of rules, interaction between legal systems, traditions and styles. The present paper does not claim to solve the multiple and extremely complex questions associated with multi-level law-making. More humbly, it attempts to contribute to this discussion by focusing on the European Union, as a textbook case study in multi-level law-making. It looks at subsidiarity as the main 'solution' provided in multi-level decision-making, examines the ways in which it has integrated law-making and in particular its position within the Better Regulation agenda and toolkit and in actual legislative practice.

II. Subsidiarity: the key solution to the dilemmas of multi-level law-making

The European Union is a textbook case study for multilevel law-making. In this sophisticated legal universe Treaties, Regulations, Directives, national Constitutions, laws and regulations co-exist and interact in a complex and unique 'European legal order'. The hierarchy is clear: Treaties lay down the 'basics' in terms of objectives, institutions, decision making and allocation of competencies while secondary EU legislation regulates issues that derive from the treaties either with automatic and uniform applicability to all EU countries (Regulations) or by setting common results while leaving the

8 Alexandre Flückiger, Concluding Remarks (2010) 4:2 Legisprudence at 213–218.

9 H. Schulze-Fielitz, Paths Towards Better Legislation, Detours and Dead Ends in K. Messerschimdt & A. D. Oliver-Lalana (Eds) *Rational Lawmaking under Review. Legisprudence According to the German Federal Constitutional Court* (Springer 2016) at 35- 36.

10 OECD, 'The Challenges of Efficient Regulation in a Multi-level Governance Context' (OECD Reviews of Regulatory Reform: Italy 2009) at 233.

choice of means to lower levels (Directives). Delegated and implementing Acts are exceptionally used to reinforce and facilitate uniform application of EU law. In the European legal order, legislative action is required both by the European and the national legislator, and the two are in a relationship of mutual dependence. The European Commission initiates the legislative process, the Council and the European Parliament decide on the Commission's proposals and the Member States are responsible for the timely and correct transposition, application, implementation and enforcement of EU law. The supremacy of EU law affects national legal orders, and national laws and regulations need to ensure that EU provisions are applicable and effective.

At the heart of this multi-level law-making system lies a fundamental agreement about the allocation of powers and competencies. In the European Union this translates into a triad of principles: the principles of conferral, subsidiarity and proportionality (article 5 TEU). Conferral deals with the 'existence' of a competence, subsidiarity deals with the 'exercise' of concurrent competencies and proportionality with the 'intensity' of EU action[11]. Subsidiarity 'goes to the heart of what the Union does'[12] and sets the ground rules for the use of conferred competencies: in areas of shared competence, the Union acts only if the objectives pursued cannot be sufficiently achieved by the Member States. In principle, decisions are to be taken at the lowest possible level of governance and actions adopted at higher (EU) level require rigid justification. As an enforceable principle that aims to function as a 'doorstopper' for the EU lawmaker[13], subsidiarity has received criticism with regard to its effectiveness[14].

Given that much of EU action takes the shape and form of legislation, subsidiarity has inevitable implications for law-making. Who can and should legislate? on what? Following the Treaties of Amsterdam and Lis-

---

11 Gabriél A. Moens and John Trone, 'The Principle Of Subsidiarity In EU Judicial And Legislative Practice: Panacea Or Placebo?' (2015) 41:1 Journal of Legislation at 67.

12 European Commission, The principles of subsidiarity and proportionality: Strengthening their role in the EU's policymaking, Communication from the Commission to the European parliament, the European Council, the European Economic and Social Committee and the Committee of the Regions, COM(2018) 703 final at 3.

13 Oxana Pimenova, 'Subsidiarity as a 'regulation principle' in the EU' (2016) 4:3 The Theory and Practice of Legislation 381–398.

14 Moens & Trone (n 11) at 72.

bon[15], subsidiarity evolved as a *legislative principle* that was integrated in the law-making process in three ways: firstly, through the early involvement of national Parliaments in EU legislative activity through the advance scrutiny of documents and the possibility to raise objections with regard to the observance of the principle of subsidiarity. Secondly, through the obligation to consult and consider regional and local dimensions for draft legislative acts. And thirdly, through the detailed justification of compliance with subsidiarity and proportionality for every draft legislative act[16]. In the Interinstitutional Agreement on Better Law-Making of 2016, the European Parliament, the Council and the Commission reaffirmed their commitment to ensuring that subsidiarity and proportionality remain at the heart of European decision-making and that they are fully respected throughout the legislative process. During the pre-legislative phase, the quality of subsidiarity and proportionality analysis are subject to the control performed by the Regulatory Scrutiny Board. In fact, the Board has on several occasions commented on the need for further justification of the evidence associated with subsidiarity or proportionality. Ex post, the application of the principles is monitored by the European Commission through dedicated annual reports[17]. And although subsidiarity is considered to hold more potential as a legislative principle compared to a principle of judicial review[18] reality suggests that it is not entirely true.

Subsidiarity remains ambiguous and volatile[19] with a *lack of common understanding of its content, competing interpretations* and a lack of *consistency* in the ways it is addressed[20]. Many of the reasoned opinions raised by national Parliaments mask differing policy preferences rather than subsidiarity

---

15 Protocol on the application of the principles of subsidiarity and proportionality, OJ C 310/207.

16 According to article 3 of Protocol 2 'draft legislative acts' refer to proposals from the Commission, initiatives from a group of Member States, initiatives from the European Parliament, requests from the Court of Justice, recommendations from the European Central Bank and requests from the European Investment Bank, for the adoption of a legislative act.

17 Annual Reports on subsidiarity and proportionality, available at: http://ec.europa.eu/dgs/secretariat_general/relations/relations_other/npo/subsidiarity_reports_en.htm.

18 Moens & Trone (n 11) at 65.

19 European Commission, Annual Report 2017 on Subsidiarity and Proportionality, COM (2018) 490 final at 3; European Commission, Annual Report 2016 on Subsidiarity and Proportionality, COM (2017) 600 final at 4–6.

20 European Union, Active Subsidiarity (n 1); Moens & Trone (n 11) at 89.

concerns, bringing back to the fore the prevailing *political* notion of the concept and its use as a 'tool' to claim a seat in the decision making table.

'Active' subsidiarity is the 'new' solution to the old problem. A 'new way of working' that will strengthen participatory contribution to EU policy and law-making and bring more consistency and uniformity in the examination of subsidiarity and proportionality at all levels of governance. The main 'tool' is a 'model assessment grid' (checklist) that will be used consistently by all levels. The checklist examines whether a proposal was preceded by consultation, the existence of statement justifying the added value for action at Union level, the adequacy of justifications on the effectiveness of national action, the identification of transnational/cross-border aspects of a problem, conflicts with Treaty objectives, ability of Member States to adopt appropriate measures, variations of the problem and its causes, capacity of Member States to achieve the desired objectives, the effect, benefits, economies of scale, impact of action at EU level etc. In October 2018 the Commission announced changes to strengthen subsidiarity and proportionality[21] by integrating the assessment grid in the better regulation guidance, enabling more effective scrutiny by national Parliaments, ensuring more active involvement of local and regional authorities in consultation, improving the assessment and presentation of territorial impacts and integrating the perspective of subsidiarity in the evaluation of legislation.

Taking a critical stance towards subsidiarity as a legislative principle, its main weakness is that it offers a *procedural solution to a substantive problem*. Is the existence of consultation a guarantee that regional concerns have been taken into account and that they have made a difference in decision making? It is striking that as the procedural integration of subsidiarity in the legislative process becomes more and more sophisticated, substantive issues associated with its content remain unclear and ambiguous. With regard to the most recent initiatives, the systematization of the questions associated with the content of subsidiarity is a welcome development but does not bring something fundamentally new in the equation.

In other words, the principle of subsidiarity as a legislative principle brings EU and national lawmakers in a relationship of co-actorship, and co-dependency. This relationship extends far beyond the dilemma of whether to legislate or not to cover the actual legislative design, content and the implementation of rules. To this moment, the effort to 'manage'

---

21 European Commission, Communication – The Principles of subsidiarity and proportionality: Strengthening their role in EU policymaking COM(2018) 703 final.

this complex relationship relies on a sophisticated system of procedures whose aim is to demonstrate that subsidiarity has been considered. But is this enough to ensure laws that will be effective in a multi-level environment?

A third dimension of the principle of subsidiarity is that of a *better regulation principle*. 'Better regulation' policies, processes and institutions evolved to address the concerns around quality in EU lawmaking. Better Regulation aims to produce policies and laws that achieve their objectives at minimum cost[22] and is a 'tool to provide for timely and sound policy decisions' through evidence-based and well-designed measures that deliver tangible benefits[23] and are prepared in an open and transparent manner, informed by evidence and backed by the involvement of stakeholders[24]. This ambitious claim covers the whole policy cycle and is pursued through three main fundamental processes: impact assessment of important legislative and non-legislative measures, stakeholder consultation and consistent evaluation of legislation in force[25].

Since the Report by the Mandelkern Group on Better Regulation, subsidiarity and proportionality have become core elements of the BR policy in Europe. In the Better Regulation Guidelines of 2015, the Commission called subsidiarity a 'general principle of better regulation' and took steps to internalise it in better regulation policy. Since then, a subsidiarity analysis is required for every new (legislative or non-legislative) initiative and when evaluating existing interventions and is addressed in impact assessments, consultations, explanatory memoranda etc. Impact assessments and consultations, as the main tools used in lawmaking, integrate the subsidiarity concerns in their rationale and processes of preparing new legislation. Has subsidiarity as a better regulation principle been successful in this?

22 European Commission, 'Better regulation for better results — An EU agenda' COM (2015) 215 final; European Commission, 'Completing the Better Regulation Agenda: Better solutions for better results' COM (2017) 651 final; K. Wegrich, 'Which Results? Better Regulation and Institutional Politics' (2015) 6:3 European Journal of Risk Regulation 369–371.

23 COM(2015) 215.

24 Better Regulation Guidelines, SWD (2017) 350 at 4–5.

25 Ibid.

1. *Impact Assessment*

Impact assessment is a structured thinking framework[26] that connects the definition and analysis of a problem to the objectives of a policy or law, examines the costs and benefits of alternative options and chooses the option that works best. Their added value lies in the enhancing evidence base for decision making, transparency[27], taming 'bureaucratic drift', ensuring accountability, policy learning and symbolic politics[28]. However, they are a flexible tool that can function as a control mechanism for regulatory powers, a procedural device to align trade-offs in lawmaking[29], a tool to ensure coherence in policy design, transparency, communication and information[30]. Much depends on how Impact Assessments are used.

Impact Assessments in the European Union are an integral part of the Better Regulation agenda. They are used for all major legislative and non-legislative initiatives and evolve around seven questions that deal with the problem to be addressed and the reasons behind it, the reasons for EU action, the desired objectives, the available options and their (economic, social and environmental) impacts, the comparison of the different options in terms of effectiveness and the selection of the preferred option.

Subsidiarity and proportionality are well integrated in Impact Assessments. The question whether the EU should act is asked early on and the analysis evolves around the transnational aspects of a problem, the potential of Member States to adequately address them and the potential scale or effectiveness benefits of action at EU level. Tool #5 of the Better Regu-

---

26 Stephan Naundorf and Claudio Radaelli, 'Regulatory Evaluation Ex Ante and Ex Post: Best Practice, Guidance and Methods', in U. Karpen & H. Xanthaki, *Legislation in Europe. A comprehensive Guide for Scholars and Practitioners* (Hart Publishing 2017) at 187–211.

27 OECD, 'Regulatory Policies in OECD Countries: From Interventionism to Regulatory Governance' (OECD Publishing 2002) 47; OECD, 'Building an Institutional Framework for Regulatory Impact Analysis (RIA): Guidance for Policy Makers' (OECD Publishing 2008) 24–25.

28 Claire Dunlop and Claudio Radaelli, 'The politics and economics of regulatory impact assessment' in Claire Dunlop and Claudio Radaelli (Eds) *Handbook of Regulatory Impact Assessment* (Edward Elgar Publishing 2016) 8–14.

29 A. Meuwese & S. van Voorst, 'Regulatory Impact assessment in legal studies' in C. Dunlop & C. Radaelli (eds) *Handbook of Regulatory Impact Assessment* (Edward Elgar Publishing 2016) 22, 24.

30 P Andrews, 'Are Market Failure Analysis and Impact Assessment Useful?' in Stephen Weatherill (ed) *Better Regulation* (Hart Publishing 2007) 49ff cf Alberto Allemanno, 'A Meeting of Minds on Impact Assessment' (2011) 17:3 European Public Law 495.

lation Toolkit titled 'Legal Basis, Subsidiarity and Proportionality' lists a number of questions on the variations of a problem across national, regional and local levels, its spread, its underlying causes and their similarity across the EU, preferred courses of action, the capacity of Member States to enact appropriate measures and the impact of national action, including potential costs or problems if action is left to the Member States. The examination of EU added value on the other hand, assesses whether the objectives of the proposed action can be better achieved at Union level, the benefits of EU action, economies of scale, efficiency and impacts on the functioning of the internal market. The subsidiarity test consists of two main elements: articulating at least one justification and supporting by 'relevant' evidence of reasonable quantity and quality.

However, as many examples highlight, assessing subsidiarity is hardly ever a case of clear -cut, black and white decisions. Evidence rarely unequivocally points in one direction and the assessment is more likely to be an iterative process. Apart from few cases, arguments in favour and against subsidiarity, might be equally plausible, sustained with equal rigor and backed by different types of equally strong evidence. Resolving the dilemma will essentially involve political and subjective judgment.

For example, the Impact Assessment on the Framework Equality Directive[31], a major Directive prohibiting discrimination in employment on the basis of a number of grounds such as disability, age, religion etc, concluded that the adoption of a Directive would be compliant with subsidiarity and proportionality as there is a justified case for European-level action on discrimination and wide latitude is left to the Member States. In the same vein, the explanatory memorandum of the FED claims that the objectives of the proposal cannot be sufficiently achieved by the Member States and only a Community–wide measure can ensure a minimum standard level of protection against discrimination and ensure legal certainty for economic operators and citizen. Yet no compelling evidence is brought forward to actually unequivocally back these statements, while counter arguments are not examined. The only area where subsidiarity is used as an argument to restrain the (expansive) action of the EU legislator is with regard to the material scope of the Directive. It is the main justification for leaving out 'hard' issues such as the organisation and content of education, recogni-

31 Commission staff working document accompanying the proposal for a Council directive on implementing the principle of equal treatment between persons irrespective of religion or belief, disability, age or sexual orientation – Impact assessment SEC(2008) 2180, available at: https://eur-lex.europa.eu/legal-content/EN/TXT/?uri=CELEX:52008SC2180.

tion of marital or family status, adoption, reproductive rights, activities of churches and other religious organisations and other similar questions[32].

Much in the same line, the Impact Assessment of the Victim Directive[33], another major legislative initiative in the field of criminal law, concludes that there is a need for EU action on the basis of the transnational aspects of the issue which cannot be dealt with by Member States and the benefits of EU action in terms of scale and effectiveness[34]. Detailed evidence to justify these conclusions is not presented. The Victims Proposal has been criticized for failing to offer 'adequate reasoning' and 'relevant evidence' with regard to the subsidiarity test and that EU harmonization of national domestic criminal procedures has not been driven by the concerns explicitly brought forward (cross-border problems of judicial cooperation) but instead by concerns for creating a common European sense of justice[35], that marginally falls within EU competence.

Apart from the point that an objective justification of subsidiarity appears to be a tough exercise, it becomes obvious that asking the questions (proceduralisation) is only the formal part of the solution. Engaging in a reflective process around the questions and the potential answers to them is the only way to integrate subsidiarity concerns in the thinking that leads to policy and lawmaking. In the opposite case, the related analysis appears to be pre-fabricated, perfunctory, purely symbolic or to mask 'hidden' agendas or concerns. Within multi-level systems, Impact Assessments need to examine subsidiarity-related arguments into more depth, in a more balanced way and taking into account national legislation and contexts.

32 European Commission, Proposal for a Council Directive on implementing the principle of equal treatment between persons irrespective of religion or belief, disability, age or sexual orientation, COM(2008) 426 final.

33 Directive 2012/29/EU of the European Parliament and of the Council of 25 October 2012 establishing minimum standards on the rights, support and protection of victims of crime, and replacing Council Framework Decision 2001/220/JHA, OJ L 315, 14.11.2012, p. 57–73.

34 European Commission, Commission Staff Working Paper Impact Assessment, SEC/2011/0580 final, available at: https://eur-lex.europa.eu/legal-content/EN/TXT/?uri=CELEX:52011SC0580.

35 Ö Jacob, 'Subsidiarity and EU Procedural Criminal Law' (2015) 5(1) European Criminal Law Review 19–45.

2. *Consultation*

Consultation is the two-way relationship between governments and citizens[36]. Article 11 of the Treaty on European Union provides that 'the European Commission shall carry out broad consultations with parties concerned in order to ensure that the Union's actions are coherent and transparent'. As a tool of openness, transparency and participation it has played an important role in the effort to improve governance and the quality of the regulatory environment[37]. Participation of stakeholders and interested parties in the formulation of policies and legislation promotes good governance, enables socio-political interaction, encourages partnerships and joint solutions and increases the efficiency and legitimacy of decisions[38]. Especially as part of the legislative process, consultation has the potential to improve transparency, enhance legitimacy, test the feasibility of proposed solutions, engage in fact finding and improve the implementation and practicability of legislation[39].

Consultation holds a key position in the effort to address subsidiarity as a legislative and a better regulation principle. Protocol No. 2 on the application of the principles of subsidiarity and proportionality provides that 'before proposing legislative acts, the Commission shall consult widely' in order to capture the views of the regional and local authorities. In the EU, stakeholder consultation is a formal and continuous process of collecting information and views[40] and is mandatory for a number of initiatives. Consultations target a wide range of stakeholders affected by or having a stated interest in a policy[41], with a special focus on organisations representing regional, local and municipal authorities or sub-national entities.

36 OECD, 'Citizens as Partners. Information, Consultation and Public Participation in Policy-Making' (OECD Publishing 2001) at 22.

37 Anne Meuwese, 'Embedding Consultation Procedures: Law or Institutionalization?' (2011) 17:3 European Public Law 531 at 534.

38 D. Obradovic and J. Alonso Vizcaino, 'Good Governance Requirements concerning the Participation of Interest Groups in EU Consultations' (2006) 43 Common Market Law Review at 1050.

39 F. Uhlmann & Ch. Konrath, 'Participation' in U. Karpen & H. Xanthaki (Eds) *Legislation in Europe. A Comprehensive Guide for Scholars and Practitioners* (Hart Publishing 2017) at 76–81.

40 Better Regulation Toolbox, Guidelines on Stakeholder Consultation available at: https://ec.europa.eu/info/sites/info/files/better-regulation-guidelines-stakeholder-consultation.pdf.

41 Tool 53 The Consultation Strategy, available at: https://ec.europa.eu/info/sites/info/files/file_import/better-regulation-toolbox-53_en_0.pdf at 2.

Views are sought on the problem to be tackled, subsidiarity and EU dimensions, policy options, efficiency improvements of existing interventions, simplification measures and impacts[42]. The BR Toolbox provides specific guidance on how to formulate a consultation strategy, conduct consultations, analyse data, use it to inform policy making and provide feedback to stakeholders.

However, consultation as a lawmaking tool is not only about hearing as many actors as possible but mostly about asking the right questions. The lack of a clear vision of what is sought in relation to lawmaking, static questions and conflicting objectives[43] might make it a superficial exercise. When it comes to subsidiarity the important thing is to ask the right questions in order to get useful answers – and to integrate these answers in decision making. But does consultation in its present form ensure that?

For example, the consultation on the FED, as presented in the IA, provided information on the spread of the problem, the impact of uniform protection on free movement, the need for the same level of protection from discrimination and the distinct wishes of specific audiences. However, the consultation findings do not unequivocally point to the need for a common EU act or that this is what most stakeholders consider the best solution. Further, how can one verify whether and how the results of consultation have influenced the final decisions? The point is that consultation is a highly flexible data collection tool. Much depends on what is asked, who will actually respond, and how this information will be used. Guidance offers a clear procedural framework for conducting consultations (eg how to make consultation 'targeted', when to publish, time limits to be respected, acknowledgement of feedback etc)[44] but does not offer any guidance on what are the meaningful questions to ask. Or how to integrate them in decision making.

So? Is the integration of the subsidiarity principle in impact assessments and consultations a guarantee that subsidiarity concerns are actually taken into account?

The previous analysis suggests that the integration of subsidiarity in the better regulation package, in particular in impact assessments and consul-

42 Guidelines on Stakeholder Consultation (n 40) at 75.

43 F. Blanc & G. Ottimofiore, Consultation in Claire Dunlop and Claudio Radaelli (Eds) *Handbook of Regulatory Impact Assessment* (Edward Elgar Publishing 2016) 155–176 at 155–157.

44 Ibid.

tation, guarantees neither that it functions as a 'doorstopper'[45] for the EU lawmaker nor that it influences decision making nor that it contributes to improved quality of rules. IAs and consultations collect information but there is no evidence that this is the right information or relevant information. And while it is impossible to give definite answers to indefinite questions like those posed by subsidiarity, what impact assessments and consultation can positively contribute is evidence and justification that explains the particular constellation of interests at a specific moment in time. Acknowledging this relative approach appears to be a more honest, grounded and practical solution to improve legislative decision making.

III. Subsidiarity in legislative practice

The previous sections explored the position of subsidiarity in the theoretical and procedural aspects of EU policy and lawmaking. The concerns embedded in the concept are formally integrated and operationalized into existing decision making procedures through requirements for consultation, justification and the opportunity for participation and early exchange with national actors. But what about legislative practice? For example, do Directives, as the most exemplary specimen of EU multi-level lawmaking, facilitate or hinder the coordinated interaction that subsidiarity requires between norms of distinct levels?

When it comes to legislative practice, there is no doubt that the nature of European and national legislation is very different: beyond the nature of decision making and the multiplicity of actors involved, European law is mostly the result of diplomacy, negotiations conducted on political terms and compromise[46]. Legislation is often couched in political rather than legal language and with a degree of vagueness that allows room for different approaches. Its complexity is often the cause of difficulties for transposi-

45 Oxana Pimenova, Subsidiarity as a 'regulation principle' in the EU (2016) 4:3 The Theory and Practice of Legislation 381–398.

46 CWA Timmermans, 'How to Improve the Quality of Community Legislation: the Viewpoint of the European Commission' in A Kellerman, G Ciavarini-Azzi, S Jakobs and R Dayton-Smith (eds) *Improving the Quality of Legislation in Europe* (Kluwer Law International 1998) at 41.

tion at national level[47]. Drafting EU legislation is the work of many hands, and minds[48].

The distinctive features of multi-level legal instruments are particularly evident in the sui generis nature of Directives. Directives determine the common results or minimum standards to be achieved, while national legislation chooses the means that will best 'transform' these into effective national rules[49]. In this relationship, the European and national legislators play an equally important – and complementary – role. The European legislator sets the broader framework and determines the end goals, while the national legislator translates this into national norms that can work in the legal order and culture of a Member State. Directives are the common 'drafting instructions' within which national legislators have to regulate respecting the diversity of legislative traditions and styles.

Legislative practice however demonstrates a different dynamic. Rather than a constructive dialogue, the relationship is one of tension. On the one hand, national legislators have devised over the years several ways, more or less creative, to transpose Directives[50], with a preference for 'clear' transposition options that 'copy-out' rather than 're-write' the provisions of Directives'[51] with the main (or sole) purpose to avoid infringement procedures. Yet, while this might satisfy the monitoring requirements of the Commission, it appears to serve neither the requirements of subsidiarity not those of better regulation (in terms of effectiveness) nor the function of distinct levels of rules within a multi-level system. If EU provisions are detailed enough to be directly integrated into national law, hence of general and immediate applicability, they should form part of a Regulation. If not, and only set the results to be achieved by legislation, they should allow sufficient space to national lawmakers to consider and choose the best way to transpose them.

---

47 Roberto Baratta, Complexity of EU Law in the Domestic Implementing Process (2014) 2:3 The Theory and Practice of Legislation 293–308.

48 William Robinson, Drafting EU legislation in the European Commission: a collaborative process (2014) 2:3 The Theory and Practice of Legislation 249–272.

49 J Dickson, 'Directives in EU Legal Systems: Whose Norms Are They Anyway?' (2011) 17 European Law Journal at 194.

50 Bernard Steunenberg and Wim Voermans, *The Transposition of EC Directives: A Comparative Study of Instruments, Techniques and Processes in Six EU Member States* (Leiden University, Leiden/ Research and Documentation Centre (WODC) of the Ministry of Justice 2006).

51 D Greenberg, 'The 'Copy-Out' Debate in the Implementation of European Union Law in the United Kingdom' (2012) 6 Legisprudence at 243.

It is no news that the application of EU law, especially of EU Directives, is a persistent problem. Even a superficial scanning of the Commission's Annual reports on monitoring the application of EU law highlights that problematic areas overshadow the successes with a noted emphasis on incorrect or untimely transposition[52]. The question is never a lack of EU legislation but rather the fact that Member States do not apply it correctly and effectively[53]. Although EU Commission enforcement policy is currently shifting away from punitive approaches towards strategic and compliance oriented ones, the larger picture is one of tension. Could this tension and the consistent difficulty of Member States to embed EU law be due to factors other than political or institutional ones? Could it be associated with the form and content of EU rules themselves? I think yes.

A first problematic point is the fact that the common purpose and results of Directives, eloquently marketed by the Treaties and the institutions, are not always clear, or at least, not as clear as EU lawmakers assume them to be. However, this is essential if Directives are expected to function as 'drafting instructions'. Otherwise, how can Member States orient rules towards results if these are not clear?

One question relates to the nature of these results. What are the common results of Directives? Are they substantive policy results? results considered satisfied by the existence of (transposed) legislation on a specific topic? or both? In other words, do common results refer to *the existence of legal remedies* or frameworks or to *real life results*? And if so, where are these to be found? Equality Directives have contributed to the development of national frameworks in a number of areas including equal pay, discrimination, among many other issues but also the development of national law, opportunities to challenge policy and interpretative choices of institutions. Is their purpose fulfilled? Or do they go beyond that to *substantive* results, for example to improve substantive equality, remedy discrimination or ensure equality of opportunities? Looking at legislation, there is no clear answer. Equality Directives aim 'to lay down a general framework for com-

52 The Annual reports on monitoring the application of EU law are available at https://ec.europa.eu/info/publications/annual-reports-monitoring-application-eu-law_en (last accessed 13/05/2019). The Single Market Scoreboard presents data on areas of the Single Market and offers a performance overview for the Member States, the results achieved etc. The information is accessible at: http://ec.europa.eu/internal_market/scoreboard/ (last accessed 13/05/2019).

53 European Commission, 'Member States compliance with EU law: not yet good enough', Press Release 6 July 2017, available at: http://europa.eu/rapid/press-release_IP-17-1846_en.htm.

bating discrimination on the grounds of religion or belief, disability, age or sexual orientation as regards employment and occupation, with a view to putting into effect in the Member States the principle of equal treatment'. This includes both the aspiration to 'lay down a framework for combating discrimination' but also refers to the objective of putting into effect the principle of equal treatment. What does that mean? Does the reference to effective equal treatment point towards substantive understandings of equality? Does it refer to minimum common results? Does it mean that citizens should have a real and effective, as opposed to a formal, opportunity to be treated equally? Or is it enough that procedures and remedies are in place? There is no obvious answer to these questions[54]. The Preamble to the Directives, the initial proposals and other documents do not provide an unambiguous answer to this question.

On another front, are these results always what they claim to be? The Victims' Directive was enacted to *enable* participation of victims and *ensure* respectful, individualized, non-discriminatory and child sensitive support *in criminal proceedings* (art. 1 par. 1, Guidance and Recital 10, Recital 17) *in practice*. Even if this is sufficient as a common result, the Guidance issued by the Commission mentions that the Directive requires criminal justice systems '*to recognize victims as individuals with individual needs, acknowledge their key role in the criminal proceedings and link the protection offered solely to the status of 'victim' rather than any other characteristic*'. Although Guidance does not have binding force, it introduces *a new, and notably broader, overarching* goal of the Directive. Making the status of victim the main parameter for enjoying the rights set out in the Directive requires a profound *rethinking* and redesign of the rationale of criminal justice systems towards polycentric models that accommodate more actors beyond the accused, not to mention the cultural change required[55]. However, is criminal law reform the aim of the Directive? If so, why is not stated anywhere in the preparatory documents or preambles of the Directive?

For Directives to operate within the context of subsidiarity and ensure the required interaction between legal orders, a clear purpose and common results to be achieved are paramount. Implicit ones require deductive ex post reasoning, engage national lawmakers in a formalistic view of EU legislation, override any perception of legislative quality. For European leg-

54 Maria Mousmouti, 'Effectiveness as an Aspect of the Quality of EU Legislation: Is it Feasible' (2014) 2:3 The Theory and Practice of Legislation 311 at 315–317.

55 Bernt Bahr & Jenny Melum, EU's 'Victims' Directive' – A Legal Act for a Cultural Change? (2018) 9: 1 International Journal for Court Administration at 19.

islation to serve as 'drafting instructions' for Member States, the common 'European' result to be achieved needs to be made clear and unambiguous so that the national legislators can contribute in the correct direction.

A second question relates to the way in which European Directives frame the common concepts and standards introduced by Directives and the ways in which they borrow and use terms and semantic concepts that have strong origins and routes in national legal orders.

'European' legal concepts are often a mix of concepts with a determined content and others with an 'open' or flexible one, that develops ex-post after being 'fertilised' in case law. But does that make it clear to Member States what the standards to be respected are? For example, the Framework Equality Directive does not define the concept of disability, among many others. Being a much contested and dynamic concept, the issue was addressed by the Court in the case Chacon Navas[56]. The Court in fact raised a reasonable question: how can the Directive ensure minimum standards of protection across the EU if the content of basic notions is not clear? It acknowledged that an 'autonomous and uniform' European definition of disability would guarantee uniform treatment across Europe[57] and formulated a definition. Following severe criticism for incompatibility with the disability policy of the EU[58] and for introducing standards difficult to deviate from[59] it was re-defined in 2013 in HK Denmark (Ring and Skouboe Werge) to become aligned to the UN Convention on the Rights of People with Disabilities[60]. But isn't that what the lawmaker should have done?

On another front, the Victims' Directive uses the term 'victim' as an umbrella term ignoring the variable semantic meaning it has in some legal orders and the fact that it does not exist in others. The definition provided is too broad to give clear guidance as almost everyone would quality as a

---

56 C-13/05 Chacon Navas v. Eurest Colectividades SA [2006] ECR I- 6467.

57 Opinion of the Advocate General in Chacon Navas, paras 57, 64, 65: The persons to be protected and the delineation of the functional limitations to be considered must not vary. Otherwise, the protection afforded by that prohibition of discrimination would vary within the Community'.

58 COM (2010) 636 final.

59 L Waddington, 'Case Comment on C-13/05 Chacon Navas v Eurest Colectividades SA, judgement of the Grand Chamber of 11 July 2006' (2007) 44 Common Market Law Review 487–499.

60 Lisa Waddington and Andrea Broderick, *Combatting disability discrimination and realising equality. A comparison of the UN Convention on the Rights of Persons with Disabilities and EU equality and non-discrimination law* (European Commission 2018), available at https://ec.europa.eu/info/sites/info/files/combatting_disabiliy_discrimination.pdf.

victim under it. As a result, the EU term antagonises terms embedded in national law, inviting clashes and ineffective transposition. Concepts with a 'European' semantic content that do not provide answers to straightforward questions as to 'who is protected' and antagonise terms used in national legal orders can hardly qualify as *clear legal drafting* that contributes to legal certainty and better application.

These examples highlight that the implications of subsidiarity for lawmaking go far beyond the discussion around institutional or procedural solutions and infiltrate the way in which EU legislation is actually conceptualized and drafted. So far, existing lawmaking tools do not seem to have taken these concerns seriously. The EU lawmaker legislates in an introvertive way, assuming that national legal orders will adjust. A legislative dialogue or a common lawmaking culture does not seem to have materialized.

IV. Conclusions

Lawmaking is a challenging enterprise. In multi-level contexts it is even more so. The particular challenges from a lawmaking perspective relate not only to the scope and magnitude of the problems and the right level for interventions but more to the dynamics of interaction between different legal orders and layers of norms, the need for coordination of legislative design and implementation and the dialogue between distinct legal traditions and styles, design and techniques.

Subsidiarity has a clear position in the EU multi-level system with a triple function as a judicial review principle, a legislative and a better regulation principle. However, in practice, it does not appear to have been particularly successful either as a 'doorstopper' for the EU lawmaker or as a catalyst in the tense relationship between EU and national legal orders or in creating a common lawmaking culture.

At the moment, subsidiarity in the EU is addressed mainly through procedural solutions whose sole aim appears to be to neutralize its political nature. When it comes to lawmaking, subsidiarity raises important questions not only in relation to *what* should be legislated at each level but also as to *how* in order to create a framework that would allow the smooth interaction between different layers of norms. Despite the 50+ years since the establishment of the European Union, no common lawmaking culture has emerged nor an improved understanding of how layers of rules can work best together in a multi-level system. In other words, subsidiarity does not seem to have facilitated a lawmaking culture that promotes a smooth interaction and the dialogue between laws at different levels nor a common understanding of quality of rules.

Lawmaking in multi-level settings needs to be extrovertive (outward looking) and strategic in order to provide a meaningful framework and at the same time allow breathing space to national legal systems or lower level rules. Multi-level legislative systems can work well if action at lower levels contributes to *the achievement of broader goals and results pursued at higher level*. This offers a framework for legislative action at all levels, moves away from antagonism and invites for cooperation in order to use legislation to achieve broader goals.

The Better Regulation agenda and especially impact assessments and consultations cannot provide definite answers to the indefinite questions posed by subsidiarity. They can however contribute to the justification that explains the particular constellation of interests at a specific moment in time. Acknowledging this relative approach would be a more honest, grounded and practical solution to improve legislative decision making in multi-level settings.

Last but not least, lawmaking in multi-level systems requires a shared understanding of legislative quality to facilitate the cooperative process between the distinct levels. At the moment the EU and national lawmakers use different 'languages' and tools, never in contact and share an introvertive and isolationist view of their task. Bringing their thinking closer could contribute to the gradual formation of a common culture.

Chapter 5: Recent Developments in EU Regulation and Legislation

Karen Banks[1]

I. Introduction

Within the rather broad topic of recent developments in EU regulation and legislation, it is appropriate to focus on a number of subjects from the world of Better Regulation and from the case law of the Court of Justice of the EU which are particularly emblematic of the challenges which the staff of the EU institutions find all around them in the complex process of creating and developing EU law. This paper discusses:

1. the 2016 Interinstitutional Agreement on Better Law Making,
2. the Task Force on Subsidiarity, Proportionality and "Doing Less More Efficiently", and
3. access to documents.

II. The 2016 Interinstitutional Agreement on Better Law Making

Since the adoption of the Interinstitutional Agreement on Better Law Making in April 2016, work has been going on with a view to ensuring its effective implementation.[2] There has been very concrete progress on a number of fronts: the promised joint register of delegated acts was set up in a timely manner, and now allows the progress of a draft act to be followed throughout its life cycle;[3] the envisaged annual dialogue between the Commission and the two co-legislators to allow for better planning of the legislative process has become a reality, leading to a joint declaration

1 Deputy Director General of the Legal Service, European Commission. Any views expressed are personal and cannot be attributed to the Commission.

2 *Official Journal* 12.5.2016, L123/1.

3 Interinstitutional register of delegated acts: https://webgate.ec.europa.eu/regdel/#home.

among the three Institutions, signed by their respective Presidents.[4] However, progress on other issues is proving to be slower.

The famous struggle over delegated and implementing acts was duly reflected in the 2016 Interinstitutional Agreement, and the three Institutions undertook to enter into negotiations with a view to agreeing on non-binding criteria for having recourse to the one or the other instrument. This was of course all the more necessary after a number of judgments of the Court of Justice which made it clear that the legislator had a wide margin of discretion in its choice of method for the further elaboration of primary legislation.[5] Quite a number of meetings have taken place at technical level, and the Institutions have managed to agree – at that level – on a number of points. However, it appears that the more sensitive issues are proving intractable, and there does not appear to be any definite time frame for making substantive progress.

A related point in the 2016 Interinstitutional Agreement was the acknowledgment by the three Institutions that there was a need for the alignment of all existing legislation to the legal framework introduced by the Lisbon Treaty, and in particular for all acts still referring to the regulatory procedure with scrutiny (known by its French acronym "PRAC") to be promptly "Lisbonized". The Commission undertook to propose the latter alignment by the end of 2016. The proposal for a regulation to do that (known as the "PRAC omnibus") was duly presented in December 2016.[6] However, it has been having a slow and painful ride ever since. The Commission of course proposed that most PRAC-type empowerments be replaced by a delegation of power pursuant to Article 290 of the Treaty on the Functioning of the EU (TFEU. However, the Council of Ministers, whose enthusiasm for delegated acts has never been very great, has proven extremely reluctant to follow this rather evident path: it has tried to replace delegations of power with implementing powers; it has preferred to remove empowerments altogether rather than to agree to delegations of power; and on one rather large and important dossier, it seems to prefer to leave PRAC in place rather than agree to delegated acts. Since the Parlia-

4 See the most recent one for 2018/2019: https://ec.europa.eu/commission/publications/joint-declaration-eus-legislative-priorities-2018_en.

5 Case C-427/12, Commission v. Parliament and Council; C-88/13, Commission v. Parliament and Council; C-65/13, Parliament v. Commission.

6 Proposal for a Regulation adapting a number of legal acts providing for the use of the regulatory procedure with scrutiny to Articles 290 and 291 of the Treaty on the Functioning of the European Union (COM(2016)799.

ment also has to agree to the ultimate outcome, I am afraid it is hard to envisage swift progress.

Finally, in relation to the 2016 Interinstitutional Agreement, impact assessment remains a vexed topic. One of the challenges for the Commission has been to induce the co-legislators to engage in their own impact assessment in relation to amendments they propose to Commission legislative proposals. In the 2016 Interinstitutional Agreement, the Parliament and Council agreed that they would carry out such impact assessments, "when they consider this to be appropriate and necessary for the legislative process", and only in relation to their "substantial amendments", the definition of "substantial" being of course a matter for the Institution in question to determine.[7]

In the time which has elapsed since the 2016 Interinstitutional Agreement was concluded, the Parliament has continued to take the matter of impact assessment rather seriously. It has carried out a considerable number of impact assessments on its own proposed amendments to Commission proposals. It has also launched a full impact assessment to support its demand for an administrative law for the Institutions.

The Council however has been making much slower progress. Since January 2018, it finally has provided itself with the capacity to outsource assessments of substantial amendments via external consultants, under a framework contract covering a range of consultants. The budget is very limited, giving the possibility to carry out assessments of only about two-thirds of Council substantial amendments in any meaningful depth. There has been no discussion yet as to how this framework contract might be used across the different formations of the Council, or on what topics. There are of course considerable differences of view among Member States' delegations as to the wisdom and usefulness of carrying out impact assessments, so it may still be some time before the newly acquired capacity is actually put to some use.

III. The Task Force on Subsidiarity, Proportionality and "Doing Less More Efficiently"

Moving on now from the Interinstitutional Agreement, the recent report from the Task Force on Subsidiarity, Proportionality and "Doing Less More Efficiently" should be mentioned. This Task Force was set up follow-

---

7 See point 15 of the 2016 Interinstitutional Agreement.

ing President Juncker's State of the Union address in September 2017,[8] in order to explore more fully one of the options for the future of Europe set out by the President in that address, i.e. "Doing Less More Efficiently". In this scenario, the Union would focus its attention and limited resources on a reduced number of areas so as to be able to act quickly and decisively in those chosen priority fields. The Task Force was set up in November 2017 under the Chairmanship of Vice-President Timmermans. Its members were drawn from national parliaments and from the Committee of the Regions. The Task Force was asked to look into three topics:

a) How to better apply the principles of subsidiarity and proportionality in the work of the Union's Institutions, notably regarding the preparation and implementation of Union legislation and policies.
b) The identification of any policy areas where, over time, decision making and/or implementation could be re-delegated in whole or in part or definitively returned to the Member States.
c) The identification of ways to better involve regional and local authorities in the preparation and the follow up of Union policies.

The Task Force met seven times, always conducting its discussions on the basis of a paper prepared by one of its members or by its secretariat. Its members engaged in considerable outreach, and the Task Force received an impressive array of contributions from the political, legal and academic worlds. It delivered its final report to President Juncker on 10 July.[9] Its conclusions concerning the topics of proportionality and subsidiarity, and the connected task of involving local actors in a more meaningful way in the development of EU law, are well worth reading. It explains in a very persuasive manner how a more active approach to subsidiarity could bring about greater ownership of EU policies at all levels of governance. There are interesting passages on the trade-off between a possibly excessive "density" of EU legislation, leaving little room for local choices, and its necessary effectiveness. Most tellingly, however, from the point of view of the challenges facing the EU law maker, the Task Force concluded that "there is EU value added in all existing areas of activity and did not, therefore,

8 The full text is available at http://europa.eu/rapid/press-release_SPEECH-17-3165_en.htm (last accessed 8 January 2019).

9 Report of the Task Force on Subsidiarity, Proportionality and "Doing Less More Efficiently", 10 July 2018, available at https://ec.europa.eu/commission/sites/beta-political/files/report-task-force-subsidiarity-proportionality-and-doing-less-more-efficiently_en.pdf (last accessed 8 January 2019)..

identify any competences or policy areas that should be re-delegated definitively, in whole or in part, to the Member States."[10]

That leaves the EU institutions to struggle on with the effort to find the right balance, over an enormous swathe of competences, between action at EU, national and local levels. In that struggle they have to rely on the principles of subsidiarity and proportionality as they may be developed on the basis of the Task Force's report.

IV. Access to documents

As to the topic of access to documents, two recent judgments, one from the General Court and the other from the Court of Justice, have made it clear that the principle of transparency has far-reaching consequences both for the legislative process itself, and for the Commission's work in preparing legislative proposals.

The *De Capitani* case concerned a request for access to the four-column tables which are generally prepared during so-called "Trilogue" negotiations between the Council and the Parliament.[11] Parliament had granted access to all the documents requested except for the fourth column of two of the tables. The fourth column contains a possible compromise position between the Institutions, or the comments of one Institution on the position of the other. The Parliament based its refusal on the provision in the "access to documents" regulation[12] which provides for such refusal where access is sought to a document relating to a matter where the decision has not yet been taken by the Institution in question if disclosure "would seriously undermine the institution's decision-making process".

The Parliament advanced a number of arguments as to why access to the fourth column of a Trilogue table would seriously undermine the legislative process. Apart from the sensitivity of the topics under negotiation, the Parliament notably argued that its confidential collaboration with the Council would be seriously put at risk if there were a danger that the provisional outcome of their negotiations would have to be revealed to the public before the negotiation had been terminated. It also explained that its members risked coming under considerable pressure if the detail of en-

10 Executive Summary, p. 4 or point 3.5 on p. 19.

11 Case T-540/15, *De Capitani v. Parliament* (CFI, 22 March 2018).

12 Regulation (EC) No 1049/2001 of the European Parliament and of the Council of 30 May 2001 regarding public access to European Parliament, Council and Commission documents (OJ L 145, 31.5.2001, p. 43), Article 4(3).

visaged compromises became public, with negative consequences for the chance of flexible negotiation.

The Court rejected first of all any idea that there could be a general presumption of non-disclosure on these grounds. It emphasised the importance of the principle of transparency, more particularly in the legislative field, and the need to construe any exceptions narrowly. It therefore required the Parliament to show how access to the concrete parts of the documents which were the subject matter of the case could undermine "specifically and actually," the Institution's decision-making process.[13] It then went on to reject the Parliament's claim that the particular sensitivity of the topic being regulated – data protection in the context of police cooperation – could warrant a refusal to disclose. The Court carried out a precise examination of the concrete content of the fourth columns in question, and could find nothing of special sensitivity there. As for the argument that allowing public access, during a Trilogue, to the fourth column of the documents at issue would allow public pressure to be brought to bear on the rapporteur and all other MEPs participating in the process, the Court's reply was that "in a system based on the principle of democratic legitimacy, co-legislators must be held accountable for their actions to the public. If citizens are to be able to exercise their democratic rights, they must be in a position to follow in detail the decision making process within the institutions taking part in the legislative procedures and to have access to all relevant information".[14] Strangely enough, after that declaration of principle, the Court went on to admit that the risk of external pressure <u>can</u> constitute a legitimate ground for restricting access to a document. It said however that "the reality of such external pressure must be established with certainty, and evidence must be adduced to show that there is a reasonably foreseeable risk that the decision to be taken would be substantially affected owing to that external pressure".[15] In the particular case at hand, the Court found no "tangible evidence" of a likelihood of particular pressure.[16] Similarly, it dismissed as theoretical and not concretely demonstrated the Parliament's argument about the loyal collaboration of the Council with its co-legislator being undermined by access to their agreed tentative compromises.

---

13 Para 62.
14 Para 98.
15 Para 99.
16 Para 99.

If one had to summarize the effect of this judgment – against which no appeal was lodged – it would be that, as regards the legislative process, there is a strong presumption of access to all documents, a presumption which can only be dislodged if there are very concrete and exceptional circumstances which would allow one of the co-legislators to demonstrate that granting access to a particular document or part of one would really be likely to undermine its own decision-making, or the legislative process more broadly. Something very concrete and demonstrably probable would be required, as the Court is not willing to be persuaded even by intelligent speculation that legislators are going to be less willing to commit themselves in writing to a compromise if that compromise risks being made public.

The second case, which is the *ClientEarth* judgment, goes even further.[17] . This case concerned a request for access to a Commission impact assessment report, as well as to a draft of such a report, together with the corresponding opinions of the Impact Assessment Board. The Commission had refused these requests because they were made at a time when it had not yet completed its deliberations as to whether to make legislative proposals in the areas which were under consideration, and if so, as to the precise content of those proposals. The General Court which, as seen above, is very stern with the co-legislators, was much kinder to the Commission. It upheld the Commission's decisions on the basis that the Commission must have a certain "space to think" so that it could make independent decisions without undue external pressure. It therefore decided that, so long as the Commission had not reached a conclusion concerning the making of a legislative proposal, the documents in question should benefit from a general presumption of confidentiality.[18] ClientEarth appealed this judgment to the Court of Justice and was successful.

The Court of Justice first considered that, even if impact assessments are carried out upstream of any legislative proposal, and at a time when it is not certain that such a proposal will ever be made, nevertheless such documents are intimately connected with the legislative process and fall therefore to be treated as "legislative documents" to which the widest access possible should be permitted. This was all the more true, according to the Court, because the legislative proposals under consideration concerned environmental matters, to which specific transparency provisions apply. The

---

17 Case C-57/16P, *ClientEarth v. Commission*, 4 September 2018.

18 Joined Cases T-424/14 and 425/14, *ClientEarth v Commission* (CFI 13 November 2015).

Court then proceeded to dismantle the general presumption of confidentiality established by the General Court. While it recognised that access to the documents in question during the time when the Commission was still engaged in the decision-making phase possibly leading to a legislative proposal could lead to third parties attempting to influence or exert pressure on the policy choices to be made, and that it would even allow those having already participated in the upstream consultative process to try to intervene further in relation to the options now being considered by the Commission, the Court did not feel that such considerations warranted a general presumption of confidentiality. It seems to have considered that the Commission would just have to ignore any such representations if they were made. It said, in so many words, that the general obligation for the Commission to maintain an open and transparent dialogue with representative associations and civil society does not mean "that the Commission is required to respond, on the merits and in each individual case, to the remarks it may have received following disclosure of a document" under the access regulation governing access to documents.[19]

Needless to say, having disposed of the general presumption against disclosure, the Court made short work of the concrete arguments put forward in order to justify confidentiality in the particular case. Notably, in response to the Commission's argument that disclosure of the documents in question to certain interested parties, before the end of the impact assessment procedure, would lead to the interests of those parties being over-represented and having a disproportionate influence, the Court responded that it was up to the Commission to prevent such an outcome by taking due account of all interests.[20]

This judgment places the Commission in a very uncomfortable position. Rather than being able to grant itself a period of "purdah" between the broad consultation phase and the moment when it actually makes a proposal, it seems that it has to hand out preparatory documents to anyone who wants to read them, and irrespective of their provisional or final character, with the inevitable consequence of provoking further representations, criticisms, lobbying, etc. It is all very well for the Court to say that the Commission is not legally obliged to respond to such representations; in order not to do so, the Commission would have to put itself in breach of its own code of good conduct under which it has undertaken to respond to all correspondence. And that is not all. Even if the Commission were to

19 Case C-57/16P, *ClientEarth v. Commission*, 4 September 2018, para 107.
20 At para. 124.

decide not to react to representations made by a lobby group following access to an impact assessment report, it is impossible to exclude the human factor : the effect of reading representations from one side of an argument only may very well be to influence the judgment of those working on a file at a time when they ought to be weighing impartially the pros and cons of every option. The Court asks in effect for a superhuman standard of lucidity, objectiveness and impartiality on the part of the Commission's civil servants. And one may wonder to what end the Court makes it clear that the purpose of allowing access to pre-legislative documents is to allow citizens to make their views known regarding choices being considered by the Commission before those choices have been definitively adopted. In other words, the whole point of access is to allow citizens to influence outcomes. But how can they do that if the Commission is obliged to steel itself against being unduly influenced, and to refuse to answer correspondence ? In summary, one can say that this judgement can only produce useful effects in the unlikely case that the citizen seeking access to an impact assessment report is one who has not already participated in the prior consultation process, and who may therefore have something new to say, of which the Commission should indeed take account. For the rest, the Court has essentially created new pressures for the Commission during the phase in which it needs to work calmly and impartially, and has furthermore ordered the Commission not to allow itself to be swayed by those pressures.

V. Conclusion

The selection of topics in this paper was designed to illustrate some of the difficulties encountered in the efforts made to engage in Better Regulation, and in the world of EU law-making more broadly. It is to be hoped that this pot-pourri of subjects has served to highlight some of the complexities of that world, but also to demonstrate the extreme interest of the work involved. The perfecting of the process of EU law-making is certainly a work in progress, but it is one which engages the imagination and challenges the ingenuity of all those who strive to find better ways forward. Critical comments on this process are to be welcomed with great interest, especially because the development of EU Regulation has always depended on an approach of improving what is improvable.

Chapter 6: A critical analysis of EU regulation

Markéta Whelanová[1]

I. Introduction

The EU law is a very extensive and complex legal order. It includes about 35 000 legal acts published in the L series of the Official Journal of the EU[2] adopted by the EU institutions and about 35 000 judgements and orders[3] adopted by the Court of Justice of the EU.

For that legal order to function properly it is essential for all EU law to be implemented correctly and in good time in the national legal orders of all the Member States. Thus, implementation is an obligation of the Member States. However, to permit proper implementation it is vital that all EU legislation be drafted to a high standard.[4]

The EU institutions therefore adopted the Interinstitutional Agreement of 22 December 1998 on common guidelines for the quality of drafting of Community legislation setting out the basic principles for drafting[5] (hereinafter "IA") and a Joint Practical Guide for persons involved in the drafting of European Union legislation[6] (hereinafter "JPG"), which is a hand-

---

1 I would like to thank William Robinson for his constructive comments on this article and his great help concerning language corrections.

2 Data from the ISAP database – see Methodical Instructions for the Organisation of Work when Meeting the Legislative Obligations Ensuing from the Membership of the Czech Republic in the European Union, Decision of the Czech Government of 12 October 2005 No. 1304, as amended by Decisions No. 1344/2009, 19/2018 and 138/2018.

3 See <https://curia.europa.eu/jcms/jcms/P_80908/en/> accessed 2.1.2019.

4 U Karpen and H Xanthaki (eds), *Legislation in Europe* (Hart Publishing, 2017), H Xanthaki, 'The Problem of Quality in EU Legislation: What on Earth Is Really Wrong?', (2001) 38 *Common Market Law Review* 651, W Voermans, 'Concern About the Quality of EU Legislation: What Kind of Problem, by What Kind of Standards?', (2009) 1 Vol. 2 *Erasmus Law Review* 59, P Popelier, 'Governance and Better Regulation: Dealing with the Legitimacy Paradox', (2011) 17 No. 3 *European Public Law* 555, W Robinson, 'Time for Coherent Rules on EU Regulation', (2015) 3 No. 3 *Theory and Practice of Legislation* 257.

5 [1999] OJC 73/1.

6 <https://publications.europa.eu/en/publication-detail/-/publication/3879747d-7a3c-411b-a3a0-55c14e2ba732> accessed 2.1.2019.

book of drafting practice. They are a good basis for achieving the necessary standard of quality of drafting.[7] Unfortunately, all too often they are not followed in practice as they are outweighed by political issues during the negotiation procedure. Both the Member States and EU institutions frequently attach more importance to achieving compromise and agreement on aspects of policy than ensuring the clarity and comprehensibility of the legal text.

As a consequence there are quite a lot of cases in which EU legislation has not achieved a high standard of legal drafting and therefore caused difficulty during the implementation process in the Member States.

The defects in EU drafting that pose problems in the national legal orders relate in particular to ambiguity or lack of clarity, incompleteness and defects of form. They are discussed in the following sections.

II. Ambiguity or lack of clarity

Ambiguity (lack of clarity) is a very broad concept and it may therefore be useful to analyze what causes ambiguity.[8] Ambiguity can be caused by formal reasons or by substantive reasons.

1. Ambiguity due to formal reasons

Ambiquity due to formal reasons appears in such cases as when provisions are too long and complicated, when provisions are overly technical or when the text is poorly structured. That is not acceptable and therefore Guideline 4 of the IA provides that *"Provisions of acts shall be concise and their content should be as homogeneous as possible. Overly long articles and sentences, unnecessarily convoluted wording and excessive use of abbreviations should be avoided."*

---

7 Nevertheless, on the expert level it is recommended to update and revise the IA whose text has been changed by the revised text of JPG – W Robinson, 'Renegotiation by the United Kingdom of its constitutional relationship with the European Union – Issues related to Competitiveness and Better Law-Making' (Study, European Parliament 2016 [53]), <http://www.europarl.europa.eu/thinktank/en/document.html?reference=IPOL_STU(2016)556939> accessed 5.1.2019.

8 See also W Robinson, 'Making EU Legislation Clearer', (2014) 16 No. 3 *European Journal of Law Reform* 610.

Unfortunately this requirement is not always complied with. The example of Council Directive (EU) 2016/1164[9] demonstrates that EU law does not always reach the requisite high standard of quality. Article 2 (1) of that Directive provides:

> *For the purposes of this Directive, the following definitions apply:*
> *(1) 'borrowing costs' means interest expenses on all forms of debt, other costs economically equivalent to interest and expenses incurred in connection with the raising of finance as defined in national law, including, without being limited to, payments under profit participating loans, imputed interest on instruments such as convertible bonds and zero coupon bonds, amounts under alternative financing arrangements, such as Islamic finance, the finance cost element of finance lease payments, capitalised interest included in the balance sheet value of a related asset, or the amortisation of capitalised interest, amounts measured by reference to a funding return under transfer pricing rules where applicable, notional interest amounts under derivative instruments or hedging arrangements related to an entity's borrowings, certain foreign exchange gains and losses on borrowings and instruments connected with the raising of finance, guarantee fees for financing arrangements, arrangement fees and similar costs related to the borrowing of funds.*

This definition, which is central to Directive (EU) 2016/1164, takes more than 10 lines in the official version. It is very verbose and contains certain terms – like Islamic finance – not known to some national legal orders. Furthermore, it is not even exhaustive since the final part refers to *"similar costs related to the borrowing of funds"*. Despite its length, therefore, the definition is merely indicative. Such a definition is very difficult to transpose to most national legal orders in a way that would be understandable and clear enough to the individuals who are the addressees.

Also problematic are overlong titles of EU legal acts. This problem can be illustrated by the delegated directives to Directive 2011/65/EU.[10] For example, the title of Commission Delegated Directive 2014/7/EU[11] reads as follows:

---

9 Council Directive (EU) 2016/1164 laying down rules against tax avoidance practices that directly affect the functioning of the internal market [2016] OJ L193/1.

10 Directive 2011/65/EU of the European Parliament and of the Council on the restriction of the use of certain hazardous substances in electrical and electronic equipment [2011] OJ L174/88.

11 [2014] OJ L4/57.

Commission Delegated Directive 2014/7/EU of 18 October 2013 amending, for the purposes of adapting to technical progress, Annex IV to Directive 2011/65/EU of the European Parliament and of the Council as regards an exemption for lead in solders, termination coatings of electrical and electronic components and printed circuit boards, connections of electrical wires, shields and enclosed connectors which are used (a) in magnetic fields within the sphere of 1 m radius around the isocentre of the magnet in medical magnetic resonance imaging equipment, including patient monitors designed to be used within this sphere, or (b) in magnetic fields within 1 m distance from the external surfaces of cyclotron magnets, magnets for beam transport and beam direction control applied for particle therapy

The very long title itself has an impact on national legal orders since the Member States are obliged to make a reference to a directive when transposing it.[12] Therefore they usually cannot avoid using the long and verbose expressions.

Another example of excessively technical and poorly structured provisions can be found in Council Directive 2014/107/EU.[13] Article 1 of that Directive provides:

Directive 2011/16/EU is amended as follows:
(1) In Article 3, point 9 is replaced by the following:
'9. "automatic exchange" means the systematic communication of predefined information on residents in other Member States to the relevant Member State of residence, without prior request, at pre-established regular intervals. In the context of Article 8, available information refers to information in the tax files of the Member State communicating the information, which is retrievable in accordance with the procedures for gathering and processing information in that Member State. In the context of Article 8(3a), Article 8(7a), Article 21(2) and Article 25(2) and (3) any capitalised term shall have the meaning that it has under the corresponding definitions set out in Annex I.'[14]

12 See for example Article 2 of the above-mentioned Commission Delegated Directive 2014/7/EU: "*When Member States adopt those provisions, they shall contain a reference to this Directive or be accompanied by such a reference on the occasion of their official publication. Member States shall determine how such reference is to be.*"

13 Council Directive 2014/107/EU amending Directive 2011/16/EU as regards mandatory automatic exchange of information in the field of taxation [2014] OJ L359/1.

14 Emphasis added.

The definition of automatic exchange in Article 1 of Council Directive 2014/107/EU therefore specifies that certain terms should be interpreted as provided for in Annex I to Directive 2011/16/EU and that those terms should be construed in a way that corresponds to the terms written there in bold letters. That technique is not user-friendly and is contrary to Guidelines 14 and 15[15] of IA as well as to Guideline 22 of JPG which provides that

> *"Technical aspects of the act shall be contained in the annexes, to which individual reference shall be made in the enacting terms of the act and which shall not embody any new right or obligation not set forth in the enacting terms."*

The ambiquity due to formal reasons is therefore very undesirable as it gravely undermines the clarity and comprehensibility of the text. It is normally easy to detect since the long and poorly structured provisions are generally seen straight away.

2. *Ambiguity due to substantive reasons*

The EU rules may also be unclear due to substantive reasons. Ambiguity based on substantive reasons can be caused by such features as vagueness, especially as to the scope, or reliance on clarification in the recitals; inclusion of soft-law provisions in legally binding acts or indicative lists and provisions resembling political planning; provisions which have not been updated or unclear links between legal acts; or indirect amendments. They are discussed in the following subsections.

---

15 *"14. Where the terms used in the act are not unambiguous, they should be defined together in a single article at the beginning of the act. The definitions shall not contain autonomous normative provisions.*
15. As far as possible, the enacting terms shall have a standard structure (subject matter and scope – definitions – rights and obligations – provisions delegating powers and conferring implementing powers – procedural provisions – measures relating to implementation – transitional and final provisions). .... ".

2.1. Vagueness, especially as to the scope, or reliance on clarification in the recitals

Concerning the vagueness as to the scope, an example can be shown in General Data Protection Regulation.[16] Article 2 of that Regulation provides as follows:

> *Material scope*
> *1. This Regulation applies to the processing of personal data wholly or partly by automated means and to the processing other than by automated means of personal data which form part of a filing system or are intended to form part of a filing system.*
> *2. This Regulation does not apply to the processing of personal data:*
> *(a) in the course of an activity which falls outside the scope of Union law ;*[14]

According to Article 2(2), the General Data Protection Regulation does not apply to the processing of personal data in the course of activities falling outside the scope of the EU law. This condition is very vague as it is not always clear what falls outside and what inside the scope of the EU law. In areas like direct taxation which are not directly regulated by secondary legislation but in certain aspects by case law, certain legal relationships fall inside the scope of the EU law only where the cross-border element is present.[17] Similarly, the area of social security, which is governed by the principle of coordination and not harmonization, does not have a global impact in national law. There may thus be uncertainty as to the application of the EU rules.

Another example can be shown in the use of the term 'public body' in the General Data Protection Regulation. Article 37 provides as follows:

> *Designation of the data protection officer*
> *1. The controller and the processor shall designate a data protection officer* [14] *in any case where:*
> *(a) the processing is carried out by a public authority or body,* [14] *except for courts acting in their judicial capacity;*

16 Regulation (EU) 2016/679 of the European Parliament and of the Council on the protection of natural persons with regard to the processing of personal data and on the free movement of such data (General Data Protection Regulation) [2016] OJ L119/1.

17 See for example the judgement of the Court of Justice of the EU in Joined Cases C-53 and C-80/13 *Strojírny Prostějov v Odvolací finanční ředitelství* (ECLI:EU:C:2014:2011).

Since the term "public body" is not defined by the Regulation, it is uncertain how broad the obligation to designate a data protection officer is. Does it apply to a public university? And to a private university? Does it apply to health insurance companies operating on the principle of solidarity? And what about transport companies owned by municipalities?

Vagueness caused by the fact that clarification of legal relationships is to be found in the recitals is unfortunately also quite common. There are even cases in which provisions of other EU acts are applicable on the basis of a recital. An example can be found in Regulation (EC) No 1610/96[18] which states in recital 17:

> *(17) Whereas the detailed rules in recitals 12, 13 and 14 and in Articles 3 (2), 4, 8 (1)(c) and 17(2) of this Regulation are also valid, mutatis mutandis, for the interpretation in particular of recital 9 and Articles 3, 4, 8 (1) (c) and 17 of Council Regulation (EEC) No 1768/92,* [14]

Regulation (EEC) No 1768/92 was later repealed and supplemented by Regulation No 469/2009.[19] When doubts concerning the meaning of Regulation No 469/2009 were raised in a case before the Court of Justice,[20] the Court stated that Regulation No 469/2009 should be interpreted having regard to recital 17 of Regulation No 1610/96.[21]

Clarity and comprehensibility also cannot be attained in cases when the EU act is approved on the EU level even though certain questions concerning its core parts still remain unresolved. The example can be cited of Council Directive (EU) 2017/1852[22] whose relationship to the rulings of national courts is vague though the Directive envisages it in general terms (e.g. in Articles 7 and 16).

---

18 Regulation (EC) No 1610/96 of the European Parliament and of the Council concerning the creation of a supplementary protection certificate for plant protection products [1996] OJ L198/30.

19 Regulation (EC) No 469/2009 of the European Parliament and of the Council concerning the supplementary protection certificate for medicinal products (Codified version) [2009] OJ L152/1.

20 See Case C-492/16 *Incyte Corporation v Szellemi Tulajdon Nemzeti Hivatala* (ECLI:EU:C:2017:995).

21 *"Nevertheless, having regard to recital 17 of Regulation No 1610/96, Article 18 of Regulation No 469/2009 must be interpreted in the light of Article 17(2) of Regulation No 1610/96."* [para 37].

22 Council Directive (EU) 2017/1852 on tax dispute resolution mechanisms in the European Union [2017] OJ L265/1.

2.2. Inclusion of soft-law provisions in legally binding acts or political planning and indicative lists

In EU law it is possible to find provisions which resemble political wishes or desires. Provisions of such a declaratory nature cause problems in the implementation process on the national level because they do not obtain any clearly defined obligation to be fulfilled.[23] Accordingly, such provisions cannot be duly enforced. In addition, penalties related to such provisions cannot be accepted in Member States governed by the rule of law where precise norms are required in those cases. Consequently, provisions of a soft-law nature should be eliminated from the EU's legally binding acts.

An example of soft law provisions in a legally binding act is to be found in Regulation (EU) No 1305/2013[24] Article 28(4) of which provides as follows:

> *(4) Member States shall endeavour to ensure [14] that persons undertaking to carry out operations under this measure are provided with the knowledge and information required to implement such operations.*

A similar example is in Directive (EU) 2016/800[25] Article 12(6) of which provides:

> *(6) Member States shall endeavour to ensure [14] that children who are deprived of liberty can meet with the holder of parental responsibility as soon as possible, where such a meeting is compatible with investigative and operational requirements. This paragraph shall be without prejudice to the nomination or designation of another appropriate adult pursuant to Article 5 or 15.*

---

23 See IA, Guideline 12: "*The enacting terms of a binding act shall not include provisions of a non-normative nature, such as wishes or political declarations…*".
JPG, point 12.1.: "*Binding acts should lay down rules, including provisions setting out the information (for example: the scope and the definitions) necessary to understand and apply those rules correctly. Anything else is superfluous: desires, intentions and declarations do not belong in the enacting terms of a binding act.*"

24 Regulation (EU) No 1305/2013 of the European Parliament and of the Council on support for rural development by the European Agricultural Fund for Rural Development (EAFRD) [2013] OJ L347/487.

25 Directive (EU) 2016/800 of the European Parliament and of the Council on procedural safeguards for children who are suspects or accused persons in criminal proceedings [2016] OJ L132/1.

Directive (EU) 2016/680[26] also fails to formulate certain provisions in a clear way. For example Article 12(2) provides as follows:

> *2. Member States shall provide for the controller to facilitate the exercise of the rights* [14] *of the data subject under Articles 11 and 14 to 18.*

It may further be pointed out that the EU directives providing for certain methodical guidelines and planning which should be followed by the Member States are difficult to transpose. Such directives concern the fulfilment of general objectives by the Member States and mostly regulate mutual cooperation between them and the European Commission. They resemble more political planning and support rather than a legal text since specific rights and duties which should be imposed on individuals are mentioned in very vague terms. An example can be found in Article 9 and 10 of Directive 2010/31/EU.[27]

Similarly, incorporation of 'appropriate measures' or 'policies' in the legal text normally does not attain a good standard of clarity. This can be demonstrated by the above-mentioned Directive (EU) 2016/680 Article 19(2) of which provides:

> *Obligations of the controller*
> *2. Where proportionate in relation to the processing activities, the measures referred to in paragraph 1 shall include the implementation of appropriate data protection policies by the controller.* [14]

Clarity is also rarely reached by 'indicative lists' appearing in the EU legislation which are coupled with the imposition of obligations. For instance, Council Directive 2013/59/Euratom[28] sets up a system based on a high level of protection which must be ensured by the Member States and on certain regulatory controls such as licensing and authorization. Those procedures should be precise so that legal certainty and legal expectations are not undermined throughout the EU. The Directive provides, however, on-

26 Directive (EU) 2016/680 of the European Parliament and of the Council on the protection of natural persons with regard to the processing of personal data by competent authorities for the purposes of the prevention, investigation, detection or prosecution of criminal offences or the execution of criminal penalties, and on the free movement of such data [2016] OJ L119/89.

27 Directive 2010/31/EU of the European Parliament and of the Council on the energy performance of buildings [2010] OJ L153/13.

28 Council Directive 2013/59/Euratom laying down basic safety standards for protection against the dangers arising from exposure to ionising radiation [2014] OJ L13/1.

ly that the Member States are to take into account 'the indicative lists' contained in various Annexes to the Directive. For example, Article 29(2) of the Directive provides that *"in the case of licensing and when determining what information must be provided under paragraph 1, Member States shall take into account the indicative list in Annex IX."*

If the list of information for licence applications is only indicative, to what extent must it be followed and complied with? Which items can a Member State choose to omit or depart from? Is it still possible for a uniform standard to be reached if each Member State chooses different criteria from the indicative lists?

2.3. Provisions which have not been updated or unclear links between legal acts

It occurs far too often in EU legislation that a provision in one EU act refers to another EU act which has already been repealed. For instance, Directive (EU) 2016/681[29] provides in Article 3 as follows:

> *Definitions*
> *For the purposes of this Directive the following definitions apply*
> *(8) 'terrorist offences' means the offences under national law referred to in Articles 1 to 4 of Framework Decision 2002/475/JHA;* [14]

The problem is that Framework Decision 2002/475/JHA is not in force anymore. It was repealed by Directive (EU) 2017/541.[30] Anyone reading the Directive (EU) 2016/681 therefore has to perform a bit of detective work and find out what should apply instead of the repealed Framework Decision.

But not all cases can be resolved by detective work: there are cases when after a certain provision had been repealed, no new provision was approved. Then a legal gap is created which is highly undesirable. Such a practice is also not in conformity with EU legislative drafting rules.[31]

29 Directive (EU) 2016/681 of the European Parliament and of the Council on the use of passenger name record (PNR) data for the prevention, detection, investigation and prosecution of terrorist offences and serious crime [2016] OJ L119/132.

30 Directive (EU) 2017/541 on combating terrorism and replacing Council Framework Decision 2002/475/JHA [2017] OJ L88/6.

31 See for example IA, Guideline 16: *"References to other acts should be kept to a minimum. References shall indicate precisely the act or provision to which they refer. Circular references (references to an act or an article which itself refers back to the initial provi-*

To support this, the example can be given of Council Directive 92/57/EEC,[32] Article 1(2) of which provides as follows:

> *(2) This Directive shall not apply to drilling and extraction in the extractive industries within the meaning of Article 1 (2) of Council Decision 74/326/EEC[14] of 27 June 1974 on the extension of the responsibilities of the Mines Safety and Health Commission to all mineral-extracting industries.*

The problem is that Decision 74/326/EEC had been repealed at the end of 2003 by Council Decision 2003/913.[33] Unfortunately, Decision 2003/913 does not carry over provisions of the Decision 74/326/EEC so the scope of Directive 92/57/EEC remains unclear since the scope of the exemption in Article 1(2) for drilling and extraction in the extractive industries is unclear.

Many problems arise when an EU act approved on the EU level does not repeal or amend all of the earlier EU acts which become obsolete or at least unclear in the light of the new EU legislation. This loophole usually appears in cases of broad regulations on the EU level which affect many EU acts. For example, Regulation (EU) 2017/625 (the Official Controls Regulation)[34] repeals in Article 146 Regulation (EC) No 882/2004[35] with effect from 13 December 2019. But the implementing Commission Regulation (EC) No 669/2009[36] which provides for references to Regulation No. 882/2004 remains unchanged.

---

sion) and serial references (references to a provision which itself refers to another provision) shall also be avoided."

32 Council Directive 92/57/EEC on the implementation of minimum safety and health requirements at temporary or mobile construction sites (eighth individual Directive within the meaning of Article 16 (1) of Directive 89/391/EEC) [1992] OJ L245/6.

33 Council Decision 2003/913 setting up an Advisory Committee on Safety and Health at Work [2003] OJ C218/1.

34 Regulation (EU) 2017/625 of the European Parliament and of the Council on official controls and other official activities performed to ensure the application of food and feed law, rules on animal health and welfare, plant health and plant protection products (Official Controls Regulation) [2017] OJ L95/1.

35 Regulation (EC) No 882/2004 of the European Parliament and of the Council on official controls performed to ensure the verification of compliance with feed and food law, animal health and animal welfare rules [2004] OJ L165/1.

36 Commission Regulation (EC) No 669/2009 implementing Regulation (EC) No 882/2004 of the European Parliament and of the Council as regards the increased level of official controls on imports of certain feed and food of non-animal origin [2009] OJ L194/11.

2.4. Indirect amendments

Vagueness is often caused by indirect amendments, cases in which a provision of one EU act supplements a provision of another EU act without a precise specification of this other EU act or its provisions.

An example of this kind of defect can be found in Directive (EU) 2016/1148[37] Article 1(1) and (7) of which provide as follows:

> *Subject matter and scope*
> *1. This Directive lays down measures with a view to achieving a high common level of security of network and information systems within the Union so as to improve the functioning of the internal market. ...*
> *7. Where a sector-specific Union legal act requires operators of essential services or digital service providers either to ensure the security of their network and information systems or to notify incidents, <u>provided that such requirements are at least equivalent in effect to the obligations laid down in this Directive, those provisions of that sector-specific Union legal act shall apply.</u>* [14]

Article 1(7) therefore refers to other EU acts and states that these other EU acts or their provisions shall not apply unless they lay down requirements which are at least equivalent in effect to those ones laid down by Directive 2016/1148. Obviously, among 35 000 EU acts it is difficult to determine which provisions of which other EU acts are at least equivalent in effect. It causes the provision of Article 1(7) of Directive 2016/1148 to be barely applicable and very unclear.

Another example can be found in Regulation (EU) 2016/1191[38] Article 17 of which provides as follows:

> *Relationship with other provisions of Union law*
> *1. This Regulation is without prejudice to the application of other provisions of Union law on legalisation, similar formality, or other formalities, and shall be complementary to such provisions.*
> *2. This Regulation is without prejudice to the application of Union law on electronic signatures and electronic identification.*

---

37 Directive (EU) 2016/1148 of the European Parliament and of the Council concerning measures for a high common level of security of network and information systems across the Union [2016] OJ L194/1.

38 Regulation (EU) 2016/1191 of the European Parliament and of the Council on promoting the free movement of citizens by simplifying the requirements for presenting certain public documents in the European Union [2016] OJ L200/1.

> *3. This Regulation is without prejudice to the use of other systems of administrative cooperation established by Union law which provide for exchange of information between the Member States in specific areas.*

This provision, despite the fact it should regulate relationships with other EU acts, does not formulate clearly what will happen if a conflict between EU acts arise. Even though that question is very important and should not be left to a mere interpretation, it is only partly resolved by the recitals to the Regulation. Recital 44 states:

> *The relationship between this Regulation and existing Union law should be clarified. In that regard, this Regulation should be without prejudice to the application of Union law which contains provisions on legalisation or similar formality, or other formalities, such as Council Regulation (EC) No 2201/2003. … If the provisions of this Regulation conflict with a provision of another Union act governing specific aspects of simplification of the requirements for presenting public documents, and simplifying such requirements even further, such as* [14] *Directive 2005/36/EC of the European Parliament and of the Council, Directive 2006/123/EC of the European Parliament and of the Council and Regulation (EC) No 987/2009 of the European Parliament and of the Council, the provision of the Union act which provides for further simplification should prevail.* [14]

The problem is that in varying EU acts aiming at different objectives it can be unclear what can be "specific aspects of simplification" or "further simplification". The examples given in recital 44 are only of a demonstrative character and do not cover all the cases which could be applicable. Therefore, legal certainty is not guaranteed. The practice is also contrary to Guideline 18 of the IA.[39]

III. Incompleteness

It is becoming more frequent that EU acts are incomplete because they include broad empowering provisions for the Commission or other bodies to specify the scope of the rules or to define basic terms used in the rules.

39 *"Every amendment of an act shall be clearly expressed. Amendments shall take the form of a text to be inserted in the act to be amended. Preference shall be given to replacing whole provisions (articles or subdivisions of articles) rather than inserting or deleting individual sentences, phrases or words. An amending act shall not contain autonomous substantive provisions which are not inserted in the act to be amended."*

Completion is usually supposed to be carried out by delegated or implementing acts under Articles 290 and 291 of the Treaty on the Functioning of the EU. Accordingly, to cover the whole scope of the EU act it is necessary to await clarification of the key parts in future implementing or delegated acts.

This approach has broad impacts on national legal orders. First, it should be pointed out that a lot of rules approved at EU level are, without the future implementing or delegated acts, lacking in detail – there is no precisely stated obligation or material or personal scope of application in them. Nevertheless, the implementation (transposition) period is running.

Examples can be found in the Tobacco Directive, Directive 2014/40/EU[40] and in Regulation (EU) No 1143/2014.[41]

Article 7 of the Tobacco Directive provides as follows:

> *Regulation of ingredients*
> *1. Member States shall prohibit the placing on the market of tobacco products with a characterising flavour.*
> *Member States shall not prohibit the use of additives which are essential for the manufacture of tobacco products, for example sugar …*
> *2. The Commission shall, at the request of a Member State, or may, on its own initiative, determine by means of implementing acts whether a tobacco product falls within the scope of paragraph 1.* [14] *Those implementing acts shall be adopted in accordance with the examination procedure referred to in Article 25(2).*
> *3. The Commission shall adopt implementing acts laying down uniform rules for the procedures for determining whether a tobacco product falls within the scope of paragraph 1. …* [14]

Article 4 of Regulation (EU) No 1143/2014 provides as follows:

> *List of invasive alien species of Union concern*
> *1. The Commission shall adopt, by means of implementing acts, a list of invasive alien species of Union concern ('the Union list'),* [14] *on the basis of the criteria laid down in paragraph 3 of this Article.*

---

40 Directive 2014/40/EU of the European Parliament and of the Council on the approximation of the laws, regulations and administrative provisions of the Member States concerning the manufacture, presentation and sale of tobacco and related products [2014] OJ L127/1.

41 Regulation (EU) No 1143/2014 of the European Parliament and of the Council on the prevention and management of the introduction and spread of invasive alien species [2014] OJ L317/35.

It follows from those examples that provisions of these EU legal acts approved by European Parliament and the Council (hereinafter 'basic EU act') leave the important matters of the scope or the core terms to be decided at a lower level.

There are two problems resulting from this legislative technique. The first one relates to rules applied in certain national legal orders with strict rules on the delegation of rulemaking powers. The second problem concerns timely implementation.

The Czech Republic is one of those Member States that apply a strict legality principle. Therefore, certain provisions in this Member State have to be laid down in the form of a statute – an act of the Czech Parliament. This approach follows from the national constitutional rules.[42] Accordingly, important matters like rights and obligations imposed on individuals and ensuing sanctions or competency of state bodies cannot be left to lower level acts (government regulations or ministerial decrees) but have to be incorporated in statutes. Furthermore, to issue any ministerial decree, a very precise empowering provision has to be formulated in a respective statute, and government regulations cannot go beyond the scope of a statute.[43]

This imperative is difficult to fulfill during the national implementation process when the EU rules are incomplete and provide for broad empowering provisions for the Commission or other bodies as regards such matters as the creation of new obligations, the establishment of basic definitions[44] or the extension of the scope of application to other areas. Proposals for Czech statutes cannot contain any vague references to future EU

---

42 For example, Article 79 (1) of the Czech Constitution (Constitutional act. No. 1/1993 Coll.): *"The ministries and other administrative offices may be established, and their powers provided for, only by statute."* Article 4 (1) of the Czech Charter of Fundamental Rights and Freedoms (Constitutional act No. 2/1993 Coll.): *"Duties may be imposed only on the basis, and within the bounds, of a statute, and only while respecting the fundamental rights and freedoms."*

43 Article 79 (3) of the Czech Constitution: *"If they are so empowered by statute, the ministries, other administrative offices, and bodies of territorial self-governing units may issue legal acts on the basis of and within the bounds of that statute."* Article 78 of the Czech Constitution: *"In order to implement statutes, and while remaining within the bounds thereof, the government is authorized to issue regulations."*

44 See for example point III of Annex I to Commission Implementing Regulation (EU) 2015/2403 establishing common guidelines on deactivation standards and techniques for ensuring that deactivated firearms are rendered irreversibly inoperable ([2015] OJ L333/62) which provides: *"In order to ensure a correct and uniform application of the deactivation operations of firearms, the Commission shall elaborate definitions in cooperation with the Member States."*

acts which might regulate important features reserved for statutes. References may be made only to directly applicable EU acts (regulations) whose content is known and is clear and precise. No exceptions to that principle should be accepted. It is very important for enforcement since the imposition of sanctions for non-compliance with a vague future obligation could be held contrary to the principle of rule of law.

Provisions of basic EU acts which are devoid of content and depend on future implementing or delegated Commission acts providing for important features cannot therefore be implemented during the period for implementation of those basic EU acts.

Nevertheless, if it is known that a delegated Directive will be merely of a technical nature, it is possible in the Czech statute to formulate a precise empowering provision for the issue of a decree by one Ministry, or to issue a Governmental regulation encompassing a number of Ministries. Similarly, if it is known that a delegated EU regulation will be precise, a reference to this Regulation can be formulated as well.

Unfortunately, all too often it is not at all clear during the implementation of a basic EU act what subsequent delegated or implementing acts will be adopted and what form they will take. Will it be a regulation or a directive[45]? And if it is a regulation, will it be precise enough to have direct effect?

To avoid any such ambiguity, it is vital that provisions conferring powers on the Commission are circumscribed narrowly. It would also assist the national implementation process if proposals for basic EU acts included, for the information of the Member States, drafts of the future delegated or implementing EU acts that will be required or at least the main elements of those acts.

Since in certain cases immediate implementation of an EU act is not possible due to constitutional imperatives following from the principle of the rule of law, the solution would be to defer implementation until the delegated or implementing act of the Commission is adopted. Nevertheless, that approach is also problematic: delegated or implementing acts of the Commission are all too frequent and if those Commission acts affect

45 While delegated or implementing acts are usually adopted in the form of regulations other types of acts, like directives, can be found as well. See for example Commission Delegated Directive 2014/1/EU amending, for the purposes of adapting to technical progress, Annex IV to Directive 2011/65/EU of the European Parliament and of the Council as regards an exemption for lead as an alloying element for bearings and wear surfaces in medical equipment exposed to ionising radiation [2014] OJ L4/45.

matters reserved for statutes (for example when those Commission acts make it necessary to extend sanctions for individuals or to confer competences on ministries or other administrative offices), the Czech statute would have to be changed. That would entail a high frequency of amendments to the Czech statutes which would undermine the stability of the Czech legal order.[46]

Another problem concerns timely implementation. Delegated or implementing acts very often have short implementation (transposition) deadlines, normally up to a couple of months.[47] In several Member States, it is difficult to comply with those deadlines if it is necessary to amend a statute. For example, in the Czech Republic, it takes about a year for a statute to go through the procedures in the two chambers of the Czech Parliament and to obtain the signature of the Czech president; this is usually too long to provide timely implementation.

IV. Defects of form

Some EU rules are not in legally binding form because they are not published in the Official Journal of the EU.

In other cases the form chosen for EU acts is incorrect, such as when directives are amended by regulations; regulations are in fact concealed directives; decisions are of a hybrid nature (with some resembling regulations but others being closer to directives). They are discussed in the following subsections.

---

46 See numbers of legislation in the capital market sector – pages of the Czech Ministry of finance <https://www.mfcr.cz/cs/soukromy-sektor/kapitalovy-trh/pravni-ramce>, accessed 2.1.2019.

47 E.g. Commission Implementing Regulation (EU) 2017/2470 establishing the Union list of novel foods in accordance with Regulation (EU) 2015/2283 of the European Parliament and of the Council on novel foods [2017] OJ L351/72, Commission Implementing Regulation (EU) 2019/66 on rules on uniform practical arrangements for the performance of official controls on plants, plant products and other objects in order to verify compliance with Union rules on protective measures against pests of plants applicable to those goods [2019] OJ L15/1 or Commission Delegated Directive mentioned in footnote 45.

1. No legally binding form

Unfortunately, it is possible to find 'legal acts' of the EU which provide for important matters like the competences of certain authorities or obligations imposed on individuals but are not published in the Official Journal.

One example is Commission decision C(2008) 8657 laying down a certificate policy as required in the technical specifications on the standards for security features and biometrics in passports and travel documents. That Decision concerns, among other things, obligations of the Member States regarding the competences of Certification or Registration Authorities of the Member States. That Decision, which is referred to in Article 6 of Council Regulation (EU) No 1417/2013 of 17 December 2013 laying down the form of the laissez-passer issued by the European Union,[48] is published on the European Commission web pages[49] but not in the Official Journal of the EU. Strangely enough, that Commission Decision is accompanied on the web pages with the following title:

Brussels,
22.12.2008
C(2008) 8657 final
NOT TO BE PUBLISHED

Another example of dubious practice is the Commission Implementing Decision of 15 December 2017 on technical standards for security features applied to tobacco products (C/2017/8435 final). It contains additional definitions to the above-mentioned Tobacco Directive and provides for further obligations for Member States, manufacturers and importers. Article 3 of that Commission Implementing Decision provides as follows:

> *Security feature*
> *1.Member States shall require security features to be composed of no less than five types of authentication elements ,*[14] *of which at least:*
> *(a)one is overt;*
> *(b)one is semi-covert;*
> *(c)one is covert.*
> *2.Member States shall require at least one of the authentication elements, referred to in paragraph 1, to be provided by an independent third-party provider meeting the requirements laid down in Article 8.* [14]

48 [2013] OJ L353/26.

49 <http://ec.europa.eu/transparency/regdoc/index.cfm?fuseaction=list&coteId=3&year=2008&number=8657&language=en> accessed 2.1.2019.

> *3. Each Member State shall communicate to manufacturers and importers of tobacco products the combination or combinations of authentication elements that are to be used in security features applied to unit packets of tobacco products placed on its market. …* [14]

Surprisingly, Commission Implementing Decision, though it was published on the internet straightaway, was not published in the L Series of the Official Journal of the EU until 4 months later,[50] long after Member States could be assumed to have started the implementation process. What was the status of such an 'Implementing Decision' before its official publication?

Unfortunately, rules not published in the Official Journal of the EU are appearing more frequently than before. A new challenge is posed by non-legislative rules such as technical norms or guidelines issued by agencies or other bodies. They are not legal acts under Article 288 of the Treaty on the Functioning of the EU and they are not published in the Official Journal either. Often they do not exist in all the official languages of the EU countries. From the point of legal certainty, the binding nature of such rules is at first sight questionable.

As regards technical norms, one example is to be found in Annex II to Directive (EU) 2016/1629.[51] It provides as follows:

> *MINIMUM TECHNICAL REQUIREMENTS APPLICABLE TO CRAFT ON INLAND WATERWAYS OF ZONES 1, 2, 3 AND 4*
> *The technical requirements applicable to craft are those set out in ES-TRIN standard 2015/1.*

Similarly, technical norms are used as binding rules also in Directive (EU) 2016/2102[52] Article 6 (1) of which provides as follows:

> *Presumption of conformity with the accessibility requirements*
> *1. Content of websites and mobile applications that meets harmonised standards or parts thereof the references to which* [14] *have been published by the Commission in the Official Journal of the European Union in accordance with Regulation (EU) No 1025/2012 shall be presumed to be in con-*

50 [2018] OJ L96/57.

51 Directive (EU) 2016/1629 of the European Parliament and of the Council laying down technical requirements for inland waterway vessels [2016] OJ L252/118.

52 Directive (EU) 2016/2102 of the European Parliament and of the Council on the accessibility of the websites and mobile applications of public sector bodies [2016] OJ L327/1.

formity with the accessibility requirements set out in Article 4 that are covered by those standards or by parts thereof.

Examples of guidelines of bodies and agencies are to be found in non-legislative rules in the financial sector. Bodies like the European Banking Agency (EBA), the European Securities and Market Authority (ESMA) or the European Insurance and Occupational Pensions Authority (EIOPA) can issue guidelines and recommendations which are governed by the "comply or explain" principle.[53] Those guidelines and recommendations form part of obligations for individuals which are stated in particular directives or regulations like Directive (EU) 2015/2366.[54] Article 96 provides as follows:

Incident reporting
1. In the case of a major operational or security incident, payment service providers shall, without undue delay, notify the competent authority in the home Member State of the payment service provider.
3. By 13 January 2018, EBA shall, in close cooperation with the ECB and after consulting all relevant stakeholders, including those in the payment services market, reflecting all interests involved, issue guidelines in accordance with Article 16 of Regulation (EU) No 1093/2010 addressed to each of the following: [14]
(a) payment service providers, on the classification of major incidents referred to in paragraph 1, and on the content, the format, including standard notification templates, and the procedures for notifying such incidents;
(b) competent authorities, on the criteria on how to assess the relevance of the incident and the details of the incident reports to be shared with other domestic authorities.

---

53 For example Regulation (EU) No 1093/2010 of the European Parliament and of the Council establishing a European Supervisory Authority (European Banking Authority) [2010] OJ L331/12:
Article 16
Guidelines and recommendations
1. The Authority shall, with a view to establishing consistent, efficient and effective supervisory practices within the ESFS, and to ensuring the common, uniform and consistent application of Union law, issue guidelines and recommendations addressed to competent authorities or financial institutions.
3. The competent authorities and financial institutions shall make every effort to comply with those guidelines and recommendations.

54 Directive (EU) 2015/2366 of the European Parliament and of the Council on payment services in the internal market [2015] OJ L337/35.

The above-mentioned examples show that according to certain EU acts individuals are to be bound by 'rules' which are of a non-legislative nature. However, the binding nature of such rules is problematic in the light of the case law of the Court of Justice. According to its judgment in the *Skoma-Lux* case,[55] the following principles should apply:

> *48 However, although Community legislation is indeed available on the internet and individuals are using this means more and more frequently to acquaint themselves with it, making the legislation available by such means does not equate to a valid publication in the Official Journal of the European Union [14] in the absence of any rules in that regard in Community law.*
> *49 Moreover, it must be emphasised that although various Member States have adopted electronic publication as a valid form, it is the subject of legislation or regulations which organise it in detail and set out exactly when that publication is valid. Accordingly, as Community law now stands, the Court cannot consider that form of making Community legislation available to be sufficient for it to be enforceable. [14]*
> *50 The only version of a Community regulation which is authentic, as Community law now stands, is that which is published in the Official Journal of the European Union , such that an electronic version predating that publication, even if it is subsequently seen to be consistent with the published version, cannot be enforced against individuals . [14]*

It follows that an EU 'legal' act regulating obligations of individuals cannot be legally binding if it is not published in the Official Journal of the EU since only the text published in the Official Journal is authentic. Moreover, such an act has to be published in the official languages of the Member States concerned. Therefore, non-legislative rules of the kind described above represent a dangerous threat to legal certainty.

2. Incorrect choice of form

2.1. Regulations as concealed directives

Though a regulation might appear to present fewer problems for implementation at national level, that is not always the case. In practice it happens quite often that regulations are formulated in the same way as directives. It should not be overlooked that expressions specific to directives

55 Case C-161/06, [2007] ECR I-10841, paras 48–50.

which serve to impose general obligations on the Member States (such as "*The Member States shall ensure/designate/establish*") often cannot be directly applicable on their own despite being set out in a regulation. Such provisions have to be duly implemented into national legal orders to become effective. They have to be supplemented with provisions clearly stating who must fulfil them, in what manner, in what timeframe, according to what criteria, and so forth. Such provisions have to be laid down by national laws and that causes many problems regarding the timely implementation of the regulation concerned.

Though the EU legislative drafting rules address those problems,[56] many EU acts do not comply with those rules. One example is Article 5 of Regulation (EU) No 598/2014 which reads as follows:[57]

> *(2) Member States shall ensure that the Balanced Approach is adopted in respect of aircraft noise management at those airports where a noise problem has been identified. To that end, they shall ensure that:* [14]
> *(a) the noise abatement objective for that airport, taking into account, as appropriate, Article 8 of, and Annex V to, Directive 2002/49/EC, is defined;*
> *(b) measures available to reduce the noise impact are identified;*
> *(c) the likely cost-effectiveness of the noise mitigation measures is thoroughly evaluated;*
> *(d) the measures, taking into account public interest in the field of air transport as regards the development prospects of their airports, are selected without detriment to safety;...*

---

56 JPG, point 2.2:
" *2.2. The drafting style should take account of the type of act.*
2.2.1. Since Regulations have direct application and are binding in their entirety, their provisions should be drafted in such a way that the addressees have no doubts as to the rights and obligations resulting from them: references to intermediary national authorities should therefore be avoided, except where the act provides for complementary action by the Member States.
2.2.2. Directives are addressed to the Member States ... Furthermore, they are drafted in a less detailed manner in order to leave Member States sufficient discretion when transposing them. If the enacting terms are too detailed and do not leave such discretion, the appropriate instrument is a regulation, rather than a directive."

57 Regulation (EU) No 598/2014 of the European Parliament and of the Council on the establishment of rules and procedures with regard to the introduction of noise-related operating restrictions at Union airports within a Balanced Approach [2014] OJ L173/65.

Another example is in Article 60 of Regulation (EU) 2016/2031[58] which provides as follows:

> *Article 60*
> *Designation of quarantine stations and confinement facilities*
> *1. For the purposes referred to in Articles 8, 48, 49 and 58, Member States shall take one or more of the following actions,* [14] *taking into account the relevant pest risk:*
> *(a) designate in their territory quarantine stations or confinement facilities;*
> *(b) authorise the use of designated quarantine stations or confinement facilities in another Member State, provided that, where applicable, that other Member State has agreed to such authorisation;*
> *(c) designate* [14] *temporarily the premises of professional operators or other persons as confinement facilities for the pests, plants, plant products or other objects and their relevant uses as set out in Articles 8, 48 and 49.*

Regulations also contain many non-obligatory provisions (options) which are very often represented by formulations like *"Member States may"*[59]. It should be noted that a Member State which decides to avail itself of an option usually has to initiate its national legislative procedures to state clearly in the national law that an option has been used. According to the Court of Justice ruling, it would be problematic to do otherwise, even though an EU regulation is concerned, since legal certainty would be prejudiced.[60] Therefore, provisions of EU regulations which provide for certain options for Member States cannot be directly applicable and require more time for national implementation in the Member States which decide to avail themselves of such an option.

Further examples of problematic practices are to be found in cases where one field is regulated by different types of EU acts. For example in the field of copyright Regulation (EU) 2017/1563[61] provides for many legal

---

58 Regulation (EU) 2016/2031 of the European Parliament of the Council on protective measures against pests of plants [2016] OJ L317/4.

59 Ibid, Article 8(1): *"By way of derogation from Article 5(1), Member States may, on application, temporarily authorise the introduction into, the movement within, and the holding and multiplication in, their territory of Union quarantine pests or pests subject to the measures adopted pursuant to Article 30(1) for official testing, scientific or educational purposes, trials, varietal selections, or breeding."*

60 See Case C-528/15 *Policie ČR v Salah Al Chodor* (ECLI identifier: ECLI:EU:C:2017:213).

61 Regulation (EU) 2017/1563 of the European Parliament and of the Council on the cross-border exchange between the Union and third countries of accessible

institutions which are similar to those under Directive (EU) 2017/1564[62] in the same field. It was therefore illogical to choose two different types of EU legal act, especially since, for instance, the obligations of authorized entities provided for in Article 5 in both the Regulation and the Directive are almost the same.

2.2. Amendment of EU directives by EU regulations

Other legislative drafting defects affecting implementation in national legal orders (such as the Czech Republic) arise when EU law mixes different types of EU acts, especially if directives are amended by regulations and vice versa.

According to Article 288 of the TFEU, directives are binding, as to the result to be achieved, upon each Member State to which they are addressed, but are to leave to the national authorities the choice of form and methods of implementation. Regulations on the other hand are, according to the same article, of general application. They are binding in their entirety and directly applicable in all Member States.

The characteristics of directives and regulations differ. It is therefore not surprising that mixing of these two types of legal acts leads to problems and is not recommended by the EU drafting rules.[63]

format copies of certain works and other subject matter protected by copyright and related rights for the benefit of persons who are blind, visually impaired or otherwise print-disabled [2017] OJ L242/1.

62 Directive (EU) 2017/1564 of the European Parliament and of the Council on certain permitted uses of certain works and other subject matter protected by copyright and related rights for the benefit of persons who are blind, visually impaired or otherwise print-disabled [2017] OJ L242/6.

63 IA Guideline 2: "*The drafting of Union acts shall be appropriate to the type of act concerned and, in particular, to whether or not it is binding (Regulation, Directive, Decision, Recommendation or other act)*".
JPG point 18.6: "*In general, it is preferable for an amending act to be of the same type as the act to be amended. In particular, it is not recommended to amend a regulation by a directive.*".

Regrettably, the EU drafting rules are often not followed in practice. An odd situation can be shown on Commission Directive 2006/141/EC[64] Annex III which was amended both by a regulation[65] and by a directive.[66]

Another example can be presented on Directive 2009/48/EC of the European Parliament and of the Council on the safety of toys[67] which was amended in the case of limit values for barium by Commission Regulation No 681/2013.[68]

Recital 11 to the amending Regulation states:

> *In order to ensure the best possible protection of health and life of humans, in particular children, it is necessary to apply those lower migration limits for barium within the shortest possible delay. Therefore, the Directive should be amended by a Regulation which enters into force on 20 July 2013, thus avoiding a longer period of transposition of a Directive during which different migration limits would apply.* [14]

Unfortunately, no account was taken of the fact that the Member States had been under an obligation to transpose Directive 2009/48/EC and so they should have already incorporated the old limit values for barium in their legal orders. To implement the new limit values in Regulation No 681/2013 correctly, it is necessary to remove the old limit values from national legal orders first. Such a change cannot be made overnight and takes some time, definitely more than the two days allowed by Regulation No 681/2013.

This approach creates problems for the Member States concerning the temporal application of the EU rules. But there are even more serious consequences for individuals. The individuals are bound by both the old limit values for barium which form part of the national transposition provisions – until they are removed – and by the new limit values for barium laid

64 Commission Directive 2006/141/EC on infant formulae and follow-on formulae [2006] OJ L401/1.

65 Commission Regulation (EC) No 1243/2008 amending Annexes III and VI to Directive 2006/141/EC as regards compositional requirements for certain infant formulae [2008] OJ L335/25.

66 Commission Directive 2013/46/EU amending Directive 2006/141/EC with regard to protein requirements for infant formulae and follow-on formulae [2013] OJ L230/16.

67 Directive 2009/48/EC of the European Parliament and of the Council on the safety of toys [2009] OJ L170/1.

68 Commission Regulation (EU) No 681/2013 amending part III of Annex II to Directive 2009/48/EC of the European Parliament and of the Council on the safety of toys, [2013] OJ L195/16.

down by the amending EU Regulation. Since those rules are in conflict, individuals are denied legal certainty.

2.3. Hybrid nature of decisions

Many questions arise when it comes to EU decisions. Some decisions are in the form of individual acts (such as those in the field of competition) but many decisions are of general application.

EU decisions of general application play an important role as regards implementation at national level. The problem is that some of those decisions resemble regulations but others are closer to directives. The question is whether decisions can be directly applicable at national level in the same way as regulations, that is to say without being duly transposed into the national legal orders.

The problems arise in the case of a decision that is a quasi-directive, that is when the decision is addressed to Member States and at the same time it provides for rights and obligations of individuals. A classic example is Commission Decision 2007/777/EC.[69]

That Decision provides for health conditions and requirements for imports into the EU of meat products and other similar products. Although the Decision is, according to its Article 10, addressed only to the Member States, it has a major impact on individuals.

Since the Decision is addressed only to the Member States it cannot be applied directly to individuals and cannot be directly binding on them. For the individuals to be bound by the rules, the Member States must first transpose the Decision, at least as regards obligations for individuals. That takes time. It follows, therefore, that decisions which are quasi-directives need a certain time for their implementation in national legal orders, similar to the transposition period in the case of directives.

---

69 Commission Decision 2007/777/EC laying down the animal and public health conditions and model certificates for imports of certain meat products and treated stomachs, bladders and intestines for human consumption from third countries [2007] OJ L312/49.

V. Conclusion

Ambiguity or lack of clarity, incompleteness and defects of form are shortcomings of the EU legislation which pose problems in the EU Member States during their implementation process. Both the EU institutions and the Member States seem to acknowledge this but they are not always successful in approving an intelligible, unambiguous and well structured text.

To improve this situation and thus to safeguard legal certainty, which is a component of the rule of law, it is necessary for all the EU institutions to follow strictly all the EU legislative drafting rules. They should aim to achieve the highest standard of clarity in their legal acts and to avoid formal defects. Further, non-legislative rules should be reduced to a minimum since they cannot be legally binding if they are not published in the Official Journal of the EU. Last but not least, the EU institutions should ensure that provisions conferring powers on the Commission are narrowly circumscribed and that proposals for EU legislative acts are accompanied by drafts of the delegated or implementing acts that will be required.

Chapter 7: Hybrid and neutral language(s) in EU Multi-Level Legislative Drafting[1]

Agnieszka Doczekalska (Kozminski University)

I. Introduction

EU drafters and national legislators transposing EU directives face the challenge of lawmaking in multi-level settings. EU law and the national law of Member States independent from each other are drawn up in the same languages, since the official languages of Member States usually become the official languages of the institutions of the European Union. It is necessary to draft legal acts in official language(s) at a national and supranational level. As EU and national legislation is applied within the same territory and legal system of a Member State, the question arises whether languages applied at different legislative levels are actually the same and how they influence each other. This chapter focuses on terminological and conceptual choices made by EU and national legislators when drafting and transposing EU law (Part IV and V). Prior to presenting an analysis, an overview is given of the legal languages of the EU and national legal systems (Part II) and of various levels and stages of EU legislative drafting and transposition (Part III).

To better illustrate legislative decisions and demonstrate how drafting languages interact with each other at the EU and national level, the focus of the analysis will be on EU directives which must be transposed into the legal systems of Member States. However, very similar finding apply to the drafting of EU regulations. The differences in language use that can appear in the two types of legal instruments result from the nature of directives and regulations. Regulations are directly binding in Member States and are drafted in more precise language than directives, which as a rule must provide national legislators with the requisite leeway in the transposition process.[2]

---

1 The work of the author has been supported by the Polish National Science Centre funds allocated on the basis of decision no. DEC-2013/11/D/HS5/01822.

2 A translator at the Commission during the interview (January 2016) admitted that although the same effort is made generally to correctly translate directives and reg-

II. Languages of the Member States' national law as compared to language(s) of EU law

Domestic law of the EU Member States is drawn up in highly culturally-embedded national languages which reflect national legal cultures and traditions. It is important to note that the language of national legislation develops its own system of legal concepts whose meanings have been shaped by tradition over time. This makes legal translation and comparative legal research very challenging.[3] Due to conceptual incongruence between legal systems, even those systems whose legal traditions are closely related, certain terms – especially ones designating legal concepts specific to a particular legal culture and system – are untranslatable.[4] These terms are referred to as system-bound or culture-bound terms, sometimes also as culture-specific terms.[5] Such terms usually have no counterparts in other legal systems.[6] Even if the same general language, e.g., English, is applied to draft law in different legal systems (e.g., in the United Kingdom and in the United States), each of the systems still develops its own legal language (e.g., British legal English and American legal English). Authors of a *Study on Lawmaking in the EU Multilingual Environment* observe that a single language (e.g., English) "may represent more than one legal system".[7] It

---

ulations, in the case of doubts about what meaning should be rendered less precise language is used in directives, since it is not the directives but the national legal acts transposing them that are directly binding and the national acts may use wording different from that used in the directive, which can clarify the meaning.

3 O Brand, 'Language as a Barrier to Comparative Law' in F Olsen, A Lorz, D Stein (eds), *Translation Issues in Language and Law* (Palgrave Macmillan 2009) 18–34. Methods of comparative law are applied when legal texts are translated, see S Šarčević, 'Challenges to the Legal Translator' in P Tiersma, L Solan (eds) *The Oxford Handbook of Language and Law* (OUP 2012) 194.

4 S Šarčević, 'Challenges to the Legal Translator' in P Tiersma, L Solan (eds) *The Oxford Handbook of Language and Law* (OUP 2012) 194. On translation techniques for culture-bound terms, see M Harvey, *A beginner's course in legal translation: the case of culture-bound terms* (Bern/Genève ASTTI/ETI 2000) 357–369.

5 The terms 'culture-bound term' and 'system-bound term' have been introduced in the area of legal translation theory by S Šarčević 'Translation of Culture-Bound Terms in Laws', (1985) 4(3) *Multilingua* 127–133.

6 A Doczekalska, 'Drafting or Translation — Production of Multilingual Legal Texts' in F Olsen, A Lorz, D Stein (eds), *Translation Issues in Language and Law* (Palgrave Macmillan 2009) 121.

7 J Várnai, A Bérczi, R Somssich, *Study on lawmaking in the EU multilingual environment*, (Luxembourg: Publications Office of the European Union 2010) < http://www.termcoord.eu/wp-content/uploads/2013/08/Study_on_lawmaking_in_the_EU_multilingual_environment.pdf > accessed 10 December 2018, 2.

should be noted that the example of the English language applied to draft legal acts in the United Kingdom and in the United States does not fully illustrate the challenges that drafters of supranational law have to face. There are twenty-four languages that supranational legislators use to draft EU legal acts, and those languages represent not only the supranational legal order of the European Union, but also the national legal systems of Member States. Moreover, supranational law which should be interpreted uniformly in all Member States is applied within the same territory where national law is binding.[8] Hence, EU legislators make careful decisions on how to use a language when drafting EU law. The process of creating autonomous terminology which is neutral for legal systems of Member States requires deculturalisation of a legal language which means that terms and expressions which are culturally neutral in national legal systems and cultures of Member States are used. The task of the national drafters transposing EU directives into the legal systems of Member States is no easier. They have to find a balance between, on the one hand, the need for sufficient transposition which respects national legislative techniques, the national legal language and its terminology, and, on the other hand, meet the requirement to apply EU autonomous concepts uniformly in all Member States. Thus, national legislators need to decide how far the language of the national acts will diverge from the language of the directive.

III. Levels and stages of EU drafting and transposition

As far as EU directives are concerned, the term 'multi-level legislative drafting' used in the title of this chapter refers to law-making at a supranational level where EU law (in directives) is drafted and to a national level where EU law (in directives) is transposed into the legal systems of Member States. However, while discussing language use and terminological challenges in two-level legislative drafting, it should be explained that neither of the two levels is purely supranational or purely national.

EU legislation does not aim at creating a legal order disconnected from national legal systems, but rather aims at harmonizing the national laws of Member States to facilitate functioning of the internal market. EU law is not applied in a vacuum, but within Member States' legal systems. Thus,

8 J-C Piris, 'Union européenne: comment rédiger une législation de qualité dans 20 langues et pour 25 États membres' 2005 (5) *Revue du Droit Public de la Science Politique en France et à l'Étranger*, 475–491.

an EU lawmaker must take into consideration legal norms that exist at a national level. Sometimes a new norm, not based on any national solution, is introduced by EU law, but often EU legal measures are inspired by existing legislation in one or more Member States. An illustration of the former is the consumer protection introduced by the *Unfair Commercial Practices Directive*,[9] while an illustration of the latter is the function of Advocate General at the Court of Justice of the EU, which is based on the French model. Thus, a legal measure might have a hybrid or mixed character, based on national experience, but then developed at a supranational-law level to facilitate harmonization of national laws or to fill a gap in an area where appropriate legislation at a national level is lacking. When decided which legal measure will be adopted, an EU legal act is drafted in the official languages of the EU. However, these languages are also official and legislative (legal) languages in Member States. At this stage, a drafter has to decide how to choose proper terms. This is a major challenge in both cases, whether a wholly new norm is adopted or one based on national solutions. In both cases, an important consideration is that EU law should be uniformly interpreted and adopted in all Member States. The challenge is great because national and supranational legislation is formulated in the same official (general) languages. Hence, when EU law is drafted, the legal traditions and legal languages of Member States are present in this process, continue to interact, and as a result create hybrid supranational legislative texts.

At a national level, when EU directives are transposed, the process is not purely national either. A national lawmaker must fulfil supranational aims indicated in a directive by enacting a national legal act. In doing so, decisions are taken on how far the wording of the national act will differ from the language of the directive. On the one hand, national drafters must follow national legislative rules and techniques. On the other hand, they must remember that the EU concepts in the directive, unless stated other-

9 Directive 2005/29/EC of the European Parliament and of the Council concerning unfair business-to-consumer commercial practices in the internal market and amending Council Directive 84/450/EEC, Directives 97/7/EC, 98/27/EC and 2002/65/EC of the European Parliament and of the Council and Regulation (EC) No 2006/2004 of the European Parliament and of the Council, [2005] OJ L 149/22–39. See G Abbamonte, 'The Unfair Commercial Practices Directive and its General Prohibition' in S Weatherill, U Bernitz (eds) *The regulation of unfair commercial practices under EC directive 2005/29: new rules and new techniques*, Studies of the Oxford Institute of European and Comparative Law, (Hart Publishing 2007) 31.

wise, are autonomous concepts of EU law and have the same meaning in all Member States. Hence, hybrid EU legislative text already imposes, while being transposed, a further hybridization of a national legislative text which applies EU terminology, expressions and some legislative techniques that are not known in national law. For instance, when directives were transposed, British legislators started to use general clauses not known previously in the English legal system.[10]

Furthermore, within supranational and national legislative drafting there are more levels and stages that can be observed. As noted by Reed Dickerson[11], and recently by Martina Bajčić[12], in a drafting process a conceptual level should be distinguished from a verbal (terminological) one. Although some legal scholars do not follow this distinction,[13] an awareness of these levels is essential in order to analyse the language applied in multi-level EU drafting. Especially in multilingual settings like the European Union, it is not sufficient to just create a new concept or introduce a borrowed concept, but it is also necessary to find an appropriate term that denotes this concept. The following sections of this chapter explain terminological choices made by legislators drafting directives (Part IV) and transposing them (Part V).

In this chapter, although the general terms "legislator" or "drafter" are used, usually more than one institution is involved in the process of legislative drafting. Moreover, within each institution, the drafting task is conducted by various experts. Examination of supranational drafting[14] reveals three institutional levels of legislative drafting. EU legislative acts (regulations, directives and decisions) are generally adopted under an ordinary legislative procedure, in which the European Parliament and the Council jointly adopt the act on a proposal from the Commission.[15] Since only in

10 S Whittaker, 'Theory and Practice of the "General Clause" in English Law: General Norms and the Structuring of Judicial Discretion' in S Grundman, D Mazeaud (eds) *General Clauses and Standards in European Contract Law* (Kluwer Law International 2006) 58–59.

11 R Dickerson, *The Fundamentals of Legal Drafting*, 2nd edition (Boston, Toronto: Little, Brown and Company 1986) 5.

12 M Bajčić, *New Insights into the Semantics of Legal Concepts and the Legal Dictionary* (John Benjamins Publishing Company 2017).

13 JKoronkiewicz, *Terminologia podatkowa a prawidłowość implementacji dyrektyw unijnych w Polsce* (Wolters Kluwer 2015).

14 Analyzing national drafting would demand an investigation of legislative procedures in 28 Member States which is beyond the scope of this paper.

15 Consolidated Version of the Treaty on the Functioning of the European Union (TFEU), Art. 289(1).

specific cases provided by the Treaties can a regulation, directive or decision be adopted under a special legislative procedure,[16] the ordinary procedure is the one most often applied.[17] Taking account of the actors taking part in the legislative procedure, there are three institutional levels of EU drafting: (1) drafting of the proposal in the Commission; (2) amendments and adoption of a legal act by the Parliament; and (3) amendments and adoption of a legal act by the Council. Moreover, legislative drafting in each institution also includes the following stages: (1) drafting in one language; (2) translating into all official languages; and (3) revision of language versions. Each of the institutions taking part in the ordinary legislative procedure has its own translation and legal-linguistic revision services.

The distinction between drafting and translation stage facilitates the explanation of terminological choices and the development of EU legal language(s). Although from a legal perspective, due to the principle of equal authenticity,[18] no official language version of an EU legal act can be considered a translation, however, a translation process is *de facto* inevitable for drafting law in twenty-four languages and in fact it is constantly present during EU legislative procedures.[19] For practical reasons, a proposal in the Commission, amendments in the European Parliament, common

---

16 TFEU, Art. 289(2).

17 According to the *Handbook on the Ordinary Legislative Procedure* (2017), PE 608.827 <http://www.epgenpro.europarl.europa.eu/static/ordinary-legislative-procedure/en/ordinary-legislative-procedure/handbook-on-the-ordinary-legislative-procedure.html> accessed 27 December 2018, during the 7th legislative term of the European Parliament and in the first half of the 8th term almost 90% of legislative proposals adopted by the Commission were subject to the ordinary legislative procedure. According to statistics on legislative procedures voted in plenary during the 8th parliamentary term 2014–2019, issued on 8.8.2018, by the European Parliament – Directorate For Plenary Sessions, <http://www.europarl.europa.eu/plenary/en/bilan-statistic.html> accessed 27 December 2018, the Parliament voted the procedures 971 times including ordinary legislative procedure voted 259 in first reading and 45 in second reading; budget voted 304 times and other procedures voted 363 times (including consent – 7, consultation – 58, non-legislative procedure – 227, others – 71).

18 This principle was developed in EU case law. See Case 283/81 *Cilfit* [1982] ECR 3415, para 18, where the ECJ stated "it must be borne in mind that Community legislation is drafted in various languages and that the different language versions are all equally authentic".

19 R Correia, 'Translation of EU Legal Texts' in Antonio Tosi (ed.) *Crossing Barriers and Bridging Cultures. The Challenges of Multilingual Translation for the European Union* (Multilingual Matters Ltd. 2003) 41.

positions of the Parliament and the Council, opinions over legislative proposals, and other legislative documents are drafted in one language and then translated into others. Although the equality of language versions is granted to all official languages and they are all given a status of working languages,[20] there is no variety in language choice when the documents are drafted. From the beginning, the French language was *de facto* the main drafting language. Nowadays, its role has been taken over by English. English became an official language and a working language in 1973 when the United Kingdom and Ireland joined the European Community. Before their accession, the UK and Ireland had to translate existing *acquis communautaire* into English.[21] At this time, EC terminology was already established mainly on the basis of French texts.[22] For a long period, French remained the main working as well as drafting language in the EU institutions. The change in this situation was introduced by the accession of new Member States in 1995 and then in 2004.[23] Nowadays, the majority of EU texts (including legislative drafts, like proposals) are drafted in English.[24]

---

20 Council Regulation No 1 determining the languages to be used by the European Economic Community, [1958] OJ 17/385, art 1.

21 EEC's *acquis communautaire* consisted at that time of around 2,500 pages, see V Miller *How much legislation comes from Europe?* RESEARCH PAPER (2010) 10(62), 8 <https://researchbriefings.parliament.uk/ResearchBriefing/Summary/RP10-62#fullreport> accessed 14 December 2018.

22 J Várnai, A Bérczi, R Somssich, *Study on lawmaking in the EU multilingual environment*, (Luxembourg: Publications Office of the European Union 2010) < http://www.termcoord.eu/wp-content/uploads/2013/08/Study_on_lawmaking_in_the_EU_multilingual_environment.pdf > accessed 10 December 2018 (98).

23 The change is reflected in the statistics: in 1986, 58% of documents (including legislative ones) were drafted in French and 26% were drafted in English; see R Phillipson, *English-Only Europe? Challenging Language Policy* (London and New York: Routledge 2003) 130. The increase of drafts in English can be observed in the following years: in 1997–45.4%, 2004–62%, 2006–72%; and decrease of drafts in French: 1997–40.4%, 2004–26%, 2006–14%; see Directorate-General for Translation, *Translating for a Multilingual Community*, 2007 <https://www.lu.lv/materiali/biblioteka/es/pilnieteksti/dazada/Translating%20for%20a%20Multilingual%20Community.pdf> accessed 3 January 2019, 6.

24 In the paper published in 2012 Manuela Guggeis and William Robinson observe that more than 80% of texts are drafted in English and only 10% in French, M Guggeis, W Robinson, ' 'Co-revision': legal-linguistic revision in the European Union 'co-decision' process' in C J W Baaij (ed) *The Role of Legal Translation in Legal Harmonization Process* (Kluwer Law International 2012) 78. Now almost all texts are drafted in English, see W Robinson, 'Translating legislation: the European Union experience' (2014) 2(2), *Theory and Practice of Legislation*194; A Felici, 'Translating EU Legislation from a Lingua Franca: Advantages and Disadvan-

However, the English used is not the legal English of the UK, Ireland or Malta, where laws are drafted in English as well. Instead a new variety of English is used. On the one hand, it is a neutral legal language, not reflecting specific features of the common law, but instead denoting EU legal concepts (EU English).[25] On the other hand, it is English 'contaminated' by foreign influences coming in particular from the French language,[26] as well as from the drafters' native languages. Before a proposal is translated into all the official languages and adopted by the Commission, it is prepared and discussed by expert groups.[27] The members of those groups can come from any of the Member States and have various mother tongues other than English. Their competence in English can also vary, since they are chosen because of their technical expertise, not their language skills. A similar situation applies to members of the European Parliament, and it would be anti-democratic if they were chosen on the basis of their language knowledge. Although full multilingualism is assured for meetings of

---

tages' in S Šarčević (ed.), *Language and Culture in EU Law. Multidisciplinary Perspectives* (Ashgate: Surrey 2015) 123–124, M Bajčić, 'The Role of EU Legal English in Shaping EU Legal Culture', 2018 (7) *International Journal of Language & Law* 13.

25 See, for instance, an example of neutral English term given by M. Bajčić. She refers to the term 'account preservation order' used in EU Regulation 655/2014 of the European Parliament and of the Council of 15 May 2014 establishing a European Account Preservation Order procedure to facilitate cross-border debt recovery in civil and commercial matters, OJ L 189/59–92, instead of 'freezing injunction' (UK legal English) or 'bank account seizure warrant' (US legal English); M Bajčić, 'The Role of EU Legal English in Shaping EU Legal Culture', 2018 (7) *International Journal of Language & Law*, 17.

26 C J W Baaij, *Legal Integration and Language Diversity: Rethinking Translation in EU Lawmaking* (OUP 2018) 63 ft.37. The examples of EU English expressions and terms mis-used or over-used due to the French influence are listed, for instance on the European Commission's website including the Information Providers Guide intended for people involved in the creation of online content for EUROPA. Not all of them are used in EU legal acts. The examples include the following terms: actors (overused, often it would be better to apply the term "stakeholders"), social dialogue (literal borrowing from French), rapporteur (used instead of 'monitor'); state aid(s) (from French *aide d'état*); cohesion; enlargement (from French *élargissement*); see EU jargon in English and some possible alternatives, <http://ec.europa.eu/ipg/content/tips/words-style/jargon-alternatives_en.htm> accessed 5 January 2019.

27 Expert groups can include national governments or private-sector experts, lobbyists, representatives of companies, trade unions, consumer groups or universities, C J W Baaij, *Legal Integration and Language Diversity: Rethinking Translation in EU Lawmaking* (OUP 2018) 63.

parliamentary bodies, especially for plenary sittings and priority political meetings,[28] amendments are usually drafted in English[29] and then translated into other official languages. In the Council, interpretation into all languages is available during debates and documents are translated into all official languages.[30] In actual practice, however, discussions are usually held in English on English versions of a document.[31]

English – the predominant language in the EU drafting process – has experienced the most influence from other languages (due to French influence, use by non-native speakers, and need to adjust an English version to make it translatable into other languages). Moreover, it is in this *de facto* drafting language that terms are shaped and thereby English also influences other official languages of the European Union. This is especially visible at the terminological level. For example, the English language allows one to create short and elegant terms that are sometimes not easy translatable into other languages. For instance, EU concepts – such as 'gender mainstreaming', 'timeshare' or 'flexicurity' – have been formulated in English. In the translation process, two strategies are used to translate these kinds of terms. One approach is to give a descriptive, sometimes wordy, equivalent. Sometimes it is complemented with an English equivalent in brackets. For example, in the Polish version of the *Regulation on establishing a European Institute for Gender Equality*, the term 'gender mainstreaming' is rendered as '*włączanie problematyki płci do głównego nurtu polityki* (gender mainstreaming)'.[32] The English equivalent in brackets is used only once, when the term 'gender mainstreaming' appears for the first time in the text of the Regulation.

---

28 Article 2 of the *Code of Conduct on Multilingualism*, Bureau Decision of 16 June 2014, <www.europarl.europa.eu/pdf/multilinguisme/coc2014_en.pdf> accessed 14 December 2018.

29 C J W Baaij, *Legal Integration and Language Diversity: Rethinking Translation in EU Lawmaking* (OUP 2018) 64.

30 Language use during meetings in the Council depends on the level of the meeting. For instance, interpretation for the Council working groups and preparatory bodies is based on the request-and-pay system. According to this system, Member States, which partially pay for interpretation, decide whether they need interpretation and for which languages; see A Doczekalska 'Legal Languages in Contact: EU Legislative Drafting and Its Consequences for Judicial Interpretation' in S Marino, Ł Biel, Ma Bajčić, V Sosoni (eds) *Language and Law. The role of language and translation in EU Competition Law* (Springer 2018), 170.

31 C J W Baaij, *Legal Integration and Language Diversity: Rethinking Translation in EU Lawmaking* (OUP 2018), 65.

32 Regulation (EC) No 1922/2006 of the European Parliament and of the Council on establishing a European Institute for Gender Equality, [2006] OJ L 403/9–17.

The other approach is to use an English calque. For instance, in the Dutch version of the *Regulation on establishing a European Institute for Gender Equality*, the term 'gendermainstreaming' is used. Sometimes, that term enters into the national legal system through the transposition process. For instance, the term 'timeshare' is applied in the Polish version of the *Directive on the protection of consumers in respect of certain aspects of timeshare, long-term holiday product, resale and exchange contracts*,[33] as well as in the Polish statute transposing this Directive.[34]

The use of calque in other language versions reveals the language in which the term was coined. The following section explains the terminological challenges that EU drafters must face.

IV. Linguistic and terminological choices at EU level – drafting of EU law

As explained, the development of EU autonomous terminology in languages which are also natural languages applied to draft national legislation of Member States requires 'deculturalisation' of these languages. Due to the reduction of cultural embedding of Member States' legal languages, it is possible to develop terminology which is neutral towards the national legal systems of Member States.

However, the legislative languages used to draft EU law are not purely neutral, but rather hybrid. There are two reasons for linguistic hybridity. Firstly, as explained, it is possible that a term used in an EU legal act purposively and expressly refers to national concepts of Member States. For instance, *Regulation 2016/1103* clearly states that "this Regulation does not define 'marriage', which is defined by the national laws of the Member States".[35] Hence, the term 'marriage' is not an autonomous concept of EU law and its meaning can differ depending on the national law of a Member State that is concerned.

Secondly, EU legal concepts, although autonomous, might be borrowed from the national legal systems of Member States. Hence, to choose a cor-

33 Directive 2008/122/EC of the European Parliament and of the Council on the protection of consumers in respect of certain aspects of timeshare, long-term holiday product, resale and exchange contracts, [2009] OJ L 33/10–30.

34 *Ustawa z dnia 16 września 2011 r. o timeshare* (Statute of 16 of September 2011 on timeshare), Dz.U. 2011.230.1370.

35 Regulation (EU) 2016/1103 implementing enhanced cooperation in the area of jurisdiction, applicable law and the recognition and enforcement of decisions in matters of matrimonial property regimes, [2016] OJ L 183/3, Recital 17.

rect term, a drafter (including a translator) must be aware of the character of the concept to be decoded in a legislative text. One might expect that the legislator should not have doubts about the meaning of concepts used in its legal act. However, the ordinary legislative procedure is a complex process involving three EU institutions. Participants include the Parliament whose members safeguard the interests of EU citizens and the Council where national government representatives safeguard the Member States' interests and are involved in tough debates and negotiations over the Commission's proposal. Sometimes it is not easy to achieve agreement on the wording of a legal act and its meaning. After enactment, a legal act is applied and interpreted by national courts. However, the ultimate decision on the meaning of EU legal instruments is reserved to the Court of Justice of the European Union. The rule of interpretation indicating whether a concept used in an EU act has its national meaning or is an EU autonomous concept seems easy to apply. As a rule, the terms of EU law denote autonomous concepts and it is only in exceptional cases, in which a reference is expressly or implicitly made to definitions laid down by the legal systems of the Member States, that the terms of EU law are to be interpreted by reference to national concepts.[36] However, two observations reveal that it is not always obvious that the term denotes an autonomous concept of EU law. Firstly, a EU legislator sometimes decides to clarify directly in the EU legal act which concepts are autonomous. This is a rare practice, however, it started to appear from 2007, mainly in recitals of EU regulations dealing with criminal and private law.[37]

---

36 See Case C-373/00 Adolf Truly GmbH v Bestattung Wien GmbH, [2003] ECR I-1931, para 30.

37 A search of "autonomous concept" and "autonomously interpreted" on Eur-lex < https://eur-lex.europa.eu > within treaties, legal acts and international agreements resulted in six documents in the area of criminal and private law: one directive and five regulations. See the following examples: "a criminal offence" is "an autonomous concept of Union law as interpreted by the Court of Justice of the European Union" according to Directive (EU) 2016/680 of the European Parliament and of the Council on the protection of natural persons with regard to the processing of personal data by competent authorities for the purposes of the prevention, investigation, detection or prosecution of criminal offences or the execution of criminal penalties, and on the free movement of such data, and repealing Council Framework Decision 2008/977/JHA, [2016] OJ L 119/89–131; "a non-contractual obligation" is an autonomous concept according to Regulation (EC) No 864/2007 of the European Parliament and of the Council on the law applicable to non-contractual obligations (Rome II), [2007] OJ L 199/40–49; "'proceedings in criminal matters' is an autonomous concept of Union law interpreted by the Court of Justice of the European Union, notwithstanding the case law of the

Secondly, national courts may ask the CJEU for a preliminary ruling on questions about whether the definition of the term used in a EU legal act should be derived from the national legal system of the Member State or whether the term has its own independent meaning in EU law. Sometimes, the answer to that question poses difficulties for the CJEU as well.[38] However, not only judges skilled in methods of legal interpretation, but also EU translators, who are not even required to have a legal background, must consider whether a concept is autonomous when they search for a correct terminological equivalent. They cannot ask the CJEU for the interpretation, since they do not have standing to do so, and moreover, an act which is in the course of being translated has not yet been enacted. Nevertheless, they can ask directly a drafter (author) of a legal act what is the meaning behind a term or expression in it. Interviews with translators in the Commission and the Council revealed that although translators and terminologists use such an opportunity, the outcome they receive does not always provide helpful answers. Drafters are often aware of the difficulties in rendering the meaning in a legal act and may be very reluctant to pro-

---

European Court of Human Rights" according to Regulation (EU) 2018/1805 of the European Parliament and of the Council on the mutual recognition of freezing orders and confiscation orders, PE/38/2018/REV/1, [2018] OJ L 303/1–38. Moreover, "the 'authenticity' of an authentic instrument should be an autonomous concept" according to Regulation (EU) No 650/2012 of the European Parliament and of the Council on jurisdiction, applicable law, recognition and enforcement of decisions and acceptance and enforcement of authentic instruments in matters of succession and on the creation of a European Certificate of Succession, [2012] OJ L 201/107–134, Council Regulation (EU) 2016/1104 implementing enhanced cooperation in the area of jurisdiction, applicable law and the recognition and enforcement of decisions in matters of the property consequences of registered partnerships, [2016] OJ L 183/30–56, and Council Regulation (EU) 2016/1103 implementing enhanced cooperation in the area of jurisdiction, applicable law and the recognition and enforcement of decisions in matters of matrimonial property regimes, [2016] OJ L 183/1–29. The latter states as well that "the term 'matrimonial property regime' should be interpreted autonomously".

38 For instance, the CJEU stated that the concept of 'joint and several liability for the payment of fines' was wrongly considered as an EU autonomous concept by the General Court in the Joined Cases T-122/07 to T-124/07 Siemens Österreich, para 155, see para 67 of Case C-231/11P Siemens Österreich [2014]; A Doczekalska 'Legal Languages in Contact: EU Legislative Drafting and Its Consequences for Judicial Interpretation' in S Marino, Ł Biel, M Bajčić, V Sosoni (eds) *Language and Law. The role of language and translation in EU Competition Law* (Springer 2018) 175, ft. 58.

vide any explanation.[39] It can be difficult to answer translators' questions, because, as noted by William Robinson, "there is no single author" of a legislative draft, and therefore "even the Commission expert [...] can no longer be sure of the precise meaning of all parts of the text".[40]

If there is no direct indication in a legal act that the term renders national legal meanings, translators should assume that the term denotes an autonomous concept, not a national one. Therefore, translators should avoid legal terms that are too closely linked to national legal systems in accordance with guidelines featured in the *Joint Practical Guide* (Point 5.3.2.),[41] *Commission Manual on Legislative Drafting* (rule 1.2.)[42] and in the Council's *Manual of precedents for acts established within the Council of the European Union* (rule 2).[43] This guideline is addressed not only to translators, but also to drafters. This not only respects the autonomy of EU law and the principle of uniform application of European law, but also facilitates multilingual legal drafting. The Council and Commission manuals allow for the use of a less elegant term as long as it is translatable into all official languages. Translators start their search for the equivalent by checking whether an equivalent legal term exists in national legal language. In classical legal translation, translators would probably choose a national legal term which performs the same function in both the source and target legal system.

However, EU translators try to replace the national term with another one to enable anyone interpreting the EU legal act to recognize that the term denotes the EU concept, and not the national one.[44] This is an example of the deculturalisation of a national legal language. This practice, however, is not welcomed in Member States, because a deculturalised EU legal act is not familiar to a national legal system. Therefore, national experts, if consulted by EU translators or terminologists, usually suggest or

39 Common replies include: "translate word by word", "translate what you see".

40 W Robinson, 'Translating legislation: the European Union experience' (2014) 2(2) *Theory and Practice of Legislation*, 200.

41 Joint practical guide of the European Parliament, the Council and the Commission for persons involved in the drafting of European Union legislation, available at https://publications.europa.eu/en/publication-detail/-/publication/3879747d-7a3c-411b-a3a0-55c14e2ba732, accessed 12 April 2019.

42 Available at http://ec.europa.eu/smart-regulation/better_regulation/documents/legis_draft_comm_en.pdf, accessed 12 April 2019.

43 Available at https://publications.europa.eu/en/publication-detail/-/publication/431ccffd-00c2-491a-b423-ce709af0d6c3 accessed 12 April 2019.

44 Information received during interview (December 2015) with translators at the Commission and the Council.

even impose the choice of national instead of neutral terms. One of the interviewed translators observed during consultations the tension between EU translators guarding the EU legal language and national experts who would like EU legal language to satisfy national needs and expectations.[45] The interviewed translators and terminologists in the Commission and Council admitted that despite national experts' suggestions, they will rather use neutral terms instead of national ones. This is also the rule applied by lawyer linguists, who revise translations of EU legal acts in order to remove any mistakes, especially incongruences between language versions. However, it rarely happens that lawyer-linguists change neutral terms into national ones, because the use of national terminology in a particular case does not jeopardize the principle of uniform interpretation.[46]

Both the drafters of the first version in one language and translators must make a decision in how to render the autonomous concepts in EU legal acts. The method applied might depend on the origin of the concept, which can be new, originally created within EU legal system, or can be borrowed from national legal systems. The former is rather rare.[47] New concepts might cover EU institutions or procedures, or certain legal principles specific to a supranational legal system. Much more often concepts known in one or more legal systems are applied. New terms can be introduced to denote new concepts, but also to designate borrowed concepts, especially in the language of a national legal system to which the concept is not known. However, the practice of creating neologisms (euronyms) is not common.[48]While taking into consideration the origin of concepts and terms denoting them, as well as the transfer of the meaning, or in other words, changes in the original meaning of the term, we can observe the following categories. Firstly, a new concept denoted by a new term can be

---

45 An EU translator mentioned during an interview (December 2015) the statement given by the national expert that was consulted: "apply national terminology, because we will change it into national legal language during transposition, anyway".

46 Information obtained during interview (December 2015) with lawyer linguists in the Council.

47 S Šarčević, 'Basic Principles of Term Formation in the Multilingual and Multicultural Context of EU Law' in S Šarčević (ed.) *Language and Culture in EU Law: Multidisciplinary Perspectives* (Ashgate: Surrey 2015) 186.

48 Jean-Claude Piris, 'Union européenne: comment rédiger une législation de qualité dans 20 langues et pour 25 États membres' (2005) 5 *Revue du Droit Public de la Science Politique en France et à l'Étranger*, , 475–491.

mentioned; for example, 'planification' and 'internal market'[49]. Secondly, a new concept denoted by a term borrowed from a national legal system(s) can appear. In this situation resemantisation of the term is required, i.e., a new meaning is given to the term borrowed from the national system. Martina Bajčić gives an example of the term 'proportionality' (in the EU the principle of proportionality) used with different meanings at national and EU levels.[50] Thirdly, both a concept and a term are borrowed from one or more national legal systems. Within this category the following subcategories can be observed depending on whether and how the meaning of a borrowed term has been changed. First, one can observe resemantisation of a term which means that a new EU meaning – sometimes considerably different from the national meaning – is given to the borrowed term. For instance, in the case of Advocate-General (French term "*avocat général*") – both the concept and the term are borrowed from the French legal system.[51] According to Article 252 TFEU, the Advocate-General should make in open court, acting with complete impartiality and independence, reasoned submissions on cases which, in accordance with the Statute of the Court of Justice of the European Union, require the involvement of the Advocate-General. The function of Advocate-General was modelled on the basis of similar tasks performed by the *Commissaire du Gouvernement* at the French *Conseil d'État*.[52] Meanwhile, the French *avocat général*, plays the role of prosecuting counsel in a French criminal procedure, especially in the court of appeal and the *Cour de cassation*.[53] Hence, the French meaning of the term *avocat général* has been changed into a EU meaning (resemantisation).

Second, a new layer of meaning can be added to borrowed terms. For instance, 'worker', 'employee', or 'consumer', became autonomous concepts of EU law and often are defined in EU legal acts, but are also known and sometimes defined in national legal systems. The example of

---

49 Examples given by Annarita Felici, 'Translating EU Legislation from a Lingua Franca: Advantages and Disadvantages' in Susan Šarčević (ed.), *Language and Culture in EU Law. Multidisciplinary Perspectives* (Ashgate: Surrey 2015) 127.

50 M Bajčić, 'Conceptualization of Legal Terms in Different Fields of Law: The Need for a Transparent Terminological Approach' *Research in Language*, 2011, 9.

51 For more information see K Borgsmidt, 'The Advocate General at the European Court: A Comparative Study' ELR (1988) 13 (2) 106–119 and Gerhard Bebr *Development of Judicial Control of the European Communities.* (BRILL 1981).

52 K Borgsmidt 'The Advocate General at the European Court: A Comparative Study' (1988) 13 (2) ELR 106–119.

53 See C Elliott, C Vernon, E Jeanpierre, *French Legal System* (Pearson Education 2006) 242.

'worker' or 'employee'[54] is an interesting one, since in some EU legal acts it is used in a national meaning,[55] and in others it is defined as autonomous concept of EU law,[56] while in others it is questionable whether the concept is autonomous.[57]

Finally, common-core concepts are considered "sufficiently common to various legal systems of Member States".[58] Hence, there is no need to introduce a new term or to add an extra meaning layer. Šarčević indicates "consumer", "contract", "damage" or "good faith" as examples of common-core concepts. Indeed, national terms referring to the above-mentioned concepts have a common point of reference. However, at the same time, there are also differences between these concepts in various Member States. Therefore, sometimes to better serve the objectives of a EU legal act or to ensure uniform application of the act, their meaning must be clarified and a new meaning layer is added. For instance, the term 'consumer' has been defined in various EU directives.[59] It should be taken into consid-

54 In English versions of various EU legal acts two terms are used, 'worker' and 'employee', whereas in other language versions such a differentiation does not always take place. On the meaning of these terms see E Verhulp, *The Notion of 'Employee' in EU-Law and National Laws*, The European Centre of Expertise (ECE) in the field of labour law, employment and labour market policies, 2017, M Risak and T Dullinger, *The concept of 'worker' in EU law. Status quo and potential for change* (ETUI 2018).

55 See Council Directive 2001/23/EC on the approximation of the laws of the Member States relating to the safeguarding of employees' rights in the event of transfers of undertakings, businesses or parts of undertakings or businesses, [2001] OJ L 82/17, art 2(1)(d) which defines 'employee' as "any person who, in the Member State concerned, is protected as an employee under national employment law".

56 See the definition of worker provided in Council Directive 89/391/EEC on the introduction of measures to encourage improvements in the safety and health of workers at work, [1989] OJ L 183/3, art 3(a).

57 In the case of the term 'worker' used in the Council Directive 98/59/EC on the approximation of the laws of the Member States relating to collective redundancies [1998] OJ L 225/16–21, the ECJ had to answer whether this term refers to an autonomous concept. The ECJ decided that that this concept is autonomous C-229/14 Ender Balkaya v Kiesel Abbruch- und Recycling Technik GmbH, para 33.

58 Susan Šarčević 'Coping with the Challenges of Legal Translation in Harmonization' in C. J. W. Baaij (ed) *The Role of Legal Translation in Legal Harmonization Process* (Kluwer Law International 2012) 98.

59 See the table of definitions of consumer in EU directives in J Várnai, A Bérczi, RSomssich, *Study on lawmaking in the EU multilingual environment*, (Luxembourg: Publications Office of the European Union 2010) <http://www.termcoord.eu/wp-content/uploads/2013/08/Study_on_lawmaking_in_the_EU_multilingual_environment.pdf> accessed 10 December 2018, 98.

eration that sometimes different terminological choices will be made when a search of the term is done in various languages. For instance, the term 'timeshare contract' was used in the English version of Directive 2008/122/EC to denote the concept of a contract of a duration of more than one year under which a consumer, for consideration, acquires the right to use one or more overnight accommodation for more than one period of occupation.[60] The term 'timeshare' was previously used in Directive 94/47/EC[61] which was the first step in harmonizing a trans-frontier timesharing market. The concept of timeshare or vacation ownership was not new in Member States. However, only four Member States – France, Greece, Portugal and the UK – regulated the timesharing sector at that time and two – Italy and Spain – were working on legislation for timesharing.[62] Timesharing, nevertheless, was a different legal concept in each Member State having laws in this area.[63] In French law it was considered as a personal right, in Greek law as a right of tenancy, in Portuguese law as a real property right, and in the UK it was based on the regulations for a club trustee system. When Directive 2008/122/EC entered into force and replaced Directive 94/47/EC, the concept of timesharing was known to all Member States including those which joined the European Union after 1994 and introduced this institution into their legal systems to harmonize their national law with Community law before their accession. Different States chose different ways to render the concept of a timeshare contract. In the Polish version a calque was used: *umowa* timeshare. In the Czech version, a descriptive equivalent is followed with the term "timeshare" in brackets which clearly indicates which language served as a terminological source.[64] In the German version, although the term 'Timesharing-*Vertrag*'

60 Directive 2008/122/EC of the European Parliament and of the Council on the protection of consumers in respect of certain aspects of timeshare, long-term holiday product, resale and exchange contracts, [2009] OJ L 33/13, art. 2.1(a).

61 Directive 94/47/EC of the European Parliament and of the Council on the protection of purchasers in respect of certain aspects of contracts relating to the purchase of the right to use immovable properties on a timeshare basis [1994] OJ L 280/83–87.

62 Opinion of the Economic and Social Committee on the proposal for a Council Directive concerning the protection of purchasers in contracts relating to the utilization of immovable property on a timeshare basis, [1993] OJ C 108, paras 1.2 and 1.4.

63 Proposal for a Council Directive concerning the protection of purchasers in contracts relating to the utilisation of immovable property on a *timeshare* basis, COM/92/220FINAL – SYN 419, [1992] OJ C 222, Recital 7.

64 *smlouva o dočasném užívání ubytovacího zařízení* (timeshare).

does exist in the German language, the term '*Teilzeitnutzungsverträgen*' was chosen. In the Spanish version the extra information is added in a descriptive term which clarifies that properties are to be used for touristic reasons.[65] In the UK, the term 'timeshare agreement' was used in both the *Timeshare Act 1992* and in the *Timeshare Regulations 1997 No. 1081*. However, in the *Timeshare, Holiday Products, Resale and Exchange Contracts Regulations 2010 No. 2960* which transposed Directive 2008/122/EC, the term 'timeshare contract' (as used in the Directive) is used instead.

The above examples demonstrate that EU legal language is not only neutral, but also hybrid. The transposition of an EU directive can remove a supranational layer from the language used or cause further hybridization of national legal language. The following section addresses these issues.

V. *Linguistic and terminological choices at a national level – transposing EU law*

As mentioned, EU directives are binding only "as to the results to be achieved". In other words, directives describe the aim that is to be accomplished and leave the choice of the most appropriate forms and methods to the Member States.[66] In order to achieve the prescribed results, national legislation transposing a directive does not necessarily have to use the same concepts that are used in the directive.[67]

Accordingly, two stages of a search for equivalents can be distinguished. Firstly, when a directive is drafted, equivalents are sought at the EU level in the twenty-four languages of the European Union. Secondly, when a directive is transposed, equivalents are chosen, at the national level, in a Member State's legal language (or languages in the case of a bilingual or multilingual country).[68] Generally, in order to transpose a directive, the existing legislation is changed or a new legal act is adopted. At the terminological and conceptual level, three different solutions can be applied in

---

65 *contrato de aprovechamiento por turno de bienes de uso turístico*.

66 Case 48/75 Jean Noël Royer [1976] ECR 00497, paras 73 and 75.

67 Case C-300/95 Commission v United Kingdom of Great Britain and Northern Ireland, ECR 1997 I-02649, para 12 in which it was noted that the Commission "accepted the right of a Member State to choose its own wording to implement a directive, provided that the national rules achieved the intended result".

68 A. Doczekalska, *All Originals: Fiction and Reality of Multilingual Legal Drafting in the European Union and Canada*, doctoral thesis (European University Institute 2009) 242–3.

the transposition process, along with three different transposition techniques.

Firstly, we can observe the transfer of an EU concept and the term. This is usually based on a copy-out technique or literal transposition which means that exactly the same or slightly changed wording of a directive appears in a national act transposing the directive. In order to precisely transpose EU law that is expressed in directives and to avoid interpretative uncertainty, a national legislator uses the same definition as the EU directives do, especially in the case of definitions of concepts that are new or have never been defined before in national law. Transfer of the concept and the term by copying out the definition from the directive can be illustrated with the definition of 'timeshare contract' copied in the Polish *Statute of 16 of September 2011 on timeshare*.[69]

Secondly, the concept is transferred, but it is denoted with a national term. Usually, a mixed technique of transposition is used here. For instance, the Polish *Act of 23 August 2007 law on prevention of unfair market practices*[70] which transposes the *Unfair Commercial Practices Directive*[71] into Polish law, repeats the definition of 'transactional decision' in terms almost identical to those used in the Directive, with just slight stylistic changes. However, the Polish legislator did not follow the Polish equivalent of 'transactional decision' used in the Directive, i.e., '*decyzja dotycząca* ***transakcji***', but used the term '*decyzja dotycząca* ***umowy***', since it is the word *umowa* ('contract') that is a legal term applied in the Polish *Civil Code* whereas the term *transakcja* ('transaction') belongs instead to economic terminology.[72]

Thirdly, to fulfil the objectives of the directive, a national legislator can apply national concepts and relevant terms. Then a transformation technique is used which means that the wording of a directive is aligned to national legal terms. For instance, while transposing the *Directive on the protection of consumers in respect to certain aspects of timeshare, long-term holiday*

---

69 *Ustawa z dnia 16 września 2011 r. o timeshare*, Dz.U. 2011.230.1370, art 2(1).

70 *Ustawa z dnia 23 sierpnia 2007 o przeciwdziałaniu nieuczciwym praktykom rynkowym*, Dz.U.2007.171.1206.

71 Directive 2005/29/EC of the European Parliament and of the Council concerning unfair business-to-consumer commercial practices in the internal market and amending Council Directive 84/450/EEC, Directives 97/7/EC, 98/27/EC and 2002/65/EC of the European Parliament and of the Council and Regulation (EC) No 2006/2004 of the European Parliament and of the Council [2005] OJ L 149/22.

72 A Doczekalska, 'Wielojęzyczność prawa a konwergencja kultur prawnych w Europie i Kanadzie' in O Nawrot, S Sykuna, J Zajadło (eds), *Konwergencja czy dywergencja kultur i systemów prawnych?* (C.H. BECK 2012) 176–181.

product, resale and exchange contracts, the Polish legislator did not transfer from the Directive the legal definition of trader and consumer, but instead referred to the definitions of these concepts in the Polish Civil Code.[73]

There are various reasons behind the changes made in EU legal language when directives are transposed. Three such reasons are illustrated below with examples from Polish legislative practice.

The first example is when a concept embodied in the EU directive exists in Polish law and the term denoting this concept in Polish law differs from the Polish equivalent used in the EU directive. Then the term from Polish law is used instead of the Polish equivalent in the directive. For instance, instead of *staranność zawodowa* – which is the literal equivalent of 'professional diligence' – applied in the *Unfair Commercial Practices Directive*, the term *dobre obyczaje* ('good manners' or 'good practices'), which is known in Polish law, is used in the Polish *Act of 23 August 2007 law on prevention of unfair market practices*[74] transposing the Directive into the national legal system.[75]

A second example is when a Polish term used in the directive already exists in Polish law, but conveys a different meaning from that given to this term in the directive. The Polish equivalents of 'legal aid' used in the Polish version of the *Unfair Commercial Practices Directive* and in the Polish Act[76] transposing this Directive into the national system are a good example illustrating this situation. According to Article 2 of the *Unfair Commercial Practices Directive*, legal aid consists of pre-litigation advice, legal assistance and representation in court and exemption from, or assistance with, the cost of proceedings. The Polish term *pomoc prawna* – used in the *Directive* – is the literal equivalent of the English term 'legal aid'. The term *pomoc prawna* is known in the Polish legal system. However, the literal equivalent *pomoc prawna* does not reflect the meaning of the term 'legal aid' in the *Directive*. Moreover, the meaning of the term *pomoc prawna* in Polish law is ambiguous. On the one hand, the term means legal assistance ren-

---

73 Ustawa z dnia 16 września 2011 r. o timeshare (Statute of 16 of September 2011 on timeshare), Dz.U. 2011.230.1370, art 6.2 and 6.4.

74 *Ustawa z dnia 23 sierpnia 2007 o przeciwdziałaniu nieuczciwym praktykom rynkowym*, Dz.U.2007.171.1206.

75 A Doczekalska, *All Originals: Fiction and Reality of Multilingual Legal Drafting in the European Union and Canada*, doctoral thesis (European University Institute 2009) 247.

76 *Ustawa z dnia 23 sierpnia 2007 o przeciwdziałaniu nieuczciwym praktykom rynkowym* (Act of 23 August 2007 law on prevention of unfair market practices), Dz.U.2007.171.1206.

dered by a professional representative[77], but not exemption from the cost of proceedings. Hence, it does not convey the entire meaning that the Directive gives to 'legal aid'.[78] On the other hand, the term *pomoc prawna* is used in the sense of judicial assistance for Polish courts from foreign courts (Article 1130 of the *Code of Civil Proceedings*)[79]. Thus, it conveys a completely different meaning to the 'legal aid' in the EU Directive. Therefore, the Polish legislator decided to use a different term from the Polish equivalent of 'legal aid' used in the *Unfair Commercial Practices Directive*. The term that has been applied in the Polish Act transposing the Directive – *prawo pomocy* ('right to assistance') – had been already used in another Polish act, i.e., in *Act of 30 August 2002 on procedure before administrative courts* (Article 2441 § 1)[80] where the assistance includes legal assistance and the exemption from costs of proceedings. Hence, the meaning is very close to the meaning of 'legal aid' in the *Unfair Commercial Practices Directive*.[81]

A third example is where a Polish term used in the EU directive is not known in Polish law, but has some connotations with a Polish legal concept, which, however, differs from the concept used in the directive. An example illustrating this situation is the term 'undue influence' used in the *Unfair Commercial Practices Directive*. The Polish equivalent for 'undue influence' applied in the Directive is the term *bezprawny nacisk* (that can be back-translated into English as 'illegal influence'). In the draft of the Polish *Act of 23 August 2007 law on prevention of unfair market practices*, which transposed the *Unfair Commercial Practices Directive*, the term *bezprawny nacisk* was used. This term – unknown in Polish law – can, however, be associated with the concept of unlawful threat that is a crime under the Polish Penal Code.[82] The *Law on prevention of unfair market practices* provides for a fine in the case of undue influence, which is a less strict penalty than that provided in the Polish Penal Code (see Article 190 of the Penal Code). Consequently, according to the rule that the law that is more lenient on the perpetrator should be used, if the illegal threat was used towards a con-

---

77 See, for example, *Ustawa z dnia 26 maja 1982 r. – Prawo o adwokaturze* (Act of 26 May 1982 – Law on the Bar), consolidated version Dz.U. 2002.123.1058.

78 Compare especially with *Prozesskostenhilfe* – the German equivalent of 'legal aid' used in the *Unfair Commercial Practices Directive*.

79 *Kodeks postępowania cywilnego* Dz.U.64.43.296.

80 *Ustawa z dnia 30 sierpnia 2002 Prawo o postępowaniu przed sądami administracyjnymi*; Dz.U.2002.153.1270.

81 A Doczekalska, *All Originals: Fiction and Reality of Multilingual Legal Drafting in the European Union and Canada*, doctoral thesis (European University Institute 2009) 248–9.

82 Act of 6 June 1997 the Penal Code (*Kodeks karny*), Dz.U.97.88.55.

sumer, the less strict provisions of the *Law on prevention of unfair market practices* would be applied. Therefore, the legislator eventually decided to use the term *niedopuszczalny nacisk* ('inadmissible influence'). Hence, there is no doubt that in the case of unlawful threat, which is conducted towards a consumer, the Penal Code should be applied.[83]

VI. Conclusions

Multilingual law of the EU is drafted in twenty-four languages which are also official languages of Member States. However, EU autonomous legal system needs its own language and terminology. One way to achieve this is to add an extra layer of meaning to national terms in order to give them uniform denotation in all Member States. The layer can be recognized at the drafting process when a term is defined or at the interpretation process when a term is recognized as an autonomous concept of EU law. The use of neutral terms which are not specific to any national legal system (deculturalisation) is another way to develop EU legal terminology. Neutral language helps not only to ensure uniform meaning but also to render this meaning in twenty-four languages.

EU legal language, although very much influenced by national legal languages, is neutral, not specific to any legal system of Member States. However, EU language is also hybrid, since it is built over national legal languages and sometimes intentionally uses national legal concepts. When EU directives are transposed into national legal systems, this hybrid or deculturalised language can be changed according to national legislative techniques or cause further hybridization, not only because new concepts are introduced into national systems but also because the exact wording of a directive is used in a national legal act.

---

83 A Doczekalska, *All Originals: Fiction and Reality of Multilingual Legal Drafting in the European Union and Canada*, doctoral thesis (European University Institute 2009) 249.

Chapter 8: European Commission's Soft Law Instruments: In-between Legally Binding and Non-binding Norms

Florin Coman-Kund (Erasmus School of Law, Rotterdam) and Corina Andone (Amsterdam Centre for Language and Communication, University of Amsterdam)

I. Introduction

Law is a fundamental feature of the multilevel system of governance of the European Union (EU). In order to achieve its objectives and develop its policies, the EU has enacted a vast number of instruments, mostly in the form of 'hard law' such as regulations, directives and decisions. Nowadays, the EU is relying increasingly in the exercise of its regulatory powers also on formally non-binding instruments, such as recommendations, opinions, communications, notices or guidelines commonly labelled as 'soft law.' Remarkably, more than 10% of current EU law consists of such soft law instruments.[1] These tools are arguably highly valued for their flexibility, particularly suitable to deal with the complexity and diversity of European affairs,[2] useful where the intensity of EU competence is rather low, and capable of producing important legal and practical effects.[3] EU soft law instruments, in particular those enacted by the European Commission,

1 O Stefan, *Soft Law in Court. Competition Law, State Aid and the Court of Justice of the European Union* (Wolters Kluwer 2013) 12.

2 See A Schäfer, 'Resolving Deadlock: Why International Organisations Introduce Soft Law' (2006) 12(2) *European Law Journal* 195–196 who contests this view.

3 F Snyder, 'Interinstitutional Agreements: Forms and Constitutional Limitations' in G Winter (ed.), *Sources and Categories of European Union Law: a Comparative and Reform Perspective* (Nomos Verlags-Ges 1996) 463. Legal effects include, among others, binding the enacting institution and the addressees, creating expectations that the enacting institutions will comply with the rule. Practical effects include, for instance, policy changes in the Member States.

are also being referred to frequently in CJEU's judgments[4] and they are increasingly challenged before European courts.[5]

Soft law instruments co-exist alongside hard law instruments in EU governance for relatively long. Yet the status, functions and role of soft law instruments, and especially the precise delineation between soft and hard law instruments, are all subject of great debates and disagreement among scholars and practitioners. There are different and often contradictory views on the distinction between soft and hard law, and rarely, if ever, a definite answer is provided that is theoretically informed and empirically supported. Most legal scholars will only agree that the use of hard and soft law reflects a wider normative variety through formulating rules robustly or softly.[6] Also, they will agree that the distinction between hard and soft law is vital for the proper functioning of a legal system, particularly in the case of such a complex multilevel system as the EU.[7] Any imbalance between the intended meaning of the legal norms and their expression is likely to affect legal certainty and raise intricate legal questions regarding institutional balance, as well as the limits and exercise of EU competences. As a result, national administrations and judges, who are the key actors interpreting and applying EU law in the Member States, are unsure if and how to apply these legal instruments.[8]

This chapter contributes to the discussions on EU soft law instruments by examining their normative content as an essential factor for delineating between hard and soft law. It focuses on the analysis and evaluation of legal instruments, which despite their classification as legally non-binding display a hard law-like content. The emphasis lies on soft law instruments enacted by the Commission because these seem to be most contested as to their legal nature and effects. Section 2 outlines the conceptual and legal ambiguity surrounding EU soft law. Section 3 explains, by relying on the relevant case law of the Court of Justice (CJEU) and EU law drafting guidelines, why and how the normative content is a key factor for determining the legal nature of EU acts. Section 4 examines the normative content of recommendations and other 'non-binding' acts of the Commission, which are legally problematic in that they oftentimes resemble hard law

---

4 See landmark Case C-322/88 *Salvatore Grimaldi v Fonds des maladies professionnelles* EU:C:1989:646.

5 Most recently in Case C-16/16P *Belgium v Commission* EU:C:2018:79.

6 See J Klabbers, 'Why not to Study Soft Law' Paper presented at the first conference of the European Network on Soft Law Research, Helsinki (2017) 2.

7 See Stefan (n 1) 20–21.

8 See Opinion of Advocate General Bobek in Case C-16/16P EU:C:2017:959 para 15.

instruments. Essential normative content elements include their structure, the strength of the obligations prescribed to addressees, the level of detail and precision of their substantive provisions, and the compliance/enforcement mechanisms attached to them. Special attention is paid to the argumentation used in Commission soft law instruments, based on the assumption that their effectiveness and intrinsic quality should largely depend on the persuasive force of their justificatory reasons.[9] Finally, some of the implications deriving from the Commission's symptomatic 'hardened' soft law instruments for the quality of EU lawmaking are discussed. In Section 5, the focus is on legal problems and concerns related to the principle of legal certainty, the principle of legality, the principle of conferral and institutional balance, legal scrutiny and review. In Section 6, a clearer delineation between EU soft law and hard law through an increased role for argumentation as a means to foster compliance is promoted.

II. The 'murky' EU soft law

The concept of 'soft law' aims at capturing the increasing complexity of the current legal normative landscape by relativizing the traditional positivist distinction between legally binding and non-binding instruments. It bears the promise of a more nuanced and 'down to earth' explanation of current lawmaking, but at the same time, it runs the risk of bringing additional complications and ambiguity. So far existing legal-political science scholarship has raised more questions than answers about the status, functions and role of EU soft law instruments.[10] Particularly significant are the debates between those viewing soft law as limited to mere non-binding

9 C Andone and S Greco, 'Evading the Burden of Proof in European Union Soft Law Instruments: the Case of Commission Recommendations' (2018) 31(1) *International Journal for the Semiotics of Law* 79.

10 Among others, F Snyder, 'The Effectiveness of European Community Law: Institutions, Processes, Tools and Techniques' (1993) 56(1) *The Modern Law Review* 19–54, L Senden, *Soft Law in European Community Law* (Hart Publishing 2003); D Trubek et al., 'Soft Law', 'Hard Law', and the EU Integration: Toward a Theory of Hybridity' (2005) 05 *Jean Monnet Working Paper* 1–42; V Fegus, 'The Growing Importance of Soft Law in the EU' (2014) 1(1) *InterEU Law East* 145–161; O Stefan, 'Soft Law and the Enforcement of EU Law' in A Jakab and D Kochenov (eds.), *The Enforcement of EU Law and Values: Ensuring Member States' Compliance* (OUP 2017) 200–217.

norms with legal relevance,[11] those defining soft law as involving politically binding norms,[12] and those combining these two views.[13] The first category of scholars seems to oversimplify the complexity of the current situation, because soft law instruments may have more than a non-binding character as they impose certain obligations on their addressees. The second category points at political rather than legal norms, which blurs the precise legal nature of soft law instruments. The third category embraces an unsolvable perplexing duality by suggesting that non-binding norms have legal relevance but do not reach a sufficient level of 'bindingness' to constitute hard law.

Given the existing lack of clarity about EU soft law instruments, Terpan rightly points out that "soft law is not a clear-cut and uncontested category."[14] It is arguably only known with certainty that soft law consists of "rules of conduct which, in principle, have no legally binding force, but which nevertheless may have practical effects"[15] and "legal effects"[16]. Unlike hard law, these rules are not formally binding as a matter of law: their addressees, mainly the Member States, have the political rather than legal

11 See Senden (n 10); U Mörth, 'Soft Law and New Modes of EU Governance – A Democratic Problem?' (2006) Online paper presented in Darmstadt November 2005 1–25; A Peters, 'Soft law as a New Mode of Governance' in U Diedrichs, W Reiners and W Wessels (eds.), *The Dynamics of Change in EU Governance* (Edward Elgar 2011) 21–51.

12 M Cini, 'The Soft Law Approach: Commission Rule-making in the EU's State Aid Regime' (2001) 8(2) *Journal of European Public Policy* 192–207; J Skjaerseth, O Stokke and J Wettestad, 'Soft Law, Hard Law and Effective Implementation of International Environmental Norms' (2006) 6(3) *Global Environmental Politics* 104–120, C Rose, 'Non-binding Instruments and Democratic Accountability' in H Cullen, J Harrington and C Renshaw (eds.), *Experts, Networks and International Law* (CUP 2017) 205–229.

13 F Terpan, 'Soft Law in the European Union – the Changing Nature of EU Law' (2015) 21(1) *European Law Journal* 68–96. There are also authors who are critical of soft law in general, including EU soft law instruments, such as Klabbers, dismissing it as "a beautiful invention, a veritable Humpty Dumpty term which, as Humpty Dumpty himself would aver, can mean anything we want it to mean" (Klabbers (n 6) 3). Klabbers has often pointed at "the redundancy of soft law" and "the undesirability of soft law" (see 'The Redundancy of Soft Law' (1996) 65 *Nordic Journal of International Law* 167–182 and 'The Undesirability of Soft Law' (1998) 67 *Nordic Journal of International Law* 381–391), going as far as advocating that soft law is not worth studying (n 6). While some of Klabbers' points of criticism may be correct, others remain open for debate (see Stefan (n 1)).

14 Terpan (n 13) 70.

15 Snyder (n 10) 32; see also Senden (n 10) 112.

16 See Stefan (n 1) 16.

obligation to base their future conduct on their provisions. Yet things become less clear when some of these instruments provide that a certain course of action needs to be taken within a certain timeframe. If this does not occur, Member States need to justify why a different, or no course of action is taken.[17] By the same token, in legal practice there seem to be much 'harder' commitments imposed on the basis of soft law instruments, which the author of the act or the addressees need to fulfill. Illustratively, Stefan argues that European competition soft law instruments are a matter of hard principles in that they are taken into account by courts for enforcing general principles of law. Thus, for the European Courts, the mere existence of Commission's notices creates legitimate expectations, such as companies assuming that they may conclude agreements satisfying certain criteria mentioned in the notice.[18] In other cases, the measures prescribed in soft law instruments are 'hardened' via legally binding acts laying down follow-up enforcement mechanisms and actions, such as the setting of clear time limits for compliance and the possibility to adopt legally binding decisions in case of non-compliance by the addressee.[19] Things become even more confusing where EU legislation prescribes the adoption of recommendations by the Commission via binding implementing acts, for instance in the very specific context of reintroduction of internal border controls within the Schengen area.[20] Last but not least, according to the *Grimaldi* jurisprudence, national courts are bound to consider EU soft law

17 S Saurugger and F Terpan, 'Studying Resistance to EU Norms in Foreign and Security Policy' (2015) 20(2/1) *European Foreign Affairs Review* 1–20.

18 O Stefan, 'European Competition Soft Law in European Courts: A Matter of Hard Principles?' (2008) 14(6) *European Law Journal* 766; see for instance Joined Cases C-189/02 P, C-202/02 P, C-205/02 P to C-208/02 P and C-213/02 P *Dansk Rørindustri A/S v Commission* EU:C:2005:408.

19 See for an example Article 13(6) and (8) of Regulation (EU) 2016/1624 of the European Parliament and of the Council on the European Border and Coast Guard and amending Regulation (EU) 2016/399 of the European Parliament and of the Council and repealing Regulation (EC) No 863/2007 of the European Parliament and of the Council, Council Regulation (EC) No 2007/2004 and Council Decision 2005/267/EC [2016] OJ L251/1; another example envisages the complex legal framework laid down under the '6 Pack on Economic Governance' where soft Commission recommendations and reports are significantly 'hardened' by the possibility to trigger "a 'shadow' of possible sanctions later on in the process"; T van den Brink and L Senden, 'Checks and Balances of Soft EU Rule-making' (2012) in European Parliament, Policy Department C: Citizens' Rights and Constitutional Affairs 53.

20 See Articles 21 and 29(4) of Regulation (EU) 2016/399 of the European Parliament and of the Council on a Union Code on the rules governing the movement

instruments for interpreting legally binding provisions or, even more, when such instruments supplement binding EU legal acts.[21]

III. Normative content as a key factor for determining the legal nature of EU (soft law) acts

The previous overview shows that the ambiguous legal nature of EU soft law instruments creates a significant degree of uncertainty as to the existence and extent of their legal effects. Since EU law is still premised, at least for the purpose of legal review, on the distinction between legally binding and legally non-binding acts,[22] one way forward is to attempt to determine on a case-by-case basis to which of the two categories (Commission's) soft law instruments belong. This brings us to the question of which criteria or standards are relevant for clarifying the genuine legal nature of EU acts, and in particular of these 'in-between' formal soft law instruments with a hard dimension. The usual criteria encompass the formal title and other external aspects of the instrument (e.g., organization of the text in parts and paragraphs) as well as the wording and substance of the instrument. To these, one may add more contextual elements, such as the adoption procedure, publication, the broader legal framework, the role and competence of the author of the act, or the implementation practice.

From a jurisprudential perspective, the CJEU expressed already in *ERTA* a preference for a 'substance prevails over form' approach[23] in order to determine the real legal nature of EU acts.[24] This approach has been applied with some degree of flexibility over time with regard to various Commission acts[25], such as recommendations,[26] letters and statement of objec-

---

of persons across borders (Schengen Borders Code) (codification) [2016] OJ L77/1.

21 Case C-322/88 (n 4) para 18; Joined Cases 317/08–320/08 *Alassini v Telecom Italia* EU:C:2010:146 para 40.

22 The CJEU does not acknowledge soft law as a specific category of legal acts, but rather focusses on determining whether EU legal instruments qualify as legally binding or legally non-binding, while admitting that in certain circumstances even non-binding EU acts may produce certain legal effects, derived from broader EU rules and principles, such as legitimate expectations or the principle of sincere cooperation (e.g., *Grimaldi* (n 4)).

23 See Opinion of Advocate General Bobek in Case C-16/16P (n 8) para 63.

24 Case 22/70 *Commission v Council* (ERTA) EU:C:1971:32 para 42.

25 See also Opinion of Advocate General Bobek (n 8) paras 62–63.

26 Case C-322/88 *Grimaldi* (n 4).

tions,[27] communications,[28] guidelines,[29] codes of conduct,[30] notices.[31] It should be noted that 'content' has been the decisive criterion for the legal diagnosis of both instruments outside the official nomenclature in the Treaties and soft law instruments expressly listed as non-binding acts in the Founding Treaties.[32] Most recently, in Case C-16/16P *Belgium v Commission*, the CJEU confirmed an 'Article 288 TFEU' recommendation may by virtue of its content not represent a genuine recommendation, but an act that produces binding legal effects.[33]

As to the more concrete factors taken into account for determining the genuine legal nature of an EU legal instrument based on its normative content, the CJEU looks primarily at the wording and substance of its provisions.[34] As a complementary tool, the European courts also consider contextual elements, such as the relevant legal-policy framework to which the legal act belongs, the powers of the adopting institutions or the publication of the legal instrument.[35] These elements enable a more fine-tuned as-

---

27 Case 60/81 *IBM v Commission* EU:C:1981:264; Case C-147/96 *Netherlands v Commission* EU:C:2000:335.

28 C-57/95 *France v Commission* EU:C:1997:164, C-301/03 *Italy v Commission* EU:C:2005:727.

29 *Dansk Rørindustri* (n 18); Case C-520/09P *Arkema v Commisison* EU:C:2011:619.

30 Case C-303/90 *France v Commission* EU:C:1991:424.

31 Case C-226/11 *Expedia v Autorité de la Concurrence and Others* EU:C:2012:795.

32 I.e., recommendations and opinions according to Articles 288 and 263 TFEU; in this respect, Advocate General Bobek distinguishes between 'typical' and 'atypical' (soft law) acts depending on whether they are listed or not in the Treaties – see Opinion of Advocate General Bobek (n 8) para 55.

33 Case C-16/16P (n 5) paras 29–31. Advocate General Bobek astutely noticed a discreet but arguably significant change in the initial *ERTA* test for determining the legal nature of an EU act from 'legal effects' in the ERTA Judgment, to 'binding legal effects' in subsequent case law (paras 69–71). This entails a narrowing down of the 'legal nature' test of EU acts, which has the effect of excluding from legal review most of soft law instruments capable of producing (some) legal effects in an era of unprecedented proliferation of such instruments, see Opinion of Advocate General Bobek (n 8) paras 72–73.

34 See Case C-16/16P (n 5) paras 37 and 52 and Case T-721/14 *Belgium v Commission* EU:T:2015:829 paras 19–35; see also the case law overview at para 18. See in the same vein Opinion of Advocate General Bobek (n 8) para 65. This is particularly the case when the Court assesses the legal nature of EU acts that are final, in that they lay down definitively the position of the adopting institution, see for instance, Case C-301/03 EU (n 28); Case C-57/95 *France v Commission* EU:C:1997:164 and Case C-303/90 (n 30).

35 See Case C-16/16P (n 5) paras 32 and 36–37 and Case T-721/14 (n 34) paras 18 and 36.

sessment of the intention of the author of the act as to its legally binding effects, and seem to fulfill a confirmatory function of the analysis based on wording and substance.[36] The application of these criteria is subject to variations depending on the particular facts and circumstances of each case.

Yet, one may distil some commonalities in the application of these criteria. Regarding the *wording*, the CJEU usually checks whether the legal instrument is drafted in imperative or non-mandatory terms in order to reach a conclusion on its legal nature.[37] In this respect, the expression of obligation through the use of 'shall/will' language is likely to correspond to instruments intended to have legally binding effects,[38] whereas a conditional 'should' language or references to 'proposed rules' suggests non-binding provisions.[39] Concerning the *substance*, the Court examines the scope of the provisions, the level of detail of the conduct prescribed to addressees, as well as the existence and design of implementing tools, such as reporting requirements, monitoring and compliance/enforcement mechanisms. The more detailed and prescriptive the provisions and implementing mechanisms of the instrument, the more likely it will qualify as a legally binding instrument.[40] As to the interplay between wording and substance in CJEU's assessment, a definite conclusion is difficult to draw. Suffice it to say that sometimes the Court found the legal instrument to be binding based on its substance even against the 'should' wording of the document[41] whereas more recently the CJEU seems to attach more weight to the conditional wording of its provisions.[42]

Deviating from the CJEU's stance, Advocate General Bobek proposes a somewhat unconventional test for assessing the legal nature of EU legal acts.[43] In essence, he posits first that the wording of the instrument should not play a decisive role and outweigh the substance and context of the in-

---

36 See Case C-16/16P (n 5) paras 36–37 and Case T-721/14 (n 34) para 36.

37 E.g., Case C-16/16P (n 5) para 34 and Case T-721/14 (n 34) paras 21–28; Case C-301/03 (n 28) paras 21–22; Case C-57/95 (n 34) para 18.

38 Ibid.

39 E.g., Case C-301/03 (n 28) paras 21–22.

40 E.g., Case C-303/90 (n 30) paras 17–25.

41 E.g. Case C-303/90 (n 30) paras 17–25.

42 E.g. Case C-16/16P (n 5) paras 32 and 36–37 and Case T-721/14 (n 34); see Opinion of Advocate General Bobek (n 8) para 65.

43 Opinion of Advocate General Bobek (n 8) paras 110–122. In this respect the AG displays more receptivity to the category of soft law, unlike the CJEU which insists, at least for the purpose of judicial review under Article 263 TFEU, on the issue whether the act has binding legal effects.

strument.[44] Second, the analysis of the legal effects of the instrument should, in his view, focus on the capacity of the instrument to induce compliance or otherwise to affect the position of the addressee.[45] In his version of the *ERTA* test, normative content remains decisive, but AG Bobek suggests placing more emphasis on the logic, substance, context and purpose of the instrument instead on the mere wording.[46] Hence, if its formal denomination is removed, does the instrument look like an act capable of producing legal effects and inducing compliance by the addressees?[47] In operationalizing the test, AG Bobek considers both external and internal aspects of the normative content of the legal instrument.[48] External elements include the overall structure of the act (e.g., the division between preamble and prescriptive part; the division in articles/paragraphs) and wording. The internal dimension concerns the substance of provisions, including purpose, scope, prescriptive character, level of detail and degree of precision, as well as monitoring, reporting, compliance mechanisms. Applying this test, AG Bobek concluded, contrary to the CJEU, that the overall analysis of the elements pertaining to content and context entails, in spite of its soft inviting language, that the recommendation at issue in case C-16/16P[49] produces legal effects and it should be a reviewable act.[50]

It is obvious from the above that the quest for clarifying the correct legal nature and effects of Union's acts, and in particular of the Commission's legal instruments, requires a combined assessment of a number of factors pertaining to the form, content and context of the instrument. In an ideal world, premised on perfect consistency between the form, content and context of the instrument[51] no particular problems should arise as to the application or weight of these criteria. Yet the reality of decision-making features situations of apparent discrepancy between these dimensions

44 Ibid paras 111 and 114.

45 Ibid paras 111 and 113.

46 According to Advocate General Bobek, too much emphasis on the "'inviting' wording" in soft law instruments would rather favour a 'form prevails over substance' approach with the practical effect that soft law instrument could never be subject to legal review (n 8 para 114).

47 Opinion of Advocate General Bobek (n 8) paras 123–124.

48 Ibid, para 116–122 for the criteria *in abstracto* and paras 123–143 for the application of the test.

49 Commission Recommendation 2014/478/EU on principles for the protection of consumers and players of online gambling services and for the prevention of minors from gambling online [2014] OJ L214/38.

50 Ibid paras 140–143.

51 See Case *Grimaldi* (n 4) para 14.

of a legal act, in particular as regards the Commission's soft law instruments. In such cases, the prevalent or decisive criterion clarifies the legal nature and effects of the twilight legal instrument. In this respect, the Court's approach that content should prevail by all means over the form of the instrument for the purpose of determining its genuine legal nature and effects is indeed persuasive.[52] An obvious reason is that this allows detecting and reviewing, beyond non-binding 'window dressing', measures genuinely intended to produce far-reaching legal effects. For the same reason, we also side with Advocate General Bobek's view that, in case dissonance persists, more weight should be given to substantive (internal) elements of the normative content of the instrument as compared to external aspects of that content, such as the wording (in particular the expression of obligations) and the structure of its provisions.[53] Hence, a conditional 'should' language should not obscure the actual legal effects resulting from highly detailed and precise prescriptive provisions, as well as from elaborated monitoring, reporting and implementing mechanisms intended to compel addressees to comply.[54] An additional argument that 'should' language should not be taken *per se* as the 'gold standard' for determining the non-binding nature of an EU legal act is that such language can sometimes be found also in hard law instruments.[55]

Somewhat surprisingly, despite the amount of scholarship pointing to the unsettled nature of soft law and the significant legal and practical problems created by these instruments leading increasingly to litigation before CJEU, little attention seems to be paid to soft law in daily EU decision-making. As will be seen later in more detail, existing EU (better) lawmaking and drafting guidelines do little more than stating generically the obvious: (1) that non-binding acts should not be prescriptive, and (2) that they

52 Also when the title of the instrument corresponds to a category of non-binding acts explicitly qualified so by EU law.

53 Opinion of Advocate General Bobek (n 8) para 114.

54 For instance, if a mere replacing of 'should' with 'shall' throughout the instrument would make it resemble a typical EU binding act, that could be taken as a strong indicator that the soft law instrument is actually intended to change the legal situation of the addressees – see also Opinion of Advocate General Bobek (n 8) para 135.

55 See for example, Articles 13(7) and 39(9), 55(1) and 75(13) of Regulation (EU) 2016/1624; should one then conclude that these provisions in the Frontex Regulation amount to non-binding provisions?

should not resemble too much legally binding acts.[56] At the same time, rather inconsistently with the features of EU non-binding acts,[57] Tool #18 mentions the importance of ensuring detailed monitoring and evaluation mechanisms of the implementation by the Member States. The feeble consideration in EU institutional practice for the normative content and drafting of soft law instruments contributes in our view to the ambiguity, inconsistencies and legal problems raised by these tools, as shown in the next section.

IV. Assessing the normative content of Commission's soft law instruments

This section exemplifies and assesses the main aspects related to the normative content of Commission soft law instruments with a special emphasis on recommendations. Our focus on these instruments stems mainly from the fact that they are part and parcel of Union's better governance efforts as formally non-binding tools, but at the same time they play an important role in the EU legal order, having far-reaching objectives, as well as considerable practical and legal significance. Incidentally, we consider other Commission soft law instruments such as guidelines, notices and codes of conduct, when deemed appropriate.

Recommendations are mentioned explicitly in Art. 288 TFEU as instruments "which shall have no binding force," and are often presented in the literature as lying "somewhere between general policy statements […] and legislation […]."[58] Recommendations are used by the Commission in a wide array of policy fields ranging most famously from competition law and state aid,[59] to other policy areas, such as the environment and con-

---

56 See Annex I of *Joint Practical Guide of the European Parliament, the Council and the Commission for Persons Involved in the Drafting of European Union Legislation* <https://publications.europa.eu/en/publication-detail/-/publication/3879747d-7a3c-411b-a3a055c14e2ba732/language-en> (2015) 8, accessed in March 2019, and Commission, 'Better Regulation Guidelines' SWD (2017) 350, "Toolbox" 2018, Tool #18 The choice of the policy instrument 115, <https://ec.europa.eu/info/better-regulation-toolbox_en> accessed in March 2019.

57 Advocate General Bobek pointed out that "the Court demonstrated a particular sensitivity towards inserting compliance or monitoring mechanisms into various atypical instruments" and that "[o]n at least two occasions, it annulled atypical Commission acts because they regulated reporting requirements in detail and arguably went beyond what was appropriate for that type of act" (n 8) para 131.

58 Cini (n 12) 194.

59 See Stefan (n 1) 24.

sumer protection,[60] for which hard law instruments have been typically used.[61] The functions that Commission recommendations normally fulfil are to complement hard law, ensure its effectiveness, supplement the lack of hard law in certain policy areas, or as alternatives to hard law when the latter cannot be used, for example because the EU has no competence to act.[62]

In line with Section 3, this analysis considers both external and internal aspects of the normative content of Commission's recommendations and other soft law instruments. It looks into the structure of the act, the overall wording and, in particular, the expression of obligation prescribed to the addressee, the substance of the provisions including the degree of details prescribed, as well as the compliance/enforcement mechanisms attached to these instruments. Last but not least, the role and quality of the argumentation advanced to support a prescribed course of action are examined as particularly important elements conferring added value to Commission's soft law instruments. Our analysis is based on EU drafting guidelines and manuals, as well as empirical insights from interviews with Commission experts.

1. *Structure*

Unlike hard law instruments, soft law instruments do not necessarily follow a strict template. Because they are drafted by the Directorates General responsible for a particular policy area, there may be variations with regard to their structure. Commission experts explain that no strict format applies as in the case of directives or regulations, precisely because these are flexible instruments which are not constrained by a binding content and form.[63] The same idea is underlined in Section I(1) of the Commission's *Legislative Drafting Manual* (LD)[64] mentioning that "the form of non-bind-

60 See Commission Recommendation 2011/136/EU providing guidelines for the implementation of data protection rules in the Consumer Protection Cooperation System [2011] OJ L57/44.

61 Cini (n 12) 193.

62 European Commission (n 56).

63 Interviews with Commission experts from the Legal Service and Secretariat General, January 25, 2019.

64 European Commission. *Legislative Drafting. A Commission Manual* 1997. http://ec.europa.eu/smart-regulation/better_regulation/documents/legis_draft_comm_en.pdf.

ing legal acts [...] is not prescribed and can vary according to circumstances." Yet the *Joint Practical Guide for Persons Involved in the Drafting of European Union Legislation* (JPG)[65] specifies that "in non-binding acts, [...] a structure or presentation too close to that of a binding act, must not be used" (2.3.3) In the same vein, the LD stipulates that "in non-binding acts [...], the basic unit is not the article but the *point*" (6.3.1 (c)). Apart from making this minor and in practice almost unobservable distinction,[66] LD surprisingly also points out that "recommendations and resolutions should, however, be drawn up in a form modelled on that of binding acts" (I(1)).

This last remark strikes not only as obviously inconsistent with the previous guidelines according to which the form of the soft law instruments should not be cast in a fixed template, but also points at how such instruments are structured and presented *de facto*. The degree of formalization seems to be such that soft law instruments resemble to a great extent, if not sometimes fully mirroring, the form of a legally binding act.[67] Thus, the structure of recommendations resembles routinely that of directives with its delineation between a preamble and a prescriptive part, the latter further being subdivided into 'points' about 'Definitions', 'Requirements', 'Supervision', 'Reporting', etc. One wonders if the use of points, rather than articles, in non-binding acts is sufficient to conclude that the format of such an act is completely different from a binding act and cannot be reasonably perceived as producing binding legal effects. After all, this perception by the addressees has occurred in practice on various occasions. Illustrative cases include the Czech Republic, as explained by Whelanová[68] who discusses the consequences of such formal aspects for legal certainty at national level. Also in Case C-16/16P, the resemblance between the Commission Recommendation 2014/478 EU and a directive made Belgium argue that the act should be challengeable before European courts for the purpose of annulment.

---

65 *Joint Practical Guide* (n 56).

66 Looking at the provisions of some recommendations or other soft law instruments of the Commission, one notices no difference whatsoever in the form of the instrument from the articles of directives and regulations. Commission experts conveyed that sometimes, despite the Commission's efforts to be clear about the legally non-binding nature of the instrument, recommendations very much resemble directives (n 63).

67 See also Opinion of Advocate General Bobek (n 8) para 126.

68 See M Whelanová's contribution in this volume.

2. *Degree of detail and precision*

EU lawyers know all too well that hard law instruments, such as directives and regulations, are particularly detailed in prescribing a certain behavior that they impose or authorize. These sometimes outline both the intended objective and the means of achieving it (regulations and decisions). At other times, they specify only the objective to be achieved by the Member States, leaving the choice of the form and the method of the transposing legal instrument to the Member States (directives). In both situations, the obligations laid down must be complied with in light of their wording and purpose outlined in the instrument. In Kratochwil's[69] words, such obligations are categorical, meaning that "the actor cannot exempt himself/herself by a simple disclaimer."

The existing drafting guidelines refer to the degree of details as concerns directives and regulations. Thus, JPG clarifies that too detailed formulations point at regulations and need to be avoided in directives (2.2.2). The drafting rules leave aside any explicit mention as to the degree of detail in the provisions of non-binding instruments. Yet, based on the guidelines for directives and regulations, it makes sense to assume that non-binding instruments should not be too detailed and prescriptive, if only to distinguish them formally from hard law instruments. Yet another reason would be that, if detailed and prescriptive, the addressees may confuse them with hard law instruments, even in cases in which non-binding language prevails. In his Opinion in Case C-16/16P, Advocate Bobek notices that Recommendation 2014/478/EU, though cast in non-binding language, abounds in details and requirements for operators' gambling websites, including the kind of information that should be displayed on their page and the number of clicks it takes to access each piece of information are provided (Point III), as well as further detailed requirements for minors (Point IV).[70] The General Court also admitted that this recommendation was very detailed, though dismissing that this could be a factor to consider the legal instrument something else than the title indicates.[71] If one looks at other recommendations, however, it takes little to notice that detailed provisions are the norm rather than the exception[72] and that the concrete

69 F Kratochwil, *Rules, Norms and Decisions. On the Conditions of Practical and Legal Reasoning in International Relations and Domestic Affairs* (CUP 1989) 96.

70 Opinion of Advocate General Bobek (n 8) paras 129–130.

71 Case T-721/14 (n 34) para 72.

72 Three recent examples: Commission Recommendation (EU) 2018/177 on the elements to be included in the technical, legal and financial arrangements between

provisions of these recommendations are remarkably detailed and precise. Moreover, such details also concern, as will be shown in subsection 4.4, comprehensive supervision and reporting obligations on the part of the addressees, which brings them even closer to hard law instruments.

3. *Strength of obligations*

EU drafting manuals and guidelines as well as Commission experts[73] underline that non-binding instruments should not be worded too similarly to binding instruments and should include only provisions having no binding force (JPG 2.2.4, 2.3.3). A close analysis of recommendations of the Commission[74] confirms that suggestions are made in these instruments by employing modal expressions that are admittedly less strong than in the case of hard law instruments such as directives. Although a course of action is prescribed in recommendations,[75] the way in which such prescriptions are made is definitely milder if one examines strictly the modal content. More often than not, *should*, which points at weak obligations, is used, while *must*, which imposes strong obligations, as well as *shall*, which is considered the strongest in terms of obligations imposed on addressees, have a very low distribution. However, other soft law instruments such as Commission communications are drafted in modal terms that are indistinguishable from directives and regulations in that the use *shall* and *must* are rather the norm.[76]

Member States for the application of the solidarity mechanism under Article 13 of Regulation (EU) 2017/1938 of the European Parliament and of the Council concerning measures to safeguard the security of gas supply [2018] OJ L32/52; Commission Recommendation (EU) 2018/234 on enhancing the European nature and efficientconduct of the 2019 elections to the European Parliament [2018] OJ L45/40; Commission Recommendation (EU) 2018/334 on measures to effectively tackle illegal content online [2018] OJ L63/50.

73 Interview with the Legal Service (n 63).

74 Andone and Greco (n 9).

75 See, for example, "The European Commission [...] *recommends* that Member States: Organise and implement policies to address child poverty and social exclusion, promoting children's well-being, through multi-dimensional strategies" (italics added) (Commission Recommendation (EU) 2013/112 Investing in children: breaking the cycle of disadvantage [2013] OJ L59/5).

76 See Commission, 'Communication on the application of State aid rules to public service broadcasting' C:2009:257; Commission, 'Communication relating to the methodology for analysing State aid linked to stranded costs' SG (2001) D/290869; Commission, 'Communication on the application, from 1 August 2013,

It is in fact fairly easily noticeable that, unlike in the hard law instruments in which *shall* plays a prominent position, its use in soft law instruments is hardly observable, with many documents containing one[77] and generally no occurrences of this modal. The General Court confirmed thathe *invitation*-type wording of Recommendation 2014/478/EU indicated that there was no intent on the Commission's part to produce binding legal effects. In its reasoning, the Court underlined that the Member States are not imposed an obligation to apply the principles set out in that act and, moreover, they retained their regulatory powers in the respective field. They were only *invited* to comply with the principles laid down in the act.[78] Arguably, the detailed prescriptive provisions of the recommendations contradict the idea that only suggestions are made and mere principles are outlined without the expectancy that Member States will also comply with the proposed recommendation.

It is, however, important to notice that the type of analysis in strictly modal terms, which the Court seems to favor when examining the wording of terms as mandatory or non-mandatory, provides only a partial picture of the strength of obligation in soft law instruments. Obligations are not rendered only in modal terms, but are sometimes strategically imposed through other documents accompanying the soft law instrument. Such documents are, strictly speaking, not part of the normative content of the instrument, yet they suggest a certain interpretation of the soft law instruments, which the addressees are pressured to follow. Such is the case of Recommendation 2014/478/EU, which was accompanied by a Memorandum[79] in which it is specified that the Commission sends "a *clear message* to the Member States as to what actions are expected" (italics added). Additionally, "by setting the objectives to be attained, it should act as a catalyst for the development of *consistent principles* to be applied throughout the European Union" (italics added) and points also at "a *comprehensive and*

---

of State aid rules to support measures in favour of banks in the context of the financial crisis ('Banking Communication')' [2013] OJ C216/1.

77 See Commission Recommendation C(2014) 7174 final on relevant product and service markets within the electronic communications sector susceptible to exante regulation according to Directive [2014] OJ L295/79. Point 24 of the preamble of this recommendation, featuring the use of *shall* combined with a detailed prescription of the behavior of the Member States and the spectrum of triggering infringement proceedings in case of non-compliance, can be seen as a factor hardening the content of the recommendation.

78 Case T-721/14 (n 34) para 32.

79 Memo 14/484 of 14 July 2014, available at http://europa.eu/rapid/press-release_MEMO-14-484_en.htm.

common approach in the area of online gambling services" (italics added). Combined with the detailed provisions in the instrument mentioned before, such references indicate very specific and precise commitments being induced on the part of the Member States, even if the instrument is explicitly called non-binding.[80] And indeed, there are cases in which Member States perceive Commission's soft law instruments as binding due to such formulations either in the act or in the accompanying documents. Examples are the case of the Czech Republic,[81] the Belgian case[82] or the very recent Romanian case[83] where a Romanian judges association requested the Court to clarify whether a Commission report addressing recommendations to Romania within the Cooperation and Verification Mechanism is binding or not.[84]

Commission experts[85] also refer to such instruments as 'gentlemen's *agreements*' and examples of a 'peer *pressure*' approach, suggesting that they are not formally binding, but informally seen as such both by the enactor of the instrument and the addressee. They are aware of the fact that Mem-

---

80 See also Opinion Advocate General Bobek (n 8) para 119. Such harmonization goals are sometimes mentioned in the instruments, as well, as in the case of Commission Recommendation 2018/C252/01 on guidance for the harmonized implementation of the European Rail Traffic Management System in the Union [2018] OJ C 253/1. Another comparable example concerns Commission Recommendation (EU)2019/243 on a European Electronic Health Record exchange format [2019] OJ L39/18 which was accompanied by a press release, a fact sheet and several other accompanying documents, all pointing at the necessity of establishing a common framework for health record exchange.

81 M Whelanová, this volume.

82 Case C-16/16P (n 5).

83 Case C-83/19, Asociația "Forumul Judecătorilor Din România" (pending).

84 In providing a typology of hard and soft law norms in the EU, Terpan (n 13) 77 explains that sometimes legal obligations in soft law instruments are just as hard as in the case of hard law instruments, in other instruments they are soft, yet in others no obligations are involved. The last case is, however, not illustrated and it is difficult to imagine that no obligation is sometimes involved, since, as Terpan (n 13) 81 himself mentions, quantitative and qualitative indicators are provided, and targets and measurements aimed at translating guidelines into national programmes are indicated. One might say in this case that although no explicit verbal indicators of the obligations imposed on the addressee are available (e.g., 'must', 'should'), the quantitative and qualitative indicators indirectly point at a requirement on the part of the addressee to carry out a particular course of action. Irrespective of the nature of the obligation, whether hard or soft, Terpan (n 13) underlines that enforcement mechanisms (soft or hard) are always applicable to back up the prescriptive behaviour imposed on the addressee.

85 Interview with the Secretariat General (n 63).

ber States do sometimes interpret such instruments as binding, although admittedly the Commission tries, already at the drafting stage, to avoid this.[86] Moreover, the rather recent technique employed in some EU legal acts of conditioning certain legal effects or benefits upon compliance by Member States with soft law instruments arguably makes them perceive such instruments as binding.[87]

4. *Compliance/enforcement mechanisms*

The strength of obligations imposed on addressees in soft law instruments is also expressed in the enforcement and compliance mechanisms often associated with these instruments. Such mechanisms contribute to the suggestion that the act is binding by inviting Member States to "notify the Commission of any measure taken pursuant to the Recommendation [...] in order for the Commission to be able to evaluate the implementation of this Recommendation"[88] and/or "include information on how they take the present Recommendation into account."[89] Sometimes, "Member States are invited to give effect" to a recommendation by a specific date[90] and otherwise inform the Commission of the reasons for not taking the instru-

86 Interview with the Legal Service (n 63).

87 Interview with the Secretariat General (n 63). Such examples are: obtaining the revocation of the post-accession safeguard measures under the Cooperation and Verification Mechanism (CVM) upon meeting Commission's recommendations laid down in the periodic CVM reports addressed to Romania and Bulgaria; or avoiding sanctions under the Excessive Imbalance Procedure laid down in Regulation 1176/2011 of the European Parliament and of the Council of 16 November 2011 on enforcement measures to correct excessive macroeconomic imbalances in the euro area [2011] OJ L306/8.

88 Commission Recommendation 2014/478/EU (n 49) Point XII.

89 Commission Recommendation (EU) 2018/951 on standards for equality bodies [2018] OJ L167/28, Chapter III.

90 See Commission Recommendation (EU) 2018/2050 on aligning the scope of and conditions for general transfer licences for the purposes of demonstration and evaluation as referred to in point (c) of Article 5(2) of Directive 2009/43/EC of the European Parliament and of the Council [2018] OJ L327/89, and Commission Recommendation (EU) 2018/2051 on aligning the scope of and conditions for general transfer licences for the purposes of repair and maintenance as referred to in point (d) of Article 5(2) of Directive 2009/43/EC of the European Parliament and of the Council [2018] OJ L327/94.

ment into account.[91] Such formulations follow closely the rules in JPG, and repeated in the *Legislative Drafting Manual*,[92] according to which "acts which have no binding force, such as recommendations, do not have a date of taking effect or application; the addressee may be requested to give effect to them by a certain date."[93]

This is consistent with the Better Regulation package of the Commission[94] with its emphasis on compliance-based mechanisms for an effective implementation of EU law, which moves from legal sanctions and infringement procedures to soft law mechanisms.[95] Yet beyond the game of words, the obligation to state reasons why a Member State departs from the recommendation implies that the instrument is binding, as otherwise there would be no such expectations on the part of the Member State.[96] As an expert from the Secretariat General[97] explained, it is important for the Commission to be informed of the activity of the Member State with respect to the proposed course of action. But in this case, there need not be any formal request for such information and a reaction to it, but rather an informal exchange of views, should the instrument be intended to be merely non-binding.

5. Persuasive force of arguments

It has already been explained[98] that the effectiveness and quality of soft law instruments in general, and recommendations in particular, should rely to a great extent on the persuasive force of the arguments advanced in such instruments. The arguments advanced to encourage the addresses to follow a certain course of action should largely determine the degree to which Member States will comply with the instrument, particularly due to the

---

91 See Saurugger and Terpan (n 17). 'Comply or explain' formulations recently abound as in Commission Recommendation (EU) 2018/334 (n 72), Commission Recommendation (EU) 2018/790 on access to and preservation of scientific information [2018] OJ L134/12, Commission Recommendation (EU) 2018/951 (n 89).

92 *Legislative Drafting* (n 64) Art. 6.9.1 point (e).

93 *Joint Practical Guide* (n 56) Art. 20.16.

94 Better regulation (n 56).

95 See M Smith, 'Challenges in the implementation of EU law at national level' (2018) Briefing Requested by the JURI Committee of the European Parliament 4.

96 See also Opinion of Advocate General Bobek (n 8) para 100. See also Commission Recommendation (EU) 2018/334, (n 72) point 43.

97 Interview with Secretariat General (n 63).

98 Andone and Greco (n 9).

fact that such instruments are not supposed to display explicitly binding force. In order to ensure that addressees follow the course of action recommended by the Commission, a strong and sound argumentation is a vital component of the normative content of the instrument.

A close look at the normative content of recommendations[99] reveals an argumentative pattern in which justificatory reasons are advanced in support of a course of action. Characteristically, a standpoint is advanced requesting Member States to take certain measures. Arguments are given justifying that the proposed measures are the right way to solve an existing or potential problem, while also underlining the advantages of taking those measures. In turn, coordinative arguments explain why the proposed measures will solve an existing problem. In all cases, it is mentioned that the proposed measures are based on fundamental values which Member States have embraced. Additionally, arguments point at the advantage of removing the variations in the way in which the Member States deal with a certain matter. In rare cases, the legal basis is mentioned, alongside the fact that the principle of subsidiarity has been taken into account.[100] Oftentimes, enforcement and compliance mechanisms are included.[101]

The outlined argumentative pattern of recommendations is hardly different from the argumentative pattern prototypical of directives, providing additional proof that recommendations resemble hard law instruments. First, just like hard law instruments, Commission recommendations feature arguments only in the preamble. Second, the same form of arguing features in the preamble of hard law instruments,[102] perhaps with the only distinguishing feature that recommendations do not claim full effectiveness of the adopted instrument as directives do. Third, the main purpose of recommendations involves cooperation or coordination at EU level and harmonization of European policies.[103] As Senden explains, coordination is not aimed "so much at establishing certain national legislation," whereas harmonization aims at "aligning national legislative and administrative

99 Andone and Greco (n 9) 88 have examined closely the argumentation advanced in recommendations enacted by the European Commission after 2012.

100 Andone and Greco (n 9) 88.

101 See (EU) 2018/334 (n 72), Commission Recommendation (EU) 2018/464 on the monitoring of metals and iodine in seaweed, halophytes and products based on seaweed [2018] OJ L78/16.

102 C Andone and F Coman-Kund, 'Argumentative Patterns in the European Union's Directives: An Effective Tool to Foster Compliance by the Member States?' (2017) 6(1) *Journal of Argumentation in Context* 76–96.

103 Senden (n 10) 179–181.

provisions, particularly with a view to removing obstacles that impede the realization of the internal market and economic and monetary union."[104] One also notices that unlike the early recommendations[105] featuring general goals, most recently very precise and specific guidelines are provided as to the actions on the part of the Member States. Together with suggesting a harmonizing purpose, it makes sense to assume that Member States will likely perceive such instruments as binding similarly to a directive. Finally, the investigation into the argumentative quality of directives and recommendations,[106] clearly demonstrates that both types of instruments fall short of sound argumentation. This is particularly obvious as concerns the way in which the Commission deals with its burden of proof, which is more often than not evaded. This defect is the more significant in the case of Commission's soft law instruments precisely because of their non-binding nature, which should in turn be compensated by their persuasive force.

V. *A legally problematic 'hardening' phenomenon of EU (Commission's) soft law instruments*

Whereas the virtues of soft law to ensure increased flexibility in Commission's policy making and enhance effectiveness of EU law cannot be denied,[107] the symptomatic 'hardening' of Commission's soft law instruments[108] raises a number of important legal problems and questions.[109] Firstly, the ambiguity concerning the genuine legal nature and effects of Commission's recommendations and other soft law instruments can affect legal certainty and generate confusion among addressees with repercussions on the very effectiveness of EU action.[110] Somewhat paradoxically,

104 The first recommendations as early as the 60s were seen as a legal instrument similar to directives. They were binding with regard to the result to be achieved upon those to whom it was addressed, leaving open the choice of form and methods (see Senden (n 10) 170). This initial characterization of recommendations can partly explain their current resemblance with directives.

105 See Senden (n 10) 170.

106 See Andone and Coman-Kund (n 101), Andone and Greco (n 9).

107 See Van den Brink and Senden (n 19) 8 and 70.

108 Van den Brink and Senden (n 19).

109 See also Stefan (n 1): 201–225 and Stefan (n 18): 15–18.

110 An illustrative case are the recommendations addressed by the Commission to some Member States within the framework of the post-accession CVM leading to an Article 267 TFEU procedure on the issue whether such recommendation are legally binding.

this situation seems to be maintained also by the indirect enhancement of the legal effects of Commission's soft law instruments under the influence of general principles of EU law such as 'effet utile' and duty of loyal cooperation based on Article 4(3) TEU,[111] or legitimate expectations.[112]

Secondly, the possibility for the Commission's soft law instruments that turn into legally binding acts based on their normative content and broader legal framework triggers problems from the perspective of the principles of attributed powers and institutional balance.[113] This is the so-called 'legislation/regulation by stealth' issue, entailing that soft law instruments may circumvent the lack of EU binding powers in a certain policy area, the lack of Commission's competence to adopt legally binding acts, and formal decision-making procedures involving other institutions.[114]

Thirdly, the much lower thresholds in terms of procedural safeguards, transparency, participation requirements and scrutiny conferring the much needed flexibility to soft law as compared to hard law[115] become particularly problematic when soft law instruments disguise far-reaching legal effects or genuine binding measures. This risks to further undermine the legality and legitimacy of Commission's actions, thereby contributing to the perceived deepening of the Union's democratic deficit.

Last but not least, the phenomenon of 'hardened' soft law instruments poses specific challenges to legal protection and review. Whereas the *Grimaldi* jurisprudence makes clear that indirect judicial review based on the preliminary ruling procedure is ensured with regard to Commission's soft law instruments,[116] not the same can be said about direct review under the annulment procedure based on Article 263 TFEU. The emphasis in Ar-

---

111 *Grimaldi* (n 4) .

112 *Dansk Rørindustri* (n 18) para 211.

113 See also Opinion of Advocate General Bobek (n 8) para 94.

114 See also Opinion of Advocate General Bobek (n 8) paras 92–93. In this regard, it is noticeable that in its jurisprudence concerning Commission's soft law, the CJEU has first determined whether the legal instrument under consideration was legally binding; if so, it then examined the competence of the Commission to adopt such a binding act (often concluding that the Commission did not have such a competence).

115 Van den Brink and Senden (n 19) 36–38. See also Meijers Committee, Standing committee of experts on international immigration, refugee and criminal law, Note on the use of soft law instruments under EU law, in particular in the area of freedom, security and justice, and its impact on fundamental rights, democracy and the rule of law (CM 1806 of 9 April 2018) available at <https://www.commissie-meijers.nl/sites/all/files/cm1806_note_on_soft_law_instruments.pdf> accessed in March 2019.

116 See Case C-16/16P (n 5) para 44 and the case law cited there.

ticle 263 TFEU on the intention 'to produce legal effects vis-à-vis third parties' and the explicit exclusion from the scope of review of recommendations and opinions, interpreted strictly by the Court of Justice,[117] makes it clear that direct legal review of EU soft law remains a thorny issue. This finding is further supported by the restrictive admissibility requirements regarding individuals under Article 263 TFEU.

VI. Better lawmaking through an argumentative 'toolbox'

The problematic 'hardening' phenomenon of EU (Commission) soft law instruments requires more than concern for the legal aspects pointed out in the previous section. In view of the remarkable increase of soft law instruments and the important practical and legal effects they produce, better lawmaking initiatives need to pay closer, if not special, attention to their functions and drafting. One way forward to solve the current perplexing and legally problematic ambiguity is to mark a sharper delineation between hard law (as legally binding and prescriptive) and soft law (as non-binding but highly persuasive) instruments. This could alleviate the legal problems and bring more clarity and coherence for the benefit of the Member States, citizens and businesses throughout the Union.

The various drafting sources currently available concern almost exclusively 'hard law' instruments, with few, sometimes even no reference,[118] to non-binding instruments. In the all too rare cases in which such references are made, instead of explaining and offering precise guidelines as to how such instruments should be formulated, those involved in drafting soft law instruments are negatively advised about what they should not do rather than about what they need to do to ensure clarity and preciseness. Despite real concerns and efforts for distinguishing between soft and hard law instruments in the drafting process, it transpires from practice that this is not always easy to achieve.[119]

This study has pointed out that the difference between hard and soft law instruments is not just a matter of expressing obligations hardly or softly. As long as an obligation is expressed, and particularly in combination with the explicit 'comply or explain' or 'comply or face legal conse-

117 Ibid, paras 38–43.

118 Remarkable cases of no such references are the *Joint Handbook for the presentation and drafting of acts subject to the ordinary legislative procedure* (2018) and the *Interinstitutional Style Guide* (2011).

119 Interview with the Legal Service (n 63).

quences' mechanisms, addressees are likely to interpret soft law instruments as not just politically, but also legally binding. Drafting manuals need to move from purely stylistic concerns (points instead of articles, *should* instead of *shall*, etc.) to more concrete substantive issues by recognizing the fundamental role of sound and persuasive argumentation in soft law instruments. Particularly in the current search for better EU governance, strong and sound arguments, as a way to transform soft law instruments from prescriptive tools resembling hard law into effective persuasive tools, are urgently needed. These are crucial for enhancing the degree of compliance with legally non-binding instruments. Instead of including such argumentation only in the preamble of soft law instruments as is currently the case, a situation which hardly differs from the case of hard law instruments, justificatory reasons need to be advanced throughout the instrument, pointing at the necessity, desirability and usefulness of the instrument.

There are at least four argumentative issues that require extensive attention in EU drafting guidelines. Firstly, the content of the argumentation should not mirror the content of hard law instruments, as exemplified by the case of recommendations and directives. The argumentative patterns characterizing hard and soft law must make it possible to distinguish between the different categories of instruments rather than just revealing commonalities. Secondly, the design of soft law instruments should make clear that no legally-binding obligations apply but rather persuasive suggestions for cooperation by addressees. Such design should also move beyond the oversimplified 'shall/should' distinction and encompass other expressions of modality[120] influencing the argument strength. Thirdly, the arguments in soft law instruments should be formulated in such a way as to ensure their effectiveness and increase their persuasive force. This should ideally result in enhanced compliance by addressees. Fourthly, the soundness of arguments in soft law instruments should be ensured by developing clear-cut criteria for reasonable argumentation. This could be done, for instance, by pointing at precise criteria that enable to avoid reasons that manipulate and induce compliance through fallacious means. Precise soundness criteria are urgently needed to identify, and consequently, avoid problems such as evasion of the burden of proof, unclear and ambiguous formulations, giving the impression of agreement between addressor and addressee when that is not the case, and other fallacious situations.

120 For a comprehensive list of expressions of modality indicating necessity, certainty, probability, etc. see A Rocci, *Modality in Argumentation* (Springer 2017).

VII. Conclusion

This chapter focused on the normative content as a key factor for delineating between EU soft and hard law instruments. It clarified the interplay between the normative content and other factors relevant for assessing the legal nature of EU legal instruments, such as form and context. It then identified the various criteria related to normative content and assessed their weight, warning about the misleading overreliance on the 'shall/should' modality language as a means to determine the genuine legal nature of EU legal acts. After discussing the normative content of exemplary Commission's soft law instruments that resemble closely hard law instruments, this chapter pointed at the concerns that such ambiguity causes in legal terms, as well as from the perspective of effectiveness and democratic legitimacy of EU action. In order to remedy this, the chapter emphasized the importance of clear and sound argumentation of soft law instruments as a way to mark a proper distinction from hard law instruments. In this respect, the chapter calls for an improvement of Union's lawmaking by proposing directions for better drafting that pays closer attention to the argumentative content of EU soft law instruments to restore legal certainty and enhance compliance by addressees.

Chapter 9: The Phenomenon of 'Directive-like Recommendations' and their Implementation: Lessons from Hungarian Legislative Practice

Petra Lea Láncos (Deutsches Forschungsinstitut für Öffentliche Verwalting Speyer and Péter Pázmány Catholic University, Budapest)

I. Introduction

On the basis of the laconic wording of Article 288 of the Treaty on the Functioning of the European Union (TFEU), directives are binding legal acts of harmonization, allowing some room for Member States to choose how to implement them, both formally and substantively. The national implementing measures are then notified to, and checked by the European Commission. According to the same article, recommendations by contrast are defined as non-binding measures. According to the case-law of the Court of Justice of the European Union (CJEU) recommendations are intended to aid interpretation, prepare legislation or achieve voluntary legal alignment.[1] By their very nature, it is up to the Member States to choose whether or not to follow them. Generally, no formal notification obligations are attached to recommendations, nor does the Commission consistently and regularly check Member States' laws for compliance with them.[2]

However, differentiations such as that set out above seem less clear cut when set against the reality of the diverse legal acts. Indeed, grey zones exist between the ideal types of legal measures, resulting in a spectrum where certain attributes of legal acts converge towards each other. In this spectrum, we find, for example, full-harmonization directives which resemble regulations and merely have to be reproduced in national law and promul-

1 Grimaldi (C-322/88) [1989] ECR 4407, Commission v. Lithuania (C-274/07) [2008] ECR I-7117, Ulrika Mörth: Soft Law and New Modes of EU Governance – A Democratic Problem? Paper presented in Darmstadt (November 2005), 16 et seq.; L Senden, Soft Law in European Community Law (Hart 2004) 457 et seq.

2 Senden (n 1) 321.

gated, or recommendations containing implementation deadlines, not unlike directives.[3]

This contribution focuses on the latter category of recommendations. It delineates the subset of Commission recommendations what may be called 'directive-like recommendations' (DLR) geared towards achieving harmonization through national implementing legislation, including provisions promoting implementation by the Member States. For the purposes of this paper, 'implementation' is used to refer to efforts on the national level to enact legislation fulfilling what is set forth in an EU recommendation. Starting from the observation that the attributes of DLRs strongly resemble those of directives, this contribution addresses the question whether differences between DLRs and all other 'classic' recommendations have consequences for the implementation of DLRs. In other words, does the perceived aspect of the 'enhanced normativity' of DLRs make implementation more likely and more similar to that of directives? Do government bodies involved in implementation afford special attention to the implementation of DLRs? What is the leeway such government bodies enjoy in implementing DLRs? And finally, does the national legislative practice regarding the implementation of DLRs provide any evidence for the added value of this specific type of soft law measure?

To answer these questions this contribution proceeds from the general to the specific. It first introduces the phenomenon of DLRs, then turns to the general question of a possible duty to implement recommendations, before making a specific analysis of their implementation at national level. It focuses on the harmonization efforts of the Hungarian Ministry of Justice for reasons of access, proposing that the general lessons learnt from the Hungarian example may yield insights regarding other national systems as well. However, it is clear that the findings of a study restricted to one national implementation system cannot claim generality. Therefore, the present study represents a first step in a more comprehensive research agenda to map the implementation of the specific measure of DLRs.

Unfortunately, the practical side of implementing EU recommendations has been paid scant attention in scholarly literature, with no empirical data available regarding the workings and considerations of national legislative bodies. Therefore, this contribution relies on the Hungarian positive law governing harmonization, and also on interviews with 4 ministerial officials whose day-to-day work is to manage implementation required under EU law. The interviewees were selected from the relevant depart-

3 Senden (n 1) 162–65.

ments of the major government bodies involved in implementing recommendations, i.e. Ministry of Justice and the Prime Minister's Office.[4] They were asked to describe the process, and their responsibilities and considerations in the implementation of recommendations, with a particular focus on DLRs. On the basis of the data gathered this contribution outlines the implementation practice followed by the government bodies involved in implementation in respect of DLRs and classic recommendations. Based on these insights gleaned from the implementation models formulated under the law and developed in the practice of the implementing government bodies, this contribution tries to answer the research questions outlined above, and also considers the possible added value of DLRs for implementation.

II. The spectrum between directives and recommendations

The TFEU sets out the main features of the different types of secondary legislation and soft law envisaged by the Treaties (Art. 288 TFEU). It provides that directives "shall be binding, as to the result to be achieved, upon each Member State to which it is addressed, but shall leave to the national authorities the choice of form and methods." Accordingly, the TFEU expressly refers to the implementation obligation of the Member States in respect of directives, while in the case of recommendations it merely stipulates that these "shall have no binding force". Differences between directives and recommendations, however, are not always as clear-cut as the laconic formulation of the Treaty suggests.

On the spectrum between directives and recommendations conforming to the classic type described by the TFEU are DLRs. These legal measures are described and adopted as recommendations, but they exhibit one or several features characteristic of directives. These features make them appear to be 'more' than simple recommendations by seemingly increasing their normativity.

In defining DLRs, this contribution departs from Senden's findings. She concedes that often recommendations will be restricted to specific cases without general scope,[5] striving to achieve closer cooperation, coordina-

4 The Legal Harmonization Department and the EU Legal Compliance Department of the Ministry of Justice, see below.

5 Senden (n 1) 162–63.

tion or a common approach in a given field.[6] However, in some cases, it is clear that recommendations are geared towards harmonization.[7] It is within the latter category that Senden identifies certain Commission recommendations as measures strongly resembling directives. To illustrate her point, Senden collected some DLRs from the area of financial regulation,[8] however, this type of Commission recommendation is not restricted to one specific policy field. In fact, DLRs appear in very different regulatory fields, with recent examples including gambling and the protection of minors, insolvency, collective redress.[9] Consequently, it seems that it is not only one DG of the Commission drafting DLRs in a specific regulatory area from time to time, but apparently several.

---

6 Robinson notes: Recommendations "are classic instruments of soft law whose use has been encouraged as part of efforts to reduce recourse to legislation at EU level. They may also be part of efforts to coordinate policies of the Member States in an area within the scope of the Treaties which may later lead to EU legislation." W Robinson, 'Legislative Training' in U Karpen and H Xanthaki, *Legislation in Europe – A comprehensive Guide for Scholars and Practitioners* (Hart 2017).

7 Senden (n 1) 166; L Blutman, *Az Európai Unió joga a gyakorlatban* (*The Law of the European Union in Practice*) (Hvg Orac 2014) 174.

8 Senden (n 1) 163, 167. Senden herself collected some examples for recommendations mimicking directives by referring to transposition deadlines and notification in the realm of financial regulation, such as Commission Recommendation (EEC) 87/63 concerning the introduction of deposit-guarantee schemes in the Community [1987] OJ L33/16–17; Commission Recommendation (EEC) 87/62 on monitoring and controlling large exposures of credit institutions [1987] OJ L33/10–15; Commission Recommendation (EEC) 88/590 concerning payment systems, and in particular the relationship between cardholder and card issuer [1988] OJ L317/55–58; Commission Recommendation (EEC) 90/109 on the transparency of banking conditions relating to cross-border financial transactions [1990] OJ L67/39–43; Commission Recommendation (EC) 97/489 concerning transactions by electronic payment instruments and in particular the relationship between issuer and holder [1997] OJ L208/52–58; Commission Recommendation (EC) 98/288 on dialogue, monitoring and information to facilitate the transition to the euro [1998] OJ L130/29–31.

9 Commission Recommendation of 14 July 2014 on principles for the protection of consumers and players of online gambling services and for the prevention of minors from gambling online (2014/478/EU) L 214/38–46; Commission Recommendation of 12 March 2014 on a new approach to business failure and insolvency (2014/135/EU) L 74/65–70; Commission Recommendation of 11 June 2013 on common principles for injunctive and compensatory collective redress mechanisms in the Member States concerning violations of rights granted under Union Law (2013/396/EU) L 201/60–65. A recent example for a DLR in financial regulation would be Commission Recommendation of 18 July 2011 on access to a basic payment account (2011/442/EU) L 190/87–91.

Senden argues that apart from their title as recommendation, the wording, the structure and the general nature of these recommendations make it difficult to distinguish them from hard law.[10] In particular, the wording of specific elements of DLRs seem to allude to directives, when referring to "supervision and reporting"[11] Meanwhile, it is also clear, that DLRs are "worded mainly in non-mandatory terms", employing terms such as "Member States are invited to", "should" etc.[12]

Commission recommendations are generally of 'external nature',[13] usually addressed to "the member states which are called upon to implement the recommendations by any necessary measures; legislative, administrative or otherwise. ... It is therefore the member states that must ensure that any other concerned parties apply the rules contained in the recommendation".[14] An important feature of these Commission recommendations is a section or provision on implementation. This may even include a deadline, effectively enshrining 'the desire of implementation'.[15] Meanwhile, the Commission may accompany such recommendations with a 'threat' to propose binding legislation in case implementation is untimely or insufficient.[16] And "finally, as a rule, the recommendations contain requests to inform the Commission of the implementation measures that have been

---

10 Senden (n 1) 164; K Géczi, 'A közigazgatási büntetőjog szabályozási anomáliái, különös tekintettel a pszeudo normák kérdéskörére' (*Regulatory anomalies of administrative criminal law with particular attention to the issue of pseudo norms*) (2009) 3 Jog – Állam – Politika 177, 181, 185.

11 Commission Recommendation of 12 March 2014 on a new approach to business failure and insolvency (2014/135/EU) L 74/70; Commission Recommendation of 11 June 2013 on common principles for injunctive and compensatory collective redress mechanisms in the Member States concerning violations of rights granted under Union Law (2013/396/EU) L 201/65.

12 See in detail: CJEU 25 October 2015, Case T-721/14, Belgium v Commission, paras 21–27. PL Láncos: Piercing the Soft Law Veil? The Hard Truth About Directive-like Recommendations (2018), <https://www.solar-network.eu/other-publication/lancos-petra-lea-piercing-the-soft-law-veil-the-hard-truth-about-directive-like-recommendations-2018/.

13 Senden (n 1) 162.

14 Ibid 164.

15 Ibid 349.

16 Ibid 164. Ortega sheds light on this practice through the example of Commission Recommendation (EC) 2005/737 on collective cross-border management of copyright and related rights for legitimate online music services [2005] OJ L276/PAGE?. He notes: "The Recommendation seems to be designed to flesh out the existing Directives on copyright in the Information Society and rental right and lending right and on certain rights relating to copyright. Given that its main aim is to encourage multi-territorial licensing and recommend how it should be regu-

taken and of any other action to comply with the recommendation in question. It seems that in most cases one could even speak of information and notification obligations in respect of these measures, given the mandatory way in which they are often formulated."[17]

According to those officials of the Commission working in the Legal Service who I interviewed, such implementation clauses are incorporated in recommendations where the competent Directorate General preparing the draft recommendation is of the view that the given measure is of particular importance. While the Commission is acutely aware of the fact that recommendations – including provisions on implementation deadlines and reporting are not binding – it nevertheless wishes to give particular emphasis to its desire that Member States follow what is set forth in the recommendation. In summary, although recommendations are not binding, this specific form of Commission recommendation raises "the expectation that it will be implemented and complied with, and its application monitored."[18] These characteristics, taken together, strongly resemble those of directives,[19] justifying the designation of this category as DLRs.

Differences between directives and recommendations regarding the Commission's role in monitoring implementation are key also for the stance of government bodies towards the implementation and 'notification' of recommendations. As Senden notes, the Commission sometimes evaluates and reports on the national implementation of certain soft law acts, "but this is not a general or consistent practice".[20] Yet DLRs differ from other recommendations in that they expressly refer to implementation, notification or monitoring, which shifts the focus onto the Member States' legislative response (or lack thereof).

---

lated, the Commission is putting particular policy options into effect. In doing so, it must be conscious that its position as the Community Executive and guardian of the Treaties, gives its recommendation authority above and beyond its status as a nonbinding act of Community law. Indeed, the Commissioner has stated publicly that 'if I am not satisfied that sufficient progress is being made, I will take tougher action'. This is tantamount to imposing sanctions for non-compliance with a non-binding act." MM Ortega, *Institutional and legal implications of the use of "soft law" instruments, European Parliament* (Working Document) Committee on Legal Affairs (14.2.2007), DT\653346EN.doc; 5.

17 Senden (n 1) 165.

18 Ibid 164.

19 See also: E Cannizzaro and E Rebasti, 'Soft law in the EU legal order' in J Iliopoulos-Strangas and JF Flauss (eds), *The Soft Law of European Organizations (SIPE)* (Nomos 2012) 208, 221.

20 Senden (n 1) 321.

III. Duties of government bodies involved in implementation of DLRs

For the purposes of this contribution it is not necessary to elaborate on the specific reasons underlying the regulatory choice of recommendation when in fact, the effects of a directive are desired.[21] but it is worth considering the effects of DLRs. The TFEU is very terse in this regard, yet it has been supplemented by the jurisprudence of the CJEU detailing the obligations of the Member States arising from recommendations.

In view of the non-binding, voluntary nature of recommendations, the CJEU has clarified that there is no general obligation of implementation or compliance by Member States.[22] In light of the *Grimaldi*[23] and the *European emergency number*[24] case law, however, it is clear that the non-binding nature of recommendations does not mean that they have absolutely no legal effect.[25] Indeed, while recommendations cannot require Member States to use a specific method of implementation, according to the jurisprudence of the CJEU, Member States *must consider the substance* of these recommendations. In light of the principle of sincere cooperation under Article 4(3) of the Treaty on European Union (TEU), it is not merely the courts and national authorities that are obliged to consider recommendations, but national legislators as well.[26] Accordingly, government bodies involved in implementation must also duly take account of the deadlines for implementation and reporting obligations set out in DLRs.

---

21 Senden provides a detailed list of the possible reasons why the Union legislator would choose to adopt a measure in the form of recommendation instead of a directive, even where the goal is to harmonize Member State law. These reasons include preparing for adopting hard law (pre-law function), providing an alternative to binding law where "there is no desire, need or room for legislation" (para-law function), the flexibility of soft law enabling rapid adaption in face of changing circumstances, consideration for the principles of subsidiarity and proportionality; ibid 168, see also: Cannizzaro and Rebasti (n 19) 225, 229; PC Müller-Graf, 'Das Soft Law der Europäischen Organisationen: Einführung' in J Iliopoulos-Strangas and JF Flauss (eds), *The Soft Law of European Organizations (SIPE)* (Nomos 2012) 138, 147. The para-law function of soft law is also captured by the Commission's commitment to reduce legislation and rather encourage voluntary alignment of national rules. European Commission, 'European Governance – A White Paper' (Communication) COM (2001) 428, point III.3.2.

22 Senden (n 1) 346; Cannizzaro, Rebasti (n 19) 222.

23 Case C-322/88 *Grimaldi* [1989] ECR 4407.

24 Case C-274/07 *Commission v Lithuania* [2008] ECR I-7117.

25 *Grimaldi* paras 16, 18.

26 Joined cases 51–54/71 *International Fruit* [1971] ECR 1107, para 3.

As Thürer expands in general with respect to soft law, "the principle of community loyalty gives rise to certain legal obligations, such as the duty to consider and make an effort to comply with soft law and not to act against it unless good reasons for doing so are set out."[27] This approach to the definition of national obligations under EU soft law measures includes the duty to take account of the measure and the general duty to abstain from steps jeopardizing the attainment of the goals set out soft law measures, with the caveat that departing from the EU measures is possible on legitimate grounds which the national legislator may have to expressly justify. On the part of the national legislator, these duties may involve regulatory, deregulation or justification tasks, respectively.[28]

While recommendations are *per se* non-binding, an issue to consider is whether DLRs are actually hard law instruments in the soft cloak of a recommendation. In other words, is it the form or the content of the soft law measure that must determine whether or not its provisions are binding? The most recent judgment rendered by the CJEU in this respect was C-16/16 P *Belgium v Commission*,[29] which explicitly dealt with the question whether an action for annulment may be brought under Article 263 TFEU against recommendations as non-binding instruments of EU law. In its judgment, the CJEU recalls that firstly, according to Article 263 TFEU, the Court is to "review the legality of legislative acts, of acts of the Council, of

---

27 D Thürer, 'The Role of Soft Law in the Actual Process of European Integration' in O Jacot-Guillarmod and P Pescatore (eds), *L'Avenir du libre-échange en Europe: vers un Espace économique européen?* (1990 Schultess Poligraphischer Verlag) 131, 134. While Cannizzaro and Rebasti sought to refute the relevance of the principle of sincere cooperation in creating obligations for the national legislator in respect of soft law based on Case 229/86 *Brother Industries v Commission* [1987] ECR 3758, 3763, in fact, the findings of that decision cannot be generalized for all soft law sources. Indeed, the *Brother Industries* case related to a memorandum which did not "ask the national authorities to make any specific decision ... but merely asks them to reach a decision on the basis of their own national legislation. Indeed, the position could not be otherwise having regard to the fact that an obligation on the Member States to adopt specific measures cannot be created by a Commission memorandum in the absence of a particular provision in the Treaty or in binding acts adopted by the institutions." Recommendations as Treaty-based soft law acts, often enacted in connection with binding acts of the institutions, requesting national authorities to adopt legislation of a specific content clearly differ from the measure at hand in the *Brother Industries* case.

28 C Andone and S Greco, 'Evading the Burden of Proof in European Union Soft Law Instruments: The Case of Commission Recommendations' [2018] 31 International Journal for Semiotic Law 79, 86.

29 Case C-16/16 P *Belgium v Commission* [2018] ECLI:EU:C:2018:79.

the Commission and of the European Central Bank, other than recommendations and opinions". Second, under Article 288 TFEU recommendations are expressly stated to have no binding force and, according to the CJEU rather confer on institutions a "power to exhort and to persuade, distinct from the power to adopt acts having binding force".[30]

However, as the CJEU explains, it may exceptionally be the case that an act adopted in the form of recommendation "by reason of its content, does not constitute a genuine recommendation".[31] Namely, objective criteria, such as the substance of the act, the context of its adoption and the powers of the institution adopting it may lead to the conclusion that the recommendation was in fact intended to have binding effects.[32] Such an assessment includes examining the wording, content and purpose of the recommendation.[33] In particular, it should be assessed whether it is drafted in more mandatory terms or in an essentially non-binding manner.[34] In C-16/16P the Court expressly refers to the fact that the recommendation at issue did "not include any explicit indication that the Member States *were required to adopt and to apply* the principles set out therein."[35] In fact, on the basis of an analysis of the wording, the content, the context and the intention of the act, the Court arrived at the conclusion that the recommendation at issue did not produce any binding legal effects and therefore could not be the subject of annulment proceedings. Consequently, it may be stated that the Court of Justice does not differentiate between classic recommendations and DLRs and does not recognise DLRs as having an 'enhanced' normative value.

It is now appropriate first to outline the main rules governing the system of legal harmonization in Hungary, with an attempt to draw up a model describing the general implementation procedure, and then to report on the procedures for the implementation of recommendations in the practice of the government bodies involved in implementation based on the findings of interviews with staff from those bodies.

---

30 Ibid, para 26.
31 Ibid, paras 26–29.
32 Ibid, paras 31–32.
33 Ibid, para 37.
34 Ibid, para 34.
35 Ibid, para 35; italics by me.

1. The system governing harmonization under Hungarian law

The Hungarian legislator guarantees compliance with implementation obligations under EU law through a host of decrees and explanatory guidelines governing the tasks entrusted to government bodies involved in implementation. The central piece of legislation in this regard is the Harmonization Decree setting out the procedure to be followed and the tasks of the different government bodies in the course of implementation.[36] In this procedure, the Ministry of Justice takes central stage, coordinating the implementation efforts of other government bodies and arranging for notification to the European Commission.

According to Article 82, paragraph 7, point (c) of the Decree on Government members' tasks[37] it is incumbent upon the Hungarian Minister of Justice to coordinate legal harmonization procedures by determining the system for programming legal harmonization, by operating a Harmonization Database comprising harmonization tasks and by overseeing harmonization activities. The system for programming legal harmonization was laid down in the Harmonization Decree. While legal harmonization tasks are loosely connected to the Government's half yearly legislative programme, they do not form an integral part of that programme.

Harmonization programming is based on so-called harmonization proposals drawn up in respect of all EU acts 'requiring' some form of legislative action.[38] This includes the mandatory drafting of harmonization proposals where it is foreseen under EU law, but also voluntary cases where the Hungarian legislator intends to harmonize.[39] Accordingly, the system set forth under the Harmonization Decree is applicable not only to the implementation of EU directives, but also to all other EU acts in respect of which the national legislator is obliged to – or chooses to – take legislative action. The Legal Harmonization Department of the Ministry of Justice is entrusted with the task of monitoring EU legislation and calling upon the competent ministry to prepare the necessary draft harmonization proposal.

---

36 Government Decree No. 302/2010 (XII. 23.) on the fulfilment of legislative preparatory tasks necessary for compliance with European Union law (*Harmonization Decree*).

37 Government Decree No. 152/2014 (VI. 6.) concerning the task and competence of the members of the Government.

38 Harmonization Decree, art 2 paras 1–2.

39 József Petrétei, 'Magyarország jogforrási rendszerének alapjai' (*Foundations of the Hungarian system of legal sources*) [2013] 2 Kodifikáció 5, 59–60.

Harmonization proposals are drafted by the competent minister responsible for preparing the relevant legislation ensuring harmonization. Where harmonization falls under the competence of several ministries, the harmonization proposal will be drafted by the minister whose administration was involved in formulating the negotiating position in respect of the relevant EU act.[40] The harmonization proposal is then prepared and submitted to the Minister in charge of the Prime Minister's Office, the Minister of Justice and the Minister for National Economy within 30 days of the promulgation of the EU act. However, in case of urgency, this deadline may be shorter in order to fulfil obligations related to implementation or the effective execution of EU law.[41] The harmonization proposal is finalized upon agreement by the competent ministries and the harmonization tasks defined therein are uploaded by the Legal Harmonization Department into the so-called Harmonization Database.

40 Harmonization Decree, art 3 para 1.
41 Harmonization Decree, art 3 paras 3–4.

Figure 1: Implementation model of the Harmonization Decree. Source: Author.

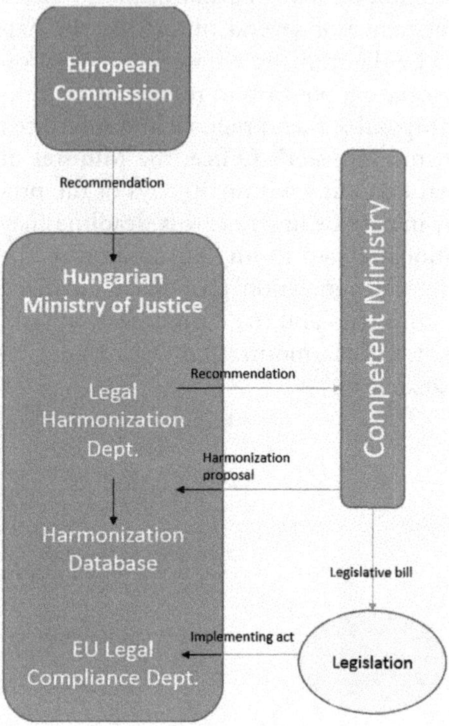

The Hungarian Ministry of Justice operates a database offering insight into the progress made in implementing EU legislation[42] since November 2005. The operation of the Harmonization Database (Harmonizációs Adatbázis) is now governed by the Harmonization Decree. Article 7 provides that the Minister of Justice is to record and publish in the database tasks pertaining to implementation as well as data related to draft legislation and final acts. While access to the full information published in the database is restricted, the Harmonization Database also has an open-access version, which features a more limited set of information. In the open-access version of the database search queries may be made with search words or data pertaining to the EU legal act, such as the CELEX number, type of act, its serial number or year of adoption. Results of search queries include the full data of

42 <https://jogharmonizacio.im.gov.hu/> accessed.

the EU act referred to and the status of the related national implementing tasks. This status may be 'completed' or 'open'. The so-called *completed legislative processes* are compiled on the basis of notifications (where available) and harmonization proposals referring to national legislation that already complies with the EU measure to be implemented or executed. *Open legislative processes* in the open-access version only refer to numerical data on the number of harmonization tasks agreed under the harmonization proposal by the competent ministries. In essence, the Harmonization Database is not a notification tool, but much rather a national instrument facilitating the coordination of harmonization tasks as well as ensuring the (restricted) transparency of the national legal system.

The competent ministry drafts the legislative bill which is then adopted according to the relevant national legislative procedure. Meanwhile, the EU Legal Compliance Department of the Ministry of Justice examines and gives opinions on legislative bills as regards their compliance with EU law with the help of correlation tables, to ensure that harmonization is carried out within the deadline foreseen.[43] According to the Decree on the drafting of laws[44] Hungarian legal acts adopted for harmonization purposes must carry a so-called *harmonization clause*. Harmonization clauses are not limited to acts implementing directives, but must be incorporated in all Hungarian acts harmonizing, executing or implementing EU law to ensure transparency within the Hungarian legal system. Such clauses indicate which EU measures the national act is intended to implement, execute or harmonize.[45] It is worth noting that the Decree formulates the obligation to attach a harmonization clause to national legislative acts with general effect, making no exceptions for soft law measures of the EU.[46]

Finally, the harmonization process ends with the notification phase. The Harmonization Decree differentiates between *notification* and *special notification*. Notification refers to the formal reporting of national implementing acts to the European Commission in the MNE-interface, the electronic notification system operated by the Commission. Such notification includes the transfer of harmonizing measures to the Commission, includ-

43 Harmonization Decree, art 6 paras 1, 3.

44 Decree No. 61/2009 (XII. 14.) of the Minister of Justice and Law Enforcement on the drafting of laws (*Decree on the drafting of laws*).

45 Ibid, arts 88–90.

46 Ibid, art 90 sets for the exceptional cases where no harmonization clause is required, these are: where implementation is carried out by means of a fundamental principle laid down in a comprehensive legal code, or where the legislative duty emanates from a decision of the CJEU.

ing the implementing act and correlation tables. The EU Legal Compliance Department has access to the MNE to upload national acts implementing directives, thereby fulfilling national notification obligations. Meanwhile, special notification covers all other "transfers of information, reports and other references to an institution of the European Union as prescribed by a Union legal act".[47]

The brief analysis of the relevant Hungarian legislation shows that the rules governing implementation are of a general nature and make no differentiation between directives and other legal acts, hard law or soft law. On that basis, recommendations should follow the implementation regime set out in the Harmonization Decree. However, as will be seen below, the regime for implementing recommendations does vary in practice.

2. *Implementation of recommendations: a mixed picture*

It is now appropriate to turn to the question of the national implementation of recommendations in practice, both classic recommendations and DLRs, attempting to sketch the model of their national implementation. The question to be answered is whether the legislator differentiates between classic recommendations and DLRs when deciding whether and how to implement them. Or with other words, are the similarities between DLRs and directives reflected in the implementation process?

To answer this question, officials of the Legal Harmonization Department and the EU Legal Compliance Department of the Hungarian Ministry of Justice were interviewed and the data obtained were compared with the statutory rules on harmonization described above. The interviews centered on the following questions: Does the Legal Harmonization Department treat recommendations in the same way as directives and send them on to the competent ministries? Does it differentiate between DLRs and classic recommendations? Does the EU Legal Compliance Department conduct special notification in respect of recommendations in general, or DLRs in particular? Why are not all implemented recommendations uploaded into the harmonization database?

As discussed earlier, the Legal Harmonization Department monitors EU legislation to identify possible legislative tasks of the government bodies involved in implementation. When faced with EU recommendations, unlike in the case of directives, the Department does not automatically have

47 Harmonization Decree, art 9.

to call upon competent ministries to take action. Indeed, it is left up to the Department staff to decide whether or not they consider the recommendation (be it a DLR or not) to give rise to 'legislative tasks'. This means that it is in the Department's discretion to specifically call the ministries' attention to certain recommendations. Accordingly, while the Legal Harmonization Department does not treat recommendations in the same way as directives, if it is of the opinion that legislative tasks 'may arise' from recommendations, it must forward the recommendations to the competent ministries.

When the Legal Harmonization Department decides to transfer the recommendation to the competent ministry *and* the latter puts forward a harmonization proposal, the implementation process must correspond to the general transposition model described above. Meanwhile, ministries monitoring EU legislation may concurrently decide that certain recommendations fall within their field of competence and that they wish to initiate implementing legislation. In this case, they either submit a harmonization proposal or they simply implement the recommendation without arranging for it to be entered into the Harmonization Database. Conversely, harmonization tasks related to recommendations must in practice be entered into the Harmonization Database if corresponding Hungarian legislation already exists. Hence, even if the legislator decides to implement a recommendation, there is not one single solution for managing the implementation of the recommendations.

Figure 2: Implementation model in government practice. Source: Author.

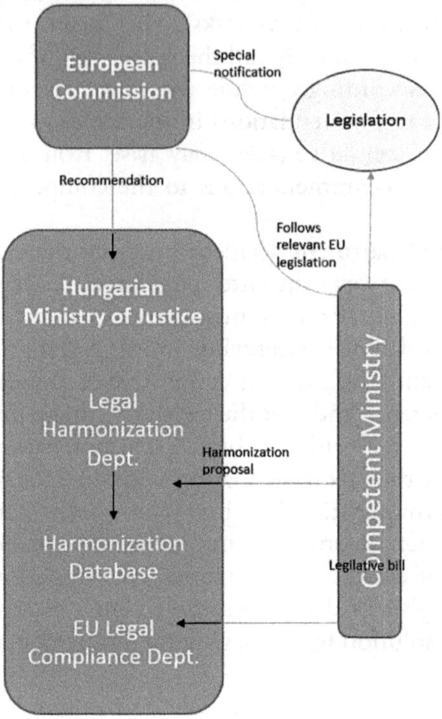

As indicated above, within the national legal order an important indicator of the EU origins of a norm and a tool for guaranteeing transparency is the harmonization clause. While the Guideline of the Ministry of Justice on harmonizing legislation has since been repealed, it sets out important points regarding inter alia the use of the harmonization clause. Although the Guideline is not enforceable, the Ministry of Justice calls the attention of government bodies involved in implementation to comply with these points if possible. In particular, point 128 of the Guideline expressly provides in respect of "national legislation related to recommendations" that it should include a harmonization clause with the wording "for compliance with ...", where the designation of the EU recommendation must be inserted.[48] However, the Guideline itself acknowledges, that "Member

48 Guideline No. 7001/2005. (IK 8.) of the Ministry of Justice, Official Gazette 2005/117/II.

States retain the right to introduce legislation corresponding to the issues regulated in the soft law measure without referring to the same." Indeed, in practice, this seems to be the norm, actually departing from the Decree on the drafting of laws.[49] This means that even if the legislator opts for the implementation of a recommendation, this will be difficult to track. With the rare exception of certain harmonization proposals regarding recommendations entered into the Harmonization Database, evidence for the fact that implementation took place is hard to find.

As far as notification is concerned, the implementation of EU recommendations does not fall under the notification obligation of the Member States. However, this specific communication between the Hungarian government bodies involved in implementation and the European Commission related to recommendations may come under the concept of special notification. Since special notification refers to conveying information to an EU institution as prescribed by an EU legal act, correspondence between ministry officials and the European Commission with respect to DLRs may be deemed a form of special notification. Special notification, i.e. communication between the European Commission and the government bodies involved in implementation regarding the EU measure will then take place 'informally', through electronic means. While the special notification is primarily handled by the EU Legal Compliance Department, competent ministries may also be directly involved in this communication alongside the Department.

The interview conducted with ministry officials and the model of national implementation practice revealed that, notwithstanding their directive-like characteristics, the implementation of DLRs is not more akin to the transposition of directives. In fact, the implementation of recommendations in general and DLRs in particular actually rather resembles the approach taken when adopting national measures for the execution of regulations.

IV. Outlook: Do directive-like recommendations have some added value?

As described above, DLRs bear some traits of both directives and recommendations, employing in varying combinations: strongly normative language, implementation deadlines, reporting duties of the government bodies involved in implementation and monitoring tasks of the European

49 Decree on the drafting of laws, arts 88–90.

Commission. The Commission relies on these directive-like characteristics for the perceived enhanced compliance pull of such recommendations. Although Member States do not consider such clauses to be binding, the Commission uses these elements to underline the desire for national implementation, channelling national efforts from the aspects of both timeliness and efficiency. By incorporating in the recommendation reporting duties the Commission lays the foundations for a streamlined communication between the Commission and the Member States regarding the implementation of the recommendation in question.

However, as the lessons from Hungarian legislative practice have shown, government bodies involved in implementation do not consider DLRs to be more binding than other recommendations. The implementation practices of Hungarian government bodies seem to demonstrate that even though DLRs are bolstered with features designed to promote implementation, on the national level, DLRs and classic recommendations are treated equally. While the European Commission seeks to reinforce the normativity of certain recommendations that are not merely intended as an interpretative aid but are meant to prompt substantive harmonization on the national level, government bodies undertaking implementation understand such measures as giving them full freedom to refrain from taking legislative action. It is apparent, that, in the view of the participating government bodies, the normativity of DLRs is not further boosted through provisions on implementation and reporting and they enjoy an absolute discretion in implementing them.

This perception of DLRs also explains the haphazard approach to their implementation and the absence of straightforward implementation procedures in their case. The Legal Harmonization Department of the Hungarian Ministry of Justice and the competent ministries all enjoy complete freedom in deciding whether or not the DLR gives rise to a need for legislative action on the national level. This non-systematic approach of Hungarian State bodies involved in implementing recommendations appears to be at odds with the *Grimaldi*[50] case-law of the CJEU, under which Member States, including the national legislator, are required to take recommendations into consideration. As such, the case may be made that the non-systematic approach followed in Hungary for considering the implementation of recommendations may be insufficient to guarantee *due consideration*. Nevertheless, even if the *Grimaldi* case-law calls for the taking into consideration of recommendations, there is nothing in the Treaty or the

---

50 *Grimaldi [Referred to in footnote 19?].*

CJEU case-law that suggests certain recommendations give rise to greater obligations on the part of the national legislator. Indeed, apart from the European Commission's clear intention to encourage implementation, neither the case-law of the CJEU nor the practice of Hungarian state bodies involved in implementation seem to suggest that DLRs should be given more weight in national implementation procedures than regular recommendations.

Since national courts and authorities are also bound to take recommendations into consideration,[51] the argument may be made that a failure to systematically indicate implementation by including a harmonization clause referring to the recommendation undermines the clarity and transparency of the legal system. Indeed, my brief survey of a handful of Hungarian judges' approach to EU recommendations revealed that due to their excessive case-load and time constraints, national judges rarely have the time to explore whether there are EU recommendations relevant to the case before them. Instead, they largely rely on the parties' pleadings, and consider only recommendations invoked by the parties. It is true, that harmonization clauses make it easier for national courts to identify applicable EU law, which they are bound to examine even where it is clear national implementation had taken place.[52] Nevertheless, the difficulties of national courts and authorities in identifying EU recommendations pertinent to their case does not allow for a conclusion that harmonization clauses should be attached to implemented recommendations. This is because national courts and authorities must take all EU recommendations into consideration, whether implemented or not, and irrespective of whether they are DLRs or classic recommendations.

Competent Hungarian bodies participating in the implementation process proceed non-systematically in respect of recommendations of any kind, giving rise to different models of implementation. While this may perhaps be criticized from an internal organizational point of view, this non-systematic approach is fully compliant with Member State obligations under EU law. Meanwhile, as discussed above, neither considerations relating to the clarity of the legal order, nor Member State duties under the principle of sincere cooperation and the *Grimaldi* case-law seem to substantiate that DLRs are more likely to be implemented than classic recommen-

51 H Grosse Ruse-Khan, T Jaeger and R Kordic, 'The Role of Atypical Acts in EU External Trade and Intellectual Property Policy' [2010] 4 EJIL 901, 909; Géczi (n 10) 188.

52 Blutman (n 7) 176.

dations. Indeed, in light of the Hungarian legislator's practice, the directive-like traits of DLRs do not give rise to a difference of treatment in the legislative process. As a result, it may be concluded that, based on the practice of national implementation, no added value of the DLR may be discerned as opposed to the form of classic recommendations.

Based on this finding, the general question may be formulated whether introducing elements intended to promote implementation by mimicking directives, such as deadlines, reporting and monitoring tasks, even makes sense in respect of soft law measures. Despite the acknowledged limitations regarding the general validity of findings of this study, the lessons from the Hungarian legislative practice nevertheless seem to demonstrate that incorporating implementation provisions in soft law measures does not serve any useful purpose. While further empirical studies focusing on implementation systems in other Member States must be conducted to ascertain the relevance of these findings for EU soft law in general, a growing body of literature suggests that in the case of soft law, the persuasion factor may be a greater incentive for national implementation than drawing on elements of hard law.[53]

53 See RA Payne, 'Persuasion, Frames and Norm Construction' [2001] 1 European Journal of International Relations 37, 40; F Amtenbrink and R Repasi, 'Compliance and Enforcement in Economic Policy Coordination in EMU' in: A Jakab and D Kochenov (eds), *The Enforcement of EU Law and Values* (OUP 2017), 145; Adone and Greco (n 28) 80.

Chapter 10: Multilevel consultation procedures at the EU level and their contribution in copyright law making

Nikos Koutras (University of Antwerp)

I. Introduction

Multilevel governance has moved beyond its European setting to become an established concept applied to a wide range of political and policy settings.[1] In addition, multilevel governance is the 'brainchild' of a period of optimism over the power of integration and the leading role of the Commission in transforming the European political order.[2] Multilevel governance approaches were first developed to consider the increasing complexity and dispersion of power amongst different levels of public institutions through the development of the European Union.[3] The multilevel governance landscape is evolving rapidly through the settlement of public consultation that is producing a new dissemination of power. Scholars argue that public consultation has pros with a potential for public good (e.g. a two-way flow of information and opinion exchange between civil society and governments).[4]

The public consultation on the review of the European copyright regulations held between 5 December 2013 and 5 March 2014 is examined, in this respect. The consultation covered a broad range of issues identified in the European Commission's communication concerning the content in

---

1 Thierry Rodon, '"Working Together": The Dynamics of Multilevel Governance in Nunavut' (2017) 5 Arctic Review <https://arcticreview.no/index.php/arctic/article/view/1048> accessed 18 July 2018..

2 George Pagoulatos and Loukas Tsoukalis, 'Multilevel Governance' [2012] The Oxford Handbook of the European Union..

3 Knud Erik Jørgensen, *Reflective Approaches to European Governance* (Springer 2016)..

4 Isabel Brusca and Juan Carlos Martínez, 'Adopting International Public Sector Accounting Standards: A Challenge for Modernizing and Harmonizing Public Sector Accounting , Adopting International Public Sector Accounting Standards: A Challenge for Modernizing and Harmonizing Public Sector Accounting' (2016) 82 International Review of Administrative Sciences 724..

the Digital Single Market (DSM)[5] i.e.: 'territoriality in the Internal Market, harmonization, limitations and exceptions to copyright in the digital age, fragmentation of the European copyright market, ways to improve the effectiveness and efficiency of enforcement while underpinning its legitimacy in the wider context of copyright reform'. The objective of the public consultation was to collect input from all stakeholders regarding the European Commission' opinion on the European copyright regulations.

The process of public consultation determines a tool based on which a society is invited (i.e. individuals, stakeholders, actors and institutions) to participate.[6] In other words, public consultations incentivize different societal layers to get involved in discussions which should be considered before start drafting policies.[7] *Ipso facto* the public consultation is distinguished from a multilevel approach which is also pluralistic. Therefore, by integrating the multilevel approach to public consultation there is potential to produced added value and benefit copyright policy makers. Hence, the added value could be more comprehensive as different societal layers are involved. And this in turn could be also effective in the context of relevant policies applied in the Member States.

In the light of the abovementioned rationale, it should be mentioned that it would be helpful to share and exchange good practices and recommendations among the Member States when a national regulation is efficient and stems from a multilayer perspective given from a multilevel consultation.

Hence, the previous discussion shows that there is potential to create a dynamic of an 'integrated approach' towards further political integration in Europe, a pending European priority. The scheme of multilevel consultations involves the dynamic of comprehensive solutions for European Member States and indicates whether multilevel governance should be promoted. Further consideration of the discussion about multilevel governance and its importance for Europe, follows below.

---

5 Mirela Mărcuţ, *Crystalizing the EU Digital Policy: An Exploration into the Digital Single Market* (Springer 2017)..

6 Rhion Jones and Elizabeth Gammell, *The Politics of Consultation* (CreateSpace Independent Publishing Platform 2018)..

7 Penny Norton and Martin Hughes, *Public Consultation and Community Involvement in Planning: A Twenty-First Century Guide* (Taylor & Francis 2017)..

II. Literature review

The reallocation of authority downwards, upwards and sideways from states has also captured the attention from an increasing number of scholars in political sciences.[8] Since 2014, the concept of multilevel governance was introduced as a guiding principle regarding all levels of government in policy design, helping to learn from each other, share best practices and further develop participatory democracy.[9]

Officially, it was adopted by the Committee of the Regions (CoR) on 3 April 2014 and supported by the Congress of Local and Regional Authorities of the Council of Europe through the Charter for Multilevel Governance. Additionally, it demonstrates a political manifesto from European cities and regions inviting all public authorities to make 'multilevel governance' a reality in day-to-day policymaking and delivery. This primarily involves working in partnership between the different levels of government (local, regional, national and European) and applying a set of principles that should guide efficient policymaking, such as participation, cooperation, openness, transparency, inclusiveness and policy coherence, all of which are essential conditions to guarantee the success of public policies in the interest of the citizens.

Given this, multilevel consultation is a tool that stems from multilevel governance. Although multilevel consultations constitute a significant part of the activities of the European Commission from a policy-shaping perspective,[10] they have not been systematically examined for their potential to improve copyright governance. In other words, multilevel consultation is likely to better participation from a multilayer governance perspective.

---

8 Edella Schlager and Christopher M Weible, 'New Theories of the Policy Process' (2013) 41 Policy Studies Journal 389; Felix Berenskoetter, *Concepts in World Politics* (SAGE 2016)..

9 Carlo Panara, *The Sub-National Dimension of the EU* (Springer International Publishing 2015)..

10 DeWayne Kurpius, 'Consultation Theory and Process: An Integrated Model' (2012) 56 The Personnel and Guidance Journal 18..

III. Public consultation as process: conceptual foundations

The participation of civil society in the legislative process is often established via the form of public consultation.[11] In contemporary times, the process of public consultation that increases stakeholders' participation constitutes a common practice in Europe.[12]

Indeed, public consultation mechanisms constitute a significant part of the activities of the European Commission from policy-shaping prior to a proposal to final implementation of a measure by the legislature and implementation on Member-State level.[13] In accordance with issues at stake, consultation is intended to provide opportunities for input from representatives of regional and local authorities, civil society organizations, the individual citizens concerned, academics and technical experts.[14]

The public consultation process has pros as well as cons.[15] Its central aim is to encourage the public to have meaningful input into the decision-making process.[16] Public participation thus provides the opportunity for communication among decision-making agencies and the public. Exchanging views could be an early warning system for public concerns, a means through which accurate and timely information can be disseminated and can contribute to sustainable decision-making.[17] Additionally, it establish-

---

11 Patrizia Nanz and Jens Steffek, 'Global Governance, Participation and the Public Sphere' (2004) 39 Government and Opposition 314; Jens Steffek and Maria Paola Ferretti, 'Accountability or "Good Decisions"? The Competing Goals of Civil Society Participation in International Governance' (2009) 23 Global Society 37..

12 Barbara Finke, *Civil Society Participation in EU Governance* (CONNEX / NEWGOV 2007); W Robert Lovan, Michael Murray and Ron Shaffer, *Participatory Governance: Planning, Conflict Mediation and Public Decision-Making in Civil Society* (Routledge 2017)..

13 Kurpius (n 10)..

14 Keith Culver and Paul Howe, 'Calling All Citizens: The Challenges of Public Consultation' (2004) 47 Canadian Public Administration 52; Christine Quittkat, 'The European Commission's Online Consultations: A Success Story?' (2011) 49 JCMS: Journal of Common Market Studies 653; Daniel Pop and Roxana Radu, 'Challenges to Local Authorities under EU Structural Funds: Evidence from Mixed Quasi-Markets for Public Service Provision in Romania' (2013) 51 JCMS: Journal of Common Market Studies 1108..

15 Fred A De Laat, Bart van Heerebeek and Jaap J van Netten, 'Advantages and Disadvantages of Interdisciplinary Consultation in the Prescription of Assistive Technologies for Mobility Limitations' [2018] Disability and Rehabilitation. Assistive Technology 1..

16 Birkland, *Introduction to the Policy Process* (ME Sharpe 2015)..

17 Denis Bouyssou and others, *Decision Making Process: Concepts and Methods* (John Wiley & Sons 2013)..

es an efficient way to collect experiences and opinions from citizens, key stakeholders and experts, in order to get a comprehensive overview of what obstacles persist and of their impact on the daily lives of people and businesses in Europe. Yet, consultations often only reach industry while they do not invite for participation by relevant stakeholders.[18] Research established that not only industry mostly responds, but also old Member States.[19] Few obstacles along the process, such as planning problems and time efficiency can be overcome by adequate coordination between the European institutions and Member States via multilevel governance therefore the role of public consultation is crucial.

IV. Multilevel governance: A conceptual analysis

The term governance has numerous concepts and principles associated with it. Weiss defines "global governance" as "collective efforts to identify, understand or address worldwide problems that go beyond the capacity of individual States to solve".[20] He asserts that global governance may be defined as "the complex of formal and informal institutions, mechanisms, relationships, and processes between and among States, markets, citizens and organizations, both inter and non-governmental, through which collective interests on the global plane are articulated, rights and obligations are established, and differences are mediated".[21]

In analogy with the definition of global governance, European Governance is characterized as a system of rules and institutions established by the European Community and private actors to manage political, economic and social affairs. The basic principles guiding European Governance, legally anchored in the Treaties, are democracy, social equity, human rights and the rule of law. These need to be reflected in institutions, rules

---

18 Christine Quittkat and Beate Kohler-Koch, *Involving Civil Society in EU Governance: The Consultation Regime of the European Commission* (Oxford University Press 2013)..

19 Jenny Stewart, *The Dilemmas of Engagement: The Role of Consultation in Governance* (ANU E Press 2009); Nathaniel Copsey and Tim Haughton, 'The Choices for Europe: National Preferences in New and Old Member States*' (2009) 47 JCMS: Journal of Common Market Studies 263..

20 Thomas G Weiss, *Thinking about Global Governance: Why People and Ideas Matter* (Taylor & Francis 2012)..

21 Thomas G Weiss, *Global Governance: Why? What? Whither?* (John Wiley & Sons 2016)..

and political systems and to be respected by all sectors of society at various levels of governance, through the lens of multilevel governance.[22]

The concept of multilevel governance is attached to the study of European integration in the nineties (e.g. Maastricht Treaty and its subsidiary principle) and the concept of decentralization.[23] The study of the European Union has been characterized by two development phases: the first one was dominated by international relations studies: the EU seen as an international organization, very much alike others (e.g. NATO, OECD, UN); in the second phase by public policies studies: the European Union seen as a unique international organization.[24]

The multilevel governance concept gives a more constructed 'shape' to the political system of the European Union with interconnected institutions that exist at multiple levels with unique policy features.[25] It contributes to the 'whole of government' approach' mentioned above. The European Union is a political system characterized by a European layer (i.e. European Commission, European Council and European Parliament, etc.), a national and a regional layer. These layers interact with each other in two ways: first, across different levels of government (vertical dimension) and second, with other relevant actors within the same level (horizontal dimension).[26]

In addition, multilevel governance serves the fundamental political objectives of the European Union: a Europe of citizens, economic growth and social progress, sustainable development, and the role of the European Union as a global actor.[27] It reinforces the democratic dimension of the European Union and increases the efficiency of the applicability of the European Union policies because it rarely applies symmetrically or homogenously.[28]

Between multi-level governance and other integration theories there are some differences and the main one is that it breaks the grey zone between

---

22 Committee of the Regions, 'The Committee of the Regions' White Paper on Multilevel Governance'..

23 Dr Yannis A Stivachtis, *The State of European Integration* (Ashgate Publishing, Ltd 2013) 107–110..

24 Mark Gilbert, *European Integration* (Rowman & Littlefield Publishers 2017)..

25 Ian Bache, *Europeanization and Multilevel Governance: Cohesion Policy in the European Union and Britain* (Rowman & Littlefield Publishers 2007)..

26 Dermot Hodson and John Peterson, *The Institutions of the European Union* (Oxford University Press 2017)..

27 Lea Pfefferle, *The EU - A Global Player?* (GRIN Verlag 2012)..

28 Erik Oddvar Eriksen and John Erik Fossum, *Rethinking Democracy and the European Union* (Routledge 2013)..

intergovernmentalism and supranationalism leaving in its place a descriptive structure. Further, multi-level governance does not address the sovereignty of states directly, but instead simply states that a multi-level structure is being created also by sub-national and supranational actors. The discussion below considers the contribution of multilevel governance to the European integration which demonstrates the central objective for Europe.[29]

1. *Multilevel governance and the European Union*

Since the emergence of the European integration, there has been a lot of discussion about both the underlying dynamics of the integration process and the nature of the emerging political system.[30] With the two most important opposing schools of thought, neofunctionalism and intergovernmentalism, earlier discussion focused on the process of integration and the final aim of the integration project.[31] However, in the aftermath of the speeding-up of the integration process with the Single European Act (1986) and Maastricht Treaty (1992), the focus of European studies has altered from aims and dynamics of the integration process to description and analysis of the actual day-to-day workings of the political system of Europe.[32]

The 'governance' turn in studies about Europe (hereinafter EU studies) has been accompanied by an opening up of this area of studies to a number of sub-disciplines of political science and public administration and to a development of new strands of research on the European Union.[33] Since then, numerous studies have addressed issues that had previously not been

29 Maurizio Carbone, *National Politics and European Integration: From the Constitution to the Lisbon Treaty* (Edward Elgar Publishing 2010)..

30 Robert Thomson, *Resolving Controversy in the European Union: Legislative Decision-Making before and after Enlargement* (Cambridge University Press 2011); K Milzow, *National Interests and European Integration: Discourse and Politics of Blair, Chirac and Schröder* (Springer 2012)..

31 Ilyas Saliba, *Neofunctionalism vs Liberal Intergovernmentalism: Are the Theories Still Valid Today?* (GRIN Verlag 2010); Borzel Tanja, *The Disparity of European Integration: Revisiting Neofunctionalism in Honour of Ernst B. Haas* (Routledge 2013)..

32 Klaus H Goetz and Simon Hix, *Europeanised Politics?: European Integration and National Political Systems* (Routledge 2012)..

33 Pamela M Barnes and Thomas C Hoerber, *Sustainable Development and Governance in Europe: The Evolution of the Discourse on Sustainability* (Routledge 2013)..

investigated, such as the impact of the European Union on the Member States, and legitimacy in Europe.

It follows that local and regional governments are effectively part of the European multilevel governance.[34] Firstly, sub-national layers are directly connected with the policy process in the area of regional policy, albeit the opportunities to shape different stages of policy vary from country to country.[35] Secondly, the Treaty of Maastricht established the Committee of Regions hence local and regional governments are formally part of the European decision-making framework.[36] Thirdly, many European policies have a direct impact on the tasks of sub-national governments (e.g. in the areas of public environment).[37] Literature with regard to European studies now are high up on the research agenda of comparative political science.[38]

They reflect two types of multilevel governance which provide a set of principles towards a more concrete interpretation of the European political system.[39] The first tradition adopts a state-centered view and argues that, like other international organizations, the EU should be treated as a forum of cooperation for Member States to enhance their problem-solving capacities.[40] Based on this type, multilevel governance pursues to construct a theory of how the distribution and functioning of political authority in the world have been and are being reshaped. This type of multilevel governance theory would highlight above all the changing role and relevance of the traditional nation-state. Accordingly, multilevel governance would be

---

34 Markus Perkmann, 'Policy Entrepreneurship and Multilevel Governance: A Comparative Study of European Cross-Border Regions' (2007) 25 Environment and Planning C: Government and Policy 861; George C Homsy and Mildred E Warner, 'Cities and Sustainability: Polycentric Action and Multilevel Governance' (2015) 51 Urban Affairs Review 46..

35 Nicholas Charron, Lewis Dijkstra and Victor Lapuente, 'Regional Governance Matters: Quality of Government within European Union Member States' (2014) 48 Regional Studies 68..

36 Thomas Christiansen and Simon Duke, *The Maastricht Treaty: Second Thoughts after 20 Years* (Routledge 2016)..

37 Philip Lynch and others, *Reforming the European Union : From Maastricht to Amsterdam* (Routledge 2014); Helen Wallace, Mark A Pollack and Alasdair R Young, *Policy-Making in the European Union* (Oxford University Press 2015)..

38 Theofanis Exadaktylos and Claudio M Radaelli, *Research Design in European Studies: Establishing Causality in Europeanization* (Palgrave Macmillan 2012)..

39 Ian Bache, *Europeanization and Multilevel Governance: Cohesion Policy in the European Union and Britain* (Rowman & Littlefield 2008)..

40 Pagoulatos and Tsoukalis (n 2)..

located among those international relations paradigms that have examined the transformations of the state-centric system over the past few decades.[41]

However, the growing body of research does not mean that it has been easy to come to grips with analyzing the political system of the European Union.[42] Considerable disagreement exists regarding the question of how to conceive the European Union.[43] Without doing much injustice to the more nuanced and detailed arguments that can be found in the literature, two broad lines of argument can be distinguished.

This sort of multilevel governance theory would be best built on a broad and abstract definition of the concept, which includes Europe as the vanguard of the political changes just described but goes beyond the European Union to capture these phenomena of political transformation in their global dimension.[44] This theory would also pay more attention to the structural dimension of multilevel governance than to its processes, in the first place due to its primary focus on the state and its loss of authority and functions in the international order, but also for the practical need to embrace and analyze a vast range of areas and empirical phenomena. Finally, and for analogous reasons, this type of theory would prioritize the study of public and territorial levels of governance over the analysis of non-state actors.[45]

The second type of multilevel governance pursues to clarify the making and implementation of public policy.[46] This is a more concrete variant of multilevel governance theory with less focus on the historical break with the Westphalian order than on the actual working of political and admin-

41 Tiziana Caponio and Michael Jones-Correa, 'Theorising Migration Policy in Multilevel States: The Multilevel Governance Perspective' (2018) 44 Journal of Ethnic and Migration Studies 1995..

42 Eriksen and Fossum (n 28)..

43 Søren Dosenrode, *The European Union after Lisbon: Polity, Politics, Policy* (Routledge 2016) 7–10, 157–159..

44 Frank H Aarebrot, *The Handbook of Political Change in Eastern Europe* (Edward Elgar Publishing 2014) 1–12; Maria T Grasso, *Generations, Political Participation and Social Change in Western Europe* (Routledge 2016) 13–25..

45 Dominic Stead, 'The Rise of Territorial Governance in European Policy' (2014) 22 European Planning Studies 1368; Natal'ya V Buley and others, 'Public Administration and Municipal Governance and Its Significance for a Modern Democratic Society' (2016) 6 International Journal of Economics and Financial Issues 220; Bob Jessop, 'Territory, Politics, Governance and Multispatial Metagovernance' (2016) 4 Territory, Politics, Governance 8..

46 Christopher Alcantara, Jörg Broschek and Jen Nelles, 'Rethinking Multilevel Governance as an Instance of Multilevel Politics: A Conceptual Strategy' (2016) 4 Territory, Politics, Governance 33..

istrative frameworks.[47] The main questions of this theoretical model would be how multilevel governance frameworks function day by day.[48]

This type of multilevel governance should be built by combining existing partial theoretical and empirical considerations of a coherent system covering several interrelated subjects. First, the origins and dynamics of political mobilization around policy concerns, with reference to those phenomena that are more specific to multilevel governance, such as subnational lobbying and the formation of political alliances (e.g. sectoral boundaries and the divide between public and private).[49] Second, the formulation, territorial structuring and temporal advancement of multilevel polices.[50] Finally, this variant of multilevel governance theory should comprise causal propositions on the mode and content of policy implementation.[51]

In the light of this scenario, the second type of multilevel governance theory would stand in the list of theories with a potential to play a critical role in the field of public policy.[52] Scholars argue that such theories could be associated with multilevel governance. This is, for example, the case of European policy subsystems and policy networks involved in public consultation concerning the review of copyright regulations review in Europe examined in this chapter.[53]

European policy networks play a central role in the formulation, deliberation, and implementation of European policies and have, thus, become objects of investigation in a fast-growing scholarly literature.[54] In a long-term perspective, the review accumulates different copyright stakeholders'

---

47 Robbie Waters Robichau and Laurence E Lynn Jr, 'The Implementation of Public Policy: Still the Missing Link' (2009) 37 Policy Studies Journal 21..

48 Homsy and Warner (n 34)..

49 Seong-Jin Choi, Nan Jia and Jiangyong Lu, 'The Structure of Political Institutions and Effectiveness of Corporate Political Lobbying' (2014) 26 Organization Science 158..

50 Elodie Fabre and Wilfried Swenden, 'Territorial Politics and the Statewide Party' (2013) 47 Regional Studies 342..

51 Donald P Moynihan and Joe Soss, 'Policy Feedback and the Politics of Administration' (2014) 74 Public Administration Review 320; Jens Newig and Tomas M Koontz, 'Multi-Level Governance, Policy Implementation and Participation: The EU's Mandated Participatory Planning Approach to Implementing Environmental Policy' (2014) 21 Journal of European Public Policy 248..

52 William N Dunn, *Public Policy Analysis* (Routledge 2015)..

53 Tanja A Börzel and Karen Heard-Lauréote, 'Networks in EU Multi-Level Governance: Concepts and Contributions' (2009) 29 Journal of Public Policy 135..

54 Michael Blauberger and Berthold Rittberger, 'Conceptualizing and Theorizing EU Regulatory Networks' (2015) 9 Regulation & Governance 367..

opinion and aims to contribute in enhanced regulation. Such regulation could be associated with 'better regulation'. Here, the concept of 'better regulation' refers to the innovations of governance that traces down the lifecycle of regulations and laws.[55] The following section discusses the concept of 'better regulation' and its implications with multilevel consultations.

2. *Innovations in governance: towards 'better regulation'*

Multilevel consultations could be considered as an additional tool towards further innovations in governance. Such perception comes from the notion to manage the regulatory state by adapting a 'whole of government' approach, from the primary stage of policy formulation to implementation. Give this, multilevel consultation could also contribute to the idea of innovations in governance, often addressed as 'better regulation' which was first introduced via a White Paper on Governance[56] and an expert group report.[57] Scholars argue that multilevel consultation affects the way in which rules are assessed before adoption, how stakeholders intervene in rulemaking, how the executive and parliaments should appraise the evidence-base of policy proposals, down to the level of inspections and enforcement.[58] This statement indicates that the rationale of 'better regulation' is well-aligned with the ideal objective for public consultation. In other words, involved participants (i.e. stakeholders) should have a word in the policy formulation, rulemaking, rules adoption and enforcement.

Proponents of the 'better regulation' scheme argue that its aim is threefold: a) to change governance and law-making processes by increasing the role of evidence in public decision making and by creating opportunities for affected interests to be consulted at an early stage, when options are being devised, b) to increase competitiveness by minimizing regulatory burdens and providing efficient regulations, and c) to address the legitimacy problems of the regulatory state by improving on procedures. Such three-

---

55 Claudio M Radaelli and Anne CM Meuwese, 'Better Regulation in Europe: Between Public Management and Regulatory Reform' (2009) 87 Public Administration 639..

56 European Commission, *COM(2001) 428 Final: European Governance : A White Paper* (2001)..

57 Mandelkern Group, 'Mandelkern Group on Better Regulation Final Report' (2001)..

58 Paul Cairney, *The Politics of Evidence-Based Policy Making* (Springer 2016)..

fold approach is a timely topic that could be adopted in the formulation of the European copyright regime.

The copyright regulations review determines a topic which has been debated in large.[59] This review could contribute in the discussion about innovations in governance towards a better copyright regulated framework for Europe. Multilevel consultation will contribute to good governance as it provides legitimacy by involving all stakeholders at all levels of governance. In particular, it should be examined i) whether all types of stakeholders were reached and not only industry; ii) whether all levels in the multilevel governance system participated and not just the old Member States; and iii) whether this has impacted on the final draft of the directive. Hence, relevant discussion follows in the next section.

V. Scientific consideration of the review on the European copyright regulations

The European copyright reform package determines a case where multilevel consultation has been applied. The objective of this multilevel consultation was to gather input from all stakeholders on the Commission's review of the European copyright rules. This chapter investigates whether multilevel consultations have the potential to improve copyright governance based on the public consultation conducted between 5 December 2013 and 5 March 2014.

In accordance with issues at stake, multilevel consultations are intended to provide opportunities for input from representatives of regional and local authorities, civil society organizations, the individual citizens concerned, academics and technical experts. It is worthy to notice that the multilevel perspective is founded via the stakeholders which were invited to participate from different Member States (see Annex 1). It should also be mentioned that among these responses there were respondents from European Member States which entered the European Union during the last decade (i.e. Slovakia 2004, Slovenia 2004, Latvia 2004, Hungary 2004, Estonia 2004, Bulgaria, 2007, Romania 2007 and Croatia 2013). Evidently,

---

59 Christophe Geiger, Oleksandr Bulayenko and Giancarlo F Frosio, 'Opinion of the CEIPI on the European Commission's Copyright Reform Proposal, with a Focus on the Introduction of Neighbouring Rights for Press Publishers in EU Law' (Social Science Research Network 2016); Víctor Rodríguez-Doncel and others, 'Legal Aspects of Linked Data – The European Framework' (2016) 32 Computer Law & Security Review 799; V Benabou and others, 'General Opinion on the EU Copyright Reform Package'..

the copyright regulations review does not only consider the 'old' Member States, but it also concerns 'younger' Member States.[60] It follows that there is quite a fair share of each type of stakeholder as there is representation from all Member States (see the Annexes below). Therefore, it is a clear result that gives evidence that the consultation allows a balancing of all interests.

Additionally, a more comprehensive picture is given through the different type of respondents involved in the consultation process. In fact, thorough analysis of the participants' origins involved (i.e. 6915 in total) illustrates that all the European Member States were involved (see Annex 2). Though, from a different layer of governance as of different type of response (i.e. as end-users, institutional users, authors, publishers, service providers, public authorities and collective management organizations).

In this context, information archiving, preserving and disseminating and relevant licensing regimes should be considered. This section interprets the results of the questionnaire used for the public consultation on the review of the European copyright regulations. Particularly, the section interprets responses on questions related to research (i.e. Questions 47 to 49). There is special focus on the field of research as the undersigned author currently investigates whether open access could be integrated to the European copyright framework in order to efficiently produce, disseminate and preserve scientific information. This in turn will enhance the scholarly scientific communication. Therefore, it is significant to examine responses by actors involved in the scholarly publishing research cycle. Hence, their perspectives should be considered in the designation of copyright regulations.[61] In particular:

a) End users/ consumers
b) Institutional users
c) Authors/ Performers
d) Publishers/ Producers/ Broadcasters and
e) Service Providers/ Intermediaries

---

60 Marc Arbyn and others, 'The Challenges of Organising Cervical Screening Programmes in the 15 Old Member States of the European Union' (2009) 45 European Journal of Cancer 2671; Copsey and Haughton (n 19)..

61 Robert K Yin, *Qualitative Research from Start to Finish, Second Edition* (Guilford Publications 2015)..

Examination of the questionnaire section about the 'research exception'

This section concerned the research exception set out in Article 5(3)(a) of the InfoSoc Directive and was intended to gather respondents' experiences of the use of copyright protected works in the context of research projects, including across borders, and their views on how problems, if identified, should be solved.

End users/consumers

Here, the terms end users or consumers refer to researchers. Researchers are generally unsatisfied with the current situation. Even though a research exception exists in some Member States, respondents still report problems in accessing scientific publications or scholarly articles.

Students and researchers highlight that access to the greatest possible range of academic publications is key for the completeness and accuracy of their research.[62] They indicate not being able to access online certain material they would need for their academic work. Some respondents consider that the more reputable and high-quality scientific journals are usually those making access to their content more difficult, through 'paywall' restrictions. The cost of subscriptions is seen as disproportionate and excessive for individual researchers.

Researchers consider that this situation is particularly difficult to accept in the case of publicly-funded research. They believe that publications which present the results of publicly funded research should always be made available without restriction.

Most respondents consider that open access publishing is a suitable solution to increase access to research content. They mention in this context some examples of open access archives and networks. At the same time, many respondents argue that there are barriers that prevent open access from working in an optimal way and consider that open access should be better supported. It is also mentioned that open access journals are sometimes considered to be not very prestigious or have low citation index

62 Ana Maria Ramalho Correia and José Carlos Teixeira, 'Reforming Scholarly Publishing and Knowledge Communication: From the Advent of the Scholarly Journal to the Challenges of Open Access' (2005) 29 Online Information Review 349; Ana Maria Ramalho Correia and José Carlos Teixeira, 'Reforming Scholarly Publishing and Knowledge Communication' [2013] Online Information Review..

scores, making it less attractive to publish in such a journal. A problem often raised by researchers is that scientific publishers often require that they (as authors of scientific publications) agree upon unduly restrictive contract conditions, for example that their work cannot be put in open access databases.

In the context of this discussion the opinion by twenty-five leading European research centers on the proposed directive, part of the European copyright regulations review, should be considered. Within an open letter addressed to Members of the European Parliament and the Council of the European Union by these research centers, a scientific consensus is identified. Specifically, the proposed exception for text-and-data-mining in Art. 3 will not achieve its goal to stimulate innovation and research if restricted to certain organizations. Additionally, the proposals for a new publishers' right under Art. 11 will favor incumbent press publishing interests rather than innovative quality journalism and that the proposals for Art. 13 threaten the user participation benefits of the e-Commerce Directive (2000/31/EC). These suggestions could be taken into account on behalf of national policy makers of the European Member States.

Institutional users

Many institutional users report problems in the practical implementation of the research exception at national level. Many find that this exception has been implemented too narrowly by some Member States, which, they argue, has resulted in a limited use of the exception by its intended beneficiaries. It is reported that only few Member States (e.g. Estonia) have applied the exception in a technology-neutral manner.

More generally, some institutional users highlight that considerable online content that is relevant for scientific research is only available for payment and is burdened with digital rights management tools. They stress that remote access to university libraries collections should be further facilitated in the area of research as it is a much more practical option than onsite consultation. Some respondents note that licenses for scientific articles often limit the number of users that can access the material at the same time. This is problematic, they say, given that research projects often involve several researchers, sometimes from different universities or institutes including across borders which need to have access at the same time. A number of institutional users, in particular from Northern Europe, report their experiences with extended collective licenses. Some point out that such mechanisms have not been very useful so far in the area of research as they are cumbersome to negotiate and limited in scope.

As a solution, these respondents consider that a mandatory and technology-neutral research exception should be adopted at EU level. More generally, they express strong support for open access publishing.

Authors/performers

The vast majority of authors – other than researchers as authors of scientific publications – consider that there are generally no problems with access to content for research purposes and with current research exception. These respondents argue that the combination of licenses and exceptions offer users considerable flexibility to access content for research purposes. Respondents argue that licenses are a good addition to whatever use would not be covered by a national exception. However, some note that it can be difficult for them to track uses and receive adequate remuneration.

Publishers/producers/broadcasters

Respondents in this category consider that the current exception works well. Any possible shortcomings with access to research publications can be easily dealt with through licensing agreements. They consider that licenses are the preferred option in the field of research as they ensure quality and security and protect against possible abuses (i.e. uses for purposes other than research). Licenses terms are broad enough to allow for the exchange of information necessary to carry out research, including across borders.[63]

Some respondents state that scientific publishers already offer 90% of their products through licensing to educational institutions, which allows researchers, students and teachers to have access to that content. Representative of Scientific Technical and Medical (STM) publishers report alternative access models that are being developed, such as 'pay-per-view' or rental for online viewing, which they consider particularly useful for researchers

63 Tomas A Lipinski, *The Librarian's Legal Companion for Licensing Information Resources and Services* (American Library Association 2013); Robert W Gomulkiewicz, *Licensing Intellectual Property: Law and Applications* (Wolters Kluwer Law & Business 2014)..

not affiliated to an institution or requiring only occasional access. Specific market-led initiatives are also mentioned, such as one in France where textbook publishers have been making works available in digital format via certain online portals (for example 'Canal Numérique des Savoirs' and 'WizWiz'). Other licensing projects mentioned include the 'RightsLink' platform and 'Conlicencia' in Spain.

Intermediaries/distributors/other service provider

This consultation is the first visible sign of the second track of the European Commission's attempt to modernize the European copyright regulations (the first track consisted of the Licenses for Europe stakeholder dialogue).[64] According to the European Commission the focus of this effort is on:

> '... *ensuring that the EU copyright regulatory framework stays fit for purpose in the digital environment to support creation and innovation, tap the full potential of the Single Market, foster growth and investment in our economy and promote cultural diversity.*'[65]

Service providers such as memory institutions, it has been obvious for a long time that the current European copyright framework is not fit for purpose for these organizations to fulfil their missions in the digital environment. The problems related to copyright have been frequently discussed in the context of Europeana and other digitisation efforts. While there has been some progress (most notably the 2012 European directive on certain permitted uses of Orphan Works),[66] there are still obstacles facing memory institutions wanting to operate in the digital environment.

From that perspective, it is therefore welcome that the European Commission is now reviewing the European copyright rules and that issues related to memory institutions are part of this review. This gives these institutions the opportunity to draw attention to the problems they are facing

64 Silja Häusermann, *The Politics of Welfare State Reform in Continental Europe: Modernization in Hard Times* (Cambridge University Press 2010); Bruno Grancelli, *Social Change and Modernization: Lessons from Eastern Europe* (Walter de Gruyter 2011)..

65 European Commission, 'Proposal for a Directive of the European Parliament and of the Council on Copyright in the Digital Single Market' (2016) 2016/0280..

66 European Parliament, 'The European Orphan Works Directive - an EIFL Guide' (2012) 55..

and to express the policy outcomes that would support them in fulfilling their public missions.

These statements could be considered as required steps that should be followed from the national policy makers to tackle the challenges related to access.[67] In other words, new models of access and use of digital collections are appropriate to respond to technological innovation that reshapes the role and mission of one type of memory institutions (i.e. museums).[68]

VI. Assessment

Considering that the world is becoming increasingly competitive and interdependent, governments, socio-economic and civil society actors, at all levels, should 'grab' opportunities to collaborate further, in fields of mutual concern with potential benefits. A paradigm-shift towards interacting and interrelated collaboration to improve the copyright governance in Europe among involved stakeholders, based on each stakeholder's competences, stems from multilevel consultations examined above. It is crucial for the European Union to be in a position to put forward, defend and flexibly adapt its unique multilevel model of governance in the changing multi-actor networked modern world.

Multilevel consultations have been reflected for several years until the examined public consultation was introduced by the European Commission (i.e. 2013). In 2016 the European Commission proposed a new Directive to update its copyright framework entitled 'Copyright in the Digital Single Market'.[69] Since then, there has been much of negotiation and several amendments to the proposal.[70] It should be noted that the most con-

67 Guy Pessach, 'Museums, Digitization and Copyright Law: Taking Stock and Looking Ahead' (2006) 1 Journal of International Media & Entertainment Law 253; Yiwen Wang and others, 'Recommendations Based on Semantically Enriched Museum Collections' (2008) 6 Journal of Web Semantics 283; Graeme Were, 'Digital Heritage, Knowledge Networks, and Source Communities: Understanding Digital Objects in a Melanesian Society' (2014) 37 Museum Anthropology 133..

68 Enrico Bertacchini and Federico Morando, 'The Future of Museums in the Digital Age: New Models of Access and Use of Digital Collections' (2011) 15 International Journal of Arts Management..

69 European Commission, 'Proposal for a Directive of the European Parliament and of the Council on Copyright in the Digital Single Market' (n 66)..

70 Staffan Albinsson, 'The Resilience of Music Copyrights: Technological Innovation, Copyright Disputes and Legal Amendments Concerning the Distribution of

troversial parts of the proposed directive are Article 11 (i.e. press publishers rights) and Article 13, which was intended to address the so-called "value gap".

In May 2018, the European Council's permanent representative committee (COREPER) agreed their amendments to the Commission's draft directive. Similarly, on 29 June 2018 the European Parliament's lead committee (i.e. the Legal Affairs Committee (JURI) agreed amendments to the Commission's proposal in consultation with three other parliamentary committees: the Committee on Civil Liberties, Justice and Home Affairs (LIBE), the Committee on the Internal Market and Consumer Protection (IMCO) and the Committee on Industry, Research and Energy (ITRE).

Before progressing to the next stage (i.e. 'trilogue' negotiations), the European Parliament had to approve and adopt the draft proposal agreed upon by the JURI committee as the formal Parliamentary negotiating position. In July 2018, the European Parliament rejected the committee's proposal. At first, this was a response to the European citizens' voice who rang, emailed and visited in significant numbers their Members of the European Parliament to ask them to oppose Article 13. The rather long titled Article 13 (i.e. *Use of protected content by information society service providers storing and giving access to large amounts of works and other subject-matter uploaded by their users*) is aimed at large consumer-focussed platforms like YouTube. The proposed Directive creates an overall obligation on the hosts of such services, where no licences are in place, to monitor what content is being uploaded to their platforms, in order to remove any infringing materials. However, the progress that followed the public consultation determines that the European Institutions got more involved with their own discussions than with the outcomes of the wide consultations that were held. Therefore, it is required to examine to what extend the objectives of the 'better regulation' scheme, which was considered previously, is part of the public consultation aftermath.

According to the rationale of the 'better regulation' scheme its first objective is (i.e. to change governance and law-making processes by increas-

---

Music' (2013) 5 Culture Unbound: Journal of Current Cultural Research 401; European Commission, 'Report on the Responses to the Public Consultation on the Review of the EU Copyright Rules' (2014) D1 Copyright <http://ec.europa.eu/internal_market/consultations/2013/copyright-rules/docs/contributions/consultation-report_en.pdf> accessed 14 May 2018; Jeremy Fleming, 'Artists Fight Internet Users over Europe's Copyright Future' (*euractiv.com*, 13 January 2015) <https://www.euractiv.com/section/digital/news/artists-fight-internet-users-over-europe-s-copyright-future/> accessed 18 March 2019..

ing the role of evidence in public decision making and by creating opportunities for affected interests to be consulted at an early stage, when options are being devised) applicable in the case study concerned. Indeed, the case study proves that the European society's perspective is going to play an important role in the context of copyright law policy making towards relevant changes. Furthermore, stakeholders (for example the Independent Film & Television Alliance-IFTA, the Association of European Research Libraries-LIBER), with potentially affected interests took part in the consultation process at a primarily stage and before transposing the Directive to national law policy making.

As far as the second objective of the abovementioned scheme is concerned (i.e. to increase competitiveness by minimizing regulatory burdens and providing efficient regulations) at this stage it is not possible to "monitor" whether such objective is in progress, on national level. In fact, the European institutions are not yet fully aware of potential regulatory burdens on national level. Additionally, the transposition phase started recently (i.e. April 2019) and it is inconvenient to capture whether the consultations have impacted on the national copyright law policy making.

The last objective for this scheme (i.e. to address the legitimacy problems of the regulatory state by improving on procedures) is not possible to be investigated on national level yet. A mechanism to address legitimacy issues nationally, has not been specified as part of the public consultation process. Given the analysis of these objectives, the examined public consultation is distinguished from several weak points that need to be improved.

To recap the weak points it should be mentioned that: i) there is lack of efficient communication of the main topic of the public consultation process to national stakeholders who potentially can have an affected interest; ii) the public consultation process lead the European Commission to focus on and engage with its own discussion (i.e. 'trilogue' process) than with the outcomes of the consultation process and iii) significant instruments in order to provide additional support to the public consultation process (i.e. to address legitimacy problems on national level) have not been introduced.

VII. Conclusion

Initially, the chapter introduced the theoretical framework of multilevel governance and interaction with public consultation process. It analysed the relevant literature in order to set up the background of the discussion concerning potential connections between multilevel governance and public consultation. Then, the argumentation required a conceptual approach for both multilevel governance and public consultation.

This chapter clarified that the instrument of multilevel consultations has the dynamic to offer more comprehensive solutions for European Member States. The wide societal approaches through a variety of national stakeholders' involvement show that multilevel governance is of paramount importance for the European Union, towards policy drafting.

To sum up, there are examples of initiatives to be undertaken by national authorities to further support the European Commission's competence and policy drafting. For instance, the establishment of an internal consultation framework on national or local level, with a step by step explanation of what and how to do, based on previous experiences, will potentially help the European Commission to conduct (in the future) an improved public consultation and it will also help to adopt a more concrete practice. Another example that could improve the process of public consultation could be the establishment of networks with comparable national and/or international authorities through which there will be exchange of ideas and information.

ANNEX 1 – Type of respondents

Through literature review the following statistics and tables have been produced by the undersigned author to reflect the accentuated multilevel perspective based on participants involved from different Member States:

A/A	TOTAL	Type of respondent	
1		End user/ consumer or Representative of end users/ consumers	4210
2		Institutional user or Representative of institutional users	219
3	Rights holders	Author/ Performer of Representative of authors/ performers	1596
4	Rights holders	Publisher/ Producer/ Broadcaster or Representative of publishers/ producers/ broadcasters	623
5	Service providers	Intermediary/ Distributor/ Other service provider or Representative of intermediaries/ distributors/ other service providers	75
6		Collective Management Organisation	47
7		Public authority	11
8		Member State	15
9		Other (please explain)	120
		TOTAL	**6915**

ANNEX 2 – Member States

Member State	**TYPE OF RESPONDENT**				
	1	**2**	**3**	**4**	**5**
1. Austria	5,2%	4,1%	18,6%	10,4%	41,3%
2. Belgium	1,1%	21%	2,9%	16%	9,3%
3. Bulgaria			0,12%	0,6%	
4. Croatia	0,23%	0.9%	0,18%		
5. Cyprus					
6. Czech Republic	2,3%	3,2%	0,9%	0,6%	
7. Denmark	0,9%	2,3%	1,9%	2,2%	1,3%
8. Estonia		1,8%	0,06%		
9. Finland	1,2%	3,6%	0,7%	0,8%	
10. France	8,8%	2,3%	12%	20,9%	2,7%
11. Germany	29,7%	8,2%	14,3%	18%	6,7%
12. Greece	0,4%	0,9%	0,62%		
13. Hungary	0,23%	0,9%	0,12%		
14. Ireland	0,47%	1,8%	0,56%	0,5%	1,3%
15. Italy	1,6%	1,8%	1,62%	3%	1,3%
16. Latvia	0.23%	0,4%			
17. Lithuania	0.23%	0,9%			
18. Luxembourg					1,3%
19. Malta					
20. Netherlands	3%	11%	8,6%	4%	4%
21. Poland	6,6%	1,8%	3,3%	4%	2,7%
22. Portugal		0.9%		1,1%	
23. Romania	0,4%	1,8%	0,2%	0,5%	
24. Slovakia	0,23%		1,4%	0,2%	
25. Slovenia	0,23%	2,7%	0,4%		1,3%
26. Spain	6,9%	10,5%	2%	2,7%	
27. Sweden	5,2%	3,2	1,8%	2%	2,7%
28. United Kingdom	7,6%	11,9%	8,1%	7,4%	5,3%
29. Not mentioned/ Not indicated	14,2%	2,7%	8,1%	5%	16%
TOTAL	**4210**	**219**	**1596**	**623**	**75**

Type of respondents (codification):

1: End-user/ consumer
2: Institutional user
3: Author/ Performer
4: Publisher/ Producer/ Broadcaster
5: Intermediary/ Distributor/ Other service provider

Part III.
Lawmaking in European Multi-level governance: The Member States' Perspective

Chapter 11: Transposition of EU Legislation into domestic law: Challenges faced by National Parliaments

Wim Voermans (Leiden University)

I. Introduction: National Parliament (enter)in(g) the EU's institutional framework

Originally, the European Treaties did not consider National Parliaments as a distinct entity of the institutional framework of the European Community/-ies, or European Union. They were more or less treated as part and parcel of the Member States and their role in European affairs rather marginal and unspecified.[1] However, with the growing influence of the EC/EU on the lives of Member States' citizens, the advent of the European Parliament (first elections in 1979) and the increasing desire for stronger democratic mandates and democratic underpinnings of EC/EU policies and laws, National Parliaments became ever more relevant both from a democratic legitimacy and a strategic point of view. Increasingly, the lack of a foothold of National Parliaments was felt as an omission in the overall institutional fabric of the EU. The situation was addressed and remedied with the adoption of the Treaty of Maastricht (1992) and the adoption of the Treaty of Amsterdam (1997).[2] A more significant change to the National Parliaments' position came with the adoption of the Treaty of Lisbon (2007).

---

1 According to Rozenberg 'National Parliaments long appeared to be the "losers" of European integration.' O. Rozenberg, *The Role of National Parliaments in the EU after Lisbon: Potentialities and Challenges*. (Bruxelles: Policy Department for Citizens' Rights and Constitutional Affairs of the European Parliament 2017) 11; N. Dörrenbächer, E. Mastenbroek, D. Toshkov, 'National Parliaments and Transposition of EU Law: A Matter of Coalition Conflict?' (2015) 53 *JCMS: Journal of Common Market Studies*, 1010–1026
p. 1010.

2 The Maastricht Treaty attached two protocols (the Declaration on the role of National Parliaments in the European Union and the Declaration on the Conference of the Parliaments ([1992] OJ C191/1), attributing a – still – very small and predominantly formal role for National Parliaments in the EU's policy and law-making processes. They are more or less a recognition of existence. The role awarded to National Parliaments by the protocols annexed to the Amsterdam Treaty (The Protocol on the role of National Parliaments in the European Union and the Protocol

The Treaty of Lisbon takes it one step further and actively involves National Parliaments into the EU legislative process and strengthens and enhances the already existing dialogue between National Parliaments and the EU institutions. The Lisbon Treaty provides National Parliaments with various rights, such as the right to information, the right to participate in various EU procedures and the right to – more or less autonomously (i.e. not in formal conjunction with the national government) scrutinise draft legislation in the field of freedom, security and justice. A 'Lisbon'-right that stands out is the right to scrutinise compliance in draft EU legislation with the subsidiarity principle (the so-called early warning mechanism with its well-known yellow card procedure). The underlying idea of the Lisbon innovations is to emancipate National Parliaments in the EU institutional framework,[3] underscore their democratic significance, and thereby strengthen the democracy of and the level of citizen involvement and participation within the EU. The Lisbon Treaty also acknowledges the inter-parliamentary cooperation of the National Parliaments, notably the Conference of Parliamentary Committees for Union Affairs of Parliaments of the European Union (COSAC) established in 1989.

The role of National Parliaments does not stop with the responsibilities and competences EU treaties provisions provide, however helpful and instrumental these provisions have already been for further engaging and committing National Parliaments in EU affairs. National Parliaments have a role in the preparation, enactment and implementation of EU policies and legislation, and the impact thereof, as well. Working together with the national government (and sometimes even other actors) they partake in preparing national positions on EU policies and legislative proposals, they inform or instruct their governments (or individual ministers) on EU-negotiations, governments are held to account by National Parliaments as regards the negotiation results, National Parliaments have varying roles in the transposition and implementation of EU legislation into the domestic legal order and responsibilities following from that, their role in setting the national budget makes them important for the EU contribution and

on the application of the principles of subsidiarity and proportionality ([1997] OJ 97/C 340/01) has more substance to it: it involves National Parliaments in the subsidiarity and proportionality review of Commission proposals. See for further details Roberta Panizza, European Parliament: Relations with the National Parliaments. Fact Sheets on the European Union 2018 (2). Brussels: European Parliament, July 2018. www.europarl.europa.eu/factsheets/en.

3 See for instance articles 10(3) and 12 Treaty on Treaty on the European Union (TEU).

funding, and in the case of Treaty revisions they have, what effectively amounts to, veto-power. All of these latter responsibilities and powers are subject to domestic (constitutional) law, conventions and traditions rather than to EU law, even though the principle of loyal cooperation hovers over them all like an umbrella. The influence of National Parliaments extends much further than what meets the eye when reading the treaties.

This chapter considers – very briefly – the role of National Parliaments in the process of *transposition* of EU legislation – a mere segment of the overall implementation process. Our aim is to give a very general idea of the different roles and responsibilities National Parliaments take on in this respect. We offer a bird's eye view of the subject matter, laying down some general notions and highlighting some interesting developments. As with all outlines the result will undoubtedly be unsatisfactorily for experts and specialists afield, as well as for those who, while eating pudding, have grown more curious for details of proof. The whole object of the chapter is, however, to give a representative overview and raise the appetite for more, because we do believe the role of National Parliaments is growing ever more critical for the EU and is still very much understudied.

II. National Parliaments and EU proposals

The involvement of National Parliaments in the transposition of EU directives (should) begin(s) very early on in the policy preparation process. For smooth transposition it is helpful if National Parliaments are well informed throughout the process leading up to a legislative act like an EU directive. An uniformed parliament runs the risk of becoming a 'surprised' parliament when confronted with an EU Directive it was unaware of, which may in turn lead to sentiments of imposed legislation – instead of a result of mutual cooperation – and delays in transposition and eventually problems with full implementation. There are indications that early involvement of National Parliaments in EU policies pays off in terms of ease and speed of transposition and implementation of EU legislation.[4]

Information is key to early involvement. At the moment the EU Commission sends out the actual legislative proposal to the Member States the policies the proposal expresses and the choices held within will already – more or less – have solidified. Until quite recently it used to be fairly com-

4 B. Steunenberg and W. Voermans, *The Transposition of EC directives: a comparative study of instruments, techniques and processes in six member states* (Leiden 2006).

plicated for National Parliaments to keep track of policy plans of the EU. It required knowledge and some expertise of the EU, its operation, the dynamics of the EU-policy cycle, the different policy and legislative instruments and the procedures to be followed. National and EU policy cycles tend not to be in-sync and they involve different actors and time-tables. On top of that it is politically not very profitable for members of national parliaments (MP's) to invest scarce resources like attention and time into the long running trains of (complicated) EU dossiers. Timing is difficult due to asymmetries in national and EU decision procedures, agendas and the generally technical subject matter of EU proposals are often distant to domestic voters. Debating and scrutinizing these dossiers to the full extent will most probably have a low electoral pay off as well: in a lot of cases the yield will only come in after the expiration of the term of office a national MP, who did only have a very slim chance of leaving a mark on the policy or proposal anyway. Domestic political forces work against early involvement of National Parliaments, not as a result of systematic euro criticism, scheming & conniving or double play of Member States, but just as a result of politics being politics.

This has been a driver for the EU and especially the European Commission to change its position as regards informing National Parliaments on EU policy developments and – ever since 2006 – opting for more direct forms of informing and communicating with them.

In 2006 the Barroso-Commission expressed that "National Parliaments must be more closely involved with the development and execution of European policy" because "the increased involvement of National Parliaments can help make European policies more attuned to diverse circumstances and more effectively implemented". Consequently the Commission launched an initiative to better inform National Parliaments, for instance by way of transmitting all new proposals and consultation papers directly to National Parliaments, with an invitation to respond to them in order "to improve the process of policy formulation".[5] This policy of (so-called) *political dialogue* with National Parliaments – now an obligation for the Commission[6] – has caught on quite well: between 2007 and 2017 National Parliaments have sent in over 4.000 opinions. Even though the

5 COM (2006) 211: *A Citizen's Agenda: Delivering Results for Europe*, notably p. 9.

6 Article 1 of the Protocol (No 1) *On the Role of National Parliaments in the European Union* states that: 'Commission consultation documents (green and white papers and communications) shall be forwarded directly by the Commission to National Parliaments upon publication. The Commission shall also forward the annual legislative programme as well as any other instrument of legislative planning or poli-

Commission is obliged to no more than merely answer to questions and comments expressed in these opinions, the dialogue itself goes well beyond mere window-dressing, as Jančić found out in 2012.[7]

Exerting influence on the transposition of EU Directives

National Parliaments are becoming more important in the EU legislative process; as mediators between the EU and their citizens 'they are of key importance for the legitimacy of European politics' as Allibrandi recently put it.[8] At present there are three different moments in the policy cycle of the EU legislative process at which National Parliaments can and do exert influence on the transposition of EU Directives – to which we will limit the discussion and analysis in this chapter: 1. The proposal phase, 2. The transposition phase and 3. The 'feedback'-stage.

The proposal stage leading up to the enactment of the EU directive

The early bird catches the worm; maximizing influence means upstreaming it in the early stages of inception of policies. National Parliaments are not well equipped to engage in the early stages of negotiations – what we label the 'informal' stage.[9] They do not have a formal role, they do – as a rule – not partake in expert groups or conferences, their informal networks in EU policy preparation are nominal, their influence is predominantly indirect and institutional. Parliamentary networking is still difficult, even though inter-parliamentary conferences and inter-parliamentary meetings for specific purposes are held more frequently. Rozenberg, in a recent EP-report, observes that in the last few years, parliamentary networks have be-

---

cy to National Parliaments, at the same time as to the European Parliament and the Council.'.

7 D. Jančić, 'The Barroso Initiative: Window Dressing or Democracy Boost?' (2012) 8 *Utrecht Law Review*, 78–91.

8 R. Alibrandi, 'Towards political integration in Europe: the involvement of National Parliaments in European Union politics and policy-making', (2018) 38 *Parliaments, Estates and Representation*, 237. See also F. Wendler, *Debating Europe in National Parliaments: public justification and political polarization* (Palgrave Macmillan 2016) 180–186.

9 It is not informal in the sense that there are no rules or procedures for the negotiations phase, but informal in the sense that National Parliaments do not have a 'formal' institutional position at this stage: only a very marginal one.

come more differentiated and clustered.[10] There are few cross-board political initiatives or programmes of Europe wide political parties represented in both the European parliament and National Parliaments to rally for or oppose EU policies or legislation. The EU does not as much suffer from a democratic deficit but rather more from political asymmetry, it seems.[11] The political dialogue set up since 2006 has brought very welcome change here – this does offer a real opportunity for National Parliaments to take a place at the negotiating table very early on, apart from the national executive who previously more or less monopolized the negotiations. The problem remaining is the one of 'making clout' early on. How to coordinate the efforts and where to find allies to politically beef up the point of view in the negotiations?

The phase of policy preparation leading up to a proposal for an EU Directive may vary in length and move at different speeds at different moments, making it extra hard for National Parliaments to monitor what is actually happening. EU and national legislative agendas are not in-sync which makes for difficult timing on the part of National Parliaments. The use of White papers and Green Papers – outlining general ideas and principles of policies considered before coming up with a detailed legislative proposal – are helpful for parliaments in this respect. Not only for the possibility to give input in an early stage, but also from a point of view of timing of the input. Getting the act of the National Parliament together at the moment the proposal of the EU Directive is sent out to the Member States and the European Parliament is no mean feat. Especially if national MP's want to consult their constituencies and stakeholders time is a constraint; the expertise and resources of national executives give them a head start and advantage at this stage.

The scrutiny phase, in which National Parliaments are offered the opportunity to vet a proposal for an EU Directive sent out to them, constitutes the more formal part of the negotiations on an EU Directive. The EU Commission sends out proposals for EU Directives to Member States pursuant to the demands of article 289 of the Treaty on the Functioning of the EU (further: TFEU). EU legislation (esp. Directives and Regulations) can only be enacted by the European legislature which consists of the EU Commission, the EU Parliament and the Council of Ministers. This latter Council represents the Member States, who are in the Council itself repre-

---

10 Rozenberg *supra* n. 1 at p. 32.

11 H.-T. *An uneven balance? a legal analysis of power asymmetries between National Parliaments in the EU* (The Hague: Eleven International Publishing 2018).

sented by the national executive, notably ministers. 'The national scrutiny systems and practices vary according to the national context and to the constitutional provisions in place' – a recent COSAC-report points out.[12] Most Member States do not consider all proposals for EU-directives at length: some of them may be very detailed and technical, some of them politically not interesting because of the subject matter, part of ongoing processes or just outright irrelevant to a country. To decide on what proposals do need parliamentary scrutiny and which do not, different *triage-systems* have been put in place).[13] Ultimately the decision to give an EU proposal full parliamentary attention or not is of course parliament's to make, but some of the national triage-systems rely on the executive to give a first impact analysis of the proposal. Government reports on the estimated impact of – especially EU directives – for the domestic legal order, the work involved in transposition, budgetary, social and economic impacts etc. come in different sorts and sizes. Some jurisdictions, like France, Spain and the Netherlands, resort to very brief summary sheets that allow parliaments to assess the impact of EU-proposals at a glance and to decide whether or not they should receive full parliamentary scrutiny (so-called *fiches*[14]). Other Member States, like the UK, have dedicated Parliamentary Scrutiny Committees put in place to advise Parliament on these matters.

Nearly all National Parliaments in the EU today have organized themselves in ways that enable them to cope with the challenges of EU legislation and policies. Most National Parliaments (and their chambers) have European Affairs Committees (EAC) that serve as observatories and junctions for the parliamentary assessment EU legislative proposals. They have an important role in the triage, scrutiny and referral of proposals to other (sectoral) Committees or the Floor. In most cases the EAC is not the sole responsible entity for scrutiny of EU legislative proposals .[15]

Parliamentary scrutiny can amount to different outcomes (and combinations thereof): (a) input for the position of the executive (Cabinet, Mini-

---

12 Conference of Parliamentary Committees for Union Affairs of Parliaments of the European Union (COSAC), *Twenty-seventh Bi-annual Report: Developments in European Union Procedures and Practices Relevant to Parliamentary Scrutiny*. Valetta 2017, p. 5.

13 Steunenberg & Voermans *supra* n. 4.

14 After the French 'fiche d'impact'.

15 Conference of Parliamentary Committees for Union Affairs of Parliaments of the European Union (COSAC), *Twenty-seventh Bi-annual Report: Developments in European Union Procedures and Practices Relevant to Parliamentary Scrutiny*. Valetta 2017.

ster or Junior Minister) in the EU Council of Ministers as part of the national position on the EU proposal, (b) a yellow or orange card (or otherwise coloured card) raised (by different parliaments) to the Commission to reconsider the proposal, (c) comment or point directly addressed at the EU Commission as an element of the political dialogue.

1. Input for the position of the executive

Typically, parliamentary scrutiny of an EU legislative proposal will take place in the setting of a debate with the government on the position of the Member State in the Council of Ministers as regards the proposal put forward. The subject matter of the debate will be the position of the Member State proper and estimates on the impact of the EU proposal and how to accommodate the transposition and implementation further down the road.[16] Research on the practice of National Parliamentary scrutiny on EU proposals over the last two decades shows that National Parliaments hardly use their powers to control government's negotiations positions,[17] even though the situation seems to have changed somewhat lately .[18] A lack of attention on the part of National Parliament can lead to different negative effects. Early input and involvement on draft legislation breeds expertise and commitment and – thus – facilitates timely transposition and increases the overall legitimacy for EU legislation as well.[19] This disuse of powers is not always the result of lacking commitment or attention. Due to asymmetries between national and EU-agenda's and procedures it is really hard for national MP's to time their input right and hold the negotiators to account once the negotiations are under way. To this end, an increasing amount of jurisdictions in the EU have established procedures allowing for 'scrutiny reserves' that call governments to a halt on negotiations on EU proposals up until the moment the proposals and national position has been debated with the National Parliaments. Some countries combine this with strict and formal mandates for government: ministers are allowed to negotiate

16 K. Auel, O. Rozenberg and A. Tacea, ' To Scrutinise or Not to Scrutinise? Explaining Variation in EU-Related Activities in National Parliaments', (2015) 38 *West European Politics* 282–304.

17 Dörrenbächer, Mastenbroek & Toshkov, *supra* n. 1 at p. 1011.

18 Wendler *supra* n. 8 at p. 19.

19 Steunenberg & Voermans, *supra* n. 4; Alibrandi *supra* n. 8.

in the Council of Ministers only as far as their mandate extends. And in case it runs out, they have to return to parliament to renew it.[20]

2. 'Cards'

The advent of the Treaty of Lisbon brought a set of instruments that aimed to give National Parliaments both a voice and an instrument in the EU's legislative process. The idea was that National Parliaments should be given possibility to raise an alarm or to issue a warning. 'A yellow card' – referring with this metaphor to one of the most popular sports in the EU: soccer. According to the Subsidiarity Protocol annexed to the Treaty of Lisbon, each National Parliament may, within eight weeks, produce a reasoned opinion stating why it considers that a European legislative draft does not comply with the principle of subsidiarity. When more than a third (or a quarter in case of draft legislative acts related to justice, freedom and security) of all National Parliaments[21] rejects a legislative proposal ('negative reasoned opinions') the proposal must be reviewed by the EU Commission.

Upon this, the EU Commission can decide to maintain, change or withdraw its proposal under an obligation to give good reasons for the decision. If the majority of the National Parliaments, however, has given a negative response to the legislative proposal, and the act to be falls under the scope of the ordinary legislative procedure of article 289 TFEU, there is a possible aftermath of the yellow card: the orange card. Should in this case the Commission decide to persist and not amend or withdraw the proposal in question, the Commission must justify this decision both to the EU Parliament and Council as to why, in the view of the Commission, the proposal does comply with the principle of subsidiarity, contrary to the view National Parliaments have taken. If, after such an explanation by the Commission, a simple majority of members of the EU Parliament, or 55% of Council members, is not convinced, the proposal will not be given further consideration. The yellow and orange card procedures – as parts of the Early Warning Mechanism – are very complex, time-pressed (8 weeks) and

20 Conference of Parliamentary Committees for Union Affairs of Parliaments of the European Union (COSAC), *Eighth bi-annual report: Developments in European Union Procedures and Practices Relevant to Parliamentary Scrutiny*. Estoril 2007.

21 Each parliament has two votes to cast. Bicameral parliaments one for each Chamber, unicameral ones two to even out the odds. All in all 56 votes can be cast: more than 19 votes against amount to more than 1/3.

require mind-boggling coordination between National Parliaments with very different setups, procedures, dynamics, culture and so on. Taken from this perspective, it is surprising that the yellow card procedure was successfully triggered three times between 2010 and 2018 with the Commission withdrawing the proposal at once.[22] The orange card procedure was never used. Aside from this meagre result of raised cards the Early Warning Mechanism did generate 354 opinions from National Parliaments on legislative proposals all validated by the EU Commission between 2010 and 2016.[23] Whether the Early Warning Mechanism is a success or not, remains to be debated,[24] but it does seem to service a lingering need.[25] The Early Warning Mechanism even has two more procedures, the green card procedure – the idea that joint National Parliaments can make a legislative proposal themselves and offer it to the Commission – or the late, or red cards procedure, amounting to blocking power of (nearly unanimously operating) National Parliaments. Both are more or less 'informal' procedures that have not been used up to date. We will therefore not deal with them here.

3. Political dialogue

Even though the political dialogue initiative is in itself not limited to the debate on legislative proposal, most opinions of National Parliaments are prompted by EU legislative proposals sent out to them. Judging by the number of opinions (in excess of 4000) the opening up of the dialogue seems to be a success: it generates information, pre-empts questions and

22 2012 on the right to take collective action, 2013 on the establishment of a European Public Prosecutor's Office and 2016 on the Revision of the Posted Workers Directive. See Remáč 2017, p. 10–16.

23 Rozenberg *supra* n. 1 at p. 25.

24 Rozenberg's report is pessimistic in this respect. 'Regarding the EWM (Early Warning Mechanism) , the survey notes that this innovative procedure has been almost redundant (…). Rozenberg *supra* n. 1 at p. 7 and p. 19. Cooper on the other hand believes that the yellow card initiatives between 2010 and 2016 evidences that National Parliaments 'have shown themselves to be a collective force in EU politics. While they do not, as a group, have the power to veto an EU proposal, they can intervene in the EU legislative process in a way that gives them influence over the final outcome.' I Cooper, 'A yellow card for the striker: National Parliaments and the defeat of EU legislation on the right to strike', (2015) 22 *Journal of European Public Policy*,1420–1421.

25 Cooper *supra* n. 24.

debates in the Council or at the moment of transposition and spurs due attention and commitment of National Parliaments within the grander scheme of the EU legislative process. Albeit that National Parliaments on their own do not have formal standing in the process, and the dialogue is, in a sense, unbalanced because the Commission and individual government are not on par, it is to be, for good reason, assessed as a positive development ,[26] especially at a moment in time where Member States and their citizens tend to take a more political and critical stance as regards the operation of the EU.

III. National Parliaments and the transposition of EU Directives

The role National Parliaments have, once an EU directive is adopted, depends on the transposition method and instrument a Member State opts for. Directives are binding upon Member States as to the result to be achieved but leave to the national authorities the choice of form and methods of transposition (art. 288 TFEU). Under EU Law, Member States are obliged to timely, full, effective, precise transposition of EU Directives, using appropriate measures. Transposition is typically done by either primary legislation or secondary legislation, with a noticeable preference for secondary (delegated or by use of statutory instruments) throughout the Union, since low ranking legislative instruments can be enacted quicker than instruments that involve different partners or imply more elaborate procedures. If and how a country can make use of secondary legislation – not requiring parliamentary involvement – for transposition largely depends on the constitutional setup of the legislative process of a country and the requirements it sets. Given the time constraints on transposition one would expect that most Member States would have made necessary constitutional legislative arrangements geared to the need of (the ever more frequent) transposition of EU Directives. The fact of the matter is, however, that most Member States do not have constitutionally enshrined provision dedicated to the transposition of EU Directives. Most Member States make do with what they (constitutionally) have got.

Countries like the Netherlands and Germany adhere to their normal constitutional principles at the occasion of the transposition of EU Directives. The principle of the *primacy* of the parliamentary legislature requires that the basic elements of any statutory system be regulated through Acts

---

26 Rozenberg *supra* n. 1 at p. 19–20.

of Parliament. Principled matters, subject matter of which the constitution requires regulation by Act of Parliament fall under this scope as well. This of course acts as an impediment on the use of lower ranking instruments when transposing EU Directives and slows things down as well. Member States do want to be quick on their feet when transposing EU Directives and have, therefore, come up with all kinds of creative uses of generis constitutional instruments and procedures to speed up the transposition process. Some use constitutional emergency procedures and related legislative emergency-instruments to sweep up transposition backlogs (France, Spain). Other countries use emergency procedures as transposition fast lanes (Slovenia). At times omnibus laws transposing bundles of EU directives into a single (yearly) Act of Parliament were popular.[27] Only a few countries have resorted to dedicated legislation and legislative procedures to speed the transposition of EU Directives (e.g. the UK) and allow for increased use of lower ranking legislative instruments to transpose EU Directives. One could criticize this by claiming that transposition EU Directives is more or less a technical act, fitting in the already debated and duly enacted EU legislation into the national legal order. Having a debate on the merit of a EU Directive at the occasion of the debate on the transposition bill is futile: the input is too late and it does no more than frustrating the pace of transposition.

On the other hand Steunenberg and Voermans c.a. have observed that most EU Member States, regardless of their constitutional system, in more or less 75% of the cases use lower ranking instruments (of secondary legislation) to transpose EU Directives and that the use of special transposition instruments of methods only marginally speed up transposition, but do tend to be controversial from a democratic point of view.[28] Furthermore, for good reasons, Member States perceive the transposition of EU Directives not as a mere technical formality. In a lot of cases important decisions have to be made in the way EU Directives are 'woven' into the fabric and frameworks of domestic legislation that sometimes are the result of long traditions and are pathways to networks and institutions of implementation and application of domestic law. Dealing with transposition as a mere semi-automatic method, an administrative conveyor belt of implementation, would seriously undermine the legitimacy of the EU legislation in question. Transposition is an act of accommodation – transferring EU law into domestic law – making it even more your own law. National Parlia-

27 Steunenberg & Voermans *supra* n. 4.

28 Steunenberg & Voermans *supra* n. 4 at p. 31–38.

ments (and Member States) still are very divergent and have (very) different traditions.[29]

In most cases, however, there will be hardly any substantial role for National Parliaments to play when EU Directives are transposed apart from the more technical details. But devils do rest in them. One of the more delicate ones, for instance, tends to be whether provisions of EU Directives should be copied out or rather elaborated in order to get a better fit with domestic legislation. Even though more and more Member States opt for copying out as much as possible, elaboration is still favoured on occasion. Another typical debate, that has died down somewhat over the last years, is whether Member States should do something 'extra' (gold-plating) on the occasion of transposition or refrain from that and only transpose the bare minimum of a Directive. Most Member States nowadays choose the latter position. As well as they try to avoid 'double banking' – i.e. inadvertently adopt two procedures (one EU and one domestic) for more or less the same subject matter.

We will be very brief on the role National Parliament play in the last (but crucial) part of the EU's legislative cycle: the feedback stages. Enacting legislation is always an exercise in proving Murphy's Law that anything that can go wrong will go wrong to the test (and sometimes even right). It is, however detailed and precise an impact analysis may be, impossible to foresee what will happen with – especially transposed – EU legislation down the road. Feedback is critical for the effective operation of EU legislation. In the EU this is however, given the political dynamics and asymmetries, very difficult to do. The political dialogue and the many opinions it yields is a valuable instrument for informal evaluation and feedback. It would be, maybe, a good idea to elaborate on.

IV. National Parliaments & comitology

In the former paragraphs, we have discussed the ways National Parliaments have emancipated themselves into the EU legislative process, in formal and more informal ways – especially on the ticket of their responsibilities in the transposition of EU Directives. The literature is clear on the outcome of this process: this has increased the democratic underpinning and

---

29 N-C. Bormann and T. Winzen, 'The Contingent Diffusion of Parliamentary Oversight Institutions in the European Union', (2016) 55 *European Journal of Political Research* 589–608.

overall legitimacy of EU legislation at this juncture of European integration. There is, however, another side to this coin, a development that seems to lead away from the democratic increase and the hold of (National) Parliaments on the EU legislative procedure, and that is the persistent reality of 'comitology'. Comitology refers to the process whereby EU legislation is modified, elaborated or adjusted by 'comitology committees' consisting of Member States 'expert' representatives without democratic mandates and chaired by the European Commission. The official term for what these comitology committees do, is enacting *implementing acts* (under the procedure laid down in article 291 TFEU). There are many of these committees (approx. 250) and their democratic legitimacy is vulnerable if not low. Even though the Lisbon Treaty tried to come up with a new system of delegation, that would offer more democratic parliamentary control on delegated legislation, for various reasons, most of the implementation legislation managed to slip away from the strict controls of art. 290 TFEU and moved across the street to the house of art. 291 TFEU, with much less parliamentary surveillance of any kind .[30] This of course presents an accountability problem and erosion of legitimacy in its wake. Neither national parliaments, nor the European Parliament are well equipped to hold comitology to account or to impose their will or mark on the process of enactment. This does pose a problem, because even conservative estimates calculate that approx. 75% of EU legislation is enacted by the European Commission (EC) in or with the aid of comitology.[31] This lack of democratic pedigree of so-called 'EU secondary legislation' causes various legitimacy-related problems at the EU level and at the national level as well. Comitology is becoming a crystallization point of criticism for Europe as a technical project run by unelected bureaucrats.[32]

V. *Key points and observations*

This chapter cannot do more than give a very sketchy overview of the role of National Parliaments in the process of the transposition of EU Directives. A moving target as such: European integration is ever dynamic, ever

---

30 W. Voermans, J.M.R. Hartmann and M. Kaeding, Michael, 'The Quest for Legitimacy in EU Secondary Legislation', (2014) 2 *The Theory and Practice of Legislation*, 5–32.

31 See Annex 1.

32 A Glencross, ' A Post-National EU? The Problem of Legitimising the EU without the Nation and National Representation', (2011) 59 *Political Studies*, 348–367.

in flux. Some observations, however, are noteworthy, we believe, at this juncture. First of all the role of National Parliaments has evolved over the last decades. National Parliaments have emancipated themselves as serious players into the whole of the EU legislative process and – to all intents and purposes – have become more actively involved at the European level. Although National Parliaments' positions and traditions vary quite substantially, they have been able to give a voice to the Member State's electorate separate from the one of governments. The role of National Parliaments in the grand scheme of the European legislative process, especially the one leading up to EU Directives, has shifted from that of a – more or less – bystander to a team player. One may read this from the amount of opinions National Parliaments have delivered to the European Commission since 2006, the way they have organized their scrutiny procedures on proposals for EU legislation, the rise of scrutiny reserves throughout post-Lisbon Europe and the practice of (formal) mandates and instructions on national positions for governments. This, the literature agrees, is helpful for the overall legitimacy and democratic underpinning of EU legislation. Another insight from the report is that some of the innovations, like the Early Warning Mechanism, did not meet with the same success as the policy of political dialogue did, and that there is no philosopher's stone to expedient transposition of EU Directives: quick fixes or methods of trying to bypass Parliament at the occasion of the transposition of EU Directives do not pay off in time gains, and come at a price in the overall legitimacy of EU legislation. A last observation is a concern: comitology, as a way of enacting legislation by predominantly unelected and unaccountable experts in its present volume, risks undermining the ever more democratic way of legislating in the EU. The critical stance the European Parliament has taken on the post-Lisbon shift to implementing acts (and away from delegating acts under art. 290 TFEU) is to be applauded in this respect.

Annex 1 EU Legislation enacted by the Commission

For the estimate of appox. 75% of the EU legislation being enacted by the Commission see a.o. the figures 4 and 5 in our article Wim Voermans, Josephine M.R. Hartmann & Michael Kaeding The Quest for Legitimacy in EU Secondary Legislation, *The Theory and Practice of Legislation*, Vol. (2)1, 2014, p. 5–32, esp. p. 29 & 30 *and* the 'mother'-figure below.

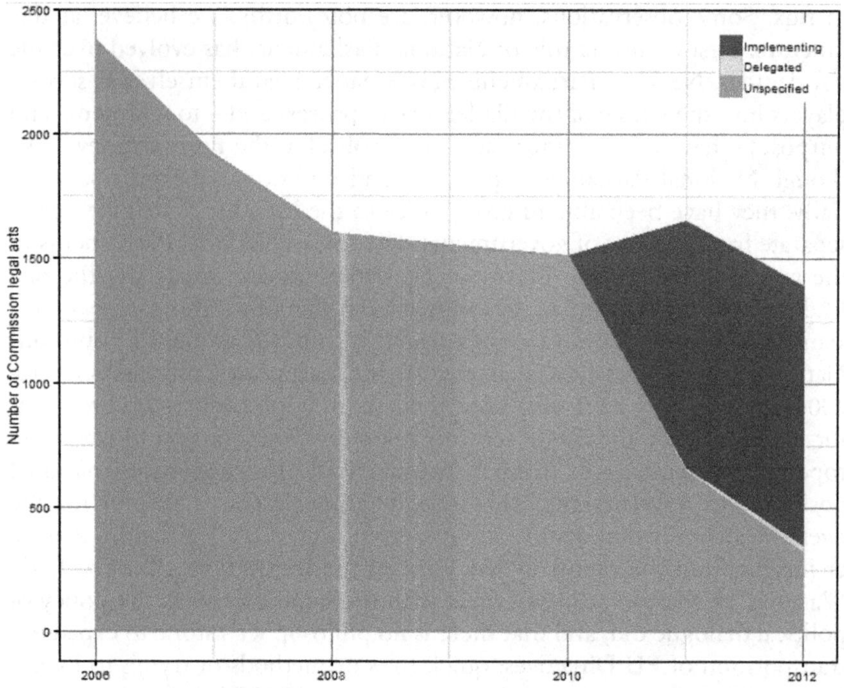

This figure is taken from the website of Dimiter Toshkov – Leiden researcher in EU decision making and EU legislation and assistant professor at the Institute of Public Administration at Leiden University. More data on the proportion and growth of Commission acts over the last 55 years can be found on his website http://www.dimiter.eu/Eurlex.html His figure 5.

Toshkov concludes (under his point 5). '(...) We see that the share of Implementing acts from all legislation adopted by the Commission is growing since their introduction. Currently, around 2/3 of all acts are Implementing legislation which provides the Commission with considerable discretion.'

The amount of Commission enacted legislation even amounts for more than 75% in total – it has increased over the years. Between 2009 the Commission was only responsible for 72% of the total EU legislation. See for the figures up until 2009: House of Commons, How much legislation comes from Europe? *Research Paper* 10/62 (by Vaughne Miller, 13 October 2010, p. 12–13, see figures below -

Adopted EU legislation 1980 to 2009: number of directives, regulations and decisions

	Commission			Council			Total
	Directives	Regulations	Decisions	Directives	Regulation	Decisions	
1980		5,901		51	312	136	6,400
1981		6,044		45	414	150	6,653
1982		5,321		42	393	128	5,884
1983		14,123		41	395	108	14,667
1984		5,190		53	351	99	5,693
1985		7,442		59	447	109	8,057
1986		12,081		74	473	184	12,812
1987		8,212		40	458	125	8,835
1988		6,799		63	434	131	7,427
1989		5,737		79	394	161	6,371
1990		6,298		65	380	169	6,912
1991		6,130		72	335	174	6,711
1992	34	1,137	385	95	381	134	2,166
1993	52	1,160	520	65	325	135	2,257
1994	24	1,579	445	17	180	72	2,317
1995	35	2,801	3,025	39	242	175	6,317
1996	39	2,341	2,806	58	247	170	5,661
1997	35	760	635	34	209	164	1,837
1998	44	733	537	53	202	196	1,765
1999	55	842	516	44	144	139	1,740
2000	38	606	557	43	182	24	1,450
2001	18	600	651	45	152	30	1,496
2002	44	602	610	149	164	57	1,626
2003	61	648	560	60	189	39	1,557
2004	59	672	468	107	858	512	2,676
2005	54	599	634	62	134	51	1,534
2006	76	1,795	781	101	238	264	3,255
2007	53	630	644	23	143	277	1,770
2008	57	1,145	791	120	239	315	2,667
2009	69	1,103	606	176	226	295	2,475

In numerical terms, the Commission, particularly Commission regulations, is the main source of EU law.[37] In 2009 the Commission was responsible for 72% of EU legislation; Commission regulations alone were 45% of the grand total. Christensen notes an increase in Commission laws in economic and social legislation since the *Treaty of Rome* and particularly since 1993.[38]

37 The Commission has delegated powers to enact legislation which is usually of a routine or mundane nature.

38 See Table 3, *Public Administration* Vol 88 Issue 1, "EU Legislation and National Regulation: uncertain steps towards a European public policy". A detailed breakdown of individual EU instruments can be found in Standard Note 5419, "EU Legislation", updated 24 March 2010.

Chapter 12: How to reconcile the drafting rules and practices of the Member-States with the rules and practices of the EU?

Rui Lanceiro (University of Lisbon)

I. The interconnection between national and EU legal drafting

In principle, the European Union (EU) relies on Member States for the implementation and safeguarding of EU law in their national legal systems or jurisdictions, as well as for ensuring compliance with national measures implementing that law, where this task has not been expressly assigned to an EU institution or body. In terms of implementation of EU law, Member States' enforcement powers, although limited by the Treaties, are higher than those of the Union. This solution was expressly enshrined in Article 291 (1) of the Treaty on the Functioning of the EU (TFEU) by the Lisbon Treaty. The same Treaty introduced the express provision that Member States must ensure the "effective implementation of Union law", which is considered "essential for the proper functioning of the Union" (Article 197 (1) TFEU).

Even before the Lisbon Treaty, this task of the Member States was recognised by the Court of Justice of the EU (CJEU), as a consequence of the principle of sincere cooperation, within the duty of Member States to ensure the full effectiveness of EU law[1], provided for in Article 5 TEEC

---

1 V.g., CJEU, Case 94/71, Schlüter & Maack v Hauptzollamt Hamburg-Jonas [1972] ECLI:EU:C:1972:45, para. 10; Cases 205 to 215/82, Deutsche Milchkontor GmbH and others v Federal Republic of Germany [1983] ECLI:EU:C:1983:233, paras. 17 e 19; Case C-290/91, Johannes Peter v Hauptzollamt Regensburg, [1993] ECLI:EU:C:1993:220, para. 8; Case C-285/93, Dominikanerinnen-Kloster Altenhohenau v Hauptzollamt Rosenheim [1995] ECLI:EU:C:1995:398, para. 26; Case C-292/97, Kjell Karlsson and Others [2000] ECLI:EU:C:2000:202, para. 27; Cases C-231/00, Cooperativa Lattepiù arl v Azienda di Stato per gli interventi nel mercato agricolo (AIMA), C-303/00, Azienda Agricola Marcello Balestreri e Maura Lena v Regione Lombardia and Azienda di Stato per gli interventi nel mercato agricolo (AIMA), and C-451/00, Azienda Agricola Giuseppe Cantarello v Azienda di Stato per gli interventi nel mercato agricolo (AIMA) and Ministero delle Politiche Agricole e Forestali [2004] ECLI:EU:C:2003:253, para. 56.

(which later became Article 10 TCE and is today, Article 4 (3) TEU)[2]. The CJEU has already stated that, "in the fields covered by European Union law, (...) the public authorities of the Member States are bound by a duty of sincere cooperation. Under that principle, they must take any appropriate measure, general or particular, to ensure fulfilment of the obligations arising out of the Treaties or resulting from the acts of the institutions of the European Union and refrain from any measure which could jeopardise the attainment of the European Union's objectives"[3].

The general duty of implementation of EU law falls on all public bodies and organs of the Member States. This means that the EU depends on national legislators, judges and public administrations to implement its policies and objectives. Determining which body or legal person is tasked to implement and apply a particular duty or obligation arising from EU law falls within the autonomy of each Member State[4]. This means that the frontier between the legislative, judicial and administrative spheres of implementation of EU law is drawn by national law – EU law is only concerned with the effectiveness and coherence of implementation.

Member State's legislative bodies have, thus, the duty to implement EU law. This duty is both affirmative, involving the enactment of legislation (namely transposing Directives or implementing Regulations) and negative, refraining from legislating against EU law. Consequently, all duties arising from Article 4 (3) TEU – obligations to implement European Union law, whether through actions or omissions, either obligations of ends or means – apply in the legislative sphere of implementation of EU law by the Member States.

For instance, the obligation to transpose a Directive does not necessarily require that its provisions are formally and literally reproduced in an express and specific national legal provision and may, depending on its content, be satisfied by a general legal regime – or even by principles of constitutional or administrative law, provided that it effectively ensures the full

2 This provision commands Member States to "take any appropriate measure, general or particular, to ensure fulfilment of the obligations arising out of the Treaties or resulting from the acts of the institutions of the Union".

3 CJEU, Case C-518/11, *UPC Nederland BV v Gemeente Hilversum*, ECLI:EU:C:2013:709, para. 59.

4 Cfr. K. Lenaerts / P. van Nuffel, Constitutional Law of the European Union, London: Sweet & Maxwell, 2005, p. 392; S. Prechal, Directives in European Community Law, Oxford: Oxford University Press 1995, p. 86.

application of the Directive[5]. It is not a condition of correct transposition that the wording of the directive be reproduced verbatim in national law, provided that there is a general legal context guaranteeing the full application of the Directive in a sufficiently clear and precise manner[6]. However, it is it is settled case-law that mere administrative practices, which by their nature are alterable at will by the national authorities and are not given the appropriate publicity, cannot be regarded as constituting the proper fulfilment of a Member State's obligations under the Treaty[7]. Hence, Directives must be transposed by means of national provisions of a binding nature (which have the same legal force as those which must be amended or revoked, if that is the case). This means that it is up to national law to determine if a legislative act is needed to implement the EU act or if an administrative regulation suffice.

Regarding the legislative power of the Member States, when, according to the principles of attribution, subsidiarity and proportionality, a subject falls within the EU's legislative sphere of competence, and there is a need for national implementing act, a link is created between national and EU legislators. Member States have the duty to legislate with the objective to achieve effective and harmonized application of EU legislation. In this context, the drafting of EU legal acts can have consequences in the national implementation stage. Some of the problems that emerge are related to the fact that there are 24 official languages in the EU, which makes the range of possible linguistic combinations enormous. All official language ver-

5 Cfr., *v.g.*, CJEU Cases 29/84, Comission v Germany [1985] ECLI:EU:C:1985:229, para. 23; Case 247/85, Comission v Belgium [1987] ECLI:EU:C:1987:339, para. 9; 252/85, Commission v France [1988] ECR 02243, para. 5; Case C-361/88 Comission v Germany [1991] ECLI:EU:C:1991:224, para. 15; Case C-433/93 Comission v Germany ECLI:EU:C:1995:263 [1995] para. 18; Case C-217/97 Comission v Germany [1999] ECLI:EU:C:1999:395, para. 31; Case C-58/02 Comission v Spain [2004] ECLI:EU:C:2004:9, para. 26.

6 CJEU, Case C-363/85, Commission v Italy [1987] ECLI:EU:C:1987:196, para. 7: "depending on the content of the directive, it is sufficient that there be a general legal context guaranteeing the full application of the directive in a sufficient clear and precise manner so that the persons covered by the directive to the extent that the directive is intended to create rights for individuals, must be enabled to ascertain the full extent of their rights and, where appropriate, rely on them before the national courts".

7 Cfr., v.g., CJEU Case 168/85, Commission v Italy [1986] ECLI:EU:C:1986:381, para. 13; Case C-334/94, Commission v France [1996] ECLI:EU:C:1996:90, para. 30; Case C-197/96 Commission v France [1997] ECLI:EU:C:1997:155, paras. 14–15; Case C-315/98, Commission v Italy [1999] ECLI:EU:C:1999:551, paras. 8 and 10; Case C-358/98, Commission v Italy [2000] ECLI:EU:C:2000:114, paras. 16–17.

sions of EU legislation are equally valid, and this can be extremely problematic when the law in question contains concepts not easily understood in at least some languages, thus creating uncertainty as to its meaning, or when there are inconsistencies between different language versions[8]. Sometimes it is difficult to convey the exact same meaning in different languages, and complex long sentences are used. National implementation is sometimes the victim of this lack of intelligibility of the drafting of EU legal texts. Beyond translation problems, another important challenge is the diversity in the legal languages of the many Member States and of the EU legal order. This means that, sometimes, legal terminology used in the EU version of one language can be somewhat different from the one used at the national level, consequently it can be not easily understood by the speakers of that language.

There is another challenge emerging from the need of Member State implementation of EU laws: the differences in legal drafting between the national and EU levels. In fact, despite some commonalities, there are no unified or harmonized legal drafting rules and practices within the 28 Member States. Such rules and practices vary considerably, largely determined by national constitutional, legal or customary rules – namely in relation to the structure of law texts or the divisions and subdivisions that an article should have. They are also different from the ones adopted at the EU level. Legal drafting rules and practices of the EU are the result of intricacies of the EU legislative process (the need for inter-institutional dialogue, for instance[9]), but also of the influence of drafting rules and practices of the Member States (through hybridization). The result is a unique set of rules that differ from the national ones.

The fact that EU acts are drafted in accordance with a different set of rules has impacts on the national implementation stage. As national actors are used to and trained to read legal texts drafted according to their national rules, the different drafting style of European legal acts can lead to problems in their wide accessibility and correct interpretation. Two types of problems may emerge, depending on the type of EU act in question. In the case of self-executing acts, it becomes a matter of correct implementation of EU law by national judges and administration. However, the core prob-

8 S. Taylor, "The European Union and National Legal Languages: an Awkward Partnership?" [2011] Revue française de linguistique appliquée XVI, 105–118; A. Čavoški, "Interaction of law and language in the EU: Challenges of translating in multilingual environment", [2017] Journal of Specialised Translation 27, 58–74.

9 The involvement of three institutions in the ordinary legislative process (the Commission, the Council and the European Parliament), brings the need to dialogue.

lem of the differences between EU and Member States' drafting rules and practices surfaces when there is a need for national legislative implementation of EU laws (transposing directives or executing regulations or decisions).

In the process of implementing EU law through legislation, there are EU derived duties that must be complied with by the Member States. According to the established case law of the CJEU, "provisions of directives must be implemented with (...) the specificity, precision and clarity necessary to satisfy the requirements of legal certainty"[10]. Member States must ensure that the legal effect of national implementing measures is sufficiently precise and clear to enable the individuals concerned to know the extent of their rights and obligations established by the EU legal order[11]. This means that there is an EU derived duty to ensure the quality of national laws drafted to implement Union legislation.

However, the principle of procedural autonomy of the Member States[12] ensures that, "according to settled case-law of the Court, in the absence of EU rules on the matter, it is for the national legal order of each Member State to establish procedural rules for actions intended to safeguard the rights of individuals"[13]. This means that a lack of harmonization is accepted. But there are limits. The principle of procedural autonomy of the Member States recognises two exceptions: the national rules must comply with the principles of equivalence and effectiveness[14]. Compliance with the principle of equivalence requires that the national rule in question ap-

10 CJEU, Case C-59/89 Commission v Germany [1991] ECLI:EU:C:1991:225, par. 24; case C-225/97, Commission v France [1999], ECLI:EU:C:1999:252, par. 37; Case C-159/99 Commission v Italy [2001], ECLI:EU:C:2001:278, par. 32; Case C-296/01 Commission v France [2003], ECLI:EU:C:2003:626, par. 54; Case C-441/02 Commission v Germany [2006], ECLI:EU:C:2006:253, par. 73; Case C-61/05 Commission v Portugal [2006], ECLI:EU:C:2006:467, par. 37; Case C-427/07 Commission v Ireland [2009], ECLI:EU:C:2009:457, par. 55; Case C-50/09 Commission v Ireland [2011], ECLI:EU:C:2011:109, par. 46; Case C-151/12 Commission v Spain [2013], ECLI:EU:C:2013:690, par. 26; Case C-281/11 Commission v Poland [2013], ECLI:EU:C:2013:855, par. 101; Case C-277/13 Commission v Portugal [2014], ECLI:EU:C:2014:2208, par. 43; Case C-29/14 Commission v Poland [2015], ECLI:EU:C:2015:379, par. 37.

11 V.g., CJEU Case C-296/01 Commission v France [2003] ECLI:EU:C:2003:626, paras 54–55.

12 CJEU Case 33/76 Rewe-Zentralfinanz eG and Rewe-Zentral AG [1976] ECLI:EU:C:1976:188.

13 CJEU, Case C-3/16 Aquino [2017], ECLI:EU:C:2017:209, para. 48.

14 V. g., CJEU, Case C-326/96, Levez, 1 December 1998, Case C-161/15, Abdelhafid Bensada Benallalicy, 17 March 2016, Case C-69/14, Dragoş Constantin Târşia, 6

plies without discrimination to actions based on implementation of EU law and those based on implementation of national law having a similar purpose and cause of action. According to the principle of effectiveness, national procedural rules are applicable on the condition that they do not make it virtually impossible or excessively difficult to exercise the rights conferred by EU law. The resulting legal framework means that, in the case of legal implementation of EU law, in the absence of EU wide rules on legal drafting and outside of the scope of these exceptions, it is up to each Member State to choose the rules and practices to follow.

Hence, when national legislators are implementing EU laws, they must transpose its letter and its spirit to the legal order of the Member State. This entails the need to adapt its content in order to ensure its correct enforcement in the context of the national legal order. But it also involves the need to adjust the legal texts drafted in accordance with EU rules in order to comply with their own legal drafting rules and practices[15]. This

October 2015, Case C-200/14, Câmpean, 30 June 2016, paras 55–56; Case 199/82, San Giorgio, 9 November 1983, para. 14. D.-U. Galetta, Procedural Autonomy of EU Member States: Paradise Lost? A Study on the "Functionalized Procedural Competence" of EU Member States, Heidelberg-Dordrecht-London-NewYork: Springer, 2010, XVI-145.

15 On the drafting problems of the national procedure for implementation through laws, v.g., B. Steunenberg & W. Voermans, The transposition of EC directives: A Comparative Study of Instruments, Techniques and Processes in Six Member States, Leiden University, 2006; J. H. Jans, "National Legislative Autonomy? The Procedural Constraints of European Law" [2009] Legal Issues of European Integration, 25 (1), 25–58 and E.B. Beenakker, The implementation of international law in the national legal order: a legislative perspective, Doctoral Thesis, Leiden University Repository 2018 (http://hdl.handle.net/1887/63079), 109. See also, G. Ciavarini Azzi, "The Slow March of European Legislation: The Implementation of Directives" in Karlheinz Neunreither and Antje Wiener (eds), European Integration After Amsterdam, OUP, 2000, 52; E. Mastenbroek, "Surviving the Deadline: The Transposition of EU Directives in the Netherlands" [2003], European Union Politics 4 (4), 371–395; B. Nowak, "Implementation of Directives into Domestic Legal System. The Case of Poland" [2005] Yearbook of Polish European Studies 9/2005 33; E. Borghetto, F. Franchino & D. Giannetti, "Complying with the transposition deadlines of EU directives: evidence from Italy" [2006] Rivista Italiana di Politiche Pubbliche 5, 7–38; S. Berglund, I. Gange & F. van Waarden, "Mass production of law. Routinization in the transposition of European directives: a sociological-institutional account" [2006] Journal of European Public Policy 13, 692–71; M. Kaeding, Better Regulation in the European Union: Lost in Translation or Full Steam Ahead? The Transposition of EU Transport Directives across Member States, Leiden: Leiden University Press (2007); T. König and B.

adjustment procedure can be difficult, especially when misalignment of EU and Member States' legal drafting rules and practices emerge.

II. A "de facto" harmonization of legal drafting techniques in the EU?

As the EU and Member States' legal drafting rules and practices are different, the misalignment between them causes drafting problems in the legal implementation procedure of EU law at national level.

Examples of this misalignment vary from one Member State to the other because some national rules and practices are closer to the EU ones than others. Typical examples of misalignment can be found in the rules governing the internal structure of the act (which set of provisions must be at the beginning or the end of the act, and which is the correct sequence), rules on referencing, rules on the existence of headings, and rules on paragraphing (if the paragraphs are numbered or not and how does the numbering work). The existence of a list of definitions is also a good example of a common feature of EU legal drafting, justified by the need to ensure a harmonized and coherent implementation throughout the European legal order, which did not exist in some Member States drafting traditions.

In some of these cases, the adjustments needed to the content of the EU legal texts to adapt them to national drafting rules are fairly simple (*v.g.*, by merely adding headings or altering the sequence of provisions). But there are also situations when major efforts were necessary. For instance, there are cases when the whole internal structure of a directive needed to be changed when transposing it to the national order[16].

Luetgert, "Troubles with Transposition? Explaining Trends in Member-State Notification and the Delayed Transposition of EU Directives" [2008] British Journal of Political Science 39, 163–194; H. Xanthaki, Drafting Legislation: Art and Technology of Rules for Regulation, Bloomsbury Publishing, 2014; N. Voulvoulis, K. D. Arpon & T. Giakoumis, "The EU Water Framework Directive: From great expectations to problems with implementation" [2017] Science of The Total Environment 575, 358–366.

16 That was the example, in Portugal, of the transposition of the EU directives on public procurement (Directive 2014/24/EU of the European Parliament and of the Council of 26 February 2014 on public procurement and repealing Directive 2004/18/EC, Directive 2014/25/EU of the European Parliament and of the Council of 26 February 2014 on procurement by entities operating in the water, energy, transport and postal services sectors and repealing Directive 2004/17/EC, and Directive 2014/23/EU of the European Parliament and of the Council of 26

As mentioned, there is some degree of harmonization and restriction of Member States' autonomy that results from the need to ensure that national implementing measures are sufficiently precise and clear. However, this is a minimum level of harmonization. There are also cases where Member States have adopted EU legal drafting solutions either through copy-out (or word for word) transpositions of Directives or through techniques that became so pervasive that they eventually became part of the legal drafting traditions of the Member States.

The Commission's strict approach and control of implementation of EU law, especially in the transposition of directives, has reinforced this trend. It is easier for a Member State to prove correct transposition of a Directive by simply copying it out, namely adopting in the implementing legislation exactly the same wording and structure as that of the Directive. Besides, the CJEU consistently states that Member States may not rely on national provisions or practices, including legislative drafting ones, to justify (alleged) failure to comply with obligations and time limits laid down in Directives. Member States have, thus, a strong incentive – for practical reasons – to use a drafting technique as close as possible to the one used by the Directive.

In several cases, the practices of the EU are integrated into the Member State's drafting rules. The EU-influenced rules became accepted as national drafting rules and are applied in the Member State even outside EU implementation. A good example is the adoption of a list of definitions in a provision at the beginning of a legislative act. This is a common feature of EU legislative acts, especially in directives, justified by the need to harmonize its interpretation in the legal orders of the Member States. Such a technique was not present in the Portuguese legal drafting tradition, as in a number of other national legal orders. However, the existence of such an initial list of definitions became so common and so ubiquitous because of the transposition of EU directives that it became "normalized" and part of the national legal drafting rules and practices, being adopted even when drafting non-EU related legal acts[17].

The adoption by the national level of EU drafting rules leads to a creeping "de facto" harmonization not only of the contents of the national laws but also of legal drafting techniques throughout the EU. Due to the very

February 2014 on the award of concession contracts) which gave rise to the Code of Public Contracts.

17 D. Duarte *et all*, Legística. Perspectivas sobre a concepção e redacção de actos normativos, Coimbra: Almedina, 2002, 258–260.

nature of being an ongoing process, it is not uniform in the sense that it works differently in the several Member States. This harmonization is not a planned outcome of EU integration, but appears as a natural spill-over consequence of the link between legal orders and legislators.

The possible emergence of European-wide common drafting rules presents several positive aspects, such as the reinforcement of a common European legal space, coherent and accessible to everyone. It would make it easier for non-national EU citizens to better understand how the laws of a Member State were drafted, promoting legal certainty for foreign investors, for instance. Better law-making practices adopted at the EU level can also be "exported" to the national level through this procedure. However, there are also a number of problems that can materialize.

National drafting traditions are part of a Member States' identities, closely connected with their constitutional, legal, social and cultural characteristics – protected under Article 4 (2) TEU. The adoption of the EU legal drafting rules with no limits would mean a loss in the diversity of the national legal orders, which is meant to be preserved.

Besides, the simple copy-out transposition of Directives, including the drafting style and technique, means that the Member States will (in the majority of cases) not use the margin of discretion given to them under this type of legal act and can also lead to the adoption of solutions not suited for a particular Member State.

The changing of stable national legal drafting traditions can also lead to unnecessary complexity in the interpretation and implementation of national rules. For instance, it can prove difficult to conjugate laws drafted according to the national traditions with the ones influenced by the EU. It can also provoke an erosion of legal certainty at the national level, because of the rapid change in the drafting rules to which national citizens and legal actors are used to. The increase in accessibility to the legal act by non-nationals needs to be balanced with the loss of accessibility to national citizens.

Finally, when the adoption of the EU legal drafting rules is not possible in accordance with national rules or is not desired by the Member State for drafting reasons, there is a danger that the drafting differences could be considered as non-compliance. That would be the case, for instance, when the Commission considers that the internal structure of the national legal act, which differs from the Directive's internal structure, leads to a least effective enforcement of its rules, namely because it makes the interpretation of the national act in accordance with the Directive more difficult. Some of the cases can have substantive consequences and should be addressed, as would be the case if a Member State would refuse to transpose a Directive's list of definitions, with the justification that its legal drafting rules do not allow for it. However, when it is merely a drafting problem, it can be easily resolved at an early stage of the infringement procedure (through the letters of notice sent by the Commission or its reasoned opinions). In that case, the misalignment of drafting rules may cause unnecessary infringement procedures that are unrelated to any opposition to the substance of the rules and only identified after the approval of the legal text.

III. Then… How to reconcile the drafting rules and practices of the Member-States with the rules and practices of the EU?

This analysis brings us back to the original question of how to reconcile the drafting rules and practices of the Member-States with the rules and practices of the EU. This is a complex problem, related with the multi-layered nature of the Union, which cannot be solved with a single solution.

One must start by recognizing that such a problem exists and that it is a distinct problem *vis-à-vis* the translation of the legal texts. The existing link between national and European legislators means that there is an interdependence of the two drafting processes (national and supranational) – they are not independent. Hence, EU legal drafting influence national laws that implement European acts, but EU legislators must take that into consideration while drafting in order to ensure effective implementation.

One possible answer lies with the Member States. EU law is not the result of an anonymous "bubble" based in Brussels. Representatives of the Member States play a role as legislators throughout the EU legislative procedure. National governments of Member States are represented on the Council by the relevant minister from each Member State depending on the subject to be discussed. In addition, Member States are represented on COREPER and working groups. These representatives should strive to make EU legislation as compatible as possible to their own legal drafting traditions. This would avoid unnecessary misalignments and bridge the gap between EU and Member States legal drafting rules and practices. When such an effort is impossible, at least EU legal drafters will become aware of the drafting concerns of the Member States.

National entities and personnel responsible for the formal legal drafting of the transposing legal acts should participate in the EU's decision-making procedure (through the respective Member State), namely during the preparation of the national language version of the secondary legislation, allowing a screening of the proposed draft and a cross-harmonization of the national and EU's legislative drafting rules and practices.

At the same time, the EU must recognize the importance of national drafting rules to ensure correct implementation by Member States. This should mainly include accepting national inputs in how to draft during the legislative process, but also take into account the diversity of national drafting traditions when evaluating correct transposition and any possible infringement of EU law.

Finally, an effort by all the involved parties to ensure strict adherence to drafting rules of clear and simple writing and structuring of legal acts would greatly facilitate the cooperation between national and EU legislators.

Chapter 13: Regulating Private Law. The Rise of Regulations and their Impact on National Codifications

Ruben de Graaff & Dorine J. Verheij (Leiden University)

I. Introduction

The spirit of codification is still strong on the continent. Over the past decades, many countries have reformed their civil codes. The Netherlands (1992), Germany (2002), Romania (2011), the Czech Republic (2014), and Hungary (2014) are just a few examples. Important new reforms are currently making their way through the legislative process. The French government wishes to complement the recently introduced law of contract with a new law of delict. The Belgian government even intends to introduce a fresh codification embracing the whole of private law.

These efforts are made against the background of an expanding body of secondary EU law. Since the 1980s, a range of directives has been introduced in order to improve the functioning of the internal market. Many of these directives regulate private law matters, such as misleading advertising, unfair commercial practices, the liability for the infringement of competition law and the return of cultural property. Over the past ten years, the Union legislature has developed a preference for using regulations rather than directives. This development can be seen in the areas of transport, consumer protection, judicial cooperation in civil matters and the internal market more broadly. As a result, important areas of private law are now governed by regulations, not by directives.

The legislative shift from directives to regulations raises important questions that have, so far, received little attention, at least not from the perspective of private law. What does the preference for regulations entail for the future of the national civil codes? What impact does this development have on the clarity, accessibility and consistency of the current systems of private law, both at the European level and within the national legal orders? How can national legislatures and courts deal with this development? How can academics pay attention to these regulations in their education and research activities? This contribution will address these questions and discuss the answers.[1]

II. Harmonisation through Directives

The core objective of the European integration project has always been to create and maintain an internal market in which the free movement of goods, persons, services and capital is ensured.[2] Over the years, the Union legislature has introduced a great number of directives in order to improve the functioning of this market.[3] In the field of private law, the attention has been fixed on the law of contract and particularly – but not exclusive-

1 This contribution is based on a prior Dutch publication: R de Graaff & DJ Verheij, 'Europese verordeningen en Nederlands vermogensrecht' (2017) Ars Aequi 988–994.

2 Art. 26 TFEU, and its predecessors.

3 Primarily based on Art. 114 and 115 TFEU, and their predecessors.

4 Council Directive 86/653/EEC on the coordination of the laws of the Member States relating to self-employed commercial agents [1986] OJ L 382/17; Directive 2002/47/EC on financial collateral arrangements [2002] OJ L168/43; Directive 2011/7/EU on combating late payment in commercial transactions [2011] OJ L48/1; Directive (EU) 2015/2366 on payment services in the internal market [2015] OJ L337/35; Directive (EU) 2016/943 on the protection of undisclosed know-how and business information (trade secrets) against their unlawful acquisition, use and disclosure [2016] OJ L 157/1.

5 Consider Council Directive 93/13/EEC on unfair terms in consumer contracts [1993] OJ L95/29; Directive 1999/44/EC on certain aspects of the sale of consumer goods and associated guarantees [1999] OJ L 171/12; Directive 2000/31/EC on certain legal aspects of information society services, in particular electronic commerce, in the Internal Market ('Directive on electronic commerce') [2000] OJ L178/1; Directive 2002/65/EC concerning the distance marketing of consumer financial services [2002] OJ L271/16; Directive 2005/29/EC concerning unfair business-to-consumer commercial practices in the internal market ('Unfair Commercial Practices Directive') [2005] OJ L 149/22; Directive 2008/48/EC on credit agreements for consumers [2008] OJ L 133/66; Directive 2008/122/EC on the protection of consumers in respect of certain aspects of timeshare, long-term holiday product, resale and exchange contracts [2009] OJ L 33/10; Directive 2011/83/EU on consumer rights [2011] OJ L 304/64; Directive 2014/17/EU on credit agreements for consumers relating to residential immovable property [2014] OJ L 60/34; Directive (EU) 2015/2302 on package travel and linked travel arrangements [2015] OJ L 326/1.

ly[4] – on consumer contracts.[5] In addition, some parts of the law of delict[6] and of the law of property have been harmonised.[7] By now, a range of different topics is regulated at the European level, such as misleading advertising and unfair commercial practices, product liability and cartel damages, the return of cultural objects and package travel arrangements.

National legislatures must transpose a directive within a given period of time. Under Article 288 TFEU, they are bound 'as to the result to be achieved' by the directive. At the same time, they remain competent to choose the 'form and methods' of implementation. Indeed, several options are available.[8] The provisions may be included in a separate act, or they may be integrated in existing statutes. The provisions may be reproduced verbatim, but their wording may also be adjusted to the terminology prevailing in the national legal system.[9] The provisions may be awarded the same scope of application, but they may also govern matters not provided for by the underlying directive. In the event of minimum harmonisation, the national legislature may even provide for a higher level of protection than the directive requires.[10]

Without any doubt, the least time-consuming approach is to incorporate directives verbatim in separate legal acts. This has been the general approach adopted in the United Kingdom, a legal system that does not, after all, have a tradition of codifying the whole of private law in a civil code. Many continental Member States have taken the implementation of directives into their national laws one or two steps further. Some of them have

---

6 Consider Council Directive 85/374/EEC on the approximation of the laws, regulations and administrative provisions of the Member States concerning liability for defective products [1985] OJ L210/29; Directive 2006/114/EC concerning misleading and comparative advertising [2006] OJ L376/21; Directive 2014/104/EU on certain rules governing actions for damages under national law for infringements of the competition law provisions of the Member States and of the European Union [2014] OJ L 349/1.

7 Consider Directive 2002/47/EC on financial collateral arrangements [2002] OJ L168/43; Directive 2014/60/EU on the return of cultural objects unlawfully removed from the territory of a Member State [2014] OJ L159/1.

8 H Rösler, 'Europeanisation of Private Law Through Directives – Determining Factors and Modalities of Implementation' (2009) XI European Journal of Law Reform, 305, 312–315; MW Hesselink, 'The Ideal of Codification and the Dynamics of Europeanisation: The Dutch Experience' (2006) 12 European Law Journal 279, 295–304.

9 Cf. Case C-59/89 *Commission v. Germany* [1991] ECR I-02607, para 18; Case C-131/88 *Commission v. Germany* [1991] ECR I-00825, para 6.

10 P Craig & G De Búrca, *EU Law. Text, Cases, and Materials* (6th edn, OUP 2015) 626–627.

grouped provisions of multiple directives together and incorporated them in national codes with a particular focus. Examples are the Austrian *Konsumentenschutzgesetz*, the French *Code de la consummation*, and the Italian *Codice del consume*. Some Member States have even tried to completely integrate the directives in the system of their respective civil codes. In the Netherlands, for instance, legislative lawyers are instructed to use the existing statutes and regulations 'as much as possible' when transposing binding EU legislation into national law.[11] In fact, the Constitution of the Kingdom of the Netherlands prescribes that private law shall be laid down in a general legal code.[12] It does not, therefore, come as a surprise that many directives have been implemented in the Dutch Civil Code. A similar approach has been followed in Germany, where the implementation of several directives has been one of the main reasons behind the reform of the general law of obligations in 2002.[13]

Each approach has its advantages and disadvantages. Reproducing the provisions of a directive verbatim in separate legal acts indicates that the rules are derived from EU law and that they should be given the same meaning as the provisions of the underlying directive. The disadvantage is that no particular attempt is made to bring these rules to the attention of the persons to whom they are addressed. Citizens and companies, and their lawyers, may expect to find the mandatory and non-mandatory rules on contract, delict and property in the civil code, regardless of whether these rules are derived from EU legislation or not. On a more fundamental level, it might be problematic that the rules themselves are not coordinated at all. Reproduction can lead to inconsistencies within the national system of private law and thus to 'internal' incoherence. Any attempt to solve these inconsistencies, however, risks impairing the 'external' coherence between the national system of private law and EU law.[14] Moreover, integrating the rules in the civil code might benefit the accessibility of private law, but risks concealing the European roots of the rules concerned.

This tension – between the demands of implementation and the ideal of codification – has troubled writers and lawmakers alike. In the Nether-

---

11 Instruction 9.7 of the 'Aanwijzingen voor de regelgeving' (Drafting instructions for legislation), to be found at <wetten.overheid.nl/BWBR0005730/2018-01-01> accessed 31 May 2019.

12 Art. 107 of the Constitution of the Kingdom of the Netherlands.

13 See, among many other contributions, R Schulze and HS Schulte-Nölke, *Die Schuldrechtsreform vor dem Hintergrund des Gemeinschaftsrechts* (Mohr Siebeck 2001).

14 Cf. Hesselink (n 8) 293–295; Rösler (n 8) 314–315.

lands, for instance, some writers defend the choice to implement directives in the civil code,[15] others prefer implementation in separate books,[16] and still others mainly criticise the impact of the directives on the internal coherence of the civil code.[17]

III. Harmonisation through Regulations

While lawyers attempted to find the proper middle course between implementation and codification, the European Commission expressed its preference for the use of regulations over directives, hinting that regulations should be used 'wherever appropriate' and that 'replacing directives with regulations can, when legally possible and politically acceptable, offer simplification'.[18] Monti endorsed this position in his 2010 report on the future of the single market:

> 'Regulation brings the advantages of clarity, predictability and effectiveness. It establishes a level playing field for citizens and business and carries a greater potential for private enforcement.'[19]

The preference for the use of regulations is caused by a dissatisfaction with the effects of directives. As provisions of directives are not directly applicable between private individuals, their effects almost entirely depend on na-

---

15 E.g. MBM Loos, 'De invloed van het Europese richtlijnenrecht op de coherentie van het Nederlandse privaatrecht' (2007) 24 NTBR 176–179; MH Wissink, 'Over volledige harmonisatie en herinrichting van het BW' (2009) 6 Vermogensrechtelijke Analyses 48, 69–70.

16 E.g. WH van Boom, 'Algemene en bijzondere regelingen in het vermogensrecht' (2003) 164 RMThemis 297, 300; MW Hesselink, 'Naar een (Europees) wetboek van consumentenrecht?' (2007) 82 NJB 850–857; JM Smits, 'Europese integratie in het vermogensrecht: een pleidooi voor keuzevrijheid' in DM Curtin and others (eds), *Europese integratie* (Kluwer 2006) 103–104.

17 E.g. C Bollen and GR de Groot, 'Verknoeit het Europese recht ons Burgerlijk Wetboek?' (1995) 12 NTBR 1–10; JE Fesevur, 'De waarde van een systeem en de noodzaak van handboeken', (2005) 22 NTBR 287; WL Valk, 'Europa en de erfenis van Meijers' (2007) 24 NTBR 45; HN Schelhaas, 'Inconsistenties in het verbintenissenrecht: de wetswijziging betaaldiensten' (2010) 27 NTBR 1.

18 Communication from the Commission – A Europe of Results – Applying Community Law, 5 September 2007, COM(2007)502 final, p. 5 and fn. 12.

19 M Monti, 'A New Strategy for the Single Market – At the Service of Europe's Economy and Society' (Brussels, 2010), to be found at <https://ec.europa.eu/docsroom/documents/15501/attachments/1/translations/en/renditions/pdf> accessed 31 May 2019.

tional implementing measures.[20] As a result, lawyers must have sufficient command of the applicable national laws and, hence, of the relevant rules of private international law. A second explanation is that directives have become more and more similar to regulations.[21] Many directives are very detailed and leave little discretion to the Member States.[22] Moreover, the case law of the Court of Justice has shown that the interpretation of national implementing measures may not lead to other results than those prescribed by a directive.[23]

Yet, compared to directives, regulations do have important advantages. A regulation is 'binding in its entirety' and 'directly applicable in all Member States'.[24] Unlike a directive, a regulation enters into force 'independent of any measure of reception into national law'.[25] In principle, Member States may not even transpose a regulation into national law, as this could endanger its direct effect and its uniform application.[26] By using a regulation, debates on national implementing measures and harmonious interpretation are, therefore, largely avoided. Nevertheless, the use of regulations cannot entirely preclude such debates from arising, as regulations can – and sometimes do – leave certain specific matters to the discretion of the

---

20 Cf. Case C-152/84 *Marshall v. Southampton and South-West Hampshire Area Health Authority* [1986] -00723, para 48, and, recently, Case C-122/17 *David Smith v. Patrick Meade and Others* [2018] ECLI:EU:C:2018:631, paras 42–43, with references to earlier judgments.

21 'Report of the Task Force on Subsidiarity, Proportionality and "Doing Less More Efficiently"' (2018), 19 to be found at <https://ec.europa.eu/commission/sites/beta-political/files/report-task-force-subsidiarity-proportionality-and-doing-less-more-efficiently_en.pdf> accessed 31 May 2019.

22 C Twigg-Flesner, 'Good-Bye Harmonisation by Directives, Hello Cross-Border only Regulation?' (2011) European Review of Contract Law 245 and F Wilman, 'The end of the absence? The growing body of EU legislation on private enforcement and the main remedies it provides for' (2016) Common Market Law Review 887–935 893.

23 Cf. Case C-441/14 *Danski Industri* [2016] ECLI:EU:C:2016:278, paras 28–34. It must be noted that the Danish Supreme Court maintained its position that Danish law cannot be interpreted in compliance with Directive 2000/78/EC establishing a general framework for equal treatment in employment and occupation: Supreme Court (Denmark) 6 December 2016, Case 15/2014 (*Danski Industri*).

24 Art. 288 TFEU.

25 Cases C-4/10 and C-27/10 *Bureau national interprofessionnel du Cognac* [2011] I-06131, para 66. See also Case 39/72 *Commission v. Italy*, [1973] -00101 para 10 and Case C-34/73 *Fratelli Variola S.p.A.* [1973] -00981 para 10.

26 The prohibition to implement regulations follows from Case 39/72 *Commission v. Italy*, [1973] -00101 para 17 and Case C-34/73 *Fratelli Variola S.p.A.* [1973] -00981 para 11.

Member States and may even require national implementing measures. Indeed, not every provision included in a regulation is formulated in such a clear, precise and unconditional way that it can be applied directly to a specific case at hand.[27]

In some areas of private law, the Union legislature has traditionally preferred the use of regulations. The rights and obligations of passengers and carriers, for instance, are largely codified in regulations. In the early 1990s, the Union legislature introduced a right to compensation and assistance for passengers in the event of denied boarding by an air carrier.[28] In subsequent years, regulations have been introduced that arrange for the rights of passengers travelling by train,[29] by sea and inland waterway[30] and by bus and coach.[31] These regulations entitle passengers to demand the performance of several services by carriers. Passengers may have a right to a refund of the ticket price, to alternative ways of transport and to care during the delay, and to compensation for the delay.[32] In addition, specific rules have been developed in respect of a carriers' liability for damage to wheelchairs,[33] for the loss of luggage and damage to luggage, and for the death and injury of passengers.[34]

---

27 See, on this topic, R Král, 'National normative implementation of EC Regulations: An exceptional or rather common matter?' (2008) European Law Review 243–256 and JA Winter, 'Direct Applicability and Direct Effect. Two Distinct and Different Concepts in Community Law' (1972) Common Market Law Review 425–438.

28 Council Regulation (EEC) No 295/91 establishing common rules for a denied-boarding compensation system in scheduled air transport [1991] OJ L 36/8 (as replaced by Regulation (EC) No 261/2004 establishing common rules on compensation and assistance to passengers in the event of denied boarding and of cancellation or long delay of flights [2004] OJ L 46/1).

29 Regulation (EC) No 1371/2007 on rail passengers' rights and obligations [2007] OJ L 315/14.

30 Regulation (EU) No 1177/2010 concerning the rights of passengers when travelling by sea and inland waterway [2010] OJ L 334/1.

31 Regulation (EU) No 181/2011 concerning the rights of passengers in bus and coach transport [2011] OJ L 55/1.

32 For an oversight of the regulations, see I Koning, MJ Boon & MDA van Bodegraven, 'Europese passagiersverordeningen. Spoor, weg, zee en binnenwateren in de slipstream van het luchtvervoer' (2011) Tijdschrift Vervoer & Recht 127–143.

33 These rules are incorporated in the regulations previously referred to as well as arranged for in specific legal instruments, such as Regulation (EC) No 1107/2006 concerning the rights of disabled persons and persons with reduced mobility when travelling by air [2006] OJ L 204/1.

34 These rules are incorporated in the regulations previously referred to as well as arranged for in specific legal instruments, such as Regulation (EC) No 889/2002 on

In recent years, the Union legislature has decided to make use of regulations in other legal areas as well.[35] The Commission's farthest-reaching proposal – the introduction of a Common European Sales Law – never entered into force.[36] However, several other proposals have been adopted, for instance in the area of financial law.[37] Consider the Regulation on credit rating agencies, which does not only impose obligations upon credit rating agencies, but also sets conditions for the civil liability of credit rating agencies towards investors and issuers. The European basis for liability introduced by this regulation exists alongside other grounds for liability established under the applicable national law.[38] Consider also the ground for civil liability contained in the Regulation on key information documents for packaged retail and insurance-based investment products, which provides a right to compensation to retail investors against manufacturers of packaged retail and insurance-based investment products.[39] In addition to financial law, part of the digital single market is also regulated by regulations. Some of these regulations involve rules of a private law nature. For example, the regulation on cross-border 'portability' of online content services in the internal market stipulates that all contractual provisions that are contrary to the regulation shall be 'unenforceable'.[40]

From the outset, it is not always clear whether a regulation involves rules of a private law nature. One would not, for instance, expect rules of substantive private law to be included in regulations in the field of judicial cooperation in civil matters. Nevertheless, the Regulation on cross-border insolvency proceedings stipulates that the insolvency practitioner is liable

---

air carrier liability in the event of accidents [2002] OJ L 140/2 and Regulation (EC) No 392/2009 on the liability of carriers of passengers by sea in the event of accidents [2009] OJ L 131/24. These regulations implement international treaties to which the EU is a party (with the exception of Regulation (EC) 181/2011).

35 Cf. T. Ackermann, 'Sektorielles EU-Recht und allgemeine Privatrechtssystematik' (2018) 25 ZEuP 741, 761.

36 Commission, 'Proposal for a Regulation of the European Parliament and of the Council on a Common European Sales Law', COM (2011) 635 final.

37 See, for examples in the area of payment services, AS Hartkamp, *Mr. C. Assers Handleiding tot de beoefening van het Nederlands Burgerlijk Recht. 3. Vermogensrecht algemeen. Deel I. Europees recht en Nederlands vermogensrecht* (Wolters Kluwer 2018) No. 192.

38 Art. 35a (5) Regulation (EU) No 462/2013 on credit rating agencies [2013] OJ L 146/1.

39 Art. 11 (2) Regulation (EU) No 1286/2014 on key information documents for packaged retail and insurance-based investment products [2014] OJ L 352/1.

40 Art. 7 (1) Regulation (EU) No 2017/1128 on cross-border portability of online content services in the internal market [2017] OJ L 168/1.

for 'any damage caused to local creditors' if he fails to comply with the regulation.[41] In addition, the Regulation on the establishment of a European Account Preservation Order procedure to facilitate cross-border debt recovery states that a creditor is liable 'for any damage caused to the debtor [...] due to fault on the creditor's part'. This ground for liability does not exclude the application of civil liability grounds established under the applicable national law.[42]

Finally, the Union legislature has also replaced several directives with new regulations. The replacement of the General Data Protection Directive with the General Data Protection Regulation is the most prominent example.[43] Since 25 May 2018, natural persons can demand access to their personal data, rectification and erasure of their personal data.[44] In addition, the regulation has created a ground for the civil liability of controllers and processors for infringements of the regulation, and has established rules on the joint and several liability of controllers and processors and on the amount of compensation.[45] Civil liability may, for instance, arise when the data subject has not given permission for processing his or her personal data.[46] The Directive on Electronic Signatures provides another example. It has been replaced with a regulation that aims to stimulate the use of electronic identification and trust services for electronic transactions in the internal market. Non-compliance with this regulation may result in the liability of a Member State or a service provider.[47]

---

41 Art. 36 (10) Regulation (EU) No 2015/848 on insolvency proceedings [2015] OJ L 141/19.

42 Art. 13 Regulation (EU) No 655/2014 establishing a European Account Preservation Order procedure to facilitate cross-border debt recovery in civil and commercial matters [2014] OJ L 189/59.

43 Regulation (EU) No 2016/679 on the protection of natural persons with regard to the processing of personal data and on the free movement of such data, and repealing Directive 95/46/EC [2016] OJ L 119/1. The current Directive on privacy and electronic communications may also be replaced by a regulation, see Commission, 'Proposal for a Regulation concerning the respect for private life and the protection of personal data in electronic communications and repealing Directive 2002/58/EC (Regulation on Privacy and Electronic Communications)' COM (2017) 010 final.

44 Art. 15–20 General Data Protection Regulation.

45 Art. 82 General Data Protection Regulation.

46 As required by Art. 6–9 General Data Protection Regulation.

47 Regulation (EU) No 910/2014 on electronic identification and trust services for electronic transactions in the internal market and repealing Directive 1999/93/EC [2014] OJ L 257/73.

IV. Clarity, Accessibility and Consistency

We have seen that regulations have gained more and more importance as a source of private law rules.[48] This development has received little attention thus far, even though it has important consequences for the study and practice of private law.

To start with, national legislatures may not transpose these rules into their national civil codes. This prohibition has important consequences for legal traditions that seek to implement EU law very precisely in their national laws, such as Germany and the Netherlands. Furthermore, this prohibition can result in the removal of so-called 'islands of EU law' from the civil codes.[49] The Dutch legislature has, for instance, removed Article 6:196b Dutch Civil Code on the liability of certification service providers, because the underlying directive has been replaced with a regulation that provides its own rules in the field of liability.[50] As stated above, it is not exceptional that national legislatures decide to codify rules of a private law nature in separate legal acts – instead of in the civil code. In the context of directives, the Dutch legislature has, for instance, implemented such rules in the Public Procurement Act,[51] in the Personal Data Protection Act[52] and in the Financial Supervision Act.[53] However, as an important differ-

48 AS Hartkamp, *Mr. C. Assers Handleiding tot de beoefening van het Nederlands Burgerlijk Recht. 3. Vermogensrecht algemeen. Deel I. Europees recht en Nederlands vermogensrecht* (Wolters Kluwer 2018) No. 192 considered the influence of regulations 'marginal', as compared to directives.

49 Cf. H Kötz, 'Rechtsvergleichung und gemeineuropäisches Privatrecht', in: PC Müller-Graff, *Gemeinsames Privatrecht in der Europäischen Gemeinschaft* (Nomos Verslagsgesellschaft 1993) 97.

50 *Kamerstukken II* 2015/16, 34413, 3, 26 (Explanatory Memorandum), in respect of Directive 1999/93/EC on a Community framework for electronic signatures, which was replaced to by Regulation (EU) No 910/2014.

51 E.g. Art. 4.15 Public Procurement Act 2012 on the voidability of contracts concluded on the basis of a contract award decision, implementing Directive 2007/66/EC amending Council Directives 89/665/EEC and 92/13/EEC with regard to improving the effectiveness of review procedures concerning the award of public contracts [2007] OJ L 335/31.

52 E.g. Art. 49 Personal Data Protection Act on the liability of the controller of personal data, implementing Directive 95/46/EC on the protection of individuals with regard to the processing of personal data and on the free movement of such data [1995] OJ L 281/31.

53 E.g. Art. 4:61p Financial Supervision Act on the liability of depositaries, implementing the UCITS V Directive (no. 2014/91/EU on the coordination of laws, regulations and administrative provisions relating to undertakings for collective investment in transferable securities (UCITS) as regards depositary functions, re-

ence, national legislatures may not take implementing decisions with regard to regulations. From that perspective, the goal of bringing together and systematising private law in national civil codes is no longer feasible.[54]

EU law itself does not distinguish public law from private law, nor does it create a coherent system of private law governing contract, delict and property. European legislative instruments are focused on and justified by specific treaty objectives. Like directives, regulations contain all kinds of different rules that the Union legislature considers apt to achieve these objectives. Private law rules may form the majority of the rules, as is the case with the regulations on passenger rights. But they may also be part of a broad legal framework, which codifies several types of obligations and mainly arranges for the public enforcement of these obligations, as is the case with the General Data Protection Regulation. In such situations, the use of regulations has a negative impact upon the clarity and accessibility of private law. But choosing a directive rather than a regulation will inevitably put the clarity and accessibility of EU law under pressure. From the perspective of EU law, the choice for a regulation can therefore be justified.

The consistency of private law can be viewed from multiple levels as well. In the first place, it is important for the body of regulations itself to be sufficiently consistent. But it is highly questionable whether that goal is currently achieved. For instance, considerable differences exist between the liability rules included in the aforementioned regulations. Whereas some of the rules are fairly detailed,[55] others only briefly describe the topic of liability.[56] Whereas some rules indicate which types of loss shall be compensated,[57] others do not provide any indications in this respect.[58] Whereas some rules address issues with respect to the applicable law,[59] jurisdic-

---

muneration policies and sanctions [2014] L 257/186) and AIFMD (no. 2011/61/EU on Alternative Investment Fund Managers and amending Directives 2003/41/EC and 2009/65/EC and Regulations (EC) No 1060/2009 and (EU) No 1095/2010 [2011] L 174/1).

54 Although it must be added that the goal of bringing together and systemising private law in national codes is in itself a difficult task to accomplish. *See* P Popelier, 'Codification in a Civil Law Jurisdiction' (2017) 19 EJLR 259–260.

55 Art. 35a Regulation (EU) no. 462/2013.

56 Art. 36 (10) Regulation (EU) 2015/848.

57 Art. 82 GDPR.

58 Art. 35a Regulation (EU) no. 462/2013.

59 Art. 13 (4) Regulation (EU) 655/2014.

tion,[60] and joint and several liability,[61] other rules do not deal with these issues.[62] Finally, whereas some rules determine the concurrence with other liability provisions, other rules remain silent in this respect.[63]

The fact that the Union legislature has, occasionally, decided to leave certain issues to the applicable national law further hampers the pursuit of consistency within the existing body of regulations. Whereas some directives are as detailed as regulations, some regulations are similar to directives. Consider Article 35a of the Regulation on credit rating agencies, which determines the conditions for the liability of credit rating agencies at the EU level, but refers the interpretation and application of core concepts as 'damage', 'intent' and 'gross negligence' back to the applicable national law.[64] Does this provision require further specification in the laws of the Member States? The Dutch legislature did not find specification necessary, while the English legislature explained the interpretation and application of Article 35a extensively in specific Implementing Regulations.[65] It is doubtful whether the main objectives pursued by the choice of a regulation – direct effect and uniform application – can be achieved in this manner.

V. *Dealing with Regulations*

The previous section has shown that, just as directives, regulations may put fundamental notions such as clarity, accessibility and consistency under pressure, both at the European level and within the national legal orders. At the same time, the use of a regulation instead of a directive may be justified if this leads to a well-functioning regulatory scheme that is directly applicable in relationships between individuals. Because of these advantages, we do expect that the impact of regulations in the field of private law will increase. In the meantime, we should ask ourselves how we should deal

60 Art. 82 (6) jo. Art. 79 (2) GDPR.
61 Art. 82 (4) GDPR.
62 Art. 35a Regulation (EU) no. 462/2013.
63 Cf. Art. 11 (5) (the provision 'are without prejudice to the liability under national law') and Art. 13 (no attention for the concurrence with other liability provisions) Regulation (EU) 910/2014.
64 Regulation (EU) no. 462/2013. The same system was adopted under Art. 11 (3) Regulation (EU) 655/2014.
65 Credit Rating Agencies (Civil Liability) Regulations 2013, to be found at <www.legislation.gov.uk/uksi/2013/1637/pdfs/uksi_20131637_en.pdf> accessed 31 May 2019.

with this development. How can we increase the accessibility and consistency of the rules regarding contract, delict and property contained in regulations?

National legislatures could, first of all, contribute to enhancing the accessibility of these rules. Even if they may not implement the rules, they may nonetheless refer to them in the existing national statutes. In the Netherlands, for instance, the legislature has referred to regulations at several places, so as to clarify the scope of application of the civil code and its relationship to EU law.[66] In Book 10, which deals with issues of private international law, the legislature has even expressly indicated that some situations are not governed by the civil code but by one or more regulations.[67] Appealing as this approach might be, the inclusion of dozens of references has a downside. Surely the civil code should not become a syllabus. It should be comprehensive, but not incomprehensible.

In any event, we should also consider using other means to enhance the accessibility of the relevant regulations. In our opinion, it is feasible and desirable to develop electronic databases that provide an overview of the relevant regulations in the different areas of private law. These databases should be readily accessible to the public – to citizens, companies, practising lawyers and scholars. They could be developed in the different Member States, in close collaboration between scholars, legislative lawyers and other stakeholders. It would seem logical if they would fall back on the existing structure of the national civil codes as a frame of reference and as a means to organise the materials.

In addition, a database could and should also be developed at the European level. After all, the existing databases – such as EUR-Lex and the websites of the European Commission and the European Parliament – do not follow a structure that is familiar to private lawyers but classify the materials according to the policy area, the responsible Directorate-General and the Committee responsible for legislative oversight. Finally, we believe that scholars should trace the relevant rules and pay attention to them in their education and research activities, in their textbooks, statute books, articles and commentaries. Keeping track of the changes made to the civil code is not sufficient anymore.

As far as the consistency of private law rules is concerned, the challenge lies, first and foremost, with the Union legislature, and therefore with the

66 Articles 3:15a BW; 6:193k BW; 6:230i (2) BW; 7:9 (4) BW; 7:50i (1) BW; 7:655 (3) BW; 7:932 (1) BW; 8:99 BW; 8:500a BW; 8:1139 BW; 8:1346 BW.

67 Articles 10:113 (b) BW and 10:114 (c) BW.

European Commission, the European Parliament and the Council of the EU. Differences between regulations may, of course, be justified if the regulations govern distinct situations. However, some differences are best avoided. This is one of the lessons we can learn from the experiences with the harmonisation of private laws through directives. For many years now, the improvement of the coherence of the existing and future acquis has been on the agenda of the Commission.[68] In fact, the Commission has just finished yet another evaluation round – the REFIT Fitness Check – in the course of which it has traced inconsistencies, unjustified overlaps, obsolete provisions and gaps in a range of consumer directives.[69] These experiences should be taken into account when drafting and evaluating regulations. It must be noted that the Commission has already taken some steps in this direction. It intends to coordinate the existing regulations in the field of passenger rights and wants to bring together the common rules in a 'Charter of basic rights'. The Commission also considers the adoption of a single EU framework regulation – an 'EU Codex' – covering passenger rights for all modes of transports.[70]

Judges and scholars may also contribute to enhancing the consistency of the rules contained in regulations. The Court of Justice could provide guidance by interpreting key concepts uniformly as much as possible. Scholars should not only reflect upon legislative proposals, but should also analyse the differences between the existing regulations and their application in the different Member States. The greater these differences, the louder the call for more uniformity will become. Eventually, the rise of regulations might even provide an impetus to the discussion about the desirability of enacting a European Civil Code.[71] Yet in spite of the efforts already made, particularly by the Study Group on a European Civil Code, this road is still long and bumpy. We therefore expect that the consistency

---

68 Commission, 'European Contract Law and the revision of the acquis: the way forward' (Communication) COM (2004) 651 final; Commission, 'Review of the Consumer Acquis', (Green Paper) COM (2006) 744 final.

69 Commission, 'Results of the Fitness Check of consumer and marketing law and of the evaluation of the Consumer Rights Directive' (*European Commission*, 29 May 2017) <https://ec.europa.eu/newsroom/just/item-detail.cfm?item_id=59332> accessed 31 May 2019.

70 Commission, 'Roadmap to a Single European Transport Area – Towards a competitive and resource
efficient transport system', (White Paper) COM (2011) 144 final, 23.

71 Consider e.g. HJ Snijders, 'NBW-vermogensrecht 25 jaar' (2017) 27 MvV 317, 319.

and uniformity of the law can only be improved one step at a time, both by the legislature and by the judiciary.

Finally, it is important to consider the relationship between regulations and the national systems of private law. Inconsistencies should, as much as possible, be avoided. Yet, the national legislatures are not encouraged to acknowledge and tackle such problems, because they are not asked, and often not even permitted, to implement the provisions contained in regulations. Even if a national legislature would adjust its laws to a regulation, there will still be two separate laws in force: the regulation and the applicable national law. To that extent, the choice for a regulation removes an important incentive to 'voluntarily' or 'spontaneously' align national laws with harmonising measures. For this reason, we expect that it will be up to the judiciary, and notably to the highest civil courts, to adjust the national laws to the requirements flowing from a regulation in a particular case.

VI. *Concluding Remarks*

Upon finalising this contribution, another proposal is making its way through the European legislative process. The European Commission intends to introduce a Regulation on a pan-European Personal Pension Product (PEPP).[72] The proposal aims to enable companies to offer pension products to consumers on a single European market. In addition to provisions concerning issues such as authorisation, supervision and administrative penalties, the proposal also contains several rules of a private law nature. The PEPP Regulation should govern the transfer of accumulated assets, the appointment and liability of the depositary, the maximum fees that may be charged when switching providers and the compensation for any losses sustained in the process, and the forms of payment of the pension itself.[73]

This example shows that the impact of regulations on private law and civil codifications is a matter of continuous concern. This contribution has demonstrated that the impact of regulations in the field of private law has increased in recent years. By now, several areas of private law have been

72 Commission, 'Proposal for a Regulation of the European Parliament and of the Council on a pan-European Personal Pension Product (PEPP)', COM (2017) 343 final. On 4 April 2019, the European Parliament has adopted its position at first reading with a view to the adoption of this Regulation, see <www.europarl.europa.eu/doceo/document/TA-8-2019-0347_EN.html>, accessed 31 May 2019.

73 Article 16, Article 41 (3), Article 48 and Article 52 of the PEPP-Proposal.

harmonised through regulations, such as the rights and obligations of passengers and carriers, the remedies for infringements of the right to privacy, the liability of credit rating agencies and the liability of insolvency practitioners involved in cross-border insolvency proceedings. These rules do not find their place in the existing national codes, because the national legislatures may, in principle, not implement the provisions contained in regulations. As a result, directly applicable European rules arise outside the realms of the national civil codifications.

The legislative shift from directives to regulations has a significant impact upon the clarity, accessibility and consistency of private law. Yet the development has, so far, received little attention. This contribution has discussed some of the consequences of this development for the coherence of the national codifications, and has indicated how scholars, legislative lawyers, judges and other practitioners may enhance the accessibility and consistency of the systems of private law – both at the national level and at the EU level.

Chapter 14: Transition from EU directives to EU regulations and the consequences for implementation at the national level. The case of the General Data Protection Regulation (GDPR)

Jeroen Van Nieuwenhove (Catholic University of Leuven)

I. Introduction

The implementation of European law by Member States often is a complex process that involves reconciling constitutional and practical constraints with the need for a uniform and transparent implementation of the newly harmonised EU rules. This EU harmonisation be initiated through directives or regulations. Both instruments have very different consequences for the implementation on the Member State level. The transition from one instrument to another (typically from a directive to a regulation) often requires wide-reaching adaptations of the legislation of the Member States. The question arises whether these consequences are sufficiently taken into consideration when the choice is made for a specific type of legal act on the EU level.

The European General Data Protection Regulation (GDPR)[1] is a good example to illustrate these implementation problems on the Member State level, because it is a regulation with wide-ranging consequences in almost every domain of legislation of the Member States. The choice for a regulation, rather than for a directive (as was the case for its predecessor), as well as the actual content of the GDPR and the margin of appreciation it leaves for the Member States has profound implications for the implementation process. This contribution examines some problems that were encountered in the implementation process (in Belgium and in the Nether-

1 Regulation (EU) 2016/679 of the European Parliament and of the Council of 27 April 2016 on the protection of natural persons with regard to the processing of personal data and on the free movement of such data, and repealing Directive 95/46/EC (General Data Protection Regulation) [2016] OJ L119/1.

lands). A prior assessment that takes into account these kind of problems at the very start of the EU legislation process seems recommendable.

II. Transition from Directive 95/46/EC to the GDPR

The GDPR is the result of a fundamental overhaul of the preceding European Directive 95/46/EC[2]. It regulates the processing of personally identifiable information (personal data) of individuals in the European Union and became applicable from 25 May 2018.

Article 288 TFEU provides that regulations are of a fundamentally different legal nature from directives. A regulation has general application and is binding in its entirety and directly applicable in all Member States. A directive, on the other hand, is only binding, as to the result to be achieved, upon each Member State to which it is addressed, and leaves to the national authorities the choice of form and methods. Directives must first be transposed in national law before they can be applied.

The reasons for replacing the 1995 Directive by a regulation were stated in recitals (9) and (13) of the the preamble to the GDPR as follows:[3]

"9. The objectives and principles of Directive 95/46/EC remain sound, but it has not prevented fragmentation in the implementation of data protection across the Union, legal uncertainty or a widespread public perception that there are significant risks to the protection of natural persons, in particular with regard to online activity. Differences in the level of protection of the rights and freedoms of natural persons, in particular the right to the protection of personal data, with regard to the processing of personal data in the Member States may prevent the free flow of personal data throughout the Union. Those differences may therefore constitute an obstacle to the pursuit of economic activities at the level of the Union, distort competition and impede authorities in the discharge of their responsibilities under Union law. Such a difference in levels of protection is due to the existence of differences in the implementation and application of Directive 95/46/EC."

"13. In order to ensure a consistent level of protection for natural persons throughout the Union and to prevent divergences hampering the free

---

2 Directive 95/46/EC of the European Parliament and of the Council of 24 October 1995 on the protection of individuals with regard to the processing of personal data and on the free movement of such data [1995] OJ L281/31.

3 Probably reflecting the explanation and justification required by the Interinstitutional Agreement on Better Lawmaking 2016 [2016] OJ L123/1, point 25.

movement of personal data within the internal market, a Regulation is necessary to provide legal certainty and transparency for economic operators, including micro, small and medium-sized enterprises, and to provide natural persons in all Member States with the same level of legally enforceable rights and obligations and responsibilities for controllers and processors, to ensure consistent monitoring of the processing of personal data, and equivalent sanctions in all Member States as well as effective cooperation between the supervisory authorities of different Member States. (...)"

This process of transitioning from a directive to a regulation occurs in many EU policy areas[4] and can even be considered as a natural evolution in the "ever closer union" to which the EU aspires. Traditionally, the harmonisation of the legislation of the Member States is achieved by means of directives, which offer the Member States a certain amount of leeway as to the means for reaching the final result. When there is a need for a more harmonised approach and sufficient consensus, regulations are considered a next step. Regulations constitute a direct legislative intervention by the EU legislature in national law, imposing a single text for the whole of the European Union, rather than requiring transposition of a directive into the law of the various Member States.

In theory, the transition from an EU directive to an EU regulation means that the Member States can simply repeal their existing transposing legislation and sit back and relax, because of the direct effect of the regulation. Even if certain provisions of national law happen to be contrary to the regulation (because they were somehow forgotten in the screening process that would normally take place), the regulation would supersede any such national provisions in case conflicts arise.

III. The GDPR is not the ultimate exhaustive regulation

In practice however, regulations are most often far from entirely self-contained bodies of law. There are obvious reasons for this, as the example of penalties or other sanctions in regulations show. Since penal law is not harmonized in the European Union, and each Member State has its own penal system, regulations almost always defer to the Member States the en-

4 For instance, a month earlier than the GDPR, regulation (EU) 2016/425 on personal protective equipment entered into force, superseding the previous directive 89/686/EEC. On 26 May 2020, regulations (EU) 2017/745 on medical devices and (EU) 2017/746 on in vitro diagnostic medical devices will enter into force, repealing the previous directives 90/385/EEC, 93/42/EEC and 98/79/EC.

actment of "effective, proportionate and dissuasive" penalties for infringements of the regulation. In most cases, this is the only condition that the regulation imposes upon Member States, leaving them a wide margin of appreciation as to the nature and severity of those penalties. In fact, the GDPR is remarkable in this regard in so far as it curtails that margin of appreciation, by specifying the administrative penalties that must be imposed by the supervisory authority of the Member States for certain infringements of the GDRP, and sets out the amount of these fines.[5] Apart from that, the GDPR provides in a more traditional fashion that the Member States "shall lay down the rules on other penalties applicable to infringements of this Regulation in particular for infringements which are not subject to administrative fines pursuant to Article 83, and shall take all measures necessary to ensure that they are implemented. Such penalties shall be effective, proportionate and dissuasive".[6]

Also, when EU regulations provide for national supervisory or regulatory authorities, they generally specify the tasks of those authorities and provide that they are to enjoy independence, but leave the precise form of the authorities to be determined by the Member States. The GDPR, for instance, contains certain conditions concerning the establishment and the independence of the supervisory authorities, the appointment of their members, as well as their competence, tasks and powers.[7] This leaves the Member States a considerable margin of discretion as to the precise form of those authorities.

Apart from these relatively obvious examples, many regulations allow and sometimes even oblige Member States to regulate certain aspects themselves. Not only does the GDPR fit in this category, it allows for relatively important aspects to be regulated by the Member States, as the following examples show.[8]

- Article 8(1) GDPR provides that children have to be at least 16 years old to give consent for the processing of personal data, but Member States may provide by law for a lower age between 13 and 16 years.
- Article 9(4) GDPR allows Member States to maintain or introduce "further conditions, including limitations, with regard to the processing of genetic data, biometric data or data concerning health", permitting a

5 Art. 83 GDPR.
6 Art. 84(1) GDPR.
7 Arts 51–58 GDPR.
8 See also, earlier in this edited volume, the contribution by M. Whelanova.

much stricter regulation of the processing of these special categories of personal data in specific Member States.

- Article 23 GDPR allows Member States to restrict "by way of legislative measure" the scope of the guarantees concerning the data subject, as well as the principles relating to the processing of personal data concerning these guarantees. Although "the essence of the fundamental rights and freedoms" must be respected, the measures must be necessary and proportionate in a democratic society to safeguard certain enumerated aims, and certain key guarantees must be upheld. This general provision substantially weakens the uniformity across the European Union that the GDPR was aiming for in the first place.
- Other, arguably less important delegations to Member States are contained in Articles 36(5), 49(5), 88, 89 and 90.

The question remains how that substantial body of exemptions for the Member States can be reconciled with the consistent level of protection for natural persons throughout the Union, that was proclaimed as the reason to transition from a directive to a regulation in the first place.[9]

IV. Further complications on the Member State level caused by the GDPR

Furthermore, this transition from a directive to a regulation leads to complications for the implementation on the Member State level.

In the first place, simply abolishing the existing national legislation transposing Directive 95/46/EC, without enacting any new legislation, was not sufficient, because the GDPR contains new obligations for Member States to regulate certain aspects of the protection for the processing of personal data. That made it necessary to carry out a careful screening of the GDPR to identify those obligations and to enact the appropriate national legislation. In those cases where the GDPR allows Member States to enact stricter measures or certain exceptions, a choice had to be made whether or not to make use of those possibilities. That also complicated the implementation process in the Member States, since political choices had to be made during the implementation process in each Member State (see further ?).

As a result, access to the actual regulation of personal data protection in any given Member State becomes more complex: instead of going through

9 See recitals (9) and (13) of the preamble to the GDPR.

a single body of national law (as is the case of the transposition of a directive),[10] the GDPR must be read in combination with the implementing legislation of the Member State concerned. The GDPR is not the single act concerning personal data protection in a given Member State, rather it constitutes a baseline degree of protection that can be enhanced or diminished by the Member States. The actual regulation of personal data protection is therefore inevitably fragmented into EU rules and rules of the Member States.

Probably in an effort to mitigate the consequences of this fragmentation, the principle of not duplicating the provisions of regulations in national legislation[11] was somewhat relaxed in the GDPR. This is, at least, what recital (8) seems to suggest, by stating that "[w]here this Regulation provides for specifications or restrictions of its rules by Member State law, Member States may, as far as necessary for coherence and for making the national provisions comprehensible to the persons to whom they apply, incorporate elements of this Regulation into their national law".

Secondly, Article 2 GDPR states that the Regulation does not apply to the processing of data in the course of an activity which falls outside the scope of Union law. This restriction is logical and necessary, because any legislative act of the EU can only be applicable within the scope of EU law as defined in the constituting treaties. One might argue that this is so obvious that it should not be expressly mentioned, but Article 2 GDPR nevertheless states a principle that has unexpected consequences for the implementation process in comparison with the transposition of Directive 95/46/EC. This might appear surprising, since Article 2 GDPR is nothing but a replication of Article 3(2) of Directive 95/46/EC. The huge difference, however, lies in the nature of the application of a regulation as compared with the transposition of a directive.

When Directive 95/46/EC was enacted and needed to be transposed, several Member States opted not to include in their transposition legislation the restriction of the rules to the scope of EU law, thereby in fact extending the scope of their transposition legislation to all processing of personal data, irrespective of whether activities within or outside the scope of EU law were concerned. This was certainly the wiser choice. If the restriction in Article 3(2) of the directive was transposed in national law, there would

10 Of course, the national legislation must comply with and be read in the light of the directive. This means that the transposition of a directive can never be seen completely separated from the directive.

11 See the CJEU case law in this regard: Case 34–73 *Fratelli Variola* [1973] ECR 981; Case 50/76 *Amsterdam Bulb BV* [1977] ECR 137.

be a loophole that would have enabled processors of personal data to contest the applicability of the directive and the transposition legislation on the ground that no EU law was involved in the given circumstances (however theoretical this might seem at first glance).

The transition from directive to regulation, however, meant that no transposition was required and that the aforementioned exception (and, accordingly, the loophole it seems to offer) simply stands as the default law of the EU. If Member States want to close this loophole, they have to enact their own legislation concerning the processing of personal data in the specific cases where no EU law was involved. One might therefore be led to expect a national version of the GDPR, applicable only for cases of processing of personal data which fall outside the scope of EU law.

To remedy this problem in an effective and convenient way, the Councils of State of both Belgium and the Netherlands suggested that a provision be inserted in the respective implementation legislation to render the GDPR equally applicable in cases where no EU law was involved. That suggestion was followed in both countries.[12]

Thirdly, for political reasons, the choice was made during the drafting of the GDPR to exclude from its scope the processing of personal data for the purposes of the prevention, investigation, detection or prosecution of criminal offences or the execution of criminal penalties.[13] For these aspects, a separate Directive (EU) 2016/680[14] was enacted that differs from the GDPR as to the degree of protection that is offered.

This is a step forwards in comparison with the aforementioned Article 3(2) of Directive 95/46/EC, that excluded the processing of personal data in

---

12 Advice 63.192/2 of the Belgian Council of State of 19 April 2018, *Kamer van volksvertegenwoordigers*, 2017–2018, No. 54–3126/001, p. 411–412, resulting in Article 2 of the *Wet betreffende de bescherming van natuurlijke personen met betrekking tot de verwerking van persoonsgegevens – Loi relative à la protection des personnes physiques à l'égard des traitements de données à caractère personnel* of 30 July 2018. Advice of the Dutch Council of State of 10 October 2017, *Tweede Kamer der Staten-Generaal*, 2017–2018, 34 851, nr. 4, p. 30–31, resulting in Article 3(1)a of the *Uitvoeringswet Algemene verordening gegevenbescherming* of 16 May 2018.

13 Art. 2(2)(d) GDPR.

14 Directive (EU) 2016/680 of the European Parliament and of the Council of 27 April 2016 on the protection of natural persons with regard to the processing of personal data by competent authorities for the purposes of the prevention, investigation, detection or prosecution of criminal offences or the execution of criminal penalties, and on the free movement of such data, and repealing Council Framework Decision 2008/977/JHA [2016] OJ L119/89.

the course of activities of the State in areas of criminal law, leaving this area to be regulated (or not) by the Member States.

There are certainly convincing reasons for adopting in Directive (EU) 2016/680 a different approach to the processing of personal data for these specific purposes in comparison with the GDPR. Nevertheless, the choice by the EU legislature to enact a *directive*, rather than another regulation (or a separate section of the GDPR, for that matter), has far-reaching consequences for the implementation by the Member States. The directive must be transposed by the Member States in national law, creating a national body of law separate from the GDPR, concerning the processing of personal data in disparate fields, since criminal offences and penalties are to be found in numerous national laws. National legislation often contains provisions concerning the penalties relating to infringements of the legislation, including the investigation of such infringements by authorized persons. As a result the protection of the processing of personal data under those national laws may be regulated in part by the GDPR and in part by the legislation transposing Directive (EU) 2016/680. To make the situation even more complex, when some infringements are punished only by administrative fines that cannot be regarded as criminal penalties, the GDPR is again applicable.

It stands to reason that these complexities in the design of the GDPR and the (only partial) transition from a directive to a regulation, make it difficult for citizens to understand the full extent of their rights and obligation concerning the processing of their personal data.

V. Delays in the implementation process

It appears that when the GDPR was enacted most Member States did not sufficiently take into account the limited timeframe (two years) for an implementation process that was vastly more complex and time-consuming than is usual for other regulations. That is clearly something for which Member States themselves must be to blame, since the complexity and scale of the task of implementation was well known beforehand. But, as we have seen, some aspects of the architecture of the GDPR and Directive (EU) 2016/680 contributed to an implementation process that resulted in a hybrid EU-Member State regulatory complex that makes it difficult to gauge correctly the scale of the necessary implementation measures and the approach to be taken.

In Belgium, for instance, the two principal laws to give effect to the GDPR were enacted on 3 December 2017[15] and 30 July 2018[16] respectively, the last one being published only on 5 September 2018, several months after the entry into force of the GDPR. Moreover, the selection of members of the supervisory authority was still ongoing some six months after the adoption of the second law. Fortunately, a transitional provision[17] was put into place to prolong the mandate of the current members of the existing privacy commission, which will provisionally perform some of the functions of the supervisory authority, even though it does not fully comply with the GDPR requirements for supervisory authorities.

VI. Conclusion

A few lessons can be drawn from the GDPR implementation experience.

First, when the EU was discussing the political outlines of what eventually became the GDPR, it should have given more consideration to the complex implementation process ahead. Was it a wise choice to transition from a directive to a regulation? It is always easy to judge with hindsight, but it could well be argued that that was a mistake. Given the choice to delegate some important aspects to Member States and to maintain a directive for criminal penalties, the end result is a fragmentation of the data protection instruments that is clearly detrimental to the transparency and the uniformity of the personal data protection legislation across the EU.

Secondly, Member States, undoubtedly, have their share of responsibility. They should have foreseen the problems that would arise and been more vigilant during the political negotiations. At the very least they should have insisted on an extension of the implementation period, longer than the standard period of two years.

Lastly, this contribution must not be understood as a criticism of regulations as an instrument. There is a place for regulations and a place for directives in the EU legal arsenal. However, for any given case the choice between the two legal instruments should be based on a prior assessment

15 *Wet tot oprichting van de gegevensbeschermingsautoriteit – Loi portant création de l'Autorité de protection des données* of 3 December 2017.

16 *Wet betreffende de bescherming van natuurlijke personen met betrekking tot de verwerking van persoonsgegevens – Loi relative à la protection des personnes physiques à l'égard des traitements de données à caractère personnel* of 30 July 2018.

17 Article 114(1) of the aforementioned Bill of 3 December 2017, as amended by the Bill of 25 May 2018.

that takes into account their respective advantages and disadvantages. The implementation process ahead and the position in which the Member States will find themselves placed in must play an important role in that assessment.

Afterword

Chapter 15: Shaping future – Reframing law-making in multilevel systems

Stephan Naundorf

I. Introduction

Scientists, politicians, lawyers, and practitioners from parliaments as well as from administrations are used to understand law-making primarily as an issue of logic, structure, process, and legitimation. They follow – by intention or unconsciously – the tradition of Max Weber's model of bureaucracy[1]. Austrian novelist Franz Kafka has created iconic monuments for this point of view on bureaucracy in literature with his novels 'The Trial' (1925) and 'The Castle' (1926). In this micro-cosmos accurate procedures are more relevant than results. These novels inspired politicians e.g. in Belgium, The Netherlands and Great Britain to label their de-regulatory projects Kafka brigades. However, this point of view might not be exclusively appropriate in modern times.

When reflecting on law-making, different branches of science, schools, and disciplines might focus on different elements or types of rationales. Constitutional law, system theory, general theory of state, political science, sociology and the like could, albeit, appear to be incompatible according to their respective constructs, but the general approach is similarly bureaucratic in general. Similar characteristics can be detected to scientific and administrative systems: both are designed to be logic, structured, process-oriented and last but not least to be legitimate. They are not so much open to related systems and not necessarily effect-driven. We could seal both hermetically and they would continue to function in a more or less self-referential fashion. In Thomas Kuhn's words[2], this type of scientific reflection is akin to 'normal science'.

1 See M Weber, *Wirtschaft und Gesellschaft* (Mohr 1922). See also F Chazel, Webers Bürokratiebegriff – neu betrachtet/Max Weber et la bureaucratie', (2010) *Trivium, Revue franco-allemande de sciences humaines et sociales – Deutsch-französische Zeitschrift für Geistes- und Sozialwissenschaften*, 1763–1820 for a critical review.
2 TS Kuhn, *The Structure of Scientific Revolutions* (University of Chicago Press 1962).

It is therefore not surprising to find that self-concepts of law-makers and reflections on law-making are more or less focussed on processes and structures. Among others, John Micklethwait and Adrian Wooldridge have challenged this rigorous system[3], when they pointedly asked what the state is actually for and when they started to look at functions to discuss criteria for success. A similar, however even more fundamental challenge, is posed by Francis Fukuyama who is asking 'What is governance?'. He concludes that even though a reliable bureaucracy is a necessary condition for democracy, science and practice lack the methods needed to measure the functionality of bureaucracies, since there is very little agreement on what constitutes high-quality government.[4]

When we look for the core-function of law, then, we might end up in a – at least in the branches of legal and political studies – widely unexplored terra incognita: innovation. In many other professional and scientific contexts, the art of design is applied to create innovations. Innovative chairs and other furniture are created by designers.[5] Digital applications are created by software designers. And of course law making is just yet another form of design. But usually law-makers would not consider themselves exactly to be designers. Thus, often they are not aware of the range of design methods they would have at their disposal. Nevertheless, since design methods appear to provide adaptive and creative solutions in other professional branches, design methods and a design attitude are recommended with growing intensity by non-governmental actors to public service-professionals; first for urban planning[6], later for general public policy and service design[7]. In consequence, public administrations around the world start at least to acquire design competencies.[8] This is a challenge in itself.

In multilevel settings like e.g. federalist jurisdictions, however, the arrangement of governance, in particular law-making elements, might be somehow more sophisticated than in one-level administrations. Nevertheless, based on experience and tradition the strength of logic is also expected

---

3 J Micklethwait and A Wooldridge, *The fourth revolution – the global race to reinvent the state* (Penguin 2015).

4 F Fukuyama 'What Is Governance?' (2013) CGD Working Paper 314; Washington, DC: Center for Global Development; <http://www.cgdev.org/content/publications/detail/1426906>.

5 L Dybdahl, *101 Danish Design Icons* (Hatje Cantz 2016).

6 P Rowe, *Design Thinking* (Mit Press Ltd 1986).

7 S Junginger, *Transforming Public Services by Design – Re-Orienting Policies, Organizations and Services around People* (Routledge 2017).

8 C Paulick-Thiel, *Mapping Innovation Units, Export Report to the International Monetary Fund* (Washington D.C., International Monetary Fund 2018).

to guide those engaged comfortably through the jungle of state levels, direct or indirect legitimation, and linguistic challenges. If strict logic would be the essence of law-making, it is just consequent to discuss for example, whether legislation might be even done more reliable or become more rigid if executed by algorithms instead of human beings.[9]

This chapter invites the readers of this book to assume another point of view when reflecting on law-making and digesting the scientific contributions presented. It asks for the core-function of law-making and how science feeds into the narratives resulting from these points of view: Simply said, law-makers are dedicated to changing the future. They intend to design innovations from within their respective governance systems. In multilevel systems law-makers, particularly, appear to share challenges but not necessarily solutions.

II. Law-makers intend to change the future

When law is made, the constituencies of law-makers expect something to be different in the real world after rules are adopted. Law-makers themselves expect impact[10]. People and organizations shall behave according to the (new) rules in future. Thus, laws and rules shall be publicly available to everybody, also to make sure that those potentially concerned might have a chance to request changes during deliberation. But first of all, law intends effectiveness: the air shall be cleaner, the world shall be fairer, products shall be safer, the cities we live in shall be healthier places, and the like. Thus, law-makers are nothing else but innovators. And those who benefit from rules and laws elect, legitimate, and control those who make and execute these well intended rules.

If we wonder why innovation provided by law-making is not appreciated or more appropriately reflected, we might find some orientation in exploring the success factors of innovation. Most studies agree on one central key factor for success – not logic, not structure, not process – it is simplici-

---

9 L Andrews et. al., *Algorithmic Regulation*, Center for analysis of risk and regulation discussion paper No. 85, London School of Economics and Political Science, 2017; R Mohabbat Kar, BEP Thapa, Basanta and P Parycek (eds), *(Un)Berechenbar? Algorithmen und Automatisierung in Staat und Gesellschaft* (Kompetenzzentrum Öffentliche IT 2018).

10 L.M. Friedman, *Impact, How Law Affects Behavior* (Cambridge, Cambridge University Press 2016).

ty[11]. Innovations are expected to be simple, functional and reliable especially by those who are supposed to use them. If innovations meet these criteria, innovators are most likely successful.

In contrast, the dominant attitude to law-making says: a world with ever growing complexity requires adequately complex rules. Interestingly, this mind-set is welcomed, supported, even rewarded by the corresponding systems of judiciary, media and in politics. It creates the need for ever more specialising expertise, which allows to defend experts from external influence. However, this development has some downside effects as well. Codebooks are growing, becoming more and more detailed. Politicians in good intention become experts. Those concerned do not understand anymore how they are expected to behave and loose trust in the political and administrative system. Accordingly, the profession of being a civil servant is not terribly attractive. And many of those concerned seem to suffer from a lack of control on their own well-being, thus, calling for radical solutions. The call for closed borders and re-focussing on national interests could in consequence be interpreted as re-constructing firewalls against the overwhelming complexity of world.

Some tools and techniques help professionals to be innovative. In addition to being logical, structured, process-oriented, and knowing one's legitimate room to 'manoeuvre', innovators shall also be able to use and understand data, to utilize tools of strategic foresight, to collaborate with diverse people. As Herbert A. Simon stated: Everyone, who devices courses of action to turn an existing situation into a preferred one, is a designer.[12] This way, innovators in public administration, particularly those who feed into law-making or implementing law follow inherently concepts of human-centred design. They may utilize tools like rapid-prototyping or crowd funding, using collective intelligence to collect ideas for problem solving. Last but not least, innovators in public administration constantly refresh their creativity by reaching out and by re-calibrating their views[13]. Many

---

11 E.g. A Düben, R Ziegler, B Kremer and R Kellermann, *Ergebnisbericht Partizipative Interventionen/Inhaltliche Empfehlungen und Einstellungsänderungen durch die Teilnahme an Partizipationsverfahren* (TU Berlin 2017), http://zukunftsticket.berlin/wp-content/uploads/VERS-Ergebnisbericht-Partizipative-Interventionen_FINAL.pdf.

12 HA Simon, *The Sciences of the Artificial* (MIT Press 1969).

13 See for example the Innovationsmeteret, developed in Denmark, now utilized all over Scandinavia; OB Lykkebo, *Innovationsbarometeret – højere effektivitet og kvalitet i den offentlige sektor gennem innovation* (Udgivet af Center for Offentlig Innovation og Jurist- og Økonomforbundets Forlag 2016), www.innovationsbarometer.coi.dk.

governmental and non-governmental innovation labs around the world proof the attractiveness of these concepts[14]. And those, who prefer to really dive deep into the technical aspects of this developments, might draw attention to legal tech-offers, heading, for example, for legal hackathons.

Innovative law-making might be understood as the art of designing truly human-centred societal solutions for a near immediate future. But it appears that law-makers hardly can imagine themselves to be protagonists of a hackathon or a foresight seminar. Similarly, science does not appear to analyse, reflect and comment whether law meets their expectations in the future. However, it is amazing that legislative systems do not pay systematic attention to the real-life impact of their innovative, future-shaping action. According to OECD-studies in 2015 and 2018 only a minority of OECD member states invest systematically capacity in ex post evaluation of the effectiveness of their policies and legal initiatives[15].

III. Law-makers provide innovation for huge, diverse though interested audiences

Law-makers often understand themselves and their profession dealing with highly specialised rather technical subject matter. They know that many people are concerned in a general way, but assume that only few of them are really interested in their field of expertise. And as they consider themselves primarily as hard-working experts, the self-perception of being a fancy, hip innovator – the way innovators tend to be portrayed in the media – is not an image they identify with. Law-making is about 'dry' if not boring problem-solving, guided or potentially restricted by political preferences. It appears to be a demanding decision-making processes, which often enough is based on convictions or anecdotal evidence rather than on facts and figures. The reality that this demanding job is done in multilevel settings also makes matters even worse: Aside from the burden of providing high level expertise, law-makers also need to be alert that other levels stay within their respective competences. It might happen, that more energy is

14 Paulick-Thiel (no 8); O Ibert, S Schmidt, V Brinks, A Kuebart, and J Kühn, *Open Creative Labs in Deutschland: Typologisierung, Verbreitung, Entwicklungsbedingungen und politische Gestaltung*, (Erkner 2018), <https://leibniz-irs.de/forschung/projekte/projekt/open-creative-labs-in-deutschland/>.

15 OECD, OECD Regulatory Policy Outlook 2018 (OECD Publishing 2018), <https://doi.org/10.1787/9789264303072-en>; OECD, OECD Regulatory Policy Outlook 2015 (OECD Publishing 2015), http://dx.doi.org/10.1787/9789264238770-en.

invested in the demarcation of powers and responsibilities than in the subject matter. The conclusion from the self-concept of law-makers as experts is quite obvious: Laws are made by experts for experts: other lawyers, judges, and core community members.

Nonetheless, a reality-check reveals that 'normal' people actually do read laws. There are many more people beyond those legal experts who would want to read and understand law for themselves. Many more than expected want to understand what code-books and provisions require them to do and not to do. When they do not understand and cannot access these codes, people tend to blame themselves, not the products of law-making that were poorly designed. For example, when people do not understand paper forms, they blame themselves first for not being capable to understand the logic of the form and its legal basis[16]. One of the unintended consequences is that people have a tendency to re-direct their anger towards an abstract administration. Yet this can be read as nothing else but self-protection.[17] It is an axiomatic assumption that experiences like this cause the notion of losing control, which might foster the demand for radical solutions.

All this adds complexity in domestic as well as multilevel settings due to actors or interest groups who may or may not be well organized. Different traditions and cultures of 'if, how, and when' the involvement of stakeholders is appropriate add again further complexity. The call for meaningful involvement of those concerned might already constitute a challenge on the local level. Due to the size, complexity and inherent diversity involvement is much more a challenge in multilevel systems. Against this background for many actors, it is too tempting to blame different levels for problems instead of re-considering their own contribution to the joint endeavour.

Though, involvement and participation are intensely discussed by civil society and politicians around the globe, law-makers and their scientific

16 Bundesregierung, *Wirksam regieren; making the law accessible* (2019), https://www.bundesregierung.de/breg-en/issues/wirksam-regieren-with-citizens-for-citizens/topics/making-the-law-accessible-317284. Two summaries available 3 February 2019 in German only: h *Open Creative Labs in Deutschland: Typologisierung, Verbreitung* <https://www.bundesregierung.de/resource/blob/975272/317242/d21df6a090dd92efaea7d57b0991cd08/2018-02-27-recht-verstaendlich-machen-onsite-befragung-data.pdf?download=1> and https://www.bundesregierung.de/resource/blob/975272/317254/03239f11929ea4f421f76f599a439362/2018-02-27-recht-verstaendlich-machen-befragung-data.pdf?download=1.

17 S Grünewald, *Wie tickt Deutschland ? Psychologie einer aufgewühlten Gesellschaft* (Kiepenheuer&Witsch 2019).

observers appear to struggle to engage. One of very few truly legislative answers to the perception of a growing distance between law-makers and their constituencies is the French initiative for a 'loi pour un état au service d'une sociéte de confiance, adopted at 10 August 2018, which changes e.g. the 'code des relations entre le public et l'administration'.[18]

Albert Camus[19] once irritated his audience, when he invited us to consider Sisyphus being a lucky man. Couldn't we consider law-makers being fancy, hip innovators? Couldn't we consider legal texts being an interesting, even exciting source of insight and guidance? One that holds the potential to shape the future like few others?

When we challenge our self-concepts, we might end up in a context, with different requirements and options. In addition to professional experience, innovative law-makers deserve cutting-edge training and digital support to make sure, they have time to focus on what only the best could do: provide human-centred solutions on the basis of expertise and empathy. Appreciation appears to be a key for success in this context.

Since today's law-making takes a more or less direct effect on everybody's future, it is hard to imagine a hipper, more relevant profession. It deserves up-to-date scientific reflection and the consideration of new methods appropriate to fulfil these demands.

IV. Multilevel legal environments in a sharing world

Some years ago, many jurisdictions were astounded with a new concept: sharing. Sharing economy, sharing societies were 'en vogue'. Concepts like open data and open government, too, are based on the principle of sharing. And sharing appears to be the logic concept in an interconnected world. In an ideal world, sharing means: everybody gives, everybody takes or receives mutually. We understand that reciprocal sharing has huge benefits. Trade is just one form of sharing. The free movement of people, who share experience and life conditions, presents another form of sharing. From this perspective e.g., the European Union is nothing but a truly sharing political system.

---

18 Z Ait-el-Kadi et al., *Code des relations entre le public et l'administration 2019, annoté et commenté* (Dalloz 2018).

19 A Camus, *The Myth of Sisyphus (Le mythe de Sisyphe*,1942), English translation by J O'Brien (Hamish Hamilton 1955).

The central idea is not really new, though. Rudolf Martin has described 1910 in the context of an early foresight exercise that a joint European legislation provided by a European parliament based on a European constitution will be the necessary result of increasing European trade particularly via air traffic[20].

Today, however, we also have experienced, that sharing does not lead automatically to perfect balance. Sometimes, many people share and just one person or centre of organization takes and gives. Some business – and even political – concepts rather look like the perfect imbalance instead of the perfect balance because only a few people have the capacity, power or the competence to process or organize what others share. Whether big data and artificial intelligence provide promises or threats depends on the level of openness and sharing. If the winner takes it all, we might have many losers.

The positive effect on innovation in science and business is well reflected in literature. Some contributions even go back to 19th century evidence[21] Other, more populist authors describe diversity as the mother of innovation[22]. However, the effect of multilevel systems on capacities and competencies for innovation seems to be discussed in the context of organisational studies of industrial transformation[23]. Literature in political or legal studies could not be identified. Thus, we need to conclude from more general observations and considerations.

In a multilevel law-making context, we see quite clearly that some decisions might be taken legitimately on top-level. The perception of 'sharing' depends on the procedures, which ensure, that all levels concerned have their respective share in joint decision making. This also refers to the role of legislative bodies at different levels within multilevel systems. Some jurisdictions prefer a clear differentiation of competencies, other provide similar powers to legislatures at different levels. The latter, however, re-

---

20 R Martin, 'Der Krieg in 100 Jahren' in A Brehmer (ed), *Die Welt in 100 Jahren* (Buntdruck 1910), 68.

21 https://www.nyas.org/history-highlights/contents/editorial/fostering-scientific-innovation-through-diversity/; referring to the Annals of the New York Academy of Sciences, Volume 323, Issue 1, published in April 1979.

22 E.g. J Baumgartner, http://www.innovationmanagement.se/imtool-articles/why-diversity-is-the-mother-of-creativity/.

23 F Geels, Multi-Level Perspective on System Innovation: Relevance for Industrial Transformation, ISBN 1-4020-4418-6_9, in Understanding Industrial Transformation: Views from Different Disciplines (https://www.researchgate.net/publication/226512683_Multi-Level_Perspective_on_System_Innovation_Relevance_for_Industrial_Transformation).

quires stronger effort for co-ordination. If there is no culture of co-ordination, these systems will be challenged by even more and faster growing legal complexity.

Top level decisions appear particularly to be legitimate when it comes to implementing measures referring to e.g. shared values of humanity and non-discrimination. In addition, decisions everybody is directly concerned with – like roaming-fees or banning geo-blocking as well as many rules designed to ensure level-playing fields – are good examples within the EU-context for how such sharing might look like. However, the on-site implementation of measures to regain control of climate change might be different according to the local climate zone. Despite their obvious benefits for many if not all, sometimes top-level decisions might appear to be out of democratic control.

Multilevel law-making is, as we know, neither self-explanatory nor self-justifying. In addition, actors in multilevel settings are often quite pre-occupied – even obsessed – with getting competencies and procedures organised to ensure that each level keeps its stakes. But 'stake-holding' is very distinct from 'share-holding'.

If we understand law-making as an innovative, collaborative task in a truly sharing setting, we once again might end up with a different story. Resources and requirements for innovative law-making might be much easier provided in a sharing multilevel environment than in a world of jealously alerted stake-holders. For example, data, knowledge of design tools and design processes, as well as platforms for collaborative outreach of practitioners could easily be shared across the levels of a multilevel system, like shared values and joint procedures. Sharing these assets would not limit the potential of providing local solutions, respecting real-life conditions, cultures and competences, even celebrating variety and diversity at each place and each level of a truly joint multilevel system. However, it is relevant to underline, that sharing does not mean, advertising and distribution one's individual solution bluntly to the rest of the world. A 'take it or leave'-approach ought not to be mixed up, with the collaborative character of 'sharing', even when taking is topped-up by additional incentives like money or political support.

This article calls for a change, at least completion of the scientific perception of legislation[24] asking for a more practical, impact-oriented and

24 H Xanthaki, 'Emerging Trends in Legislation in Europe', in U Karpen and H Xanthaki (eds.), *Legislation in Europe – a Comprehensive Guide for Scholars and Practitioners* (Hart 2017) 275–296.

forward-looking point of view. Scientific reflection of legislation could then provide relevant impulses not only for deeper understanding of processes and structures but also for further development of practice. Textbooks then could do, what Franz Kafka expects books to do in general. He wrote on 27 January 1904 in a letter to his friend Oskar Pollack:[25]

> 'Altogether, I think we ought to read only books that bite and sting us. If a book we are reading doesn't shake us awake like a blow to the skull, why bother reading it in the first place?'

25 F Kafka, *Letter to Oskar Pollak* (1904). Source of translation: <http://languagehat.com/kafka-on-books/>; source of original text: <https://homepage.univie.ac.at/werner.haas/1904/br04-003.htm>.

The Contributors

The Editors

Patricia Popelier is senior professor of constitutional law and legislative studies at the University of Antwerp and chair of the research group on Government and Law. She is vice-president of the International Association of Legislation, Chair of the Flemish Centre for Legislation (ICW), co-promoter of the Jean Monnet Centre of Excellence ACTORE, Convenor of the Standing Research Group on 'Subnational Constitutions in Federal and Quasi-Federal Systems' of the International Association of Constitutional Law, Member of the Scientific Committee of EURAC Institute for Federalism in Bolzano, Italy, Member of the Scientific Committee of the Impact Assessment Observatory in Rome, and spokesperson for the Research of Government and Law's Membership of the International Association of Institutes for Federalism Studies. She is also member of the editorial board of several journals and book series, including the journals *Theory and Practice of Legislation* and *Tijdschrift voor Wetgeving* (Journal for Legislation).

William Robinson is an Associate Research Fellow at the Institute of Advanced Legal Studies in London. After studies in law and legal translation in London he worked for 35 years in the field of EU law and language for the European institutions, at the European Court of Justice, the European Patent Office and then at the European Commission. In the Commission's Legal Service he coordinated a team of 20 lawyers who revised the Commission's draft legal acts and legislative proposals. Since 2010 he has been engaged in research into EU legislative drafting issues and language at the Institute of Advanced Legal Studies and teaching legislative drafting, in particular to the staff of the EU institutions.

João Tiago Silveira is Professor at the Lisbon Law School of the University of Lisbon, where he teaches in the fields of Administrative Law, legislative drafting/better regulation and Constitutional Law. He is Deputy President of the institute of Lisbon Law School (*Instituto de Ciências Jurídico-Políticas*) and member of the board of the International Association of Legislation. He has relevant activity in the private sector as Partner in the law firm Morais Leitão, Galvão Teles, Soares da Silva & Associados as well as arbitrator. He has played an active role in public positions, namely as State Secretary of Justice, State Secretary of the Presidency of the Council of Ministers and Director of the Legislative Policy and Planning Office of the Ministry of Justice. During this role he conceived and executed policies on cutting red tape and simplification of registries and notaries, new technologies in courts, better regulation, simplification of legislative procedures, urban rehabilitation and reform of administrative litigation. João Tiago Silveira has published several articles and regularly performs interventions in seminars and postgraduate courses in Administrative Law, Administrative Litigation, better regulation and legislative drafting.

Felix Uhlmann holds a chair for constitutional and administrative law as well as legislative theory at the Law Faculty of the University of Zurich, Switzerland. He is the director of the Centre for Legislation in Zurich and he is a board member of the Swiss Society for Legislation, of the Swiss Society for Parliamentary Questions and of the International Association of Legislation. Together with Georg Muller, he has published the standard treatise on legislation in Switzerland (*Elemente einer Rechtssetzungslehre*). He teaches the subject in courses at the university, educational programs for Parliamentary staff and civil servants both in Switzerland and abroad.

Helen Xanthaki, PhD, is the Dean of Postgraduate Laws Programmes of the University of London; Professor (PTF and Hon) at UCL;; Visiting Professor at QMUL and Senior Associate Research Fellow at the Sir William Dale Centre for Legislative Studies. She is President of the International Association for Legislation and author of several publications in the field of legislative studies, including *Drafting Legislation: Art and Technology of Rules for Regulation*. She is the editor of *Thornton's Legislative Drafting* and member of the editorial board of *Theory and Practice of Legislation, European Journal of Law Reform,* and *Novalogos*.

The Authors

Corina Andone is an Assistant professor of Language and Communication at the University of Amsterdam, and a senior researcher of the Argumentation and Rhetoric Group (ARGA) at the Amsterdam Centre for Language and Communication (ACLC). Her primary research interests, concerning the analysis and evaluation of legal-political argumentation, combine theoretical insights from argumentation scholarship and EU legal-political studies with empirical insights from 'real-life' reasoning. Most recently, she has been conducting research on probative obligations in political accountability, reports of the European Parliament's committees of investigation, and the use and quality of argumentation in European Union directives and recommendations. She is in the editorial board of *Argumentation* (Springer) and *Journal of Argumentation in Context* (Benjamins).

Karen Banks is Deputy Director General of the Legal Service of the European Commission. Prior to that, she was Director responsible for running the AGRI-FISH team of the Legal Service. She has also worked in the areas of competition law, social law, intellectual property and the external relations aspects of EU law. Karen took her first law degree in Dublin in 1978 (University College Dublin) and a Master's Degree in 1982 at London University (the London School of Economics). She worked as a solicitor in general practice before joining the Commission.

Florin Coman-Kund is an Assistant Professor in European Union Law at Erasmus School of Law Rotterdam. He obtained his PhD degree at Maastricht University and published a monograph on "European Union Agencies as Global Actors. A Legal Study of the European Aviation Safety Agency, Frontex and Europol" (Routledge 2018). He currently focuses on the functions and limits of law in multilevel governance, legitimacy and accountability of EU (external) executive action, expert-based regulatory processes and the rule of law. He is pursuing legal research in context, by using empirical qualitative methods and case study research, and by integrating legal approaches with insights from other disciplines such as political science, public administration and argumentation theory.

Agnieszka Doczekalska is an assistant professor at the Law School of Kozminski University in Warsaw (Poland). She obtained Ph.D. in law at the Law Department of the European University in Florence (Italy) and holds also diploma in translation studies from the University of Lodz (Poland) and the University of Strasbourg (France). She conducts the research on the relations between EU legal language and national legal languages.

Ruben de Graaff, LL.M. (Leiden), is a PhD candidate and lecturer at the Institute for Private Law of Leiden University, the Netherlands. His research has been awarded with the VBR Publication Prize (2016) and with the biannual NJV Publication Prize (2017). In 2017, he worked as a visiting research fellow at the Ludwig Maximilians Universität in Munich, Germany.

Elena Griglio is Senior Parliamentary Official of the Italian Senate. She teaches Legislative Drafting at the Department of Political Sciences of the LUISS University in Rome. She holds a course in "Legislative Drafting and follow-up of non-legislative acts" within the Master on Parliament and Public Policies of the LUISS School of Government and a course in "Subnational parliaments" within the Joint Master in Parliamentary Procedures and Legislative Drafting EUPADRA. Phd in Public Law, University of Turin, she has been post-doc Fellow in Public Comparative Law at the LUISS University and adjunct professor in Administrative Law at the University "Cattolica del Sacro Cuore" in Rome.

Nikos Koutras is a postdoctoral research fellow at the University of Antwerp, Research Group Government & Law, and has been Visiting Professor in European Union Law at the University of Antwerp. He studied political science at the University of Crete. He holds a master's in science of Information at the Ionian University. He also holds a PhD in Political Science (Ionian University, Greece) and a PhD in Law (Macquarie University, Australia). He has been awarded research scholarships from Macquarie University, an Erasmus International scholarship for a research visit at the University of Trento (Faculty of Law) and a research grant from the University of Antwerp for an ACTORE short research visit.

Rui Lanceiro is an Assistant Professor at the University of Lisbon Law School (since 2016). He obtained his PhD *summa cum laude*, at the same University, with a thesis on the influence of EU law on the Portuguese administrative procedure, through the principle of sincere cooperation. He is Secretary General of the Lisbon Centre for Research in Public Law (CIDP) and an advisor to the Portuguese Constitutional Court (since 2012). He is a member of the European Group of Public Law, the International Association of Legislation, and co-chair of the Portuguese Chapter of ICON-S. He worked in ministerial offices of the Portuguese Government, drafting legislation, with the State Secretary of the Presidency of the Council of Ministers (in 2008–2011).

Petra Lea Láncos is researcher of Deutsches Forschungsinstitut für Öffentliche Verwaltung (Speyer, Germany) and associate professor at **Deutsches Forschungsinstitut für Öffentliche Verwaltung Speyer**, Faculty of Law (Budapest, Hungary). Between 2006–2007 she worked as a research assistant at the Max Planck Institute for Comparative Public Law and International Law (Heidelberg, Germany). From 2013 to 2015 she was legal counsel to the Hungarian Deputy Ombudsman responsible for Future Generations. In 2015 she worked as a researcher at the Institute of Media Studies at the National Media and Infocommunications Authority. She is legal counsel at the Constitutional Court of Hungary and co-editor of the *Hungarian Yearbook of International Law and European Law*. Her areas of research include language law, European media law and European soft law.

Nicola Lupo is Professor of Public Law and Director of the Center for Parliamentary Studies at LUISS University in Rome. He holds a Jean Monnet chair on "Understanding European Representative Democracy" and is visiting professor at the Nicolaus Copernicus University in Toruń (Poland). His publications concern sources of law, parliamentary rules of procedures, legal drafting, budgetary procedures, regional councils, parliaments in the EU. Co-author, with Andrea Manzella, of *Il Parlamento europeo. Una introduzione* (Luiss University Press, 2019) and, with Luigi Gianniti, of a textbook on Italian Parliamentary Law (*Corso di diritto parlamentare*, 3rd ed., Il Mulino, 2018), he has recently co-edited *Interparliamentary Cooperation in the Composite European Constitution* (with Cristina Fasone, Hart, 2016) and *The Italian Parliament in the European Union* (with Giovanni Piccirilli, Hart, 2017).

Maria Mousmouti is Lecturer in Law at the Institute of Advanced Legal Studies of the University of London and Executive Director at the Centre for European Constitutional Law, a research center based in Athens, Greece. Her research in the field of legislative studies deals with the concepts of legislative quality and effectiveness, legislative design and mechanics and their application in areas of law like urban legislation, equality, fundamental rights, disability etc. Her first monograph titled 'Designing Effective Legislation' is due In August 2019. Her work is to support reform initiatives through research, evidence-based advice and capacity-building. She has actively worked in more than 20 countries in the EU, Southern Europe, the Middle East, Africa and Central Asia.

Stephan Naundorf belongs to the German Federal Chancellery's Better Regulation Unit since 2006. His responsibilities include the development of the Federal Government's programme on Better Regulation. Since 2008 he also advises the respective Minister of State to the Chancellor in this field. Naundorf is chair elect 2020 of the OECD's Regulatory Policy Committee. He holds a MBA and a Master of Political Sciences. Before joining the Federal Government he has worked in corporate communications in the business sector for ten years, including the emerging online and digital markets at the turn of the millennium. His writings on Better Regulation have been published in Zeitschrift für Gesetzgebung, Tagesspiegel.de, Revue Française d'Administration Publique, Acteurs Publics and Legislation in Europe.

Evelyne Schmid is an associate professor of public international law at the University of Lausanne in Switzerland. She was previously based at the University of Basel and at Bangor University in Wales and completed her PhD at the Graduate Institute of International and Development Studies (IHEID). She is the principal investigator of a research project on international law in subnational parliaments and is the author of Taking Economic, Social and Cultural Rights Seriously in International Criminal Law (Cambridge Studies in International and Comparative Law, 2015; Christiane-Rajewsky award 2016). In 2018, she was elected as a board member of the European Society of International Law (ESIL).

Jeroen Van Nieuwenhove is councilor at the Belgian Council of State (Legislation Section) and affiliated researcher at the Center for Public Law (KU Leuven, Belgium). He is member of the editorial board of the journal *Tijdschrift voor Wetgeving* (Journal for Legislation) and board member of the Flemish Centre for Legislation (ICW). His research topics are better regulation and legislative drafting, federalism and parliamentary law (including electoral law).

Dorine Verheij, LL.M. (Leiden) and MJur, is a PhD candidate and lecturer at the Institute for Private Law of Leiden University, Hazelhoff Centre for Financial Law, the Netherlands. Her PhD research concentrates on European private law in the context of the financial sector and the liability of credit rating agencies. In 2017, she worked as a visiting academic at the University of Oxford (United Kingdom) and the University Paris II Panthéon-Assas (France).

Wim Voermans is Professor of Constitutional and Administrative law at Leiden University in the Netherlands. His academic focus is on Dutch and European constitutional law, with a particular interest in the Dutch and EU legislature. Voermans is one of the three directors of the Leiden Research Profile “Political Legitimacy”.

Markéta Whelanová is the Head of the Analytical Unit of the Department for Compatibility with EU Law of the Czech Office of the Government and the Deputy Director of this Department. As a state servant she focuses on the field of implementation of EU law, especially on the methods of its implementation in the Czech legal order and related legislative drafting. Since 2015 she is the Vice-president of the Working Commission for EU Law of the Legislation Council of the Czech Government.

